A PERSPECTIVE IN THEORETICAL COMPUTER SCIENCE

COMMEMORATIVE VOLUME FOR GIFT SIROMONEY

World Scientific Series in Computer Science

Published

Volume 1: Computer-aided Specification Techniques
by J Demetrovics, E Knuth & P Rado

Volume 2: Proceedings of the 2nd RIKEN International Symposium on Symbolic and Algebraic Computation by Computers
edited by N Inada & T Soma

Volume 3: Computational Studies of the Most Frequent Chinese Words and Sounds
by Ching Y Suen

Volume 4: Understanding and Learning Statistics by Computer
by M C K Yang & D H Robinson

Volume 6: DC Flux Parametron
A New Approach to Josephson Junction Logic
by E Goto & K F Loe

Volume 8: Information, Randomness & Incompleteness — Papers on Algorithmic Information Theory
by G J Chaitin

Volume 9: P-Prolog — A Parallel Logic Programming Language
by Rong Yang

Volume 10: Intelligent Chinese Language Pattern and Speech Processing
edited by P S-P Wang

Volume 12: An Introduction to Chinese, Japanese, and Korean Computing
by J K T Huang & T D Huang

Volume 14: Computer Vision and Shape Recognition
edited by A Krzyzak, T Kasvand & C Y Suen

Volume 16: A Perspective in Theoretical Computer Science — Commemorative Volume for Gift Siromoney
edited by R Narasimhan

Forthcoming

Volume 5: Information Control Problems in Manufacturing Automation
by L Nemes

Volume 7: Syntactic and Structural Pattern Recognition — Theory and Applications
edited by H Bunke & A Sanfeliu

Volume 11: Control Theory of Robotic Systems
by J M Skowronski

Volume 13: Mathematical Logic for Computer Science
by Z W Lu

Volume 15: Stochastic Complexity in Statistical Inquiry
by J Rissanen

Volume 17: Computer Transformation of Digital Images and Patterns
by Z C Li, T D Bui, Y Y Tang & C Y Suen

Volume 18: On Visualization of Abstract Objects and Relations
by T Kamada

Series in Computer Science — Vol. 16

A Perspective in Theoretical Computer Science

Commemorative Volume for Gift Siromoney

edited by

R. Narasimhan

Senior Professor
Computer Group
Tata Institute of Fundamental Research
Bombay
India

World Scientific
Singapore • New Jersey • London • Hong Kong

Published by

World Scientific Publishing Co. Pte Ltd.,
P O Box 128, Farrer Road, Singapore 9128
USA office: 687 Hartwell Street, Teaneck, NJ 07666
UK office. 73 Lynton Mead, Totteridge, London N20 8DH

Library of Congress Cataloging-in-Publication data is available.

A PERSPECTIVE IN THEORETICAL COMPUTER SCIENCE – COMMEMORATIVE VOLUME FOR GIFT SIROMONEY

ISBN 9971-50-925-3

Cover design: Creative eye kolam

Printed in Singapore by JBW Printers & Binders Pte. Ltd.

PREFACE

Professor Gift Siromoney passed away on March 21, 1988, after a brief illness. His tragic and untimely death has resulted in the disappearance of a much-loved teacher and a highly productive research scientist with many-faceted interests. At the time of his death Dr Siromoney was the Chairman of the Department of Statistics at the Madras Christian College, Madras. In fact, he was the founder of the Department of Statistics and the architect of the Kibble Computer Centre there. For nearly four decades he taught and guided students and younger colleagues on a wide range of topics from Statistics to Computers, Epigraphy, Art, History, Linguistics, Anthropology, and Music. He was an enthusiastic amateur photographer, painter and bird-watcher, and took much interest in nature studies.

The Madras Christian College has started a *Gift Siromoney Endowment Fund* to promote research and scholarly work in the areas to which Dr Gift Siromoney himself had contributed so ably. In addition, it is proposed to publish commemorative volumes with contributions from friends, colleagues, and students in the areas in which Dr Siromoney was active. This volume is the first of such a planned series covering topics in Theoretical Computer Science. The contributors to this volume are eminent scholars well-known in this field, who were also personal friends of Dr Siromoney either as peers, colleagues, or students.

Much of the preparatory work to bring out this commemorative volume was done by Prof. (Mrs) Rani Siromoney, who was herself the foremost collaborator with her husband in his research work in Formal Grammars and Automata Theory. As the editor of this volume I am much indebted to Mrs Siromoney for her untiring assistance. Both of us are extremely grateful to all the authors who so readily agreed to contribute to this memorial volume and who, also, generously agreed to our suggestion to allow the publishers' payments by way of royalties to be consolidated and credited to the *Gift Siromoney Endowment Fund*. We would like to express our thanks to World Scientific Publishing Co. Pte. Ltd. for their enthusiastic cooperation in bringing out this volume expeditiously.

No collection of articles can do justice to the personality of Dr Gift Siromoney. Those of us who had known him closely over the years would continue to cherish the memory of the love and warmth of a dedicated teacher and a loyal friend.

R. Narasimhan

ACKNOWLEDGEMENT

The idea of bringing out a memorial volume to reflect the many-faceted research interests of Dr Gift Siromoney came from Professor J. P. Vijayathilakan, Chairman, Department of Statistics. Arul and I are grateful to him, members of the college community, the many friends and relatives, with special thanks to colleagues in the departments of Mathematics and Statistics, for the love and affection shown during Dr Siromoney's illness and the support given in bringing out this volume. A selected list of publications is included to show the broad spectrum of his contributions.

We are grateful to Prof. R. Narasimhan for agreeing to be the editor of this volume and for help at various stages of our research for the past two decades. Special thanks to all contributors who made this publication possible and to World Scientific Publishing Co. Pte. Ltd. for the excellent production.

Rani Siromoney

Professor Gift Siromoney and his wife Rani.

CONTENTS

LIST OF SELECTED PUBLICATIONS OF DR. GIFT SIROMONEY

THEORETICAL COMPUTER SCIENCE

Equal matrix languages and kleene closure, Proceedings of the Indian Academy of Sciences, Vol. 74, Sec. A, pp. 172-188, 1971, (with Siromoney, R).

Abstract families of matrices and picture languages, Computer Graphics and Image Processing, Vol. 1, pp. 284-307, 1972, (with Siromoney, R. and Krithivasan, K).

Picture languages with array rewriting rules, Information and Control, Vol. 22, pp. 447-470, 1973, (with Siromoney, R. and Krithivasan, K).

N-dimensional array languages and description of crystal symmetry - I, Proceedings of the Indian Academy of Sciences, Vol. 78, Sec. A, pp. 72-88, 1973, (with Siromoney, R. and Krithivasan, K).

N-dimensional array languages and description of crystal symmetry - II, Proceedings of the Indian Academy of Sciences, Vol. 78, Sec. A, pp. 130-139, 1973, (with Siromoney, R. and Krithivasan, K).

Array grammars and kolam, Computer Graphics and Image Processing, Vol. 3, pp. 63-82, 1974, (with Siromoney, R. and Krithivasan, K).

Radial grammars and biological systems, Proceedings of the Conference on Biologically Motivated Automata Theory, Mclean, Virginia, pp. 92-96, 1974, (with Siromoney, R).

Extended controlled table L-arrays, Information and Control, Vol. 35, pp. 119-138, 1977. Also in TR-304, Computer Science Centre, University of Maryland, May 1974, (with Siromoney, R).

Parallel O-Lindenmayer languages, paper presented at the All India Workshop and Symposium on Digital Image Processing, Bangalore, 1973. Also in International Journal of Computer Mathematics, Vol. 5, Sec. A, pp. 109-123, 1975, (with Siromoney, R).

Radial grammars and radial L-systems, Computer Graphics and Image Processing, Vol. 4, pp. 361-374, 1975, (with Siromoney, R).

Hexagonal arrays and rectangular blocks, Computer Graphics and Image Processing, Vol. 5, pp. 353-381, 1976, (with Siromoney, R).

Stochastic table arrays, Computer Graphics and Image Processing, Vol. 18, pp. 202-211, 1982, (with Siromoney, R. and Subramanian, K.G.).

Extended table matrix grammars, STAT-50/83, Madras Christian College, 1983, (with Siromoney, R. and Subramanian, K.G.).

Map generating systems, Proceedings of FST/TCS 3, Bangalore, pp. 145-170, 1983, (with Siromoney, R. and Subramanian, K.G.).

A note on an extension of matrix grammars generating two-dimensional languages, Information Sciences, Vol. 35, 1985, (with Subramanian, K.G. and Siromoney, R).

A public key cryptosystem that defies cryptanalysis, Bulletin of the European Association for Theoretical Computer Science, Vol. 28, pp. 37-43, 1986 (with Siromoney, R).

Rosenfeld's cycle grammars and kolam, Graph Grammars and Their Application to Computer Science, (Eds. H.Ehrig, M.Nagl, G.Rozenberg and A.Rosenfeld), LNCS, Vol. 291, pp. 564-579, 1987, (with Siromoney, R).

ARCHAEOLOGY

The evolution of the gopuram and the vimanam, MCC Magazine, Vol. 31, pp. 78-80, 1962.

Mahabalipuram costumes and jewellery, MCC Magazine, Vol. 39, p. 76, 1970.

Changing fashions in the Pallava art, The Sunday Standard (Madras), Feb. 28, 1971.

Pallava paintings of Kanchipuram, The Indian Express, Madras, Sep. 20, 1975, (with Lockwood, M).

Depiction of animals in Mahabalipuram sculptures, The Ethological Society of India, Souvenir, pp. 3-5, 1976.

Earliest sculpture of Kannappan, The Indian Express, March 3, 1977, (with Lockwood, M).

Musical instruments from Pallava sculptures, **Kalakshetra** Quarterly, Vol. 2, No. 4, pp. 11-20, 1979.

Computer analysis of early Chola and Pandya sculptures: An iconometric study, Proceedings of the Fifth International Tamil Conference held at Madurai in January 1981, pp. 3-7 - 3-16, (with Govindaraju, S. and Bagavandas, M).

CHARACTER RECOGNITION

Computer recognition of printed Tamil characters, Pattern Recognition, Vol. 10, pp. 243-247, 1978, (with Chandrasekaran, R. and Chandrasekaran, M).

Machine recognition of an ancient Tamil script of the Chola period, Journal of the Epigraphical Society of India, Vol. 6, pp. 18-19, 1979, (with Chandrasekaran, M. and Chandrasekaran, R).

Computer translation of South Indian music into staff notation, Proceedings of the International Symposium on Microwaves and Communications, IIT, Kharagpur, pp. 170-173, 1981, (with Chandrasekaran, M. and Chandrasekaran, R).

Machine recognition of Brahmi script, IEEE Transactions on Systems, Man, and Cybernetics, Vol. 12, 1983, pp. 648-654, (with Chandrasekaran, R. and Chandrasekaran, M).

Computer dating of medieval inscriptions: South Indian Tamil, Computers and the Humanities, Vol. 17, 1983, pp. 199-208, (with Chandrasekaran, R. and Chandrasekaran, M).

Context-dependent recognizer for handprinted Tamil characters, Proceedings of the IEEE International Conference on Systems, Man, and Cybernetics, Bombay-New Delhi, Vol. 2, pp. 786-790, 1983, (with Chandrasekaran, M. and Chandrasekaran, R).

Computer recognition of Tamil, Malayalam and Devanagari characters, Journal of the Institution of Electronics and Telecomunication Engineers, Vol. 30, No. 6, pp. 150-154b, 1984, (with Chandrasekaran, M. and Chandrasekaran, R).

EPIGRAPHY

Newly discovered Tamil inscription from the Tambaram Area, MCC Magazine, 42, 1973.

Computer techniques of image enhancement in the study of a Pallava Grantha inscription , Studies in Indian Epigraphy, Vol. 2, Journal of Epigraphical Society of India, pp. 55-56, 1975.

The invention of the Brahmi script, Souvenir of the Fourth Annual Congress of the Epigraphical Society of India, pp. 42-50, 1977, (with Lockwood, M).

A new Tamil-Brahmi inscription, The Sunday Standard, Madras, August 13, 1978, (with Emmanuel Jebarajan).

Kalvettu Ezhuthukkalil Tirukkural, Madras Christian College, Tambaram, 1980, (with Govindaraju, S. and Chandrasekaran, M).

ICONOMETRY

Iconometry of Pallava sculptures, Sunday Standard, Sep. 3, 1978.

An application of component analysis to the study of South Indian sculptures, Computers and Humanities Vol. 14, pp. 29-37, 1980, (with Bagavandas, M. and Govindaraju, S).

An iconometric study of Pallava sculptures, Kalakshetra Quarterly, Vol. 3, No.2, pp. 7-15, 1980, (with Bagavandas, M. and Govindaraju, S).

Iconometric analysis of the sculptures of the Dharmaraja Ratha, in K.V. Raman et al (Eds.), Srinidhih, Perspectives in Indian Archaeology and Culture, New Era Publications, Madras, pp. 137-150, 1983, (with Bagavandas, M. and Govindaraju, S).

Cluster analysis of facial proportions of South Indian sculptures, Advances in Information Sciences and Technology, in Dutta Majumder (Ed.), Vol. 1, pp. 137-146, 1984, (with Govindaraju, S., Bagavandas, M. and Chandrasekaran, R).

Temple carvings of Southern India, Perspectives in Computing, Vol. 5, No. 1, pp. 34-43, 1985, (with Govindaraju, S. and Bagavandas, M).

Computer analysis of bronze images of South India: an iconometric study, Tamil civilization, Vol. 3, Nos. 2 and 3, pp. 83-100, 1985, (with Govindaraju, S. and Bagavandas, M).

INDUS SCRIPT

Indus Script: challenge and response, The Sunday Standard, Madras, May 6, 1979, (with Abdul Huq).

Classifications of frequently occurring inscriptions of the Indus civilization in relation to metropolitan centres, STAT-44/80, Madras Christian College.

Cluster analysis of Indus signs - a computer approach, Proceedings of the Fifth International Tamil Conference held in January 1981, at Madurai, pp. 2-15 - 2-23, (with Abdul Huq).

Segmentation of unusually long texts of Indus writings: A mathematical approach, Journal of the Epigraphical Society of India, Vol. 9, pp. 68-77, 1982, (with Abdul Huq).

Statistical analysis of Harappan signs and sites, CALTIS-85, Special issue of Seminar on Calligraphy, Lettering and Typography of Indian Scripts, pp. 97-99, 1985, (with Abdul Huq).

Inscribed objects and Harappan signs: A computer analysis, Journal of Asian Studies, Vol. 2, No. 2, pp. 1-21, 1985, (with Abdul Huq).

Segmentation of Indus texts: A dynamic programming approach: Computers and the Humanities, Vol. 22, pp. 11-21, 1988, (with Abdul Huq).

INFORMATION THEORY

Entropy of logarithmic series distributions, Sankhya Series A, Vol. 24, pp. 419-420, 1962.

Efficient methods of telegraphy, typewriting and teleprinting in Tamil, Tamil Culture, Vol. 10, pp. 107-120, 1963.

Entropy of Tamil Prose, Information and Control, Vol. 6, pp. 297-300, 1963.

An information-theoretic test for familiarity with a foreign language, Journal of Psychological Researches, Vol. 8, pp. 267-272, 1964.

Style as information in Karnatic music, Journal of Music Theory, Vol. 8, pp. 69-74, 1964, (with Rajagopalan, K.R).

The general Dirichlet's series distribution, Journal of the Indian Statistical Association, Vol. 2 and 3, pp. 69-74, 1964.

A note on the entropy of Telugu prose, Information and Control, Vol. 13, pp. 281-283, 1968, (with Balasubrahmanyam, P).

MUSIC AND MUSICAL INSTRUMENTS

Some new light on stringed instruments of the ancient Tamil country, MCC Magazine, 34, 1965.

Computer recognition and transliteration of mridangam mnemonics, Quarterly Journal of the National Centre for Performing Arts, Vol.7, pp. 11-17, 1978, (with Chandrasekaran, M., and Chandrasekaran, R).

A Pallava musical instrument, The Sunday Standard, January 28, 1979.

Computer recognition of South Indian musical scores, MCC Magazine, 49, 1980, (with Chandrasekaran, M., and Chandrasekaran, R).

NATURE STUDIES

Some uncommon bird visitors observed in and around Tambaram, Newsletter for Birdwatchers, Vol. 3, pp. 9-10, 1963.

Bulbuls eating flowers, Newsletter for Birdwatchers, Vol. 3, p. 12, 1963.

Butterflies of Tambaram, MCC Magazine, Vol. 32,pp. 101-103, 1963.

A plea for the study of migration of butterflies, Newsletter for Birdwatchers, Vol. 4, pp. 6-7, March 1964.

The alate invasion, Motivator, No. 6, p. 27, 1967.

The Mellushian Cuckoo, Newsletter for Birdwatchers, Vol. 8, p. 9, 1968.

Medicinal plants used by the people of the Narikurava tribe (Tamil), Aaraaichi, Vol. 3, pp. 354-357, 1973, (with Giles Lal, D. and Livingstone, C).

Herbal medicines of the Narikoravas, Folklore, (Calcutta), Vol. 14, pp. 363-366, 1973, (with Giles Lal, D. and Livingstone, C).

Migratory birds of Tambaram area, Nature Lovers Newsletter, Vol. 1, No. 2, pp. 3-4, 1975.

Tambaram flora and early Tamil literature, MCC Magazine, 45, pp. 21-26, 1976.

The Neophron vultures of Thirukkalukundram, Newsletter for Birdwatchers, Vol. 17, No. 6, pp. 2-4, 1977.

Butterflies of Tambaram: a checklist STAT 35/78, Madras Christian College, 1978.

Occurrence of the Glossy Ibis at Vedanthangal, Newsletter for Birdwatchers, Vol. 24, pp. 12-13, 1984.

SOCIO - ECONOMIC AND POLITICAL SURVEYS

D.M.K. has clear edge over Old Congress, The Mail, February 19, 1971.

Savings behavior of producer-households: a study of motivations, Southern Economic Review, pp. 174-188, 1972, (with Kurien, C.T).

Student opinion on convocation and honorary degrees, MCC Magazine, 41, pp. 39-40, 1972.

Children's vision: A sample survey of children in Tamil Nadu, MCC Magazine, 45, pp. 40-41, 1976.

Surveys, MCC Magazine, 47, pp. 21-26, 1978, (with Bala, S. and Govindaraju, S).

Election prospects, ASIDE, 50, November, 1979.

Public opinion on summary punishment of criminals, MCC Magazine, 50, p. 59, 1981.

Parliamentary elections in Tamil Nadu: Report of a pre-election survey conducted in December 1979, Religion and Society, Vol. 29, pp. 58-75, 1982.

TAMIL STUDIES

Context-sensitive rules in Tolkappiam, Proceedings of the Second World Tamil Conference at Madras, pp. 314-318, 1968.

Statistical aids in Tamil Studies, Saiva Siddhanta, Vol. 3, pp. 44-48, 1968 (with Rajagopalan, K. R.).

Grammars for kernal sentences in Tamil, Foundations of Language, Vol. 7, pp. 508-518, 1971.

Computer methods of dating Tamil inscriptions, Proceedings of Fifth International Tamil Conference held at Madurai, pp. 2.7-2.13, January 1981, (with Chandrasekaran, M. and Chandrasekaran, R).

The origin of the Tamil script, Tamil Studies, Vol. 2, pp. 8-23, 1982.

Miscellaneous

Are computers a threat to man? MCC Magazine, 35, pp. 42-43, 1965.

Recommendations of the Education Commission on the study of languages, Motivator, Vol. 3, pp. 14-15, 1967.

Indian heritage, A catalogue of books (mimeo), Tambaram, 1968, (with Nirmal, C.J).

Polished stone axes: two new records, MCC Magazine, 37, No. 2, pp. 22-24, 1968.

History of the Tambaram area (Tamil), Souvenir of the Tambaram Municipality, 1970.

Iron-smelting in Tamil Nadu, ancient sites near Vandalur, The Mail, March 28, 1970.

Commemoration Day Address, MCC Magazine, 43, pp. 17-20, 1974.

South Indian kolam patterns, Kalashetra Quarterly, Vol. 1, No. 1, pp. 9-14, 1978.

Perception of structure and complexity in South Indian kolam patterns, STAT-62/86, Madras Christian College, 1986.

Hinduism and Jainism, in Douglas, J.D. (Ed.), Twentieth Century Encyclopaedia of Religious Knowledge, Second Edition, , Baker Book House, Michigan, U.S.A., 1987.

A Perspective in Theoretical Computer Science

Commemorative Volume for Gift Siromoney

Graph grammars for map generation[1]

by

Kunio Aizawa

and

Akira Nakamura

Department of Applied Mathematics
Hiroshima University
Higashi-Hiroshima, 724 Japan

ABSTRACT Recently, there have been a number of interesting papers on map and graph generating systems. The basic primitives of such systems are map and graph, respectively. They are some kinds of the formal grammars generating sets of maps or graphs as their languages. A map is defined as a finite connected planar graph. So, maps are considered to have some underlying structure corresponding to embedded space. It seems to be one of the reasons why maps are more difficult to manipulate by a computer than graphs. In this paper, we discuss a condition to reconstruct maps from corresponding graphs without any confusion. Then we propose a class of graph grammars which generate graphs with some additional informations to reconstruct maps preserving their structures from its language. At last, we show that the class of GLM systems is same as the class of a popular map generating system.

1. INTRODUCTION

Recently, there have been a number of interesting papers on map and graph generating systems[1) - 3)]. The basic primitives of such systems are map and graph, respectively. They are some kinds of the formal grammars generating sets of maps or graphs as their languages.

A graph is defined by a set of nodes and a partial relation on the set, i.e., nodes and edges, (and sometimes the labelling functions on them). Thus a graph is less affected by a specific space, e.g., an array or a plane, since it need not be embedded to

[1] This research is partly supported by the Grant-in-aid for Scientific Researches (63740120) from the Ministry of Education, Science and Culture, Japan.

such a structure. On the other hand, a map is a finite connected planar graph in which multiple edges and loops are allowed. Furthermore, for every vertex in a map there exists a closed path to itself such that going in the clockwise direction from vertex to vertex always the rightmost different edge is chosen to form the path. This definition implies the following:

(1) A map consists of a finite set of regions (faces).

(2) Each face is surrounded by a finite, circular sequence of edges (boundary).

(3) One or more edges meet in a vertex.

(4) Each edge has one or two vertices associated with it.

(5) Edges cannot cross without forming a vertex.

(6) There are no vertices without an associated edge.

(7) Every edge is a part of the boundary of a face.

(8) Two faces can have in common one or more vertices and one or more edges of their boundaries.

(9) There are no islands in faces.

From the above definition, it is not so difficult to see that maps have some underlying structure corresponding to embedded space (e.g., two-dimensional plane). It seems to be one of the reasons why maps are more difficult to manipulate by a computer than graphs. Therefore it seems useful if a map can be manipulated as a graph. In fact, it is easy to define, for a given map M, a corresponding graph M_G as the dual graph of M (see Fig. 1a-b). In general, it is not so easy, however, to reconstruct the original map M from its corresponding graph since the graph M_G is same as, for example, the graph M_G' but the reconstructed map M' from M_G' is not same as the original map M (see Fig. 1c-d).

In this paper, we discuss a condition to reconstruct maps from corresponding graphs without any confusion. Then we propose a class of graph grammars (GLM systems) which generate graphs with some additional informations to reconstruct maps preserving their structures from its language. At last, we show that the class of GLM systems is same as the class of a famous map generating system (BPM0L systems).

2. BASIC DEFINITIONS AND NOTATIONS

Basic definitions and notations of graphs and maps are reviewed in this section.

Definition 1. A *labelled graph* is a system $H = (V, E, \Sigma_V, \Sigma_E, \rho_V, \rho_E)$, where V is a finite nonempty set called the set of nodes, E is a set of pairs of two elements from V called the set of edges, Σ_V is a finite nonempty set called the set of node labels, Σ_E is a finite nonempty set called the set of edge labels, ρ_V is a mapping from V into Σ_V called the nodes labelling function, and ρ_E is a mapping from E into Σ_E called the edges labelling_function. H is called a graph over (Σ_V, Σ_E).

Definition 2. Let $A = (V, E, \Sigma_V, \Sigma_E, \rho_V, \rho_E)$ and $B = (V', E', \Sigma_V, \Sigma_E, \rho_V', \rho_E')$ over (Σ_V, Σ_E). An *isomorphism* of A onto B is a bijective mapping σ from V into V' such that $\rho_V' \circ \sigma = \rho_V$, $\rho_E' \circ \sigma = \rho_E$ and $E' = \{(\sigma(x), \sigma(y)) \mid (x,y) \in E\}$. We say that A is *isomorphic* to B.

Combinatorial definitions of maps used in this paper are almost same as those of Tutte[4).]

Definition 3. Let S be a finite set of elements called *crosses* such that the number of elements of S is to be divisible by 4, i.e., $|S|=4n$. Then the set S is partitioned in to n disjoint quarters called *edge*. If X is a cross, the other members of its cell are denoted by θX, ϕX, and $\theta\phi X$.

Definition 4. Let $A=\{X, \theta X, \phi X, \theta\phi X\}$ be an edge, then θ and ϕ are permutations satisfying the following properties:

(1) $\theta^2=\phi^2=I$ and $\theta\phi=\phi\theta$.

(2) The four crosses X, θX, ϕX, and $\theta\phi X$ are all distinct.

Here I denotes the identical permutation of S. θ and ϕ are called the *first involution* and *second involution*, respectively.

Definition 5. Let P be any permutation of S. It arranges the crosses in disjoint cyclic sequence called the *orbit* of P. The orbit through a cross X, denoted as J(P, X), is

$$J(P, X)=(X, PX, P^2X, \dots, P^{m-1}X),$$

where m is the least positive integer such that $P^mX=X$.

The involutions θ and ϕ have their orbits. In their case m=2 for each cross. We refer to the number of members of an orbit J(Q, X) as the *length of orbit*, denoted by |J(Q, X)|.

Definition 6. The permutations θ, ϕ, and P are said to define a *premap* L=L(θ, ϕ, P) on S if the following two conditions are satisfied:

(1) $P\theta=\theta P^{-1}$.

(2) For each cross X, the orbit of P through X and θX are distinct.

We say that P is the *basic permutation* of the premap L.

Definition 7. A *vertex* of a premap L=L(θ, ϕ, P) is defined as a pair v of two orbit J(P, X) and J(P, θX).

Let A={X, θX, ϕX, $\theta\phi$X} be an edge, then the unordered pairs {X, θX} and {ϕX, $\theta\phi$X} are called its two *half-edges* in L. The two half-edges of A may be absorbed by the same vertex or by two different vertices. In the first case, A is a *loop* of L, and in the second case a *link*.

Let S be a set of crosses, and Ψ_K be a group generated by the set K={θ, ϕ, P} of permutations of S. Then Ψ_K partitioned S into nonnull equivalence classes such that two crosses belong to the same equivalence class if and only if some member of Ψ_K maps one into the other. The equivalence classes of Ψ_K are called the connected components of L.

Definition 8. A premap L=L(θ, ϕ, P) on S is called a *map* on S, denoted as M(θ, ϕ, P), if L has exactly one connected component.

An example of intuitive meanings of edges, half-edges, permutations, orbits, and vertices is represented in Fig. 2. It is then found that the drawing partitions the plane into disjoint connected regions. These are called the *faces* of the map.

Definition 9. A map M is called a *proper map* if each face is bounded by a simple closed curve, i.e., there is no edge which is not a part of the boundary of a face

An example of the proper maps is shown in Fig. 3a. In Fig. 3b, we have an improper map. In the rest of this paper, we will treat proper maps only.

3. MAPS AND GRAPHS

As mentioned in the first section, maps have some underlying structure depending on embedded space and it is not necessarily true that corresponding graphs preserve the structures of original maps. In the case of simulating a map generating system by a digital computer, it seems useful if a map can be manipulated as a graph.In this section we define the corresponding graph of a given map and the reconstructed map from a graph. At first, we define isomorphism of maps.

Definition 10. [Tutte[4)]]. Let $M_1=M(\theta_1, \phi_1, P_1)$ and $M_2=M(\theta_2, \phi_2, P_2)$ be maps on sets S_1 and S_2, respectively. An *isomorphism* of M_1 onto M_2 is a bijective mapping σ of S_1 onto S_2 with the following properties:
If $\sigma X_1=X_2$, where X_1 and X_2 are crosses of S_1 and S_2, respectively, then also $\sigma(\theta_1 X_1)=\theta_2 X_2$, $\sigma(\phi_1 X_1)=\phi_2 X_2$, and $\sigma(P_1 X_1)=P_2 X_2$.
If such an isomorphism exists, we say that map M_1 is *isomorphic* to M_2.

Now, we consider to construct a corresponding graph from a given map $M=M(\theta, \phi, P)$. Regarding a given map M as a planar graph, we define the corresponding graph M_G as the dual graph of M (see Fig. 4). If edges of M are directed, the directions of corresponding edges are defined as right to left according to original edges (see Fig. 5). We also define the reconstructed map M'as the dual graph of M_G providing that the node representing the unbounded area of M becomes the environment (see Fig. 6). Note here that we treat proper maps only. The faces and edges of M are corresponding to the nodes and edges of M_G, respectively. In M_G, however, there is no counterpart to the vertices of M. Namely, M_G cannot represent the orbits of each half-edge. Thus, if we confuse the order of orbit by interchanging some edges of M_G to construct a new graph M_G' providing that they are isomorphic, the map M' reconstructed from M_G' need not be isomorphic to the original map M. From the definition of isomorphism of maps, it is obvious that if the dual graph M_G has the knowledge of orbits of the basic permutation P of M, the map M' reconstructed from M_G is isomorphic to the original map M.

In the case where the generative process of maps is emphasized, faces and edges of maps are usually labelled with a symbol. A definition of the labelled map is as follows:

Definition 11. A *labelled map* is a system $M=M(\theta, \phi, P, \Sigma_E, \Sigma_F, \rho_E, \rho_F)$, where $M(\theta, \phi, P)$ is a map, Σ_E is a finite nonempty set of edge labels, Σ_F is a finite nonempty set of face labels, ρ_E is a mapping from the set of all edges into Σ_E, ρ_F is a mapping from the set of all face boundaries into Σ_F. M is called a map over (Σ_E, Σ_F).

The isomorphic relation of labelled maps are defined as follows:

Definition 12. Let $M=M(\theta, \phi, P, \Sigma_E, \Sigma_F, \rho_E, \rho_F)$ and $M'=M(\theta', \phi', P', \Sigma_E', \Sigma_F', \rho_E', \rho_F')$ be labelled maps on sets S_1 and S_2, respectively. If map $M(\theta, \phi, P)$ is isomorphic to $M(\theta', \phi', P')$ under an isomorphism σ and $\rho_E=\rho_E'\circ\sigma$, $\rho_F=\rho_F'\circ\sigma$, we say that M is isomorphic to M'.

4. GRAPH GRAMMARS GENERATING MAPS

In the last section, we realized that the orbit J(P, X) of each half-edge is necessary for graphs to reconstruct maps. By making use of this result, a graph grammar generating graphs which preserve the nearly equal relations of maps is proposed in this section. At first, we will review the definitions of map generating systems according to Lindenmayer and Rozenberg[5] and Does and Lindenmayer[6].

Definition 13. A *binary propagating map 0L system* G, denoted by BPM0L system, is a 5-tuple

$$G=\langle\Delta, \Sigma, P, R, \omega\rangle, \text{ where}$$

Δ is a finite nonempty set of edge alphabet,
Σ is a finite nonempty set of cell alphabet,
P is a finite nonempty set of edge production rules,
R is a finite nonempty set of cell production rules, and

ω is the starting map.

Alphabet Σ and Δ are disjoint. Moreover three special symbols: ∞ (the label of the environment), and +, - (orientation signs associated with edge labels in production rules) are used. Let the *oriented edge alphabet* Δ_0 be the Cartesian product of Δ and {+, -}. For convenience we will usually write its element in the form A^+ and A^-.

Edge production rules are of the form $A \rightarrow \alpha$, where $A \in \Delta$ and $\alpha \in {\Delta_0}^+$.

Cell productions are of two kinds:

(1) *chain productions* of the form $(X, a) \rightarrow b$, where $a, b \in \Sigma$, $X \in {\Delta_0}^+$ and

(2) *division productions* of the form $(X, a) \rightarrow (X_1, b, X_2, c, D)$, where $a, b, c \in \Sigma$, $D \in \Delta_0$, and $X_1, X_2 \in {\Delta_0}^+$. X, X_1 and X_2 are all finite.

Definition 14. A *direct derivation step*, denoted by $\Rightarrow$, in a BPM0L system is performed as follows:

(1) First of all, every edge is rewritten as a sequence of edges. This rewriting is governed by an edge production rule $A \rightarrow \alpha$. For example, if the edge production is

$$A \rightarrow B^- C^+ D^-,$$

then Fig. 7 shows this derivation step.

(2) After each edge of the map has been rewritten, we apply the cell production rules.

  (a) If the set of cell production rules P contains a chain production $(X, a) \rightarrow b$, then a cell labelled a can change its label to b.

  (b) If P contains a division production $(X, a) \rightarrow (X_1, b, X_2, c, D)$, then a cell labelled a can acquire a division edge between its two vertices u_1 and u_2 only if the sequence β of directed edges leading from u_1 to u_2 in the clockwise direction is equal to X_1, and the sequence γ of directed edges leading clockwise from u_2 to u_1 is equal to X_2. The division edge will be labelled by D without its sign and its associated arrow points from u_1 to u_2 if sign of D is +, or from u_2 to u_1 otherwise.

  (c) If P contains neither a chain production nor a division production for a given cell then the label of the cell remains unchanged in this derivation step.

As usual in formal language theory, a *derivation* is the reflexive and transitive closure of ⇒, denoted by ⇒*.

The *language* of G, denoted by L(G), is defined as L(G)={M | ω⇒*M}.

Example 1.[Lindenmayer and Rozenberg[5)]]

Let G=<{0, 1, 2}, {a, b}, P, R, ω> be a BPM0L system, where

edge productions are $0 \to 0^+$

$1 \to 1^- 0^+$

$2 \to 0^+ 0^-$,

cell productions are $(0^- 1^- 0^+ 0^+ 0^+, a) \to (0^- 1^-, a, 0^+ 0^+ 0^+, b, 2^+)$

$(0^- 0^- 0^- 1^+ 0^+, a) \to (0^- 0^- 0^-, b, 1^+ 0^+, a, 2^+)$

$(0^+ 0^- 0^-, b) \to b$

$(0^+ 0^+ 0^- 0^+, b) \to b$

$(0^+ 0^+ 0^- 0^+ 0^+, b) \to b$

$(0^- 0^- 0^+ 0^- 0^-, b) \to b$,

the starting map is shown in Fig. 8.

Then the derivation steps of G is shown in Fig. 9.

Definition 15. An *extended binary propagating map 0L system* G, denoted by EBPM0L system, is a 7-tuple

$G = <\Delta, \Sigma, P, R, \omega, \Delta_T, \Sigma_T>$, where

Δ, Σ, P, R, and ω are same as in the definition of BPM0L systems,

Δ_T is a finite nonempty subset of Δ,

Σ_T is a finite nonempty subset of Σ.

The language of G is defined as

L(G)={M | ω⇒*M and M is labelled by Δ_T, Σ_T only}.

Lemma 1. For any (E)BPM0L system G, if ω is a proper map, then every element of L(G) is also a proper map.

Proof: Assume that map M∈L(G) is an improper map. Then, there exists at least one boundary ξ which is not a simple closed curve and has the length three or more in M. So the sequence of vertices which ξ passes can be written as nαnβn, where n is a vertex of M and α, β are sequences of vertices. Thus two parts nαn and nβn of ξ are connected at a vertex n. Since ω is a proper map, such structure must be constructed by the applications of production rules. Since (E)BPM0L system is a propagating system, such structure cannot be generated by the applications of edge production rules and chain productions. So it must be a division production. A division production adds an edge to a map. Thus such structure must be started as a loop. However, from the definition of division productions, $(X, a) \rightarrow (X_1, b, X_2, c, D)$, where $a, b, c \in \Sigma$, $D \in \Delta_0$, and $X_1, X_2 \in \Delta_0^+$, the division edge cannot be a loop. This is a contradiction.

Now we propose a graph generating system called "graph L system with orbital matrices". Unlike usual graph generating systems, its sentential forms and production rules are represented in a form of matrix. This matrix represents nodes and their connectedness relations of graph. Furthermore, they have another set of matrices called "orbital matrices" representing the orbit of underlying maps.

Definition 13. A *graph L system with orbital matrices*, denoted by GLM system, is a 6-tuple

$$G = \langle \Delta, \Sigma, *, E, N, \omega \rangle, \text{ where}$$

Δ is a finite nonempty set of edge alphabet,
Σ is a finite nonempty set of node alphabet ($\Delta \cap \Sigma = \emptyset$),
$*$ is a symbol for orbital matrices ($* \notin \Delta \cup \Sigma$),
E is a finite nonempty set of edge adding rules,
N is a finite nonempty set of node replacement rules,
ω is the starting graph.

As in the definitions of BPM0L systems, three special symbols: ∞ (the label for environmental node), and +, - (direction signs for edges in production rules) are used. The oriented edge alphabet Δ_0 is also defined as in the case of BPM0L systems.

(1) An edge adding rule is of form $a \rightarrow \beta$, where $a \in \Delta$ and $\beta \in \Delta_0^+$.

(2) A node replacement rule is of form $(X_1, A) \rightarrow \begin{bmatrix} (X_2, B) & e \\ & (X_3, C) \end{bmatrix}$, where $A, B, C \in \Sigma$, $X_1, X_2, X_3 \in \Delta_0^+$, and $e \in \Delta_0$.

The starting graph ω is represented by a set of matrices. One of these matrices denotes nodes and edges of ω. The oriented edge alphabet on this matrix means slightly different than that on BPM0L systems. Each edge label on a row corresponding to a node n signed with "+" if its edge emerges from n, "-" if its edge directs to n. Each of the rest corresponding to an edge (i.e., there exist the number of edges plus one matrices) represents the orbit of underlying map (orbital matrices). The edges marked with "*" on each of these matrices are the next edges in orbit for each half-edge (in clockwise direction) and the edge to which it corresponds. Therefore, there exist at most three marks on it (see Fig. 10).

A direct derivation step of GLM system G, denoted by $\Rightarrow$, is performed as follows:

(1) At first, every edge is rewritten as an ordered set of edges. For example, if an edge adding rule $e \rightarrow \beta_1 \beta_2 ... \beta_n$ is applied to an edge labelled with e, then

(a) the matrix element corresponding to the rewritten edge is partitioned into n elements and the i-th element is labelled with β_i if the sign of e is +, labelled with β_{n-i+1}^- if the sign of e is -, where β_i^- denotes β_i with opposite sign.

(b) New orbital matrices for β_1 to β_n are introduced. Each orbital matrix for β_i, $2 \leq i \leq n-1$, is marked with $*$ at β_i and β_{i+1} if the sign of e is +, β_{i-1} if the sign of e is -. The orbital matrix for β_1 is marked at β_1 and any edges excluding e itself such that their orbital matrices are marked at e, if the sign of e is +, any edges (excluding e) corresponding to any mark in the orbital matrix of e, if the sign of e is -. If the sign of e is +, the orbital matrix for β_n is same as that of β_1 for the case of -, otherwise same as for the case of -.

(c) Delete the orbital matrix for e.

(d) The matrix element corresponding to e of each orbital matrix for other edges is partitioned into n elements and marked with $*$ at β_1 if formerly marked at e and the sign of e is +, β_n if formerly marked at e and the sign of e is -.

(2) After each edge of the graph has been rewritten, the node replacement rules are applied. For example, if $(X_1, A) \rightarrow \begin{bmatrix} (X_2, B) & e \\ & (X_3, C) \end{bmatrix}$ is applied to a node n labelled with A, then

(a) An edge e_1 absorbed by the node is selected nondeterministically. The orbital matrix of e_1 can tell which edge is "the next edge" on the orbit containing e_1. So the next edge e_2 is determined uniquely. Repeating this procedure, a sequence, $e_1 e_2 ... e_m$ of all edges absorbed by n is obtained. If the concatenation of edge labels of the sequence is equal to X_1, this rule can be applied to n. Note at this time, from a view point of a node, the signs of edge labels on the column corresponding to the node is opposite to that of on the node replacement rules.

(b) At the same time of above procedure, the last edge, e_i, of X_2 and the first edge, e_{i+1}, of X_3 are selected nondeterministically.

(c) Each row corresponding to n of all matrices is divided to two rows corresponding to the node labelled with B and C. The edge between B and C is labelled with e. The edges e_1 to e_m are distributed among these two rows. e_j is on the row of B, if it is of X_2, on the row of C, if it is of X_3. Each mark on the orbital matrices is moved to the corresponding row at the same time.

(d) The orbital matrices of e_i and e_m are marked with "*" at the edge between B and C. At that time, if the number of marks becomes more than three, the mark corresponding to e_1 or e_{i+1} must be deleted.

Here, we present an example of GLM system which simulates the derivation process of the BPM0L system in Example 1.

Example 2. Let G=<{0,1,2}, {a, b}, *, E, N, ω> be a GLMsystem, where

edge adding rules are

$$0 \to 0^+$$
$$1 \to 1^- 0^+$$
$$2 \to 0^+ 0^-,$$

node replacement rules are

$$(0^- 1^- 0^+ 0^+ 0^+, a) \to \begin{bmatrix} (0^- 1^-, a) & 2^- \\ & (0^+ 0^+ 0^+, b) \end{bmatrix}$$

$$(1^+ 0^+ 0^- 0^- 0^-, a) \to \begin{bmatrix} (1^+ 0^+, a) & 2^+ \\ & (0^- 0^- 0^-, b) \end{bmatrix}$$

$$(0^+ 0^- 0^-, b) \to (0^+ 0^- 0^-, b)$$

$$(0^+ 0^+ 0^- 0^+, b) \to (0^+ 0^+ 0^- 0^+, b)$$

$$(0^+ 0^+ 0^- 0^+ 0^+, b) \to (0^+ 0^+ 0^- 0^+ 0^+, b)$$

$$(0^-0^-0^+0^-0^-, b) \to (0^-0^-0^+0^-0^-, b),$$

the starting graph is shown in Fig. 11.
The derivation steps of G is shown in Fig. 12 (also in the matrix form).

From the definition of GLM system and Example 1, 2, it is not so difficult to see that each mark on the orbital matrices represents "next" edge (in clockwise direction) on the boundary of underlying map. It is shown[4)] that the boundaries are the orbit of the permutation $P\theta\phi$. Thus the orbit of the basic permutation can be reconstructed from the orbital matrices. Then the next lemma holds immediately.

Lemma 2. All maps reconstructed from a given graph generated by a GLM system are nearly equal to each other.

From the definition of GLM systems and Lemma stated above, the proof of the following theorem is not so difficult.

Theorem. The class of the set of maps reconstructed from graph languages generated by GLM systems is equal to the class of maps generated by BPM0L systems.

5. Conclusion

In this paper, we propose graph L systems generating graphs which have underlying structure of two-dimensional maps. They are slightly different from usual graph L systems using node replacement rules and graph embedding rules. In fact, they can be regarded as a kind of map generating systems which treat orbits explicitly. However, they can be treated easily by a digital computer. It is still difficult for usual map generating systems.

From a point of view of the formal language theory, if we introduce terminal alphabet to GLM systems (i.e., EGLM systems), it is clear that they have the same class as EBPM0L systems. We conjecture that the class of EGLM system is a subclass of a usual graph L systems (perhaps with some contexts and edge replacement rules). So GLM system may shed light on the relationship between graph and map generating systems.

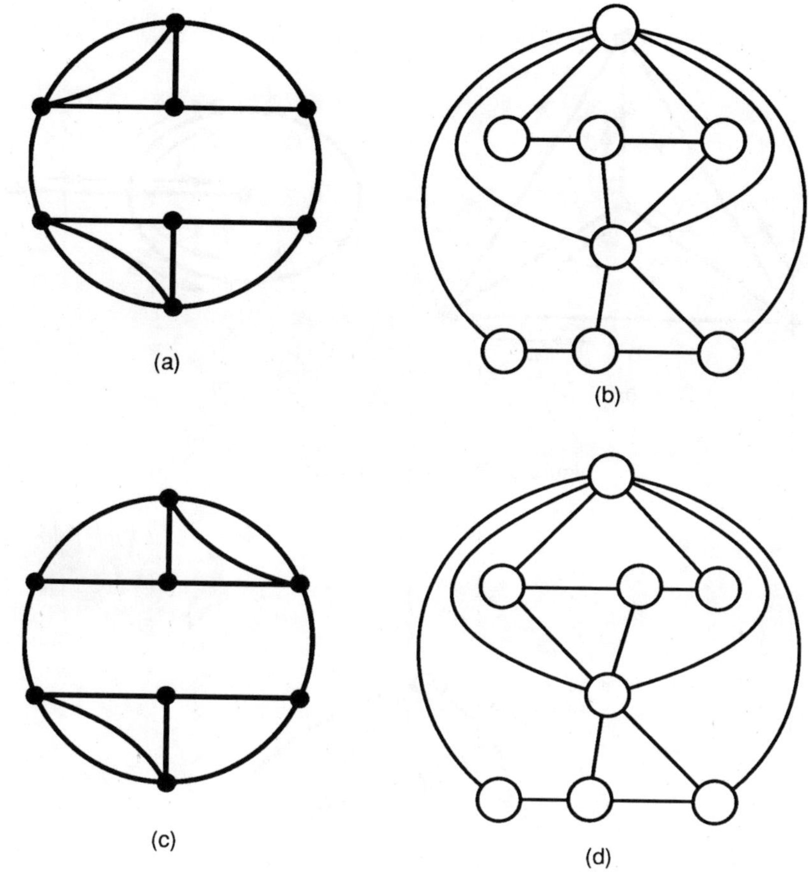

Figure 1. Maps and graphs.

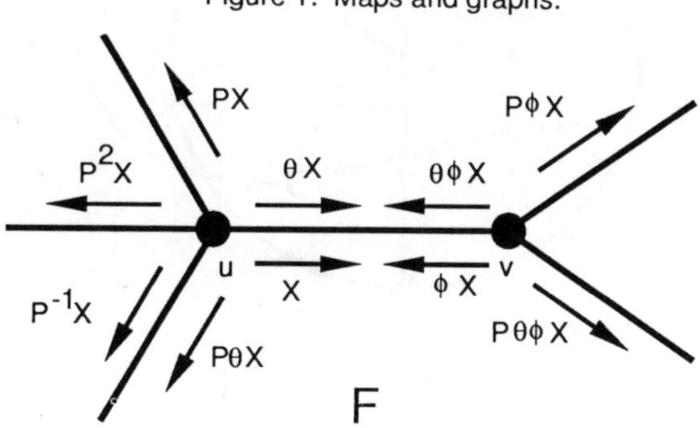

Figure 2. Drawing of a map.

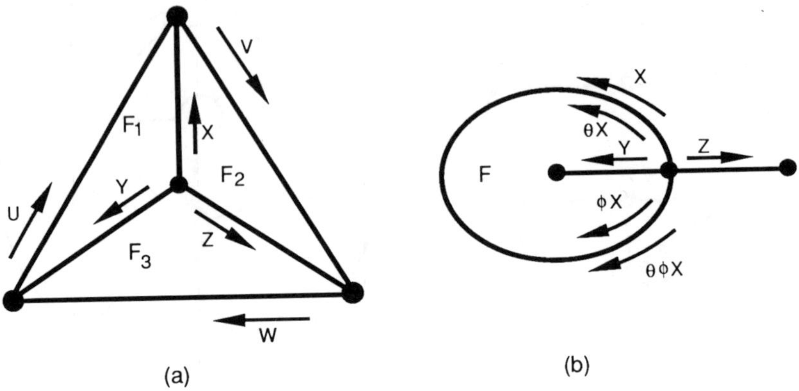

Figure 3. Proper and improper maps.

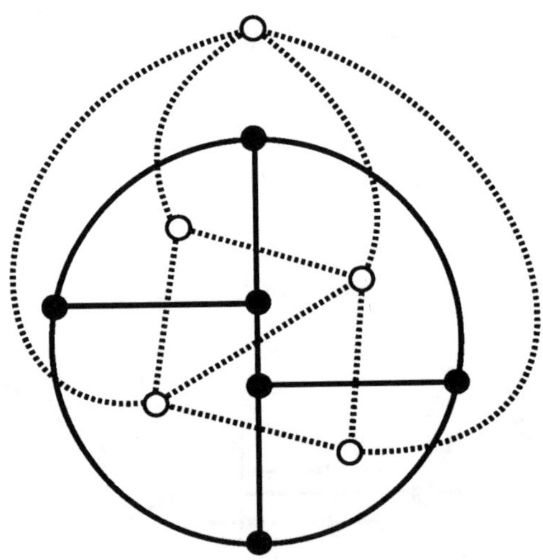

Figure 4. The dual graph of a map.

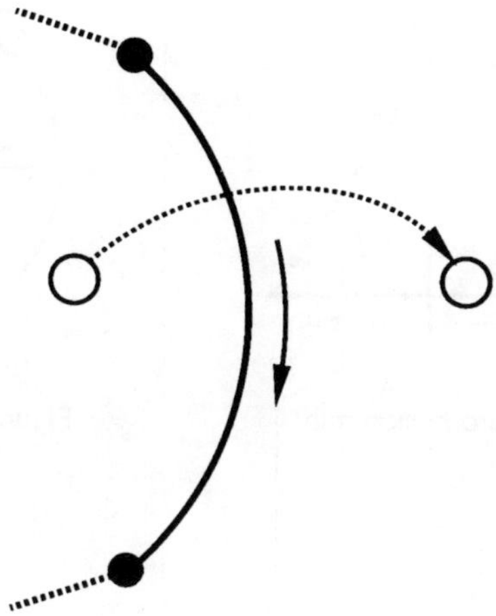

Figure 5. Direction of an edge.

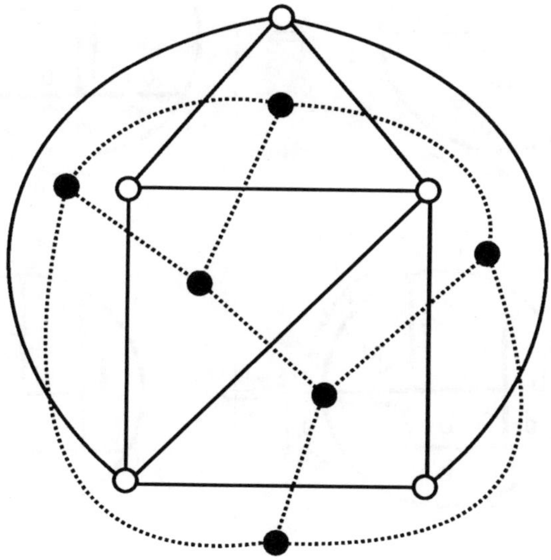

Figure 6. An underlying map of a graph.

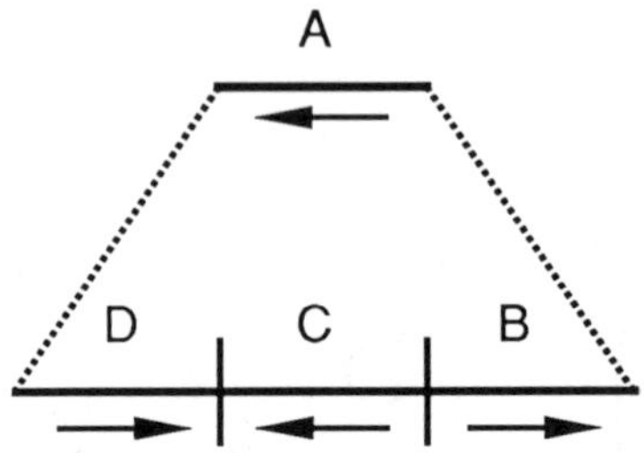

Figure 7. Edge production rule.

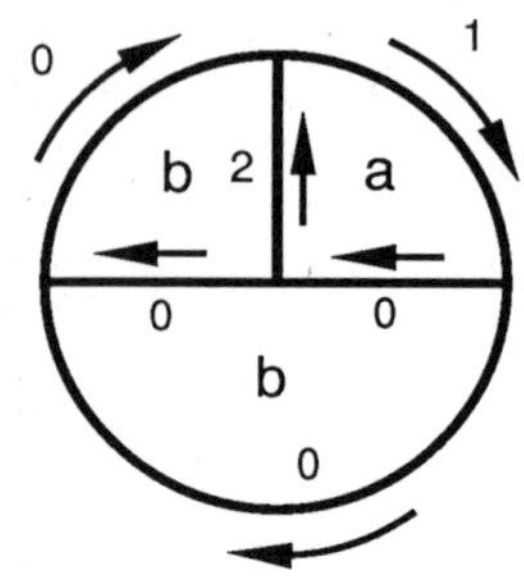

Figure 8. The starting map.

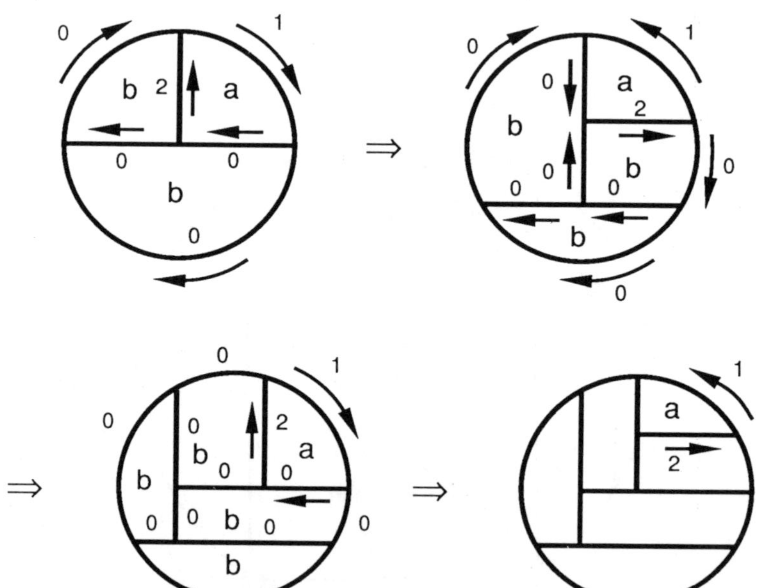

Figure 9. Derivation steps of BPM0L system.

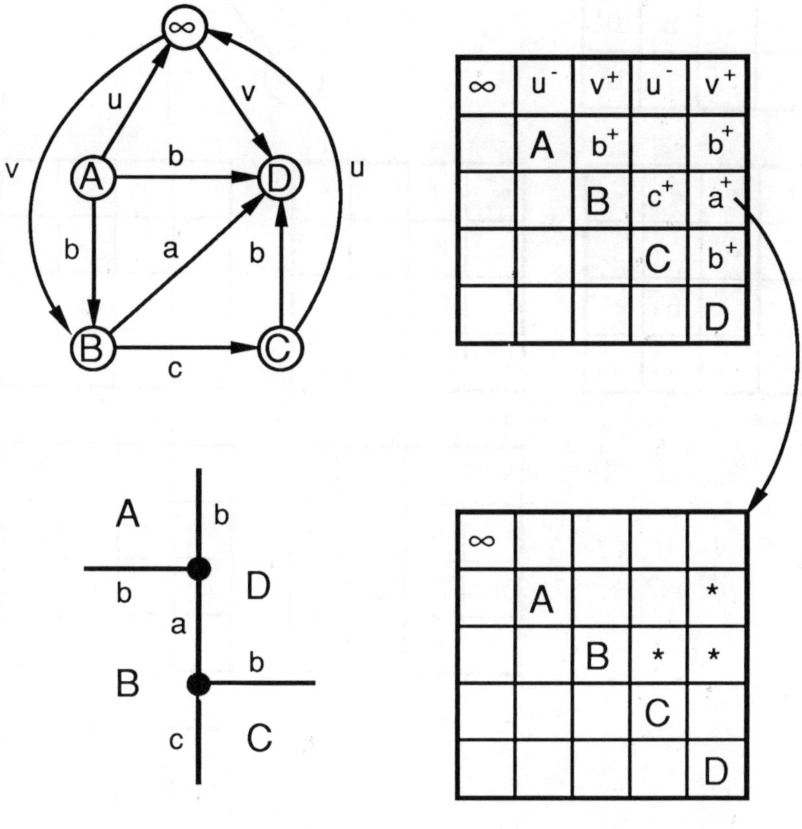

Figure 10. Matrix representation of a graph with orbital matrices.

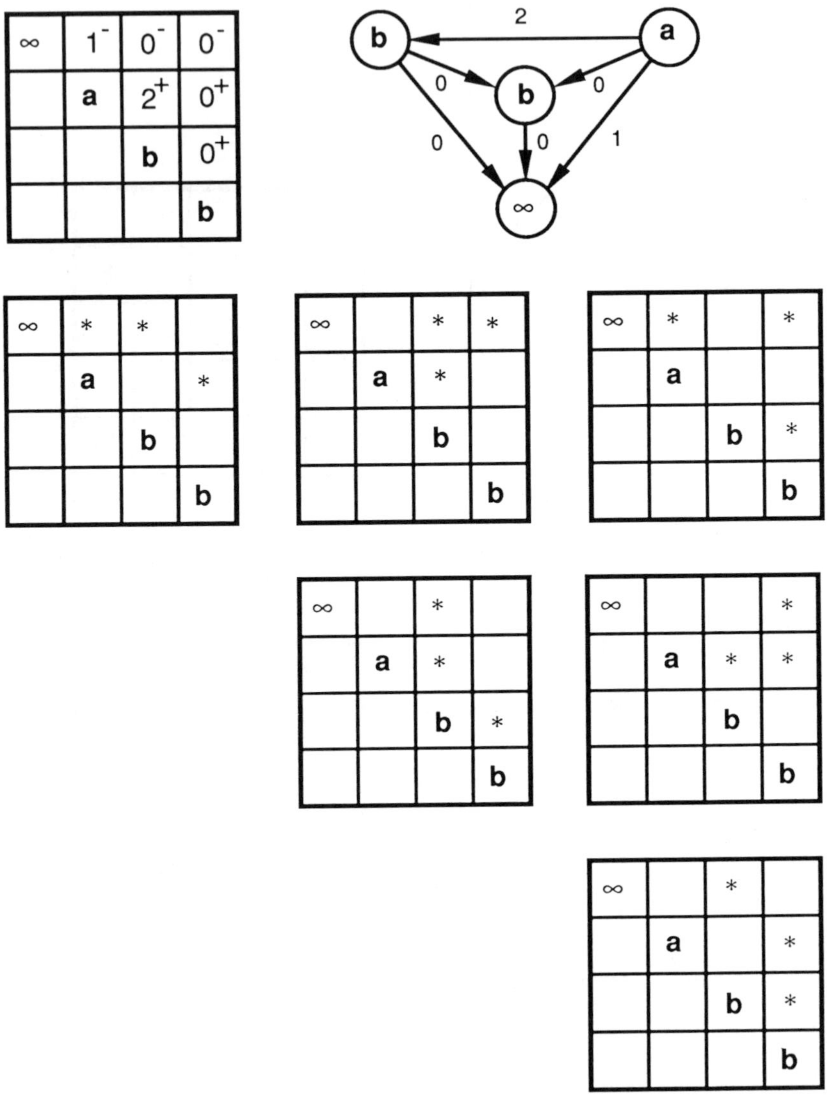

Figure 11. The starting graph.

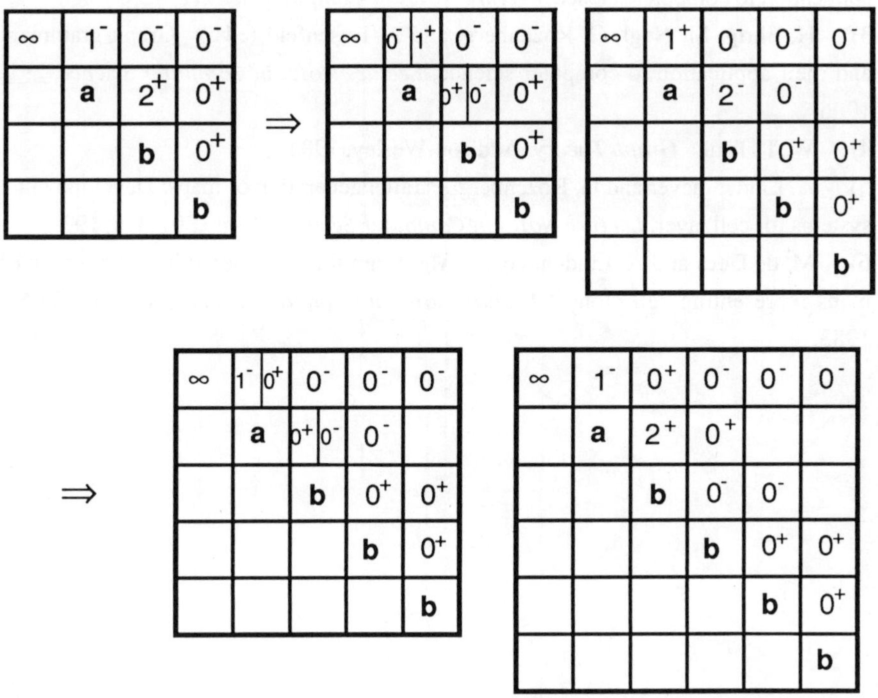

Figure 12. An example of the derivations of GLM systems.

References

1) V. Claus, H. Ehrig, and Rozenberg (eds.): Graph-grammars and their application to computer science and biology, *Lecture Notes in Computer Science*, 73, 1979.

2) H. Ehrig, M. Nagl, and G. Rozenberg (eds.): Graph-grammars and their application to computer science, *Lecture Notes in Computer Science*, 153, 1983.

3) H. Ehrig, M. Nagl, G. Rozenberg, and A. Rosenfeld (eds.): Graph-grammars and their application to computer science, *Lecture Notes in Computer Science*, 291, 1986.

4) W. T. Tutte: *Graph Theory*, Addison-Wesley, 1984.

5) A. Lindenmayer and G. Rozenberg: Parallel generation of maps: Developmental systems for cell layer, *Lecture Notes in Computer Science*, 73, pp.301-316, 1979.

6) M. de Does and A. Lindenmayer: Algorithm for the generation and drawing of maps representing cell clones, *Lecture Notes in Computer Science*, 153, pp.39-57, 1983.

A NOTE ON HDTOL LANGUAGES AND THE EQUIVALENCE OF DETERMINISTIC PUSHDOWN TRANSDUCERS*

Karel Culik II

Dept.of Computer Science
University of South Carolina
Columbia, SC 29208, USA

Juhani Karhumaki

Department of Mathematics
University of Turku
SF - 20500 Turku, Finland

ABSTRACT

We show that important decidability properties of HDTOL languages, cf. [4], and recently developed techniques of matching computations via HDTOL languages, cf. [5], can be used to solve a special case of the equivalence problem for deterministic pushdown transducers.

1. INTRODUCTION

The equivalence problem for deterministic pushdown automata (dpda's for short) is one of the major open problems of formal language theory. Much harder, but more important from the point of view of applications, is the same problem for deterministic pushdown transducers (dpdt's for short). While there are quite a number of partial solutions to the former problem, cf. [15], there are very few such for the latter one, cf. [10],[11],[3] or [12]. Indeed, even for the dpdt's with bounded domains the problem seems to be open. This should be compared to the fact that, in general, all natural problems for bounded (nondeterministic) context-free languages are decidable, cf. [8].

---

* Reported research was supported by the National Sciences Foundation Grant CCR-8702752.

Our goal in this note is two-fold. In the first place we demonstrate that quite a substantial subcase of the equivalence problem for dpdt's with bounded domains is decidable. In the second - and more important - place, we introduce a technique which potentially can be used to test the equivalence not only for dpdt's with bounded domains, but for some other family of dpdt's as well.

Our approach is based on two nice properties of the family of HDTOL languages. Firstly, as pointed out in [2], the intersection of two bounded context-free languages is an HDTOL language. Secondly, it is decidable, although computationally very hard, to test whether two morphisms, or even deterministic gsm's, are equivalent word by word on a given HDTOL language, cf. [4]. In addition to these facts we employ the techniques of matching computations via HDTOL languages originally introduced in [5] in order to attack the equivalence problem for deterministic multitape automata.

It follows that we can test for a suitably defined family of dpdt's whether they are equivalent on their common domain - a problem which is essentially harder than testing of their equivalence only. A result of similar nature has been established in [6].

2. PRELIMINARIES

We assume that the reader is familiar with the basics of formal language theory, cf. [9]. As regards to the theories of bounded context-free languages and HDTOL languages we refer to [8] and [14], respectively.

We recall the most important notions needed in this note. A DTOL language over the alphabet Σ is a language of the form

$$L_\infty = \bigcup_{i=0}^{\infty} L_i$$

where

$$L_0 = \{w\}$$

and

$$L_{i+1} = \bigcup_{j=1}^{t} h_j(L_i), i \geq 0,$$

for some word $w \in \Sigma^*$ and for a finite set $\{h_1,\ldots,h_t\}$ of morphisms of Σ^*. An HDTOL language is a morphic image of a DTOL language, i.e. of the form $g(L_\infty)$ for some morphism $g: \Sigma^* \to \Delta^*$ and a DTOL language $L_\infty \leq \Sigma^*$. Further, an EDTOL language is a language of the form $L_\infty \cap \Delta^*$ for some alphabet Δ and a DTOL language L_∞. An important property of DTOL languages is that the families of HDTOL and EDTOL languages coincide, cf. [13].

Following [8] we say that a language $L \subseteq \Sigma^*$ is bounded if there exists words $w_1,\ldots,w_n$ such that

$$L \subseteq w_1^* w_2^* \ldots w_n^*.$$

It is also shown in [8] that bounded context-free languages can be characterized in terms of semilinear sets, where the semilinearity is defined as follows. A subset of $\mathbf{N}^n$ is semilinear if it is a finite union of sets of the form

$$\{x_0 + \sum_{i=1}^{r} n_i x_i \mid n_i \geq 0 \} \quad (1)$$

for some vectors $x_0, x_1, \ldots, x_r$ in $\mathbf{N}^n$. Sets of the form (1) are called linear.

A deterministic pushdown automaton (dpda for short) consists of a finite set of states Q, a finite input alphabet Σ, a finite stack alphabet Γ, an initial state q_0, a finite set of final states, and a finite set of transitions E. Transitions are of the form

$$(p, \alpha, A) \longrightarrow (q, \gamma), \tag{2}$$

where $p, q \in Q$, $\alpha \in \Sigma \cup \{1\}$, $A \in \Gamma$ and $\gamma \in \Gamma^*$, and moreover satisfies well known determinism conditions, which guarantees for each input word at most one computation, for details cf. [9]. Our pushdown automaton accepts, as it is customary, with final states only (although the form of the acceptance is irrelevant for our considerations).

A deterministic pushdown transducer (dpdt for short) is obtained from the corresponding automaton by adding an output alphabet Δ and associating an output word to each transition of the automaton. Hence, transitions of a dpdt are of the form

$$(p, \alpha, A) \longrightarrow (q, \beta, \gamma) \tag{3}$$

where $\beta \in \Delta^*$ and the rest is like in (2).

Let T be a dpdt. We denote by $\mathrm{dom}(T) \subseteq \Sigma^*$ and $\mathrm{range}(T) \subseteq \Delta^*$ the domain and the range of the transduction defined by T. Clearly, both of them are context-free, and dom(T) is even a deterministic context-free language. Further, let $\mathrm{comp}(T) \subseteq E^*$ denote the set of all accepting computations of T. Then also comp(T) is a deterministic context-free language. Indeed, it is accepted by a dpdt which is obtained from T by replacing each transition (3) by

$$(p,(p,\alpha,A) \longrightarrow (q,\beta,\gamma),A) \longrightarrow (q,\beta,\gamma).$$

Hence, it follows that

$$\mathrm{dom}(T) = c\ (\mathrm{comp}(T)), \tag{4}$$

where c is a morphism $E^* \longrightarrow \Sigma^*$ defined by

$$c\ ((p,\alpha,A) \longrightarrow (q,\beta,\gamma)) = \alpha\ .$$

Observe, that (4) holds for nondeterministic transducers and automata as well.

Now, we define our class of dpdt's. A dpdt T is called strongly bounded if it satisfies the following two conditions:

(i) dom(T) is a bounded language,

(ii) there exists a deterministic gsm $\delta : \Sigma^* \longrightarrow E^*$ such that, for each w in dom(T), $\delta(w)$ in E^* is the unique computation of T with w as the input.

Condition (ii) above means that from input words of the transducer we can recover computations of these words via a deterministic gsm. It also follows that if such a δ exists, then necessarily

$$\delta \overset{\mathrm{dom}(T)}{\equiv} \gamma \circ c^{-1}, \tag{5}$$

where $\gamma = \{(w,w) \mid w \in \mathrm{comp}(T)\}$. That is to say, on dom(T), δ is equivalent to the composition of the inverse c and the intersection with comp(T). Clearly, this composition is a push-down transduction which is unambiguous on dom(T).

We do not know whether the existence of δ in (5) can be effectively tested. This is an unpleasant feature of the definition of strongly bounded dpdt's. However, for given gsm g it is easy to test whether g satisfies condition (ii), and therefore we can decide whether there exists such g with at most given number of states, see [3]. Also, many concrete examples of dpdt's with bounded domain are easily seen to be in our family. For example, transducers obtained from dpda's accepting the languages $\{(ab)^i a^i \mid i \geq 0\}$ and $\{a^i b^j a^i \mid i,j \geq 0\}$ in a natural way are such.

3. EQUIVALENCE OF STRONGLY BOUNDED DPDT'S

In this section we prove that the equivalence of two strongly bounded dpdt's can be effectively tested. In fact, we obtain this as a corollary of a stronger result. We say that two transducers T_1 and T_2 are weakly equivalent if they are equivalent on their common domain, i.e.,

$$T_1(x) = T_2(x) \text{ for all } x \text{ in } \mathrm{dom}(T_1) \cap \mathrm{dom}(T_2).$$

Clearly, the ordinary equivalence implies the weak one, but not vice versa.

Theorem 1 It is decidable whether two given strongly bounded dpdt's are weakly equivalent.

Proof. First of all, as we discussed above, the word "given" means here that the dpdt's T_i, for i = 1,2, in particular their transition functions δ_i, for i = 1,2, must be effectively given.

Now the decision procedure goes as follows. First we calculate the languages $\mathrm{dom}(T_i)$, for i = 1,2, in the form

$$\mathrm{dom}(T_i) = \{w_1(i)^{j_1} \ldots w_{n_i}(i)^{j_{n_i}} \mid (j_1, \ldots, j_{n_i}) \in K'\}$$

for some semilinear subsets K_i of $\mathbf{N}^{n_i}$. This can be done effectively by the theory of bounded context-free languages, cf. [8]. Then we look for the intersection $\mathrm{dom}(T_1) \cap \mathrm{dom}(T_2)$ the representation

$$\mathrm{dom}(T_1) \cap \mathrm{dom}(T_2) = \{w_1(1)^{j_1} \ldots w_{n_1}(1)^{j_{n_1}} \mid (j_1, \ldots, j_{n_1}) \varepsilon K'\} \quad (6)$$

where K' is also a semilinear set. This can be found since $\mathrm{dom}(T_2) \cap w_1(1)^* \ldots w_{n_1}(1)^*$ is (effectively) a bounded context-free language, and semilinear sets of vectors are (effectively) closed under intersection. In the third step we construct an EDTOL representation for $\mathrm{dom}(T_1) \cap \mathrm{dom}(T_2)$. Because of (6) this is easy to do, cf. also [2]. And, finally, we use the fact that each EDTOL language is also an HDTOL language, cf. [13], to obtain an HDTOL representation for the intersection $\mathrm{dom}(T_1) \cap \mathrm{dom}(T_2)$.

Now, let σ_i, for i = 1,2, be a function from the set E_i of transitions of T_i into Δ_i^* defined by

$\sigma_i(x_i)$ = the output of the transition x_i.

Then, we have:

T_1 and T_2 are weakly equivalent

iff

$$\sigma_1 \circ \delta_1(w) = \sigma_2 \circ \delta_2(w) \text{ for all } w \in \text{dom}(T_1) \cap \text{dom}(T_2) \quad (7)$$

But the mappings $\sigma_i \circ \delta_i$ are dgsm's. Consequently, (7) is the question of deciding whether or not two dgsm's are equivalent on a given HDTOL language. This was shown to be decidable in [4].

Corollary 1 The equivalence problem for strongly bounded dpdt's is decidable.

We conclude this section with a few remarks. First, in the definition of strongly bounded dpdt we can allow δ to be unambiguous finite transducer instead of dgsm. The proof of Theorem would remain the same. Second, throughout this paper we can use unambiguous pushdown transducers instead of deterministic ones. Third, in the proof of Corollary 1 only, it would be enough to test the equivalence of dgsm's on context-free language rather than on HDTOL languages. This is much easier, cf. [7] and [1].

REFERENCES

[1] Albert, J., Culik II, K. and Karhumäki, J., "Test sets for context-free languages and algebraic systems of equations", Inform. Control **52**, 172-186 (1982).

[2] Blattner, M. and Cremers, A., "Observations about bounded languages and developmental systems", Math. Systems Theory **10**, 253-258 (1977).

[3] Culik II, K. and Karhumäki, J., "Synchronizable deterministic pushdown automata and the decidability of their equivalence", Acta Informatica **23**, 597-605 (1986).

[4] Culik II, K. and Karhumäki, J., "The equivalence of finite valued transducers (on HDTOL languages) is decidable", Theoret. Comput. Sci. **47**, 71-84 (1986).

[5] Culik II, K. and Karhumäki, J., "HDTOL matching of computations of multitape automata", Technical Report TR88004, USC (1988).

[6] Culik II, K. and Karhumäki, J., "Loops in automata and HDTOL relations", Technical Report TR88003, USC (1988).

[7] Culik II, K. and Salomaa, A., "On the decidability of homomorphism equivalence for languages", J. Comput. Syst. Sci. **17**, 163-174 (1978).

[8] Ginsburg, S., The Mathematical Theory of Context-free Languages, McGraw Hill, New York (1966).

[9] Harrison, M., Introduction to Formal Language Theory, Addison-Wesley, Reading (1978).

[10] Ibarra, O., "On some decision questions concerning pushdown machines", Theoret. Comput. Sci. **24**, 313-322 (1983).

[11] Ibarra, O. and Rosier, L., "On the decidability of equivalence for deterministic pushdown transducers", Inf. Process. Lett. **13**, 89-93 (1981).

[12] Katayama, T., Tsuchiga, N. and Enemoto, H., "On the decidability of equivalence for deterministic pushdown transducers", Trans. Inst. Elect. Commun. Eng. Japan **58-D**, 760-767 (1975).

[13] Nielsen, M., Rozenberg, G., Salomaa, A. and Skyum, S., "Nonterminals, homomorphisms and codings in different variations of OL systems", Part I. Deterministic systems. Acta Informatica **4**, 87-106 (1974).

[14] Rozenberg, G. and Salomaa, A., The Mathematical Theory of L Systems, Academic Press, New York (1980).

[15] Tomita, E., "A direct branching algorithm for checking equivalence of some classes of deterministic pushdown automata", Inform. Control **52**, 187-238 (1982).

CLANS AND THE COMPLEXITY OF DEPENDENCE GRAPHS

A. Ehrenfeucht
Department of Computer Science
University of Colorado at Boulder
Boulder, CO 80309
U.S.A.

G. Rozenberg
Department of Computer Science
Leiden University
P.O. Box 9512, 2300 RA Leiden
The Netherlands

ABSTRACT

We demonstrate how to use the notion of a *clan* to establish the complexity of Γ-labelings of graphs and hence the complexity of dependence graphs.

INTRODUCTION

Dependence graphs arise in the theory of traces and in the theory of graph grammars, see, e.g., [AR1], [AR2], and [M]. Within the theory of traces the notion of dependence graph formalizes the notion of a process (in a trace system) and then a *naked dependence graph* describes the structure of a process. A characterization of naked dependence graphs is given in [ER1]. This characterization is given in terms of so called *Γ-labelings* which in turn are characterized using the notion of a *clan* (see, e.g., [ER2]).

In this note we elaborate more on this characterization and in particular we further explore the relationship between clans and Γ-labelings. We demonstrate how to use the notion of a clan in order to establish the complexity of recognizing the existence of Γ-labelings of a graph (and hence the complexity of recognizing naked dependence graphs).

We assume the reader to be familiar with [ER2] - we use without recalling the notation and terminology introduced there. The basic result from [ER2] that we use in this note is the following theorem - it is Theorem 2.2 from [ER2] (recall that a subgraph means an induced subgraph).

Theorem 1. Let Γ be a dependence alphabet and let g be a graph. There exists a Γ-labeling of g iff $\hat{h}$ is isomorphic with a subgraph of Γ, where h = *symr*(g). ■

1. THE ALGORITHM $\mathcal{A}$

In this section we will consider an algorithm for generating the partition $\hat{P}_h$ for a sr graph h ($\hat{P}_h$ is the maximal partition of the set of nodes of h into complete clans - the classes of $\hat{P}_h$ are the nodes of $\hat{h}$).

First we need an operation of splitting a set of nodes of a graph h by a node of h. It is defined as follows.

Let h = (V,E) be a graph, let $x \in V$ and let L be a nonempty subset of V. Let $L_1 = \{ y \in L : (x,y) \in E \}$ and $L_2 = \{ y \in L : (x,y) \notin E \}$. Then

$$split_x(L) = \begin{cases} \{L\}, \text{ if } L_1 = \emptyset \text{ or } L_2 = \emptyset , \\ \{L_1 , L_2\}, \text{ otherwise.} \end{cases}$$

Then given a set T of subsets of V (rather than a subset L of V), and a node $x \in V$, $split_x(T)$ is defined in the obvious way: each $L \in T$ is split by x as above yielding again a set of subsets of V; thus $split_x(T) = \cup \{ split_x(L) : L \in T \}$.

Consider now the following algorithm $\mathcal{A}$:

Input: A sr graph h = (V,E).

Computation: <u>begin</u> M := {V},

<u>for all</u> $x \in V$ <u>do</u> M := <u>split</u>$_x$(M)

<u>end</u>

Clearly the output of $\mathcal{A}$ is a partition R of V.

Let $R_0 , R_1 , \ldots, R_m$ be the sequence of "intermediate" partitions produced by $\mathcal{A}$; i.e., $R_0 = \{V\}$, and, for each $1 \le i \le m$, $R_i = split_{x_i}(R_{i-1})$, where $V = \{ x_1 , \ldots, x_m \}$. (Since h is clear from our considerations, we will use the notation $\hat{P}$ rather than $\hat{P}_h$. Also, for a partition N, $\equiv_N$ denotes the equivalence relation induced by N).

Lemma 1. $R = \hat{P}$.

Proof.

(1) For all $y,z \in V$,

$y \equiv_R z$ iff, for all $u \in V$, $(u,y) \in E$ iff $(u,z) \in E$.

This can easily be proved by induction on i ($0 \le i \le m$), because clearly, for each $0 \le i \le m$, and all $y,z \in V$

$y \equiv_{R_i} z$ iff, for all $u \in \{ x_1, \ldots, x_i \}$, $(u,y) \in E$ iff $(u,z) \in E$.

(2) For all $y,z \in V$,

$y \equiv_{\hat{P}} z$ iff $\{y,z\}$ is a clan of h and $(y,z) \in E$
iff, for all $u \in V$, $(u,y) \in E$ iff $(u,z) \in E$.

This follows directly from the definition of $\hat{P}$ and from the fact that h is reflexive.

Now the lemma follows from (1) and (2). ■

Hence $\mathcal{A}$ generates $\hat{P}$.

2. THE COMPLEXITY OF Γ-LABELINGS

In this section we establish the complexity of Γ-labelings, essentially through analyzing the algorithm $\mathcal{A}$.

Theorem 2. Let Γ be a dependence alphabet. There exsists an algorithm which given a graph $g = (V,E)$ decides in $\mathcal{O}(|V|^2)$ steps whether or not there exists a Γ-labeling of g.

Proof.

By Theorem 1, deciding whether or not a graph $g = (V,E)$ has a Γ-labeling is equivalent to deciding whether or not $\hat{h}$ is isomorphic with a subgraph of Γ, where $h = symr(g)$.

(1) Clearly constructing $h = symr(g)$ can be done in $\mathcal{O}(|V|^2)$ steps (one has to inspect and possibly "modify" each pair of $V \times V$).

(2) To construct $\hat{h} = (\hat{P},\hat{E})$ we have to construct $\hat{P}$ and $\hat{E}$.

By Lemma 1, algorithm $\mathcal{A}$ can be used to construct $\hat{P}$. Clearly, given a set M of subsets of V and a node x, constructing $split_x(M)$ can be done in $\mathcal{O}(|V|)$ steps. Since we have to go through all the nodes of h, $\hat{P}$

can be constructed in $\mathcal{O}(|V|^2)$ steps.

To construct $\hat{E}$ we consider the partition $R = \{ R_1 , \ldots, R_k \}$ constructed by $\mathcal{A}$ and from each R_i , $1 \leq i \leq k$, we choose one element, say v_i . Then we form an edge between R_j and R_s , where $1 \leq j,s \leq k$, iff (v_j,v_s) is an edge of h. Clearly, the construction of $\hat{E}$ in this way takes $\mathcal{O}(|V|^2)$ steps.

Altogether, $\hat{h}$ can be constructed in $\mathcal{O}(|V|^2)$ steps.

(3) Since Γ is fixed, checking whether or not $\hat{h}$ is isomorphic with a subgraph of Γ can be done in a constant (i.e., not dependent on $|V|$) number of steps.

Now the theorem follows from (1), (2), and (3). ■

Remark.

(1) A related result is given in [AER], where it is shown that, for a fixed dependence alphabet Γ, the class of Γ-dependence graphs is in NLOG (see Remark 4.7 of [AER]). It is easy to see from the algorithm in [AER] that, for a fixed Γ, also the class of naked Γ-dependence graphs is in NLOG (and hence in P).

(2) It is easily seen that our algorithm for constructing $\hat{P}$ is optimal in the sense that each algorithm for constructing $\hat{P}$ must take at least $|V|^2$ steps. ■

To put Theorem 2 in proper perspective we observe the following.

Theorem 3. The problem of deciding whether or not for a graph g and a dependence alphabet Γ there exists a Γ-labeling of g is NP-complete.

Proof.

It is well-known that the CLIQUE problem is NP-complete.

Obviously, the CLIQUE problem is equivalent to the problem of deciding whether or not an arbitrary complete (antireflexive and symmetric) graph g_1 is isomorphic to a subgraph of an arbitrary (antireflexive and symmetric) graph g_2 .

Clearly, g_1 is isomorphic to a subgraph of g_2 , iff $\bar{g}_1$ (the complement of g_1) is isomorphic to a subgraph of $\bar{g}_2$ (the complement of g_2).

But $\bar{g}_1$ is $\hat{h}$ for a sr graph h, and $\bar{g}_2$ is a sr graph, hence a dependence alphabet.

Consequently, CLIQUE reduces to our problem. Since obviously the problem is in NP, it is NP-complete. ■

ACKNOWLEDGEMENTS

The authors are indebted to J. Engelfriet for useful comments on the first draft of this note.

REFERENCES

[AER] Aalbersberg, IJ.J., Engelfriet, J. and Rozenberg, G., The complexity of regular DNLC graph languages, Techn. Rep. 86-03, Dept. of Computer Science, Leiden University, 1986.

[AR1] Aalbersberg, IJ.J. and Rozenberg, G., Theory of traces, *Theoretical Computer Science*, v. 60, pp. 1-82, 1988.

[AR2] Aalbersberg, IJ.J. and Rozenberg, G., Traces, dependence graphs and DNLC grammars, *Discrete Applied Mathematics*, v. 11, pp. 299-306, 1985.

[ER1] Ehrenfeucht, A., and Rozenberg, G., On the structure of dependence graphs, *in* K. Voss, H.J. Genrich, G. Rozenberg (eds.), *Concurrency and nets*, Springer-Verlag, pp. 141-170, 1987.

[ER2] Ehrenfeucht, A., and Rozenberg, G., Theory of 2-structures, Part I: Clans, morphisms, and basic subclasses, *Theoretical Computer Science*, to appear.

[M] Mazurkiewicz, A., Basic notions of trace theory, in J.W. de Bakker, W.-P. de Roever, G. Rozenberg (eds.), *Linear time, branching time and partial order in logics and models for concurrency*, LNCS 354, Springer-Verlag, pp. 258-262, 1989.

The Constructive Engine

Gérard Huet

INRIA

Rocquencourt, France

Introduction

The Calculus of Constructions is a higher-order formalism for writing constructive proofs in a natural deduction style, inspired from work of de Bruijn [4,7], Girard [21] and Martin-Löf [33]. The calculus and its syntactic theory were presented in Coquand's thesis [12], and an implementation by the author was used to mechanically verify a substantial number of proofs demonstrating the power of expression of the formalism [15]. The Calculus of Constructions is proposed as a foundation for the design of programming environments where programs are developed consistently with formal specifications[37]. This note presents in detail an implementation in CAML[18,44] of a proof-checker for the calculus. This proof-checker proceeds by operating an abstract machine, called the constructive engine.

The description in this paper is close in spirit to the inference system described in section 10.2 of [13]. The main departure is the addition of a system of constants, allowing a form of definitional equality. The implementation shown corresponds to a simplification of version 4.9 of the system. Differences with the actual implementation are discussed below.

1 Technical Preliminaries

The constructive engine is an environment machine which manipulates λ-expressions with a rich language of types. There are several sorts of variables which may appear in the terms of the calculus. The global variables, as well as the global constants, are referenced with their name, a concrete string of ASCII characters. The environment is looked up through a hash table for fast access to the declaration information of the global. The locally bound variables are represented by their binding depth, in the manner of de Bruijn[3]. Since the constructive engine works by weaving back and forth between the environment and the currently constructed term, we need to switch representations efficiently. Also, we need to be able to compare two terms modulo β-reduction, in order to implement type equality checking. This section presents various programming techniques developed for such algorithms.

1.1 λ-calculus in the de Bruijn notation

We now recall the de Bruijn's notation of λ-calculus. This abstract representation of λ-expressions was originally introduced by de Bruijn[3], and later extended to Automath's

[1] A preliminary version of this paper, describing version 4.5 of the engine, was presented as an invited lecture at CAAP88. This paper describes a simplified view of the current 4.9 implementation.

Λ structures by Jutting[29].

We first consider untyped λ-calculus. We use CAML as our specification language. The type of *concrete* λ-terms may be defined as:

```
#type concrete =
#       Var of string                   (* x *)
#   |   Lambda of string * concrete     (* [x]E *)
#   |   Apply of concrete * concrete    (* (E1 E2) *);;
Type concrete defined
     Var : (string -> concrete)
   | Lambda : (string * concrete -> concrete)
   | Apply : (concrete * concrete -> concrete)
```

Thus every variable, whether it is free or bound, is implemented by a concrete string. Such representation needs complex substitution operations, in order to guarantee the preservation of the right binding relationships. Variable renamings (called α-conversion) may be necessary, and thus new names have to be coined. In order to avoid this naming problem, we define the type of *abstract* λ-terms:

```
#type lambda =
#       Ref of num              (* variables *)
#   |   Abs of lambda           (* lambda abstraction *)
#   |   App of lambda * lambda (* apply function L1 to argument L2 *);;
Type lambda defined
     Ref : (num -> lambda)
   | Abs : (lambda -> lambda)
   | App : (lambda * lambda -> lambda)
```

Now each variable occurrence is represented by its *binding depth*, i.e. the relative depth with respect to its binding abstraction operator. A term of type `lambda` containing n free variables is valid in a context of length n, according to:

```
#let rec valid n = function
#       Ref(m)      -> m <= n
#   |   Abs(l)      -> valid (n+1) l
#   |   App(l1,l2) -> valid n l1 & valid n l2;;
Value valid = - : (num -> lambda -> bool)
```

Thus a *closed* λ-term is one which is valid in an empty context:

```
#let closed = valid 0;;
Value closed = - : (lambda -> bool)
```

We write Λ_n for the set of lambdas M such that *valid n M*.

The recursion structure of algorithm `valid` is characteristic of computations on lambdas. The corresponding induction principle may be stated as:

Contextual Induction Principle. Let P_n be a property of lambdas, indexed by a natural number n, and satisfying the closure conditions:

- $P_n(M) \wedge P_n(N) \Rightarrow P_n(App(M, N))$

- $P_{n+1}(M) \Rightarrow P_n(Abs(M))$
- $0 < m \leq n \Rightarrow P_n(Ref(m))$.

Then $P_n(M)$ for every $M \in \Lambda_n$. Here is an algorithm for translating a concrete term to its abstract representation, given a context of free variables:

```
#exception Unbound;;
Exception Unbound defined

#let index_of id = search 1
#where rec search n = function
#       (name::names) -> if name=id then n
#                        else search (n+1) names
#      | [] -> raise Unbound;;
Value index_of = - : ('a -> 'a list -> num)

#let rec parse_env lvars = abstract
#where rec abstract = function
#   Var(name)           -> Ref (index_of name lvars)
# | Lambda(id,conc)     -> Abs(parse_env (id::lvars) conc)
# | Apply(conc1,conc2) -> App(abstract conc1,abstract conc2);;
Value parse_env = - :
      (string list -> concrete -> lambda)

#(* parsing closed lambdas *)
#let parser = parse_env [];;
Value parser = - : (concrete -> lambda)
```

The abstract representation is not convenient for the human interface, and thus we assume we have declared a grammar for concrete syntax, as follows[44]:

```
#grammar concrete =
#rule entry Lambda = parse
#       Term x                        -> parser(x)
#and Term = parse
#       "("; Term_list x; Term y; ")" -> Apply(x,y)
#     | IDENT x                       -> Var(x)
#     | "["; Binder x; "]"; Term y    -> list_it (curry Lambda) x y
#     | "("; Term x; ")"              -> x
#and Term_list = parse
#       Term x                        -> x
#     | Term_list x; Term y           -> Apply(x,y)
#and Binder = parse
#       IDENT(x)                      -> [x]
#     | IDENT(x); ","; Binder y       -> x::y;;
Calling Yacc ... ........................................
Value concrete = - : (string -> Parsers)
```

```
Grammar concrete for programs defined
  entry Lambda
```

We may now give examples in concrete syntax:

```
#<<[x](x [y](x y))>>;;
('Abs
 ('App (('Ref 1),('Abs ('App (('Ref 2),('Ref 1))))))) :
 lambda
```

Remark that the two occurrences of x have different indexes 1 and 2, and that conversely the references (`Ref 1`) correspond to two distinct variables x and y.

The first fundamental algorithm concerns the recomputation of global references to global variables across n levels of binding. This is computed by the algorithm `lift` below.

```
#let lift n = lift_rec 1
#where rec lift_rec k = function
#    Ref(i)          -> if i<k then Ref(i)   (* bound variable : invariant *)
#                              else Ref(i+n) (* free variable  : relocated *)
#  | Abs(lam)        -> Abs(lift_rec (k+1) lam)
#  | App(lam,lam') -> App(lift_rec k lam,lift_rec k lam');;
Value lift = - : (num -> lambda -> lambda)
```

Now we may program substitution, as follows.

```
#let subst lam =
#let lift_lam n = lift n lam in subst_lam 1
#where rec subst_lam n = function
#    Ref(k) -> if k=n then lift_lam (n-1)      (* the substituted variable *)
#              if k<n then Ref(k)              (* bound variables *)
#              else Ref(k-1)                   (* free variables *)
# |  Abs(lam') -> Abs(subst_lam (n+1) lam')
# |  App(lam1,lam2) -> App(subst_lam n lam1,subst_lam n lam2);;
Value subst = - : (lambda -> lambda -> lambda)
```

For instance, we may now program the conversion of a solvable λ-term to its head normal form as:

```
#let rec hnf = function
#    Ref(n)          -> Ref(n)
# |  Abs(lam)        -> Abs(hnf lam)
# |  App(lam1,lam2) -> let lam'=hnf lam1 in match lam' with
#                        Abs(lam) -> hnf(subst lam2 lam)
#                     |  _        -> App(lam',lam2);;
Value hnf = - : (lambda -> lambda)
```

These algorithms are satisfactory, as executable specifications. They are nor satisfactory as efficient programs. We see two main problems with this approach. The first one is that too much unnecessary copying of structures is effected. The second one is that the operation of λ-reduction is in some sense not elementary enough: we would like to substitute occurrence by occurrence, in a maximally lazy fashion. We shall not tackle the second problem here, but will try and share as much as possible during the computation, in order to remedy the first problem. It should be noted that this very basic problem of efficient computation on λ-terms is still largely open. The sharing of combinatory dags applies only to weak reduction (where one does not reduce inside abstractions). The same is true of abstract environment machines such as the SECD, FAM or CAM machines, which furthermore compute in applicative order (innermost) as opposed to the normal order (leftmost-outermost) corresponding to the standardization theorem. Wadsworth's method[43] does not avoid unnecessary duplications. Levy's sharing of redex families[31] has not yet been implemented in a computationnally efficient way. We do not claim that de Bruijn's abstract representation will lead to the best implementations of λ-calculus. However, the sharing method which we shall now present leads to an acceptable behaviour for our application to the constructive engine.

1.2 Sharing morphisms

Let us forget λ-calculus for the sake of the current discussion, and consider the simpler case of terms built up from free constructors. For instance, consider the following algebra, corresponding to the abstract syntax of terms for some simplified arithmetic:

```
#type term =
#     Var of string
#   | Plus of term * term
#   | Minus of term
#   | Constant of num;;
Type term defined
     Var : (string -> term)
   | Plus : (term * term -> term)
   | Minus : (term -> term)
   | Constant : (num -> term)
```

Now let us consider a simple-minded implementation of first-order substitution over these terms, with substitutions represented as association lists:

```
#let naive_subst sig = subst_rec
#where rec subst_rec = function
#     Var(str)    -> if mem_assoc name sig then assoc name sig else Var(str)
#   | Plus(t1,t2) -> Plus(subst_rec t1,subst_rec t2)
#   | Minus(t)     -> Minus(subst_rec t)
#   | Constant(n) -> Constant(n);;

line 3: unbound variable name in mem_assoc name sig

line 3: unbound variable name in assoc name sig
2 errors in typechecking

Typecheck Failed
```

This method is clearly computationally absurd, since a full copy of a term is effected, even when the substitution is empty. Worst, substitution will un-share terms naturally shared on the underlying dags, such as `let M=Constant(2) in Plus(M,M)`. This may be acceptable in certain situations, for instance if we want to rewrite the two occurrences of M above in distinct ways. But if we think of these abstract terms as applicative structures, we want to profit of the possible sharing to represent in a shared fashion the substitution to a non-linear term such as `Plus(Var(x),Var(x))`.

One solution to this problem has been proposed long time ago by Boyer and Moore[1], and this "structure sharing" representation is now one of the classical ways to implement PROLOG. In this method, we manipulate substitution closures rather than terms, and this has some undesirable effects. For instance, we do not have a direct access to the top of the term anymore, and this access gets more and more costly the further we substitute. After a while, the whole structure may become completely inverted. For this reason, the "structure copying" implementation is still retained in many applications.

At the other end of the spectrum, we find the representations which share through congruence closure[40,20]. These methods are fine for *ground* terms (not containing free variables). In the case where we manipulate mostly terms with variables, congruence closure is not really applicable, and produces more overhead than it saves.

We shall now study how to share maximally in the standard representation of terms containing free variables. We shall not try and guess possible sharing through syntactic coincidences. We only care to preserve existing sharing, and to share as much as possible of a substituted version of a term with the original version. Let us first see how to implement this idea of sharing non-substituted portions of a term. Here is a simple recursive algorithm which reports, together with its result, a boolean value indicating whether sharing has been possible or not.

```
#let subst_and_share sig = fst o subst_rec
#where rec subst_rec x = match x with
#     Var(name)    -> if mem_assoc name sig then (assoc name sig,false)
#                                             else (x,true)
#   | Plus(t1,t2) -> let (t'1,b1)=subst_rec t1
#                    and (t'2,b2)=subst_rec t2
#                    in if b1&b2 then (x,true) else (Plus(t'1,t'2),false)
#   | Minus(t)    -> let (t',b)=subst_rec t
#                    in if b then (x,true) else (Minus(t'),false)
#   | Constant(n) -> (x,true);;
Value subst_and_share = - :
      ((string * term) list -> term -> term)
```

Again, we have a correct specification of what we exactly mean by sharing, but the program above is very costly in storage, since the computation of the sharing relationship builds on the side a duplicate of the structure in the shape of a tree of booleans. If the aim is to avoid building un-necessary structure, we must clearly avoid these explicit boolean values.

The next idea is to replace the values `(true,x)` above by an exception, signaling that sharing is possible. Let us define a *sharing morphism* as a term morphism, which raises a special exception `Identity` to signal that its result is identical to its argument. If `f` is such a sharing morphism, it may be applied on an argument with possible sharing with:

```
exception Identity;;
let share f x = try f(x) with Identity -> x;;
```

and now we may implement a sharing substitution with:

```
#let sharing_subst sig = share subst_rec
#where rec subst_rec = function
#    Var(name)    -> if mem_assoc name sig then assoc name sig
#                                          else raise Identity
#  | Plus(t1,t2) -> (try Plus(subst_rec t1,share subst_rec t2)
#                     with Identity -> Plus(t1,subst_rec t2))
#  | Minus(t)    -> Minus(subst_rec t)
#  | Constant(n) -> raise Identity;;
Value sharing_subst = - :
      ((string * term) list -> term -> term)
```

It is clear that we now have maximum sharing of the substituted term with its original pattern, without extra structure.

It may be objected however that the substitution algorithm is now cluttered with extra cases, which brings two problems: readability is questionable, and mistakes may occur in the transformation from a copying algorithm to its shared version. Note in particular that the case corresponding to an n-ary constructor splits into 2^{n-1} subcases. This objection may be overcome, by noticing that the transformation is systematic enough to be encapsulated in a macro.

More precisely, given two arguments, one which gives the signature of the constructors over which we want a sharing morphism effect, and the second which gives what happens on the others, we may write without difficulty a macro `morphism` which generates the full recursion. Without giving its actual code, which would be hard to understand for readers not familiar with CAML, here is the instance of its call in our example:

```
#pragma let term_signature = [("Plus",2);("Minus",1)]
        and replace_sig =
   <:CAML<function Var(x)    -> if mem_assoc x sig then assoc x sig
                                else raise Identity
                 | Constant(_) -> raise Identity>>;;
(* Macro-generated version of sharing_subst above *)
let subst sig = share #(morphism term_signature replace_sig);;
```

Remark 1. The macro `replace_sig` above is enough to illustrate the example. It is unsatisfactory in that it assumes that the argument to the `substitute` algorithm is called `sig`. A more satisfactory version of the macro, parameterized in an adequate fashion, is easy to define with the mecanism of *anti-quotation* of CAML[44]:

```
#pragma let replace_sig sig =
   <:CAML<function Var(x)       -> if mem_assoc x {^sig^} then assoc x {^sig^}
                                   else raise Identity
                  | Constant(_) -> raise Identity>>;;
```

and now the identifier `sig` is generated in its proper scope:

```
let subst sig = let SIG = <:CAML<sig>> (* abstract syntax of sig *)
                in share #(morphism term_signature (replace_sig SIG));;
```

This remark applies to the other macros explained in the next section. However, we prefer to present the more readable "unsafe" versions.

Remark 2. The sharing mechanism we present uses ML's exceptions. Other mechanisms may be thought of. For instance, if one assumes the existence of a primitive `eq` which tests for *physical* identity, we may program a sharing substitution in the following manner:

```
...
match arg with
...
 | App(x,y) -> let x'=subst x and y'=subst y
               in if eq(x,x') and eq(y,y') then arg else App(x',y')
...
```

Using one mechanism or the other may be motivated by æsthetics or implementation reasons (availability of primitives, efficiency). Somehow the user should not have to worry about such low-level detail, but obviously current implementations of functional programming languages lack the proper memory management primitives needed to express naturally this economic use of data structures.

1.3 Binding morphisms with sharing

The ideas of the previous section may be extended to algebras where certain constructors are binding in some of their arguments. For instance, in `lambda` above, `Abs` is binding in its argument, whereas `App` is not. We indicate this information with the following *descriptors*:

```
#pragma let lambda_descr = [("Abs",[true]);("App",[false;false])];;
```

We now give the code for lifting `Ref` indexes over k levels of binding:

```
#pragma let lift_k =
  <:CAML<function Ref(i) -> if i<n then raise Identity (* bound var *)
                             else Ref(i+k) (* free var is shifted *)>>;;
```

and the general case is macro-generated with the help of a macro `binding_morphism` which generalizes the idea of sharing morphisms to binding constructors implemented with de Bruijn indexes. Without boring the reader with the actual details of the macro `binding_morphism`, let us just indicate an example of macro-expansion:

```
#pragma binding_morphism lambda_descr lift_k =
<:CAML<let rec f n = function
           Abs(x1)     -> Abs(f (n+1) x1)
         | App(x2,x1) -> App(try f n x2, (try f n x1 with Identity -> x1)
                                with Identity -> x2,f n x1)
         | Ref(i)      -> if i < n then raise Identity else Ref(i+k)
      in f 1>>
```

Now we get the lift function as:

```
#let lift k lam = if k=0 then lam
#                 else share #(binding_morphism lambda_descr lift_k) lam;;
Value lift = - : (num -> lambda -> lambda)
```

Remark that we save exploring the term `lam` in the case $k = 0$, which we know beforehand to be an identity.

We now iterate this idea for substitution:

```
#pragma let subst_lam =
<:CAML<function Ref(k) -> if k=n then lift_lam (n-1) (* substituted var *)
                          if k<n then raise Identity (* bound var *)
                          else Ref(k-1)>>            (* free var *);;

#let subst lam =
#    let lift_lam n = lift n lam
#    in share #(binding_morphism lambda_descr subst_lam);;
Value subst = - : (lambda -> lambda -> lambda)
```

This substitution algorithm is still far from perfect. First we should recognize the special case when we substitute a closed term, since in that case no lifting is necessary. Further, we should share all instances of (`lift n lam`) for a given n. These ideas are implemented in the following version:

```
#pragma let subst_closed_lam =
   <:CAML<function Ref(k) -> if k=n then lam          (* lam is shared *)
                             if k<n then raise Identity (* bound var *)
                             else Ref(k-1)>>            (* free var *);;

#let subst lam =
# if closed lam
#    then share #(binding_morphism lambda_descr subst_closed_lam) lam
# else let instances = ref [] in
#      let lift_lam n = (* local memo version *)
#          if n=0 then lam
#          else (assoc n !instances (* memo effect *)
#                ? let new_instance = lift n lam
#                  in (instances:=(n,new_instance)::!instances;
#                      new_instance))
#      in share #(binding_morphism lambda_descr subst_lam) lam;;
Value subst = - : (lambda -> lambda)
```

Further optimizations are possible. For instance, the initial pass to check whether `lam` is closed or not could set up the lifting code with maximum sharing, for any relocating value n, since intuitively the shared areas are the same. The above version recomputes this information p times, where p is the number of distinct levels where the substituted variable occurs. This would not affect the quantity of sharing, it would only speed up its computation, and since the code would be significantly more complicated we shall not do it here.

Although in some sense we share maximally a term with its substituted versions, we fail to propagate this sharing, since recursive exploration of a term where certain nodes are shared does not recognize this sharing, and will therefore undo this sharing by further substitutions. In order to preserve sharing, we ought to remember in a table pairs of addresses (original-term-node, substituted-term-node), in the spirit of traditional graph-copying algorithms. We shall ignore this optimization here.

Finally, a smarter use of indexes may be imagined, where lifting and substitution are delayed as much as possible, by keeping relocation indexes in the expressions themselves. However, this idea is not as easy as it sounds, since such relocation annotations do not commute easily with abstraction, and very quickly we run into the problem of manipulating complex annotations of the form "lift by n_1 all variables greater the m_1, and ..." Clearly, we are not saying the last word on possible implementations of λ-calculus in the de Bruijn style.

2 Application to the Calculus of Constructions

2.1 Term and types

The Calculus of Constructions, originally described in Thierry Coquand's thesis[12], refers to a family of formalisms which permit to describe both objects structured with types, and natural deduction proofs of higher-order logic. We thus have naturally two levels of descriptions:

```
#type level = Object | Proof;;
Type level defined
     Object : level
   | Proof : level
```

The two levels are intermixed in uniform term structures of a typed λ-calculus, where types are themselves terms of the same nature. At the level of proofs, we use the Curry-Howard isomorphism: propositions are seen as the types of their proofs.

We thus have two kinds of judgement:

- `Judge(M,T,Object)` means "Object `M` has type `T`".
- `Judge(M,P,Proof)` means "Proof `M` proves proposition `P`".

Such judgements refer implicitly to a global context of variable declarations and constant definitions. That is, we have possibly non-closed terms of a λ-calculus with constants. We shall come back later to the structure of the global environment. We may at this point define our types of terms and judgements:

```
#type constr =
#     Rel of num                            (* bound variables *)
#   | Var of string * judgement             (* free variables *)
#   | Const of string * judgement           (* constants *)
#   | Prop                                  (* type of propositions *)
```

```
#  | Type of num                        (* universes *)
#  | App of constr * constr             (* application  (M N) *)
#  | Lambda of constr * constr          (* abstraction  [x:T]M *)
#  | Prod of constr * constr            (* product      (x:T)M *)
#and judgement = Judge of constr * constr * level;;
Type constr defined
     Rel : (num -> constr)
   | Var : (string * judgement -> constr)
   | Const : (string * judgement -> constr)
   | Prop : constr
   | Type : (num -> constr)
   | App : (constr * constr -> constr)
   | Lambda : (constr * constr -> constr)
   | Prod : (constr * constr -> constr)
Type judgement defined
     Judge : (constr * constr * level -> judgement)
```

The `Rel` variables are local variables implemented with de Bruijn indexes. The `Var` and `Const` refer to respectively variable declarations and constant definitions. Global identifiers are recognized by the parser as known in the environment as variable declarations or constant definitions, and the corresponding piece of the environment is pointed to by the corresponding term constructors `Var` and `Const`. This has the advantage of avoiding environment searches during type-checking. It has the drawback that our term structures are complicated dags sharing with the environment all the necessary information.

Both `Prod` and `Lambda` are operators which are binding in their second argument, the first one being the *type* of the bound variable. `Lambda` is λ-abstraction, whereas `Prod` is product formation for types, and universal quantification for propositions. Note our ambiguous use of the word "type", since the type of a term is either a type, i.e. a term of type `Type(i)` for a certain `i`, or a proposition, i.e. a term of type `Prop`. In this last case, we use the analogy of propositions with types, identifying a proposition with the type of it proofs. We thus have a λ-calculus at two levels. At the level `Object` abstraction is used for expressing the functionality of the mathematical objects and proposition schemes, in the spirit of Church's type theory. At the level `Proof` it corresponds to (intuitionistic) implication introduction in natural deduction.

The following function checks that its argument is a kind, i.e. of the form `Prop` or `Type(_)`, and returns the level of terms whose types are of that kind.

```
#let level_of_kind = function
#   Type(_) -> Object
# | Prop    -> Proof
# | _       -> error "Not a proposition or a type";;
Value level_of_kind = - : (constr -> level)
```

Note the similarity of our term structures with the linguistic structures of Automath. In the terminology of Automath, our structure extends Nederpelt's Λ. However, we use it with a restricted notion of level, i.e. we have a *regular* language[19]. We distinguish between `Prod` and `Lambda`, in the spirit of AutPi. This was not done in the original calculus of Coquand[12]. We prefer to make the distinction now, because this entails unicity of types. We have also constants and δ-rules, in the spirit of $\Lambda\Delta$[10]. More importantly, we have higher-order quantification, like in Girard's system $F\omega$, which makes the calculus significantly more powerful than both the Automath systems, and the Martin-Löf type theories. We may thus develop higher-order mathematics, as advocated by Scott[42]. In the jargon of proof theorists, the system is "non-predicative".

2.2 Substitution

Substitution is a straightforward generalization of the ideas given in section 1.3 above. The descriptor `lambda_descr` is simply replaced by the descriptor

```
let constr_descriptor =
    [("App",[false;false]);
     ("Lambda",[false;true]);
     ("Prod",[false;true])];;
```

which describes the binding effect of the term constructors. The functions `lift` and `subst` are appropriately adapted.

The main departure from pure λ-calculus is that we have a calculus with *constants.* We thus have several substitution functions for various uses:

```
subst1 : constr -> constr -> constr
(* (subst1 c1 c2) substitutes c1 for Rel(1) in c2 *)
subst2 : string -> constr -> constr
(* (subst2 str c) substitutes Rel(1) for Var(str,_) in c *)
subst_con : string -> constr -> constr -> constr
(* (subst_con str c1 c2) substitutes c1 for Const(str,_) in c2 *)
```

Each of these functions is programmed with the help of the macro `binding_morphism`.

2.3 Equality

Equality of terms means inter-convertibility by β-conversion. Because the calculus is confluent and nœtherian, this could be decided by comparing the normal forms of the two terms. However this is not what we want in a calculus with constants. We want to verify equivalence of terms with as little constant expansion as possible, i.e. to try intensional equality before computing unfolding the constant definitions.

For instance, consider the step of proof which consists in applying a lemma `L1` stating that every reflexive relation `R` is cyclic. We thus have, in the current context, a constant:

```
L1 : (T:Type)(R:T->T->Prop)(Reflexive R)->(Cyclic R)
```

Assume that the current context contains declarations for a type `T1`, a relation `R1` over `T1`, and a hypothesis `H1` that `R1` is reflexive. Now we want to be able to apply `(L1 T1 R1 H1)`. The last application will involve verifying equality of two instances of the proposition `(Reflexive R1)`. It would be absurd here to look up the definition of the concept `Reflexive`, and to expand to normal form the two propositions. We want to avoid going back to first principles, but to do as we usually do in first-order logic, when

Reflexive is a non-analysed binary predicate. Of course, in last resort, we must allow for possible constant expansion.

This motivates the introduction of a data type of *approximations*, which are used to compute head normal forms progressively.

```
#(* The two kinds of variables *)
#type reference =
#     Local of num
#   | Global of string;;
Type reference defined
     Local : (num -> reference)
   | Global : (string -> reference)

#type approximation =
#     Abstraction of constr * constr
#   | Product of constr * constr
#   | Variable of reference * constr list
#   | Constant of (string * judgement) * constr list
#   | Propconst
#   | Typeconst of num;;
Type approximation defined
     Abstraction : (constr * constr -> approximation)
   | Product : (constr * constr -> approximation)
   | Variable :
     (reference * constr list -> approximation)
   | Constant :
     ((string * judgement) * constr list ->
      approximation)
   | Propconst : approximation
   | Typeconst : (num -> approximation)

#(* One step of approximation *)
#let rec approx stack = hnf
#where rec hnf = function
#     Rel(n)         -> Variable(Local(n),stack)
#   | Var(name,_)    -> Variable(Global(name),stack)
#   | Const(n_j)     -> Constant(n_j,stack)  (* No expansion! *)
#   | Prop           -> if stack=[] then Propconst
#                       else anomaly "Prop cannot be applied"
#   | Type(n)        -> if stack=[] then Typeconst(n)
#                       else anomaly "Type cannot be applied"
#   | App(c1,c2)     -> approx (c2::stack) c1
#   | Lambda(c,c')   -> (match stack with
#                          []          -> Abstraction(c,c')
#                        | arg1::rest -> approx rest (subst1 arg1 c'))
#   | Prod(c,c')     -> if stack=[] then Product(c,c')
#                       else anomaly "Product cannot be applied";;
```

```
Value approx = - :
      (constr list -> constr -> approximation)

#let approxim c = approx [] c;;
Value approxim = - : (constr -> approximation)
```

We are now ready to describe type equality, which proceeds by λ-conversion and constant expansion. This last operation is delayed as much as possible.

```
#(* Constant expansion *)
#let expand = function
#  Constant((_,Judge(c,_)),stack) -> approx stack c
#| _ -> anomaly "Trying to expand a non-constant";;
Value expand = - : (approximation -> approximation)

#(* equality of terms modulo conversion *)
#let rec conv term1 term2 = eqappr (approxim term1,approxim term2)
#    where rec eqappr = function
#       (Abstraction(c1,c2),Abstraction(c'1,c'2)) -> conv c1 c'1
#                                                   & conv c2 c'2
#     | (Product(c1,c2),Product(c'1,c'2)) -> conv c1 c'1 & conv c2 c'2
#     | (Variable(n1,l1),Variable(n2,l2)) -> (n1=n2) &
#              (length l1 = length l2) & for_all2 conv l1 l2
#     | (Propconst,Propconst) -> true
#     | (Typeconst(u1),Typeconst(u2)) -> u1=u2
#     | ((Constant(s1,l1) as appr1),(Constant(s2,l2) as appr2)) ->
#         (* try first intensional equality *)
#         (eq(s1,s2) & (length(l1) = length(l2)) & (for_all2 conv l1 l2))
#         (* else expand the second occurrence (arbitrary heuristic) *)
#      or eqappr(appr1,expand appr2)
#     | ((Constant(_) as appr1),appr2) -> eqappr(expand appr1,appr2)
#     | (appr1,(Constant(_) as appr2)) -> eqappr(appr1,expand appr2)
#     | _ -> false;;
Value conv = - : (constr -> constr -> bool)
```

The next function effects one step of head normal form leading to Prop, Type, or Prod. It is used for making explicit the type of a construction.

```
#let hnftype = apprec []
#where rec apprec stack = app_stack
#where rec app_stack = function
#      Rel(_)                -> error "Typing error 1"
#    | Var(_)                -> error "Typing error 2"
#    | Const(_,Judge(c,_)) -> app_stack(c)
#    | App(c1,c2)            -> apprec (c2::stack) c1
#    | Lambda(_,c)           -> (match stack with
#                                    []       -> error "Typing error 3"
```

```
#                                | c'::rest -> apprec rest (subst1 c' c))
#      (* Prod/Prop/Type *)
#    | c                     -> if stack=[] then c
#                               else anomaly "Cannot be applied";;
Value hnftype = - : (constr -> constr)
```

2.4 Structure of the environment

The environment contains variable declarations, constant definitions, values waiting to be applied, and types waiting to be used as coercions. We shall explain the last two kinds of items in the next section.

```
#type declaration =
#     Vardecl of string * judgement
#   | Constdecl of string * judgement
#   | Value of judgement
#   | Cast of judgement
#and context == declaration list;;
Type declaration defined
     Vardecl : (string * judgement -> declaration)
   | Constdecl : (string * judgement -> declaration)
   | Value : (judgement -> declaration)
   | Cast : (judgement -> declaration)
Type context abbreviates declaration list
```

We now declare the he initial state, consisting of the empty initial context, and the initial judgement, stating that `Prop` is an `Object` of type `Type(0)`.

```
#let ENV = ref ([]:context)
#and VAL = ref (Prop)          (* The current construction *)
#and TYP = ref (Type(0))       (* Its type *)
#and LEV = ref (Object)        (* Its level *);;
Value ENV = ('ref []) : context ref
Value VAL = ('ref 'Prop) : constr ref
Value TYP = ('ref ('Type 0)) : constr ref
Value LEV = ('ref 'Object) : level ref
```

2.5 A digression on the meaning of inference rules

The constructive engine may be thought of as some kind of loom, where we weave back and forth between the environnement and the current value. The fabric is produced whenever we build a new component of the environment, by taking the current judgement to build a new variable declaration or a new constant definition. The fabric may be taken back by discharging variables as abstractions or products, forming arbitrary new patterns.

This "loom" implementation is in some way the spirit of natural deduction, as opposed to sequent calculus, in which proofs may be seen as produced by cooperating machines working in parallel. In some sense this is a deep distinction between natural deduction logical frameworks, and sequent calculus logical frameworks. For instance, compare and_intro:

$$\frac{\Gamma \vdash A \quad \Gamma \vdash B}{\Gamma \vdash A \wedge B} \qquad \textit{natural}$$

$$\frac{\Gamma \vdash A \quad \Delta \vdash B}{\Gamma \cup \Delta \vdash A \wedge B} \qquad \textit{sequent}$$

In the sequent formulation, Γ and Δ may be thought of as *sets* of propositions. In the natural formulation, Γ may be thought of as a list constructed progressively. However, the important distinction is not so much on the structural rules. It is that the two occurrences of Γ on the numerator of the natural rule do not denote two lists that somehow happen to be equal structurally: they denote the *same shared object*. Actually, the left top occurrence may be considered the binding occurrence of Γ, whereas the right top one, as well as the one in the denominator, may be considered residuals, or pointers to the data structure which was the state of the environment when applying the rule. Similarly, the occurrences of A and B in the denominator denote pointers to the propositions that have been bound to their respective binding occurrence on the numerator.

Thus we may regard inference rules of natural deduction formalisms as direct specifications of elementary machine operations, with registers for the environment, the current proof, and the currently proved proposition. This is the point of view we take for our implementation of the Calculus of Constructions.

It should be noticed that this point of view may not be adequate for theorem proving, as opposed to theorem checking. For synthesizing proofs, the sequent formulations may actually be preferable. The point we want to emphasize (and we believe has not been strongly stressed before) is first that natural versus sequent formulations of logic is not a choice based on æsthetic choice, but is important for its pragmatic use, and second that it suggests implementation techniques, since the meaning of meta-variables in the rules is quite different.

Once we notice that meta-variables in inference rules denote *shared* objects, it is natural to distinguish, in the various occurrences of such schematic variables, one *binding* occurrence, instanciated by pattern-matching, the others denoting *residuals* in the sense of λ-calculus, i.e. pointers to the corresponding substructure. For instance, consider the usual natural-deduction formulation of arrow-elim, i.e. application or modus ponens:

$$\frac{\Gamma \vdash M : A \rightarrow B \quad \Gamma \vdash N : A}{\Gamma \vdash (M\ N) : B}$$

In order to make explicit the flow of information, when using this rule for proof-checking, it is obvious that the binding occurrences of Γ, M and N are in the denominator of the rule, whereas the binding occurrence of B is in the numerator. Concerning A, we have a problem. The one in the right argument of the rule may be considered binding: "Let A be the type of term N in environment Γ." The one in the left argument, however, may not. Even if one deals with a system where unicity of types holds, we do not mean that the types of M and N should *share* a common substructure, but merely that the corresponding substructures are *equal* (and here, actually, a recursive exploration to check this fact is meant). In our case, where types are only unique up to λ-conversion, we want to say something like: "Let C be the type of term M in environment Γ. Convert C to its head normal form. Check that it has the shape $A' \to B$. Check that A and A' are convertible." We are now close to a complete specification of the proof checker. Two details remain.

The first detail concerns the order in which M and N are actually typechecked in a sequential machine. There are two possible interpretations of application as a term constructor: the *left-sequential* one (first M and then N), and the *right-sequential* one (the opposite order). In either case, some explicit memorisation of the intermediate type shall be needed. We remark that this memorisation cannot be done simply in an auxiliary stack, since the proper scoping must be enforced. We are lead to stack the corresponding judgement as an item in the environment. In our implementation, we choose the right-sequential interpretation, and we are thus lead to an inference rule (where binding occurrences are underlined):

$$\frac{\Gamma \vdash N : \underline{A} \quad \Gamma \vdash M : \underline{C} \quad C \rhd \underline{A'} \to \underline{B} \quad A \equiv A'}{\underline{\Gamma} \vdash (\underline{M}\ \underline{N}) : B}$$

which is in turn implemented as the composition of two unary transition rules, with explicit stacking in the environment:

$$\Gamma \vdash N : B \implies \Gamma; N : B \vdash \qquad \textit{stack\_value}$$

$$\Gamma; N : B \vdash M : C \implies (C \rhd A' \to B, A \equiv A') \;\; \Gamma \vdash (M\ N) : B \qquad \textit{pop\_apply}$$

In stack_value, the notation $\Gamma; N : B \vdash$ stands for stacking the current judgement in the environment without changing it. We are thus lead to the view of elementary machine operations (the conditional transition rules) corresponding to an explicit sequentialisation of inference rules. The memorisation insures that these elementary commands may be used independently of each other.

The second detail concerns conversion in the presence of the constant definitions, which are definitional equalities; in such systems the conversion depends on these equalities, and thus of the environment, in which they are declared. That is, in order to be completely rigorous we ought to write $\Gamma \vdash A \equiv A'$ above.

To a certain extent the situation may be compared to PROLOG. The inference rules, with suitable detail, correspond rather directly to PROLOG clauses. The relations $\rhd$ and $\equiv$ are executable predicates, and the underlining of binding occurrences correspond to input specifications à la Concurrent Prolog. This point of view is close to the one of the logical framework Typol[30]. The transition rules correspond to the basic instructions of a sequential PROLOG machine. One may argue that this low-level description is not really needed for the user of the logical environment. However, this amount of detail may be needed to derive useful meta-mathematical properties.

In the following, we shall describe our engine in terms of the CAML functions implementing its basic transition rules. The higher-level inference rules are given as comments.

2.6 Initialization

2.6.1 Resetting the current judgement

```
#let reset_current () =
#  VAL := Prop;
#  TYP := Type(0);
```

```
#  LEV := Object;;
Value reset_current = - : (unit -> level)
```

2.6.2 Resetting, pushing and popping the environment

```
#let reset_env () =
#  ENV := []
#and push_env declaration =
#  ENV := declaration::!ENV
#and pop_env () = match !ENV with
#    [] -> error "Empty environment"
#  | decl::env -> ENV := env; decl;;
Value reset_env = - : (unit -> context)
Value push_env = - : (declaration -> context)
Value pop_env = - : (unit -> declaration)
```

2.6.3 Searching the environment

Note that we do not need to relocate the judgements stacked in the environment, since we do not use indexes, but identifiers for the globals.

```
#let search name = search_rec !ENV
#    where rec search_rec = function
#        [] -> error(name ^ " not declared")
#      | decl::rest -> match decl with
#               Vardecl(s,_)    -> if s=name then decl else search_rec rest
#             | Constdecl(s,_)  -> if s=name then decl else search_rec rest
#             | _               -> search_rec rest;;
Value search = - : (string -> declaration)
```

2.7 The basic machine operations

There are few basic machine operations, partitioned into two kinds: the ones that build up the environment, and the ones that build up the current construction. For each such command, we give first the inference rule, then the CAML function which performs the corresponding machine instruction.

2.7.1 Introducing a new hypothesis

$$\frac{\Gamma \vdash M : Prop}{\Gamma; x : M \vdash}$$

$$\frac{\Gamma \vdash M : Type(i)}{\Gamma; x : M \vdash}$$

```
#let assume name =
#    let declaration =
#        let typ = hnftype !TYP
#        in let lev = level_of_kind typ
```

```
#           in Vardecl(name,Judge(!VAL,typ,lev))
#     in push_env declaration;;
Value assume = - : (string -> context)
```

2.7.2 Introducing a new definition

$$\frac{\Gamma \vdash M : T}{\Gamma; x = M : T \vdash}$$

```
#let declare name =
#     let declaration = Constdecl(name,Judge(!VAL,!TYP,!LEV))
#     in push_env declaration;;
Value declare = - : (string -> context)
```

2.7.3 Global Introduction

$$\frac{\Gamma = \Gamma_1; x : \Gamma_x; \Gamma_2}{\Gamma \vdash x : \Gamma_x} \qquad \frac{\Gamma = \Gamma_1; x = V : \Gamma_x; \Gamma_2}{\Gamma \vdash x : \Gamma_x}$$

```
#let consider name =
#     match (search name) with
#          Constdecl((_,Judge(_,typ,lev)) as constant) ->
#             (TYP:=typ;
#              LEV:=lev;
#              VAL:=Const(constant))
#        | Vardecl((_,Judge(typ,_,lev)) as variable) ->
#             (TYP:=typ;
#              LEV:=lev;
#              VAL:=Var(variable));;
Value consider = - : (string -> constr)
```

2.7.4 Prop intro

$$\frac{\Gamma \vdash}{\Gamma \vdash Prop : Type(1)}$$

```
#let proposition () = VAL:=Prop;TYP:=Type(1);LEV:=Object;;
Value proposition = - : (unit -> level)
```

2.7.5 Type intro

$$\frac{\Gamma \vdash}{\Gamma \vdash Type(i) : Type(i+1)}$$

```
#let universe num =
#  if num<1 then error "Illegal universe level"
#  else VAL:=Type(num);TYP:=Type(num+1);LEV:=Object;;
Value universe = - : (num -> level)
```

2.7.6 App intro

$$\frac{\Gamma \vdash M : (x : B)C \quad \Gamma \vdash N : A \quad \Gamma \vdash A \equiv B}{\Gamma \vdash (M\ N) : [N/x]C}$$

As explained above, this rule splits into two transitions rules:

```
#(* Stacks a value for future application *)
#let stack_value () =
#    let declaration = Value(Judge(!VAL,!TYP,!LEV))
#    in push_env declaration;;
Value stack_value = - : (unit -> context)

#(* Extracts the last pushed value in environment *)
#let unstack_value () =
#    match !ENV with
#          Value(j)::rest -> ENV:=rest; j
#        | _ -> error "Last item not a value";;
Value unstack_value = - : (unit -> judgement)

#let pop_apply () =
#  match hnftype !TYP with
#     Prod(typarg,typres) ->
#       let (Judge(val,typ,lev)) = unstack_value()
#       in if conv typ typarg then (VAL:=App(!VAL,val);
#                                   TYP:=subst1 val typres)
#          else error "Application would violate typings"
#   | _ -> error "Non-functional construction";;
Value pop_apply = - : (unit -> constr)
```

2.7.7 Discharging definitions

We allow forgetting a constant by replacing its value in the current judgement.

$$\frac{\Gamma; x = M : T \vdash N : A}{\Gamma \vdash [x/M]N : [x/M]A}$$

```
#let pop_const () =
#     match !ENV with
#        [] -> error "No constant in environment"
#      | Constdecl(name,Judge(val,_))::rest ->
#                 VAL:=subst_con name val !VAL;
#                 TYP:=subst_con name val !TYP;
#                 ENV:=rest
#      | _ -> error "Last item not a constant";;
Value pop_const = - : (unit -> context)
```

Variables may be discharged in two ways: for forming abstractions and for forming products. Both rules use as an auxiliary:

```
#let unstack_var () =
#    match !ENV with
#      []                   -> error "No hypothesis in current context"
#    | Vardecl(var)::rest -> ENV:=rest; var
#    | _                  -> error "Last item not a variable";;
Value unstack_var = - : (unit -> string * judgement)
```

2.7.8 Lambda Introduction

$$\frac{\Gamma; x : M \vdash N : P}{\Gamma \vdash [x : M]N : (x : M)P}$$

```
#let abs_var () =
#  let (name,Judge(typ,_)) = unstack_var()
#  in VAL:=Lambda(typ,subst2 name !VAL);
#     TYP:=Prod(typ,subst2 name !TYP);;
Value abs_var = - : (unit -> constr)
```

2.7.9 Product Introduction

Here we have the union of 3 inference rules:

$$\frac{\Gamma; x : M \vdash N : Prop}{\Gamma \vdash (x : M)N : Prop}$$

$$\frac{\Gamma \vdash M : Type(j) \quad \Gamma; x : M \vdash N : Type(i)}{\Gamma \vdash (x : M)N : Type(max(i, j))}$$

$$\frac{\Gamma \vdash M : Prop \quad \Gamma; x : M \vdash N : Type(i)}{\Gamma \vdash (x : M)N : Type(i)}$$

The last two rules appear to be binary. However, they correspond to a unary transition, since the type of M is explicit in the judgement stored in the variable declaration. Here is an example where the rules of inference do not carry enough information: we do not need to use a meta theorem saying that if $\Gamma; x : M$ is a well-formed environment, then either $\Gamma \vdash M : Type(j)$ or $\Gamma \vdash M : Prop$. This fact is actually explicit from the way the variable declarations are structured in the machine.

```
#let gen_var () =
#  if !LEV = Proof then error "Proof objects can only be abstracted";
#  let (name,Judge(typ,kind,_)) = unstack_var()
#  in (TYP:=(match hnftype !TYP with
#         Prop -> Prop (* quantification : TYP stays Prop *)
#       | Type(n) -> (* product *)
#               Type(match kind with Prop -> n | Type(m) -> max m n)
#       | _ -> error "Product allowed only on types");
#      VAL:=Prod(typ,subst2 name !VAL));;
Value gen_var = - : (unit -> constr)
```

2.7.10 Type conversion

$$\frac{\Gamma \vdash M : A \quad \Gamma \vdash B : Prop \quad \Gamma \vdash A \equiv B}{\Gamma \vdash M : B}$$

$$\frac{\Gamma \vdash M : A \quad \Gamma \vdash B : Type(i) \quad \Gamma \vdash A \equiv B}{\Gamma \vdash M : B}$$

As for application, this pair of rules splits into two transition rules:

```
#(* Stacking a type for future coercion *)
#let stack_cast () =
#    let typ = hnftype(!TYP)
#    in let lev = level_of_kind typ
#       in let declaration = Cast(Judge(!VAL,typ,lev))
#    in push_env declaration;;
Value stack_cast = - : (unit -> context)

#let unstack_cast () =
#    match !ENV with
#          []              -> error "No cast in current context"
#        | Cast(j)::rest -> ENV:=rest;j
#        | _               -> error "Last item not a cast";;
Value unstack_cast = - : (unit -> judgement)

#let cast () =
#   let (Judge(typ,_,lev)) = unstack_cast()
#   in if lev<>!LEV then error "Wrong level for coercion"
#      if conv !TYP typ then TYP:=typ
#      else error "Cannot coerce to intended type";;
Value cast = - : (unit -> constr)
```

2.8 Higher-level commands

2.8.1 Sections

The machine is equipped of a hierarchical description mechanism which permits to declare variables and define constants within a local scope. This mechanism is operated through the opening and closing of named *sections*. Variables and constants are declared with a certain *strength* controlling their lifetime as follows. When n sections are opened, the possible strengths of notions are integers between 0 and n. A notion of strength 0 is local to the current section, a notion of greater strength will survive the closing of the current section. When a section is closed, the corresponding segment of the environment is popped and processed as follows. Stacked casts and values are forgotten, with a warning. Local constants disappear by substitution. Local variables are discharged, by abstraction in values, and by product/quantification in types. Thus the variables and constants declared with a positive strength will be kept, under the same name, but with added functionality.

We shall not discuss further this sections mechanism, which would require a more precise explanation, and whose design is not considered definitive yet. For the present paper, let us just consider this structuring mechanism as high-level commands, which could be implemented by macro-generation of the elementary operations of the engine, by keeping separately the strength information. In the current implementation, however, section headers are items in the environment.

2.8.2 Inductive definitions

It is possible to describe complex inductive definitions of types, constructors of those types, and induction/recursion principles on those types. We shall not describe further this facility, which is described in [39], and which ought to be superseded in next versions of the calculus by the addition, at the terms level, of (strongly positive) recursive type definitions.

3 The mathematical vernacular

The constructive engine is generally not operated directly. Its commands are usually compiled from a higher level notation for mathematics, called the *Mathematical Vernacular.* The idea of describing mathematical arguments in a mathematical vernacular language is due to de Bruijn[8].

3.1 A small vernacular syllabus

Our mathematical vernacular is very rudimentary at present. Here is a succinct description of its main constructs.

There are two sub-languages:

- a language of *expressions*, used to denote terms, propositions, types, proofs, etc...
- a language of *commands*, used to write mathematical definitions, postulate axioms and hypotheses, state and proof lemmas and theorems.

3.1.1 Expressions

Names are identifiers in the sense of CAML. Two special identifiers "Prop" and "Type" are reserved.

Expressions are defined recursively as follows:

- names are expressions.
- $Prop$ is an expression.
- $Type(n)$ is an expression, for $n > 0$. $Type$ is an abbreviation for $Type(1)$.
- $(M \quad N)$ is an expression when M and N are expressions. It stands for "apply function M to its argument N". This notation is generalized to $(M \quad N1 \quad N2 \quad ... \quad Np)$.
- $(x : M)N_x$ is an expression if x is a name, and M and N_x are expressions. It stands for the logical proposition "for every x of type M we have N_x" when N_x stands for a proposition, and for the type "product of N_x indexed by M" when N_x stands for a type. This notation is extended to accomodate $(x1, x2, ..., xn : M)N$ as an abbreviation for $(x1 : M)(x2 : M)...(xn : M)N$. When x does not occur in N, the expression $(x : M)N$ may also be written as $M \rightarrow N$.

- $[x : M]N_x$ is an expression if x is a name, and M and N_x are expressions. It stands for the function which associates to its argument x of type M the value N_x. This notation is extended to accomodate $[x1, x2, ..., xn : M]N$ as an abbreviation for $[x1 : M][x2 : M]...[xn : M]N$.
- *let* $x = M$ *in* N_x is an expression if x is a name, M and N_x are expressions. It stands for the expression N_x, in which every occurrence of the name x is replaced by the expression M.

3.1.2 Commands

A mathematical text is seen as a list of commands to be executed. The type-checking of expressions that are arguments to commands ensures that the definitions make sense, and that the proofs prove the statements of theorems.

- Hypothesis x : T
  defines a new hypothesis x of type the expression T
- Variable x : T
  variant of the previous command
- Hypotheses x,y,z : T
  for multiple declarations sharing the type T
- Variables x,y,z : T
  idem
- Axiom x : A
  the proposition A is assumed as an axiom named x
- Type x
  Abbreviates Variable x : Type
- Proposition x
  Abbreviates Variable x : Proposition
- Definition x M
  Checks that M is well-typed, and defines it under name x
- Name x M
  Local version of Definition
- Global x : T = M
  Checks that M is well-typed consistently with type T, and defines it under name x
- Let x : T = M
  Local version of Global
- Theorem x P Proof M
  Checks that M is a proof of proposition P, and defines it under name x

- Lemma x P Proof M
  Local version of Theorem. These composite commands may be broken into parts, such as:
  Lemma x
  Statement P
  Proof M
  This permits to introduce definitions and facts local to the proof.
- Section x
  Opens a section named x
- End x
  Closes the section x

Other commands are useful for interactive use. We shall not list them here.

We do not explain in this note how the vernacular commands get parsed and translated as elementary commands of the machine. The details are relatively straightforward.

3.2 A full exemple: Newman's lemma

We give here the listing of a full exemple as written in the current system. Newman's lemma states that every nœtherian relation is confluent if it is locally confluent. The proof is the same as the one explained in [25], and given in an older version of the calculus in [15]. A discussion of the definition of induction principles in the Calculus of Constructions may be found in [27].

This section of vernacular assumes prior loading of a standard prelude, defining logical primitives.

We start with an auxiliary module of definitions concerning binary relations, where notions such as transitive-reflexive closure `Rstar` of relation `R` are defined.

```
  Variable A : Type.
  Variable R : A->A->Prop.

(* Definition of the reflexive-transitive closure R* of R *)
(* Smallest reflexive P containing R o P *)

Definition Rstar [x,y:A](P:A->A->Prop)
   ((u:A)(P u u))->((u:A)(v:A)(w:A)(R u v)->(P v w)->(P u w)) -> (P x y).

Theorem Rstar_reflexive  (x:A)(Rstar x x)
 Proof [x:A][P:A->A->Prop]
       [h1:(u:A)(P u u)][h2:(u:A)(v:A)(w:A)(R u v)->(P v w)->(P u w)]
       (h1 x).

Theorem Rstar_R (x:A)(y:A)(z:A)(R x y)->(Rstar y z)->(Rstar x z)
 Proof [x:A][y:A][z:A][t1:(R x y)][t2:(Rstar y z)]
       [P:A->A->Prop]
       [h1:(u:A)(P u u)][h2:(u:A)(v:A)(w:A)(R u v)->(P v w)->(P u w)]
```

```
        (h2 x y z t1 (t2 P h1 h2)).

(* We conclude with transitivity of Rstar : *)

Theorem  Rstar_transitive
          (x:A)(y:A)(z:A)(Rstar x y)->(Rstar y z)->(Rstar x z)
 Proof   [x:A][y:A][z:A][h:(Rstar x y)]
         (h ([u:A][v:A](Rstar v z)->(Rstar u z))
            ([u:A][t:(Rstar u z)]t)
            ([u:A][v:A][w:A][t1:(R u v)][t2:(Rstar w z)->(Rstar v z)]
             [t3:(Rstar w z)](Rstar_R u v z t1 (t2 t3)))).

(* Another characterization of R* *)
(* Smallest reflexive P containing R o R* *)

Definition Rstar' [x:A][y:A](P:A->A->Prop)
    ((P x x))->((u:A)(R x u)->(Rstar u y)->(P x y)) -> (P x y).

Theorem Rstar'_reflexive (x:A)(Rstar' x x)
 Proof   [x:A][P:A->A->Prop]
         [h1:(P x x)][h2:(u:A)(R x u)->(Rstar u x)->(P x x)]h1.

Theorem Rstar'_R (x:A)(y:A)(z:A)(R x z)->(Rstar z y)->(Rstar' x y)
 Proof   [x:A][y:A][z:A][t1:(R x z)][t2:(Rstar z y)]
         [P:A->A->Prop][h1:(P x x)]
         [h2:(u:A)(R x u)->(Rstar u y)->(P x y)](h2 z t1 t2).

(* Equivalence of the two definitions: *)

Theorem Rstar'_Rstar  (x:A)(y:A)(Rstar' x y)->(Rstar x y)
 Proof   [x:A][y:A][h:(Rstar' x y)]
         (h Rstar (Rstar_reflexive x) ([u:A](Rstar_R x u y))).

Theorem Rstar_Rstar'  (x:A)(y:A)(Rstar x y)->(Rstar' x y)
 Proof   [x:A][y:A][h:(Rstar x y)](h Rstar' ([u:A](Rstar'_reflexive u))
          ([u:A][v:A][w:A][h1:(R u v)][h2:(Rstar' v w)]
           (Rstar'_R u w v h1 (Rstar'_Rstar v w h2)))).
```

We are now ready to develop the standard notions from rewriting theory. `<A>Ex2(P,Q)>` means there exists `x:A` such that `(P x)` and `(Q x)`.

```
Definition coherence [x:A][y:A]<A>Ex2((Rstar x),(Rstar y)).

Theorem coherence_intro  (x:A)(y:A)(z:A)(Rstar x z)->(Rstar y z)->(coherence
x y)
 Proof   [x:A][y:A][z:A][h1:(Rstar x z)][h2:(Rstar y z)]
         [C:Prop][h:(w:A)(Rstar x w)->(Rstar y w)->C](h z h1 h2).
```

```
(* A very simple case of coherence : *)

Lemma Rstar_coherence (x:A)(y:A)(Rstar x y)->(coherence x y)
 Proof  [x:A][y:A][h:(Rstar x y)]
        (coherence_intro x y y h (Rstar_reflexive y)).

(* coherence is symmetric *)
Lemma coherence_sym (x:A)(y:A)(coherence x y)->(coherence y x)
 Proof  [x:A][y:A][h:(coherence x y)]
         (h (coherence y x)
            ([w:A][h1:(Rstar x w)][h2:(Rstar y w)]
                  (coherence_intro y x w h2 h1))).

Definition confluence
     [x:A](y:A)(z:A)(Rstar x y)->(Rstar x z)->(coherence y z).

Definition local_confluence
     [x:A](y:A)(z:A)(R x y)->(R x z)->(coherence y z).

Definition noetherian
     (x:A)(P:A->Prop)((y:A)((z:A)(R y z)->(P z))->(P y))->(P x).

Section Newman.

(* The general hypotheses of the theorem *)

Hypothesis Hyp1:noetherian.
Hypothesis Hyp2:(x:A)(local_confluence x).

(* The induction hypothesis *)

Section Ind.
  Variable    x:A.
  Hypothesis  hyp_ind:(u:A)(R x u)->(confluence u).

(* Confluence in x *)

  Variables   y,z:A.
  Hypothesis  h1:(Rstar x y).
  Hypothesis  h2:(Rstar x z).

(* particular case x->u and u->*y   *)
Section Newman_.
  Variable    u:A.
  Hypothesis  t1:(R x u).
```

```
  Hypothesis  t2:(Rstar u y).

(* In the usual diagram, we assume also x->v and  v->*z   *)

Theorem Diagram.
  Variable v:A.
  Hypothesis u1:(R x v).
  Hypothesis u2:(Rstar v z).

Statement (coherence y z).
Proof     (* We draw the diagram ! *)
  (Hyp2 x u v t1 u1
        (coherence y z)               (* local confluence in x for u,v *)
                                      (* gives w, u->*w and v->*w *)
        ([w:A][s1:(Rstar u w)][s2:(Rstar v w)]
  (hyp_ind u t1 y w t2 s1             (* confluence in u => coherence(y,w) *)
        (coherence y z)               (* gives a, y->*a and z->*a *)
          ([a:A][v1:(Rstar y a)][v2:(Rstar w a)]
  (hyp_ind v u1 a z                   (* confluence in v => coherence(a,z) *)
      (Rstar_transitive v w a s2 v2) u2     (* gives b, a->*b and z->*b *)
        (coherence y z)
        ([b:A][w1:(Rstar a b)][w2:(Rstar z b)]
  (coherence_intro y z b (Rstar_transitive y a b v1 w1) w2))))))).

Theorem caseRxy (coherence y z)
Proof (Rstar_Rstar' x z h2
      ([v:A][w:A](coherence y w))
      (coherence_sym x y (Rstar_coherence x y h1))  (* case x=z *)
      Diagram).                                     (* case x->v->*z *)
End Newman_.

Theorem Ind_proof (coherence y z)
Proof (Rstar_Rstar' x y h1 ([u:A][v:A](coherence v z))
        (Rstar_coherence x z h2)                    (* case x=y*)
        caseRxy).                                   (* case x->u->*z *)
End Ind.

Theorem Newman (x:A)(confluence x)
Proof [x:A](Hyp1 x confluence Ind_proof).

End Newman.
```

The complete proof-checking of this example takes 4 seconds on a SUN 3-60 in the current version 4.9 of our implementation of the calculus, using CAML version 2.6.

We would like to stress the fact that this seemingly purely declarative piece of mathematics is actually compiled and run on the constructive engine. This is an extremely concrete illustration that "the mathematician builds the universe he lives in."

Conclusion

We have presented here only a facet of our implementation of the calculus. Other uses of the system are possible. For instance, an extractor computes the information contents of proofs with special annotations. A theorem-prover, based on the proper adaptation of LCF tactics, searches for proofs under the user's guidance. The incorporation of the tactics language in the vernacular would be a first step towards a completely formal description of mathematical theories in a language close to the usual mathematics practice. Extensions of the calculus are considered, principally recursive types.

We have given in this note a rather complete description of the basic bloc, the Constructive Engine. The algorithms presented are directly executable CAML programs, taken from the actual implementation. This is a first attempt at using CAML as a publication language.

References

[1] R.S. Boyer, J Moore. "The sharing of structure in theorem proving programs." Machine Intelligence **7** (1972) Edinburgh U. Press, 101–116.

[2] N.G. de Bruijn. "The mathematical language AUTOMATH, its usage and some of its extensions." Symposium on Automatic Demonstration, IRIA, Versailles, 1968. Printed as Springer-Verlag Lecture Notes in Mathematics **125**, (1970) 29–61.

[3] N.G. de Bruijn. "Lambda-Calculus Notation with Nameless Dummies, a Tool for Automatic Formula Manipulation, with Application to the Church-Rosser Theorem." Indag. Math. **34,5** (1972), 381–392.

[4] N.G. de Bruijn. "Automath a language for mathematics." Les Presses de l'Université de Montréal, (1973).

[5] N.G. de Bruijn. "Some extensions of Automath: the AUT-4 family." Internal Automath memo M10 (Jan. 1974).

[6] N.G. de Bruijn. "A namefree lambda calculus with facilities for internal definition of expressions and segments." TH Report 78-WSK-03, Technological University Eindhoven, Aug. 1978.

[7] N.G. de Bruijn. "A survey of the project Automath." (1980) in to H. B. Curry: Essays on Combinatory Logic, Lambda Calculus and Formalism, Eds Seldin J. P. and Hindley J. R., Academic Press (1980).

[8] N.G. de Bruijn. "Formalizing the Mathematical Vernacular". Unpublished memo, Technological University Eindhoven, July 1982.

[9] N.G. de Bruijn. "Formalization of constructivity in AUTOMATH." in: Papers dedicated to J.J. Seidel, Ed. P.J. de Doelder, J. de Graaf and J.H. van Lint (1984)

[10] N.G. de Bruijn. "Generalizing Automath by means of a lambda-typed lambda calculus." Proceedings, Maryland 1984-1985 Special Year in Mathematical Logic and Theoretical Computer Science.

[11] A. Church. "A formulation of the simple theory of types." Journal of Symbolic Logic **5,1** (1940) 56–68.

[12] Th. Coquand. "Une théorie des constructions." Thèse de troisième cycle, Université Paris VII (Jan. 85).

[13] Th. Coquand. "An analysis of Girard's paradox." First IEEE Symposium on Logic in Computer Science, Boston (June 1986), 227–236.

[14] Th. Coquand. "Metamathematical Investigations of a Calculus of Constructions." Submitted to Theoretical Computer Science.

[15] Th. Coquand and G. Huet. "Constructions: A Higher Order Proof System for Mechanizing Mathematics." *EUROCAL85,* Linz, Springer-Verlag LNCS 203 (1985).

[16] Th. Coquand and G. Huet. "The Calculus of Constructions." To appear, Information and Control.

[17] Th. Coquand and G. Huet. "Concepts Mathématiques et Informatiques Formalisés dans le Calcul des Constructions." Logic Colloquium, Orsay (July 85). To appear, North-Holland.

[18] G. Cousineau, G. Huet. "The CAML Primer, Version 2.6." Projet Formel, INRIA-ENS, March 1989.

[19] D. Van Daalen. "The language theory of Automath." Ph. D. Dissertation, Technological Univ. Eindhoven (1980).

[20] P. J. Downey, R. Sethi, R. Tarjan. "Variations on the common subexpression problem." JACM **27,4** (1980) 758–771.

[21] J.Y. Girard. "Interprétation fonctionnelle et élimination des coupures dans l'arithmétique d'ordre supérieure." Thèse d'Etat, Université Paris VII (1972).

[22] R. Harper, F. Honsell and G. Plotkin. "A Framework for Defining Logics." Second LICS, Ithaca, June 1987.

[23] R. Harper and R. Pollack. "Type checking, universe polymorphism, and typical ambiguity in the calculus of constructions." CCIPL, TAPSOFT'89, Barcelona, March 1989.

[24] W. A. Howard. "The formulæ-as-types notion of construction." Unpublished manuscript (1969). Reprinted in to H. B. Curry: Essays on Combinatory Logic, Lambda Calculus and Formalism, Eds J. P. Seldin and J. R. Hindley, Academic Press (1980).

[25] G. Huet. "Confluent Reductions: Abstract Properties and Applications to Term Rewriting Systems." J. Assoc. Comp. Mach. **27,4** (1980) 797–821.

[26] G. Huet. "Formal Structures for Computation and Deduction." Course Notes, Carnegie-Mellon University, May 1986.

[27] G. Huet. "Induction Principles Formalized in the Calculus of Constructions." TAPSOFT87, Pisa, March 1987. Springer-Verlag Lecture Notes in Computer Science 249, 276–286.

[28] G. Huet. "Extending the Calculus of Constructions with Type:Type." Unpublished notes, Feb. 1987.

[29] L.S. van Benthem Jutting. "The language theory of Λ_∞, a typed λ-calculus where terms are types." Unpublished manuscript (1984).

[30] G. Kahn. "Natural Semantics." In Programming of Future Generation Computers, eds K. Fuchi & M. Nivat, North-Holland 1988.

[31] J.J. Lévy. "Optimal Reductions in the Lambda Calculus." in To H. B. Curry: Essays on Combinatory Logic, Lambda-calculus and Formalism, Eds. J. P. Seldin and J. R. Hindley, Academic Press (1980), 159–191.

[32] Z. Luo. "ECC, an Extended Calculus of Constructions." Fourth LICS, Asilomar, June 1989.

[33] P. Martin-Löf. "A Theory of Types." Report 71-3, Dept. of Mathematics, University of Stockholm, Feb. 1971, revised (Oct. 1971).

[34] P. Martin-Löf. "An intuitionistic theory of types: predicative part." Logic Colloquium, North-Holland (1975).

[35] P. Martin-Löf. "Intuitionistic Type Theory." Studies in Proof Theory, Bibliopolis (1984).

[36] P. Martin-Löf. "Truth of a proposition, evidence of a judgement, validity of a proof." Transcript of talk at the workshop "Theories of Meaning", Centro Fiorentino di Storia e Filosofia della Scienza, Villa di Mondeggi, Florence (June 1985).

[37] C. Mohring. "Algorithm Development in the Calculus of Constructions." IEEE Symposium on Logic in Computer Science, Cambridge, Mass. (June 1986).

[38] C. Mohring. "Extracting F_ω'programs from proofs in the Calculus of Constructions." Sixteenth Symposium on Principles of Programming Languages, Austin, Jan. 89.

[39] C. Mohring. "Extraction de programmes dans le Calcul des Constructions." Thèse d'Informatique, Université Paris 7, Janv. 89.

[40] G. Nelson, D.C. Oppen. "Fast decision procedures based on congruence closure." JACM **27,2** (1980) 356–364.

[41] B. Russel and A.N. Whitehead. "Principia Mathematica." Volume 1,2,3 Cambridge University Press (1912).

[42] D. Scott. "Constructive validity." Symposium on Automatic Demonstration, Springer-Verlag Lecture Notes in Mathematics, **125** (1970).

[43] C. Wadsworth. "Semantics and Pragmatics of the Lambda-Calculus". Ph.D. thesis, Oxford University, Sept. 1971.

[44] P. Weis et al. "The CAML Reference Manual, Version 2.6." Projet Formel, INRIA-ENS, March 1989.

COMPLEXITY OF ACCEPTANCE PROBLEMS FOR TWO-DIMENSIONAL AUTOMATA

Akira ITO[+], Katsushi INOUE[++], and Itsuo TAKANAMI[++]

[+]*Technical College,* [++]*Faculty of Engineering*
Yamaguchi University, Ube, 755 Japan

Abstract We investigate computational complexity of acceptance problems for several two-dimensional automata and show that there exists a fixed nondeterministic finite automaton (alternating finite automaton, nondeterministic on-line tessellation acceptor, deterministic one-way parallel/sequential array automaton) for which the acceptance problem is NLOG-complete (P-complete, NP-complete, PSPACE-complete) under appropriate transformation.

1. Introduction

It is well-known that decision problems concerning two-dimensional automata are more complicated compared with one-dimensional case. For example[1],[3],[4],

> "Emptiness problem of finite automata over binary alphabet with boundary symbols is *PSPACE-complete* for 1-dimensional case, but *undecidable* for 2-dimensional case."

Many problems such as universal, equivalence, or disjointness problems are also undecidable for 2-dimensional automata[4]-[8].

On the other hand, for decidable problems, there has been little attention paid to the question how much amount of resource complexity they require, except about two-dimensional grammars[9]-[11]. In this paper, we investigate computational complexity of acceptance problems concerning several 2-dimensional automata.

From our results, some interesting applications for open questions in 2-dimensional automata study appear. For example, consider the following questions:

"$\mathcal{L}$[2-NA]$\subseteq \mathcal{L}$[2-DM_1] ?" and "$\mathcal{L}$[2-AFA]$\subseteq \mathcal{L}$[2-NM_1] ?,"

where $\mathcal{L}$[*] denotes the class of sets accepted by two-dimensional nondeterministic finite automata, deterministic 1-marker automata, alternating finite automata, and nondeterministic 1-marker automata, respectively.

Apparently, it is natural to think that the inclusion relationships of the above would be true: Actually, (1) all the known sets accepted by 2-NA's (2-AFA's) are also accepted by 2-DM_1's (2-NM_1's), (2) all the known sets *not* accepted by 2-DM_1's (2-NM_1's) are also *not* accepted by 2-NA's (2-AFA's), (3) there exists a certain set accepted by 2-DM_1's (2-NM_1's) but *not* accepted by 2-NA's (2-AFA's), and (4) there is no known set accepted by 2-NA's (2-AFA's) but *not* accepted by 2-DM_1's (2-NM_1's).

On the other hand, if the inclusions are true, the consequences of this paper lead us to the conclusions:

NLOG=DLOG and P=NLOG,

where DLOG,NLOG, and P denote the classes of languages accepted by 1-dimensional deterministic log-space, nondeterministic log-space, and deterministic polynomial-time Turing machines, respectively.

Thus, it turns out that these unsolved problems on two-dimensional automata have close relationships to the well-known historical open problems on the computational complexity theory, and therefore to settle them affirmatively, we would require a certain development of new techniques.

2. Definitions

Definition 2.1. Let Σ be a finite set of symbols. A *2-dimensional tape* (or *rectangular tape*) over Σ is a 2-dimensional rectangular array of elements of Σ. The set of all 2-dimensional tapes over Σ is denoted by $\Sigma^{(2)}$.

For a tape $x \in \Sigma^{(2)}$, we let $\ell_1(x)$ be the number of rows of x and $\ell_2(x)$ be the number of columns of x. Particularly, if a tape $x \in \Sigma^{(2)}$ satisfies $\ell_1(x)=\ell_2(x)$, we call it a *square tape*. If $1 \leq i \leq \ell_1(x)$ and $1 \leq j \leq \ell_2(x)$, we let x(i,j) denote the symbol in x with coordinates (i,j). Furthermore, we define

$$x[(i,j),(i',j')],$$

when $1 \leq i \leq i' \leq \ell_1(x)$ and $1 \leq j \leq j' \leq \ell_2(x)$, as the two-dimensional tape z satisfying the following:

(i) $\ell_1(z)=i'-i+1$ and $\ell_2(z)=j'-j+1$,

(ii) for each k,r $[1 \leq k \leq \ell_1(z), 1 \leq r \leq \ell_2(z)]$, $z(k,r)=x(k+i-1,r+j-1)$.

We assume that, when a 2-dimensional tape x is given to any 2-dimensional automaton as an input, x is surrounded by the boundary symbol "#"s.

Definition 2.2. A *polynomial* p(m,n) of 2 variables m and n is the following form:

$$p(m,n)=\sum_{0 \leq i,j \leq k} c_{i,j} \cdot m^i n^j,$$

where $c_{i,j}$'s are real coefficients and k is a non-negative integer $(\exists i[c_{i,k} \neq 0]$ or $\exists j[c_{k,j} \neq 0])$. We denote k by deg(p(m,n)). Note that for any polynomial p(m,n) of non-negative integer variables m and n, there exists a constant c>0 such that $p(m,n) \leq c \cdot (mn)^{deg(p(m,n))}$. By "P(m,n)," we denote the set of all polynomials of m and n.

Here, we give the list of all 2-dimensional automata and their notations which appear in this paper.

2-DA ⋯ deterministic finite automaton[4],[12]

2-NA ⋯ nondeterministic finite automaton[4],[12]

2-AFA ⋯ alternating finite automaton[13]

TR2-AFA ⋯ three-way 2-AFA[13]

TW2-AFA ⋯ two-way 2-AFA[14]

2-dota ⋯ deterministic on-line tessellation acceptor[14],[15]

2-ota ⋯ nondeterministic on-line tessellation acceptor[15]

DOWPSA ⋯ deterministic one-way parallel/sequential array acceptor[12]

2-DTM(f(m,n)) ··· deterministic f(m,n) space-bounded Turing machine[13]

TR2-DTM(f(m,n)) ··· three-way 2-DTM(f(m,n))[16]

2-NTM(f(m,n)) ··· nondeterministic f(m,n) space-bounded Turing machine[13]

TR2-NTM(f(m,n)) ··· three-way 2-NTM(f(m,n))[16]

2-ATM(f(m,n)) ··· alternating f(m,n) space-bounded Turing machine[13]

DRBCS ··· deterministic rectangular bounded cellular space acceptor[17],[18]

NRBCS ··· nondeterministic rectangular bounded cellular space acceptor[17],[18]

NRBCS(f(m,n)-time)) ··· f(m,n) time-bounded NRBCS[17],[18]

DRBCS(f(m,n)-time)) ··· f(m,n) time-bounded DRBCS[17],[18]

We omit definitions of these 2-dimensional automata. If necessary, see the appropriate references.

Below, we introduce new 2-dimensional automata which have intermediate accepting powers between deterministic and full-nondeterministic 2-ota's.

Definition 2.3. Let Z (called a zone) be a subset of $N \times N$, where N denotes the set of all positive integers. We say that a 2-ota M is *Z nondeterministic-zone bounded* if for each input x, each cell of M does never do a nondeterministic transition on x, except the cells which have the coordinates $(i,j) \in Z$. By "2-ota(Z)," we denote a Z nondeterministic-zone bounded 2-ota. Note that 2-ota($\emptyset$)=2-dota and 2-ota(N^2)=2-ota. We can also define 2-ota(Z) for such zone Z as $\{1\} \times N$ (topmost-zone), $N \times \{1\}$ (leftmost-zone), $\{1\} \times N \cup N \times \{1\}$ (front-zone), or $\{(i,i) \quad i \in N\}$ (diagonal-zone). See Figure 1.

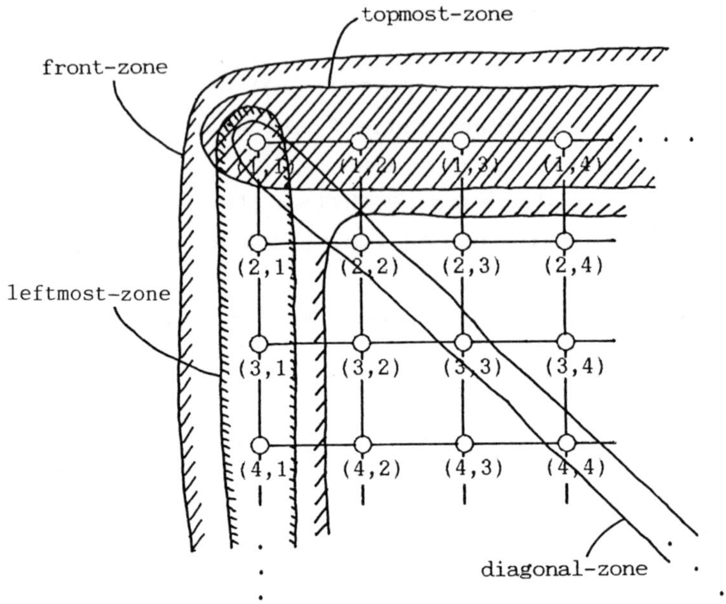

Fig.1. Several zones on 2-dimensional grid.

Among those variants of nondeterministic-zone bounded 2-ota's, we will mainly concern with 2-ota($\{1\}\times N$)'s in this paper and we abbreviate them by "2-ota(t)'s" from now on.

Definition 2.4. For any 2-dimensional automaton M with input alphabet Σ, define

$$T(M)=\{x\in\Sigma^{(2)} \mid M \text{ accepts } x\}.$$

Furthermore, we define the class of sets of tapes accepted by 2-dimensional automata. For example,

$$\mathcal{L}[\text{2-DA}]=\{T \mid T=T(M) \text{ for some 2-DA } M\}.$$

$\mathcal{L}$[2-NA],…,$\mathcal{L}$[DRBCS(f(m,n)-time)] are defined similarly. We especially define $\mathcal{L}[\text{2-DA}^s]$ as the class of sets of square tapes accepted by 2-DA's. $\mathcal{L}[\text{2-NA}^s]$,…,$\mathcal{L}[\text{DRBCS}^s(f(m)\text{-time})]$ are defined similarly. We also define,

$$\mathcal{L}[\text{DRBCS(poly-time)}] = \bigcup_{p(m,n)\in P(m,n)} \mathcal{L}[\text{DRBCS}(p(m,n)\text{-time})]$$

$$\mathcal{L}[\text{NRBCS(poly-time)}] = \bigcup_{p(m,n)\in P(m,n)} \mathcal{L}[\text{NRBCS}(p(m,n)\text{-time})]$$

Note that RBCSs which work in time m+n-1 (real-time), $O(m+n)$ (linear-time), and $O(mn)$ (area-time) are all polynomial-time bounded RBCSs[17],[18].

We also give the list of notations of the well-known language classes[2],[19]:

<u>the class of languages … accepted by 1-dimensional Turing machines</u>

DSPACE[S(n)] … in deterministic S(n) space

NSPACE[S(n)] … in nondeterministic S(n) space

ASPACE[S(n)] … in alternating S(n) space

DLOG … in deterministic logarithmic space

NLOG … in nondeterministic logarithmic space

P … in deterministic polynomial time

NP … in nondeterministic polynomial time

PSPACE … in polynomial space

DLBA … in deterministic linear space

NLBA … in nondeterministic linear space

3. Preliminary Results

In this section, we develop preliminary results which are required in the subsequent discussions.

First, we define an encoding of 2-dimensional tapes which maps 2-dimensional tapes to 1-dimensional strings.

Definition 3.1. For a rectangular tape $x \in \Sigma^{(2)}$ with $\ell_1(x)=m$ and $\ell_2(x)=n$, define

$dscr_*(x)=w_1\#w_2\#\cdots\#w_m$, where $w_i=x[(i,1),(i,n)]$ and $\# \notin \Sigma$,

and call it the *1-dimensional (split) description* of x.

Note that $|dscr_*(x)|=mn+m-1$. Further, for any set T of rectangular tapes, define

$$\mathrm{dscr}_*(T)=\{\mathrm{dscr}_*(x) \mid x\in T\},$$

Lemma 3.1. *For each $X\in \{D,N,A\}$, any function $f(m,n)$, and any set T of rectangular tapes,*

$$T \text{ is in } \mathcal{L}[2\text{-}XTM(f(m,n))] \Rightarrow \mathrm{dscr}_*(T) \text{ is in } XSPACE[\log n + g(n)],$$
$$\text{where } g(n)=\max_{n=m'n'+m'-1} f(m',n').$$

Proof. Suppose that M is an f(m,n) space-bounded 2-XTM accepting $T\subseteq \Sigma^{(2)}$. We construct a "one-dimensional" Turing machine A with read-only input tape over $\Sigma \cup \{\#\}$ such that, for each $x\in \Sigma^{(2)}$, $\mathrm{dscr}_*(x)$ is accepted by A iff x is accepted by M.

First, A checks that a given input string w has a form

$$¢u_1\#u_2\#\cdots\#u_k\$ \text{ for some } k\geq 0,$$

where $u_i\in \Sigma^*$ and ¢,\$ are the endmarkers. *A* also checks that all substrings u_i ($1\leq i\leq k$) have the same length ℓ and stores ℓ in the binary representation on the first track of the working tape. At this time, A has finished the check that w is the $\mathrm{dscr}_*(x)$ for some $x \in \Sigma^{(2)}$ with $\ell_1(x)=k$, $\ell_2(x)=\ell$. Next, A begins to simulate M at the left most position of the input string, where M should begin to move. *A* acts in the same way as M except when M would go up or go down to an adjacent row. In this case, A moves its input head just $\ell+1$ cells to the right or to the left, according to the direction of M's input head motion "up" or "down". Note that these extra actions of A can be deterministically done. *A* accepts w if and only if M accepts x. It is clear that A accepts $\mathrm{dscr}_*(T)$.

Now, let us consider the amount of space used by A. Clearly, $\ell\leq |w|$. Since M is f(m,n) space-bounded, A has used at most $f(k,\ell)$ cells of the working tape, where $|w|=k\ell+k-1$. In other words, for any input string w with length n, A uses at most $\log n + \max f(k,\ell)$, where the maximization operation undergoes over all positive k's and ℓ's satisfying $n=k\ell+k-1$.■

Lemma 3.2. *For each $X\in \{D,N,A\}$, any function $g(n)$, and any set T of rectangular tapes,*

$$\mathrm{dscr}_*(T) \text{ is in } XSPACE[g(n)] \Rightarrow T \text{ is in } \mathcal{L}[2\text{-}XTM(g(mn+m-1))].$$

Proof. Suppose that A is a "one-dimensional" g(n) space-bounded Turing machine accepting $dscr_*(T)$ over $\Sigma \cup \{\#\}$. We construct a 2-XTM M over Σ such that, for each $x \in \Sigma^{(2)}$, x is accepted by M iff $dscr_*(x)$ is accepted by A. Note that A never accepts a given input string w unless it has a form

$$¢u_1\#u_2\#\cdots\#u_k\$ \text{ for some } k \geq 0, \text{ where } u_i \in \Sigma^*$$

and unless all substrings u_i $(1 \leq i \leq k)$ have the same length ℓ. So, from now on, we only consider the inputs for A of this form. Given a 2-dimensional input tape $x \in \Sigma^{(2)}$ with $\ell_1(x)=k$ and $\ell_2(x)=\ell$, M begins to simulate A at the leftmost upper boundary corner of the input, where A should begin to move. M acts in the same way as A except when M reaches the left or right boundary area. In this case, M moves its input head from the left-hand side or right-hand side boundary area to the opposite side and move one cell up or down, according to the direction of A's input head motion "right-to-left" or "left-to-right." M accepts x if and only if A accepts w. Note that this extra actions of M can be deterministically done. It is clear that M accepts T.

Now, let us consider the amount of space used by M. Since A is g(n) space-bounded, A has used at most $g(k\ell+k-1)$ cells of the working tape. In other words, for any 2-dimensional tape x with $\ell_1(x)=m$ and $\ell_2(x)=n$, A uses at most $g(mn+m-1)$ cells of the working tape on the given 1-dimensional description, $dscr_*(x)$. It follows that M also uses at most $g(mn+m-1)$ cells of the working tape for m and n, that is, M is $g(mn+m-1)$ space-bounded.■

Theorem 3.1. *For each $X \in \{D,N,A\}$ and any set T of rectangular tapes,*

(1) $T \in \mathcal{L}[\text{2-XTM}(\log m + \log n)] \Leftrightarrow dscr_*(T) \in \text{XSPACE}[\log n]$,

(2) $T \in \mathcal{L}[\text{2-XTM}(mn)] \Leftrightarrow dscr_*(T) \in \text{XSPACE}[n]$.

Proof. (1): Suppose that T is in $\mathcal{L}[\text{2-XTM}(\log(mn+m-1))]$. From Lemma 3.1, $dscr_*(T)$ is in XSPACE[log$n$], since $\max_{n=m'n'+m'-1}\log(m'n'+m'-1) = \log n$. On the other hand, from 2-dimensional version of Space Compression Theorem[2], we can easily show that $\mathcal{L}[\text{2-XTM}(\log(mn+m-1))]=\mathcal{L}[\text{2-XTM}(\log m+\log n)]$. Conversely, suppose that $dscr_*(T)$ is in XSPACE[log$n$]. From Lemma 3.2, T is in $\mathcal{L}[\text{2-XTM}(\log(mn+m-1))]$. From

the same reason as above, $\mathcal{L}$[2-XTM(log(mn+m-1))]=$\mathcal{L}$[2-XTM(log$m$+log$n$)]. Part (1) follows from these facts.
(2): Analogously, Part (2) follows.■

For the case of square tapes, we define a special encoding, in which additional symbol "#" used in the split description is not used. From this, not only the encoding itself becomes more economical but also the arguments can be simplified.

Definition 3.2. For a square tape $x \in \Sigma^{(2)}$ with $\ell_1(x)=\ell_2(x)=m$, define

$$\mathrm{dscr}(x)=w_1w_2\cdots w_m, \text{ where } w_i=x[(i,1),(i,m)],$$

and call it the *1-dimensional (cohesive) description* of x.
Note that $|\mathrm{dscr}(x)|=m^2$. Further, for any set T of square tapes, define

$$\mathrm{dscr}(T)=\{\mathrm{dscr}(x) \mid x \in T\}.$$

Lemma 3.3. *For each $X\in\{D,N,A\}$, any function f(m), and any set T of square tapes,*

T is in $\mathcal{L}$[2-XTM^s(f(m))] $\Rightarrow$ dscr(T) is in XSPACE[log n + f($\sqrt{n}$)].

Proof. The proof technique is almost the same as one of Lemma 3.1. We only give the points different from the proof of Lemma 3.1. Suppose that M is an f(m) space-bounded 2-XTM accepting $T\subseteq\Sigma^{(2)}$. We construct a one-dimensional Turing machine A over Σ such that, for each $x\in\Sigma^{(2)}$, dscr(x) is accepted by A iff x is accepted by M.

A checks that a given input string w has length k^2 for some $k\geq 0$, and during the course of the simulation, A always witnesses whether M reaches the left or right boundary symbol by counting the present distance from the boundary. Note that these checks can be done in log space. ■

By using the same argument as in the proof of Lemma 3.2, we can get the following.

Lemma 3.4. *For each $X\in\{D,N,A\}$, any function g(n), and any set T of* *square tapes,*

$$dscr(T) \text{ is in } XSPACE[g(n)] \Rightarrow T \text{ is in } \mathcal{L}[2\text{-}XTM^s(g(m^2))].$$

From Lemma 3.3, Lemma 3.4, and the same argument as that of Theorem 3.1, we get the following.

Theorem 3.2. *For each X∈ {D,N,A} and any set T of square tapes,*

(1) $T \in \mathcal{L}[2\text{-}XTM^s(\log m)] \Leftrightarrow dscr(T) \in XSPACE[\log n]$,

(2) $T \in \mathcal{L}[2\text{-}XTM^s(m^2)] \Leftrightarrow dscr(T) \in XSPACE[n]$.

We must further define a 2-dimensional encoding of 1-dimensional strings, which maps 1-dimensional strings to 2-dimensional square tapes. This is a dual concept of 1-dimensional description of square tapes introduced in Definition 3.2.

Definition 3.3. For any string $w \in \Sigma^*$ with $|w|=n$, we define the square *embedding* of w (embd(w) in short) as the square tape x over $\Sigma \cup \{\$\}$ ($\$ \notin \Sigma$) satisfying the following:

(1) $\ell_1(x)=\ell_2(x)=m$, where m is the least integer satisfying $n \le m^2$, and

(2) for each i,j($1 \le i \le m, 1 \le j \le m$),

$$x(i,j)=\begin{cases} w((i-1)m+j) : \text{if } (i-1)m+j \le n \\ \$: \text{otherwise,} \end{cases}$$

where w(k) denote the *k*th symbol from the left boundary of w. Intuitively, embd(w) is the smallest square box enclosing the given string w. Note that $(m-1)^2<n$. Further, for any language L of strings, define

$$embd(L)=\{embd(w) \mid w \in L\}.$$

Lemma 3.5. *For each X∈ {D,N,A}, any nondecreasing function g(n), and any language L,*

$$L \text{ is in } XSPACE[g(n)] \Rightarrow embd(L) \text{ is in } \mathcal{L}[2\text{-}XTM^s(g(m^2))].$$

Proof. Suppose that A is a 1-dimensional g(n) space-bounded Turing machine accepting L over Σ. We construct a 2-XTM M over $\Sigma \cup \{\$\}$ such that, for each $w \in \Sigma^*$, embd(w) is accepted by M iff w is accepted by A. Given a 2-dimensional square tape $x \in (\Sigma \cup \{\$\})^{(2)}$ with $\ell_1(x)=\ell_2(x)=m$, M first checks by a raster-scanning on x that a non-"\$" substring w is followed by a unary substring $\{\$\}^*$. After that, M simulates A just as in the proof of Lemma 3.2. Of course, M never visits "\$" area of x through the simulation. M accepts x if and only if A accepts w. It is clear that M accepts embd(L).

Now, let us consider the amount of space used by M. Since A is g(n) space-bounded, M have used at most g(k) cells of the working tape, where k is the the size of non-"\$" area of x. Since $k \leq m^2$ and g is nondecreasing, M is $g(m^2)$ space-bounded.■

Lemma 3.6. *For each $X \in \{D,N,A\}$, any nondecreasing function f(m), and any language L,*

embd(L) is in $\mathcal{L}[2\text{-}XTM^s(f(m))]$ ⇒ L is in XSPACE[$\log n + f(\sqrt{n}+1)$].

Proof. Suppose that M is an f(m) space-bounded 2-XTM accepting $\mathrm{embd}(L) \subseteq (\Sigma \cup \{\$\})^{(2)}$. We construct a 1-dimensional Turing machine A with read-only input tape over Σ such that, for each $w \in \Sigma^*$, w is accepted by A iff embd(w) is accepted by M.

First, A computes the least integer k such that $|w| \leq k^2$ and stores k in the binary representation on the first track of the working tape. Next, A acts just as in the proof of Lemma 3.1. By utilizing the working tape, even when M enters the "\$" area of embd(w), A can continue to simulate M without leaving off the boundary of w. *A* accepts w if and only if M accepts embd(w). It is clear that A accepts L.

Now, let us consider the amount of space used by A. Since M is f(m) space-bounded, A has used at most f(k) cells of the working tape. From the inequality $(k-1)^2 < |w|$, it follows that $k \leq \sqrt{|w|}+1$ (note that $\sqrt{x}$ is the integer part of the square root of x). Since f is nondecreasing, we can say that, for any input string w with length n, A uses at most $\log n + f(\sqrt{n}+1)$ cells of the working tape.■

From Lemma 3.5, Lemma 3.6, and arguments similar to one of the proof of Theorem 3.1, we can get the following.

Theorem 3.3. *For each $X \in \{D,N,A\}$ and any language L,*

(1) $L \in XSPACE[\log n] \Leftrightarrow embd(L) \in \mathcal{L}[2\text{-}XTM^s(\log m)]$,

(2) $L \in XSPACE[n] \Leftrightarrow embd(L) \in \mathcal{L}[2\text{-}XTM^s(m^2)]$.

Theorem 3.4.

(1) $\mathcal{L}[2\text{-}DTM(\log m + \log n)]=\mathcal{L}[2\text{-}NTM(\log m + \log n)]$
$\Leftrightarrow \mathcal{L}[2\text{-}DTM^s(\log m)]=\mathcal{L}[2\text{-}NTM^s(\log m)] \Leftrightarrow DLOG=NLOG$,

(2) $\mathcal{L}[2\text{-}NTM(\log m + \log n)]=\mathcal{L}[2\text{-}ATM(\log m + \log n)]$
$\Leftrightarrow \mathcal{L}[2\text{-}NTM^s(\log m)]=\mathcal{L}[2\text{-}ATM^s(\log m)] \Leftrightarrow NLOG=P$, and

(3) $\mathcal{L}[DRBCS]=\mathcal{L}[NRBCS] \Leftrightarrow \mathcal{L}[DRBCS^s]=\mathcal{L}[NRBCS^s] \Leftrightarrow DLBA=NLBA$.

Proof. The statement "$\mathcal{L}[2\text{-DTM}(\log m+\log n)]=\mathcal{L}[2\text{-NTM}(\log m+\log n)] \Rightarrow$ DLOG=NLOG" is trivial, since 1-dimensional Turing machines are the special versions of 2-dimensional Turing machines on rectangular tapes. We next consider the statement "DLOG=NLOG $\Rightarrow \mathcal{L}[2\text{-DTM}(\log m+\log n)]=\mathcal{L}[2\text{-NTM}(\log m+\log n)]$." Suppose that DLOG=NLOG. From Theorem 3.1, if $T \in \mathcal{L}[2\text{-NTM}(\log m+\log n)]$, then $dscr_\#(T)$ is in NLOG. The assumption implies $dscr_\#(T)$ is also in DLOG. From Theorem 3.1, it follows that T is in $\mathcal{L}[2\text{-DTM}(\log m+\log n)]$. By using the same arguments, the remaining parts follow. (Note that ASPACE[log$n$]=P [19] and for each $X \in \{D,N\}$ $\mathcal{L}[XRBCS]=\mathcal{L}[2\text{-XTM}(mn)]$ ($\mathcal{L}[XRBCS^s]=\mathcal{L}[2\text{-XTM}^s(m^2)]$) [20].)■

The following lemma points out the upper bound of the complexity of reasonably time-bounded RBCS.

Lemma 3.7.

(1) $T \in \mathcal{L}[DRBCS(poly\text{-}time)] \Rightarrow dscr_\#(T) \in P$, (2) $T \in \mathcal{L}[NRBCS(poly\text{-}time)] \Rightarrow dscr_\#(T) \in NP$, (3) $T \in \mathcal{L}[DRBCS^s(poly\text{-}time)] \Rightarrow dscr(T) \in P$, and (4) $T \in \mathcal{L}[NRBCS^s(poly\text{-}time)] \Rightarrow dscr(T) \in NP$.

Proof. (1): Suppose that M is a p(m,n) time-bounded DRBCS accepting $T \subseteq \Sigma^{(2)}$, where $p(m,n) \in P(m,n)$. We can easily construct a 1-dimensional deterministic multi-tape Turing machine A over $\Sigma \cup \{\#\}$ such that, for each $x \in \Sigma^{(2)}$, $dscr_\#(x)$ is accepted by A iff x is accepted by M and A is polynomial-time bounded. Detailed construction of A is omitted here.

The other cases are proved just in the same manner.■

4. Main Results

The main purpose of this section is to show that there exist 2-dimensional automata for which the acceptance problems on square tapes are NLOG-, P-, NP-, and PSPACE-complete.

In what follows, we use the standard many-one log-space or polynomial-time reducibility, and we assume that the reader is familiar to such a notion as "NP-completeness"[1],[2].

Definition 4.1. For any collection $\mathscr{C}$ of 2-dimensional automata, the *acceptance problem for* $\mathscr{C}$ is the following:
INSTANCE: A 2-dimensional automaton M in $\mathscr{C}$ with input alphabet Σ, and a 2-dimensional tape $x \in \Sigma^{(2)}$ (rigorously, "$dscr_*(x)$" or "dscr(x)").
QUESTION: Does M accept x ?

Theorem 4.1. *There exists a 2-NA M such that the acceptance problem for {M} on square tapes is NLOG-complete.*

Proof. (Note that "Does a 1-dimensional nondeterministic finite automaton accept ε ?" is NLOG-complete[3]). We show that Graph Accessibility Problem (GAP), which is known to be NLOG-complete[2], is reducible to this particular problem with respect to log-space transformation. That is, we exhibit a log-space transducer A which for each input w, if w is an encoding of some graph G listing all node-pairs (i,j) of the directed edges in G, produces an output (M,dscr(x)) such that 2-NA M accepts x if and only if G can be accessible. We assume that G has a node set $\{1,2,\cdots,m\}$, where node 1 is the starting node (IN), and node m is the final node (OUT).

A transforms the original representation form of G to an "adjacency matrix" representation:

$$dscr(x)=w_1w_2\cdots w_m,$$

where for each $i(1 \leq i \leq m)$ $|w_i| = m$, and for each $j(1 \leq j \leq m)$,

jth symbol of w_i = 1: if there exists an arc from node i to node j,
0: otherwise,

by using the following simple algorithm:

```
for i=1 to m do begin
     for j=1 to m do begin
          if there exists a directed edge (i,j) exists
               then print "1" else print "0"
     end;
end
```

Clearly, this transformation is done deterministically in log $m \leq \log |w|$ space and G is accessible iff the (1,m) element of the "closure" of the 0-1 matrix represented by x is "1". Another work of A is the output of a 2-NA M accepting T_{GAP}, which denotes the set of square tapes produced by A from GAP. M checks that there exists a path from node 1 to node m as follows (See Figure 2):

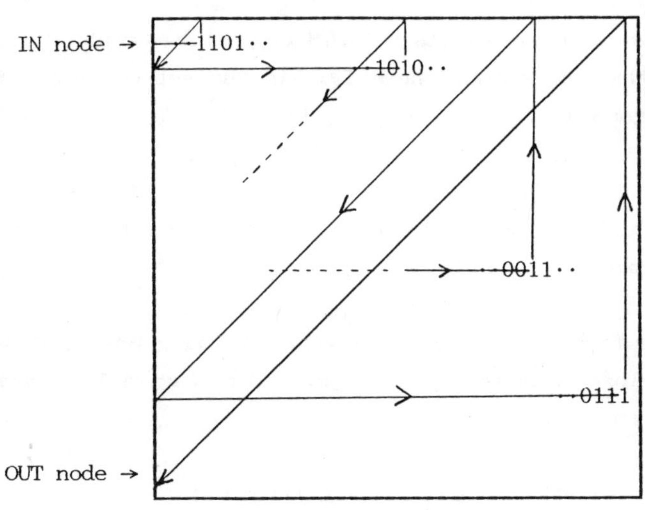

Fig.2. Action of 2-NA M on a tape in T_{GAP}.

M starts at the position (1,1). While going to the left, M non-deterministically chooses some '1' position, then it goes upward from this position. After it reaches the top boundary, M changes its direction downward with a 45° leftward slant. When M reaches the left boundary, it checks that this position is (m,1), which is for the final node. If so, it enters an accepting state, otherwise repeats the above search for '1' on the present row. It is clear that $T(M)=T_{GAP}$.

The membership in NLOG follows from Theorem 3.2.■

Corollary 4.1. *$\mathscr{L}$[2-NA^s] ⊆ $\mathscr{L}$[2-DTM^s(log m)] ⇔ NLOG=DLOG.*

Proof. "⇒" portion: Suppose that $\mathscr{L}$[2-NA^s]⊆ $\mathscr{L}$[2-DTM^s(log$m$)]. Then, from Theorem 4.1 and Theorem 3.2, we get NLOG=DLOG. "<=" portion: Suppose that NLOG=DLOG. This implies, from Theorem 3.4, that $\mathscr{L}$[2-DTM^s(log$m$)]=$\mathscr{L}$[2-NTM^s(log$m$)]. Since $\mathscr{L}$[2-NA^s]=$\mathscr{L}$[2-NTM^s(0)], it immediately follows that $\mathscr{L}$[2-NA^s]⊆ $\mathscr{L}$[2-DTM^s(log$m$)].■

Of course, even if there exists a 2-DTM^s(log m) M accepting T_{GAP}, we can conclude that DLOG=NLOG, where T_{GAP} is the set described in the proof of Theorem 4.1.

Fact 4.1 [20]. $\mathscr{L}^0$[2-NA^s] ⊆ $\mathscr{L}^0$[2-DTM^s(log$m$)] ⇔ DLBA=NLBA, where $\mathscr{L}^0$[*] denotes the class of tally sets accepted by the correspondent machines.

Compare the following upper bound with the equivalence '$\mathscr{L}$[2-NA]⊆ $\mathscr{L}$[2-DTM(log$m$+log$n$)]⇔NLOG=DLOG,' to which Corollary 4.1 is rewritten by using Theorem 3.4.

Fact 4.2 [21]. $\mathscr{L}$[2-NA] ⊆ $\mathscr{L}$[2-DTM(log m·log n)].

Remark 4.1. In contrast with Theorem 4.1, we can show that there exists a 2-DA M such that the acceptance problem for {M} on square tapes is DLOG-complete with respect to NC^1 reducibility[22],[23]. In this case, we adopt 1GAP, i.e., GAP each node of which has at most outdegree one, which is known to be DLOG-complete[24]. Note that each row of the resulting square tapes T_{1GAP} has only one "1".

Theorem 4.2. *There exists a TR2-NTM(log m) M such that the acceptance problem for {M} on square tapes is NLOG-complete.*

Proof. We can easily exhibit a transducer A which produces from an instance w in any NLOG-compete language, say GAP, an output of the following square tape z:

$$dscr(z)=w0^{m^2-m}, \text{ where } m=|w| \text{ and } 0 \text{ is a new symbol.}$$

Since, when input tapes for TR2-NTM(log m)'s are restricted to a single row, the resulting class of sets accepted by them is equivalent to NLOG, it is straightforward to design a TR2-NTM(log m) M such that M accepts z iff w is in GAP.

From Theorem 3.2, the membership in NLOG is clear.■

By using the same argument as in the proof of Corollary 4.1, we get the following.

Corollary 4.2.

$$\mathscr{L}[TR2\text{-}NTM^s(\log m)] \subseteq \mathscr{L}[2\text{-}DTM^s(\log m)] \Leftrightarrow NLOG=DLOG.$$

The above equivalence is just a 2-dimensional version of the following one.

Fact 4.3 [24]. 1-way NLOG $\subseteq$ DLOG $\Leftrightarrow$ NLOG=DLOG.

Theorem 4.3. *There exists a TW2-AFA M such that the acceptance problem for {M} on square tapes is P-complete.*

Proof. We show that Circuit Value Problem (CVP), which is known to be P-complete[2], is reducible to this particular problem with respect to log-space transformation. We assume that for a given circuit $C=\{C_1,\cdots,C_m\}$, C_1 is a variable and C_m is for the output of the circuit (if necessary, we rearrenge the order of the circuit elements in this order by using log-space).

A produces a square tape x from C, according to the following algorithm:

```
for i=1 to m do begin
      case Ci of
         'variable xr' for some r:
                  case the assignment to xr of
                        'true' : print "T";
                        'false': print "F";
                  for ℓ=2 to m do begin print "0" end
         '∧(j,k)':
                  for ℓ=1 to m do begin
                        if ℓ=j or ℓ=k then print "&" else print "0"
                  end;
         '¬(j)':
                  for ℓ=1 to m do begin
                        if ℓ=j then print "n" else print "0"
                  end;
end
```

It is clear that this transformation is done in deterministic log m space. Note that CVP satisfies the following property:

$$C_i = \wedge(j,k) \text{ or } \neg(j) \Rightarrow j,k<i. \qquad \cdots \text{(A)}$$

Thus, the upper triangular region of the resulting square tape x consists of "0"s at all.

Since $\mathcal{L}[\text{TW2-AFA}^s]=\mathcal{L}[\text{2-dota}^s]^{R2}$, where the superscript "R2" denotes 180°-rotational operation[14], we describe the behavior of a 2-dota M' accepting T_{CVP}, which is the set produced by A from CVP, rather than a TW2-AFA M itself. It is easy to change the below for 2-dota M' to one for TW2-AFA M.

M' computes the truth value of the circuit in a "PLA"-like manner: If M' meets a "T" or "F" on the leftmost column, it sends this truth value to the diagonal cell on the same row and thereafter propagates the same value downward from the diagonal cell to the bottom boundary. On any row, if M' meets one of "&"s on the *i*th row, then it holds the truth value of the upper-neighborhood cell and sends it to the right along the *i*th row. When it meets the other "&" on the same *i*th row again, it computes logical AND of the truth value sent from the left and that from the upper-neighbor cell. The resulting truth value is the output of the circuit element C_i. M' propagates this value to the right and makes it reflected at the diagonal into the downward direction. Analogously, if M' meets a NOT element "n", it computes logical NOT of the truth value of the upper-neighborhood cell. After that, M' propagates it in the same manner as the AND operation. Note that, from the property (A), when M' has to evaluate the output of any circuit element, the input of this circuit element is always provided at the upper-neighbor cell of the evaluating cell.

M' accepts x if and only if the logical value of the accepting cell C(m,m) is "T", which means the output of the circuit represented by x is 'true'. It is clear $T(M')=T_{CVP}$.

The membership in P follows from Theorem 3.2.■

By using the same argument as in the proof of Corollary 4.1, we get the following.

Corollary 4.3. *$\mathcal{L}[TW2\text{-}AFA^s] \subseteq \mathcal{L}[2\text{-}NTM^s(\log m)] \Leftrightarrow P=NLOG$.*

We next investigate the complexity of acceptance problem for time-bounded RBCSs. Note that 2-ota is the most primitive usage of RBCS which has only "2-way" communication and works in real-time.

First of all, we mention the complexity of acceptance problem for deterministic 2-ota's: From the facts described in the proof of Theorem 3.2, it is trivial that there exists a deterministic 2-ota M such that the acceptance problem for {M} is P-complete and that the equivalence '$\mathcal{L}[2\text{-dota}^s] \subseteq \mathcal{L}[2\text{-NTM}^s(\log m)] \Leftrightarrow NLOG=P$' holds.

The following theorem concerns with 2-ota(t), which is a 2-ota whose nondeterministic mechanism is allowed to use only on the first row of a given input tape.

Theorem 4.3. *There exists a fixed 2-ota(t) M such that the acceptance problem for {M} on square tapes is NP-complete.*

Proof. Determining whether a directed graph has a kernel is known to be NP-complete[1],[2]. (A *kernel* of a directed graph is a set of vertices such that 1) there is no arc from a vertex in the kernel to another vertex in the kernel, and 2) each vertex not in the kernel has an arc into it from the kernel.) We show that Kernel problem is reducible to our problem. Given a graph instance G, our transducer A produces an output (M,dscr(x)) such that 2-ota(t) M accepts x iff G has a kernel. The tape x is just the transposed adjacency matrix of G and it is easily seen that this transformation can be done in deterministic log space.

The behavior of M on a given input tape x is the following (see Figure 3).

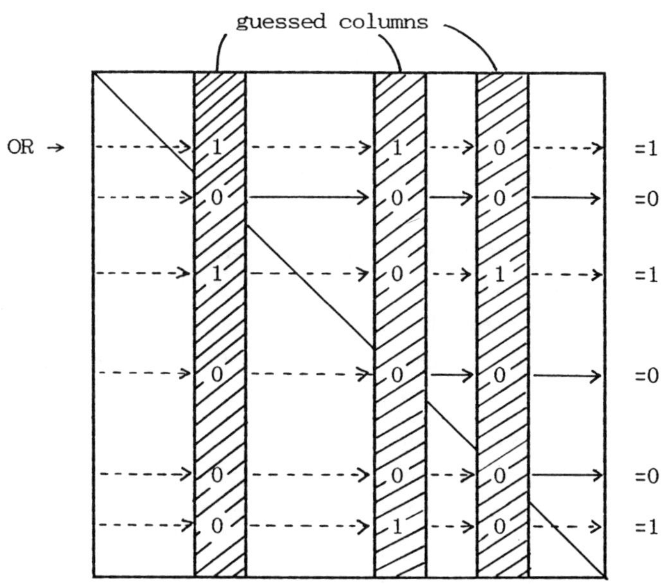

Fig.3. Action of 2-ota(t) M on a tape in T_K.

On the first row, M nondeterministically selects a set of columns $K=\{j_1,\cdots,j_k\},k\geq 1$ corresponding to the set $\{v_{j_1},\cdots,v_{j_k}\}$ of vertices which is a candidate for a kernel of G. For each $j_s \in K$, the cells on the j_sth column propagate this information vertically along the column. At the same time, horizontally from the first column on each row, M computes logical OR operations between the input symbols on the selected columns. At the last column of x, M checks on each *i*th row that ($i\in K$ and OR=0) or ($i\notin K$ and OR=1). Note that whether or not $i\in K$ is easily recognized by using the information whether the *i*th row includes the cell on which the signal on the diagonal collides with the signal from the above. If all these checks are successfully done, M accepts x; otherwise rejects. It is clear that $T(M)=T_K$, where T_K is the set of square tapes produced by A from Kernel problem. The membership in NP follows from Lemma 3.7.■

Corollary 4.4. *$\mathcal{L}[2\text{-ota}^s(t)] \subseteq \mathcal{L}[2\text{-ATM}^s(\log m)] \Leftrightarrow P=NP$.*

Proof. "⇒" portion follows from Theorem 4.3, Theorem 3.2, and the fact ASPACE[log*n*]=P. Conversely, suppose that P=NP. If T is in $\mathcal{L}$ [2-ota^s(t)], then from Lemma 3.7, dscr(T) is in NP. The hypothesis implies dscr(T) is also in P (=ASPACE[log*n*]). From Theorem 3.2, it follows that T is in $\mathcal{L}$[2-ATM^s(log*m*)].■

Remark 4.2. From Lemma 3.7, We can also state that $\mathcal{L}$[2-ota^s(t)]⊆$\mathcal{L}$ [DRBCS^s(poly-time)] ⇒ P=NP.

From corollary 4.2, it is interesting to know whether $\mathcal{L}$[2-dota]= $\mathcal{L}$[2-ota(t)], because if it were the case, we could say that P=NP. Below, we can settle this question in the negative.

Theorem 4.4. *$\mathcal{L}[2\text{-dota}^s] \subsetneq \mathcal{L}[2\text{-ota}^s(t)]$.*

Proof. The proof is shown in Appendix.

Theorem 4.5. *There exists a DOWPSA such that the acceptance problem for {M} on square tapes is PSPACE-complete.*

Proof. It is known that there exists a deterministic linear-bounded automaton (dlba) A such that the acceptance problem for {A} is PSPACE-complete[1]. Since a DOWPSA whose inputs are restricted to those with only one row is equivalent to a dlba ($\mathcal{L}$[DOWPSA^s]=$\mathcal{L}$[TR2-

$DTM^s(m)]$[16]), it is easy to see that the acceptance problem for A is reducible to this problem in polynomial-time, by using the same technique as in the proof of Theorem 4.2.

It is clear, from Theorem 3.2, that this problem is in PSPACE.■

From Theorem 4.5 and Lemma 3.7, we get the following.

Corollary 4.5. *$\mathcal{L}[DOWPSA^s] \subseteq \mathcal{L}[NRBCS^s(poly\text{-}time)] \Rightarrow PSPACE=NP$.*

5. Discussion

In this paper, we have investigated the computational complexity about acceptance problems for several two-dimensional automata and show that there exists a fixed nondeterministic finite automaton (alternating finite automaton, nondeterministic on-line tessellation acceptor, deterministic one-way parallel/sequential array automaton) for which the acceptance problem is NLOG-complete (P-complete, NP-complete, PSPACE-complete).

This means that acceptance problems of familiar classes of two-dimensional automata construct a so-called "Hierarchy of Complete Problems[3]".

We give some interesting questions concerning the topics in this paper.

(1) Does there exist a 2-DM_1 (2-NM_1) accepting T_{GAP} (T_{CVP}) ?, where T_{GAP} (T_{CVP}) is the set described in the proof of Theorem 4.1 (Theorem 4.3). See Corollary 4.1 (Corollary 4.3).

(2) Complexities of other known decidable problems of 2-dimensional finite automata[5],[7],[8].

It will be also interesting to investigate the several properties of nondeterministic-zone bounded 2-ota's introduced in this paper. For example, does the proper containment $\mathcal{L}$[2-ota(t)] $\subsetneq$ $\mathcal{L}$[2-ota] hold ?

Acknowledgment A. Ito, one of the authors, thanks Dr. Hiroshi Taniguchi of Tottori University for his stimulating discussions and frequent support.

References

[1] Garey,M.R. and Johnson,D.S., *Computers and Intractability: A Guide to the Theory of NP-Completeness*, Freeman, (1979).

[2] Hopcroft,J.E. and Ullman,J.D., *Introduction to Automata Theory, Languages, and Computation*, Addison Wesley (1979).

[3] Galil,Z., "Hierarchies of Complete Problems," *Acta Inf.* 6, 77-88 (1976).

[4] Blum,M. and Hewitt,C., "Automata on a Two-Dimensional Tapes," *Proc.8th SWAT*, 155-160 (1967).

[5] Taniguchi,K. and Kasami,T., "Some Decision Problems for Two-Dimensional Nonwriting Automata," *Trans. IECE Japan* 54-C, No.7, 578-585 (1971).

[6] Inoue,K. and Nakamura,A., "Some Decision Problems for Two-Dimensional On-Line Tessellation Acceptors and Their Variants," *Memoirs of the Faculty of Engineering Hiroshima University* 6, No.3(Serial No.20) 1-8 (February 1978).

[7] Inoue,K. and Takanami,I, "A Note on Decision Problems for Three-Way Two-Dimensional Finite Automata," *Inf.Proc.Lett.* 10, No.4-5, 245-248 (1980).

[8] Kinber,E.B., "Three-Way Automata on Rectangular Tapes over a One-Letter Alphabet," *Inf.Sci.* 35, 61-77 (1985).

[9] Morita,K.,Yamamoto,Y,and Sugata,K., "The Complexity of Some Decision Problems about Two-Dimensional Array Grammars," *Inf.Sci.* 30, 241-262 (1983).

[10] Morita,K., Nakazono,K.,and Sugata,K., "On Two-Dimensional Pattern-Matching Languages and Their Decision Problems," *Inf.Sci.* 40, 53-66 (1986).

[11] Kim,C. and Sudborough,I.H., "The Membership and Equivalence Problems for Picture Languages," *Theoret.Comput.Sci.* 52, 177-191 (1987).

[12] Rosenfeld,A., *Picture Languages -- Formal models for picture recognition*, Academic Press (1979).

[13] Inoue,K.,Takanami,I.,and Taniguchi,H., "Two-Dimensional Alternating Turing Machines," *Theoret.Comput.Sci.* 27 61-83 (1983).

[14] Ito,A.,Inoue,K.,and Takanami,I., "Deterministic On-Line Tessellation Acceptors are Equivalent to Two-Way Two-Dimensional Alternating Finite Automata through 180°-Rotation," to appear in *Theoret.Comput.Sci.*.

[15] Inoue,K. and Nakamura,A., "Some Properties of Two-Dimensional On-Line Tessellation Acceptors," *Inform.Sci.* 13, 95-121 (1977).

[16] Inoue,K. and Takanami,I., "Three-Way Tape-Bounded Two-Dimensional Turing Machines," *Inf.Sci.* 17 195-220 (1979).

[17] Beyer,W.T, "Topological Invariants by Iterative Array", Ph.D. dissertation, MIT (1970).

[18] Smith III ,A.B., "Two-Dimensional Formal Languages and Pattern Recognition by Cellular Automata," *Proc. 12th SWAT*, 144-150

(1971).

[19] Chandra,A.K,Kozen,D.C.,and Stockmeyer,L, Alternation, *J.ACM* **28**, 114-133 (1981).

[20] Inoue,K.,Takanami,I.,and Taniguchi,H., "The Accepting Powers of Two-Dimensional Automata over Square Tapes," *Trans. IECE Japan* **63-D**, No.2, 113-120 (1980).

[21] Ito,A.,Inoue,K.,and Takanami,I., "Complexity of Acceptance Problem for Two-Dimensional cellular spaces," *Tech.Rep.IEICE Japan* **COMP88**, No.301, 1-10(1988).

[22] Ruzzo,W.L., "On Uniform Circuit Complexity", *JCSS* **22**, 365-383 (1981).

[23] Cook,S.A., "A Taxonomy of Problems with Fast Parallel Algorithms", *Inf.Cont.* **64**, 2-22 (1985).

[24] Hartmanis,J. and Mahaney,S., "Languages Simultaneously Complete for One-Way and Two-Way Log-Tape Automata," *SIAM J.Comput.* **10**, No.2, 383-390 (May 1981).

Appendix

The proof of Theorem 4.4 ("$\mathcal{L}$[2-dota^s]$\subsetneq$ $\mathcal{L}$[2-ota^s(t)]").

Let $T_1=\{x\in \{0,1\}^{(2)} \mid \exists m\geq[\ell_1(x)=\ell_2(x)=2m$ & $x[(1,1),(m,2m)] \neq x[(m+1,1),(2m,2m)]$ (i.e., upper and lower half of square tape x are different)]}.

It is known[20] that (1) $T_1\notin \mathcal{L}$[2-dota^s]. We will show below that (2) $T_1\in \mathcal{L}$[2-ota^s(t)]. From these facts, we get the desired result. Below, we will construct a 2-ota(t) M accepting T_1 (see Figure 4).

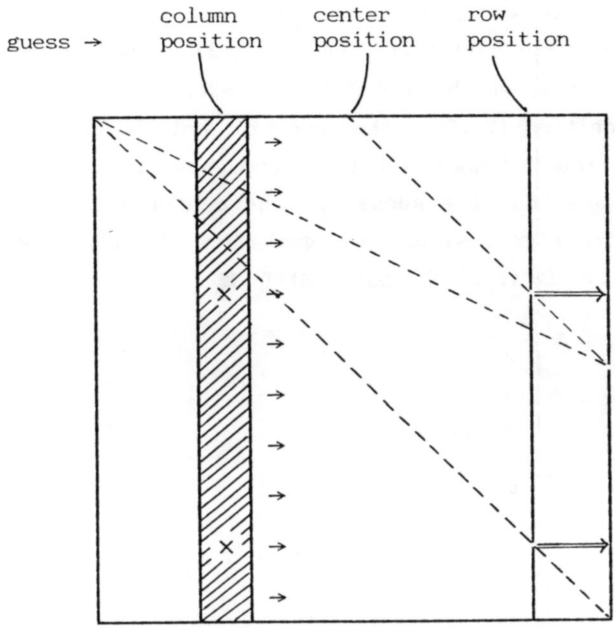

Fig.4. Action of 2-ota(t) M on a tape in T_1.

Suppose that an input tape x with $\ell_1(x)=\ell_2(x)=2m$ $(m\geq 1)$ is given to M. M must select a position (i,j) such that $x(i,j)\neq x(m+i,j)$. In order to do this, it guesses 3 matters on the 1st row of x: one is for the column position j, one is for the center position m, and the last one is for the row position i, which must be done after the guess for the center position. After the *j*th column was selected on the 1st row, the top cell of this column sends this information vertically along the column and then all cells on the *j*th column propagate their own input symbols to the right. The *i*th cell on the top row which was selected for the row position, sends this information vertically along the *i*th column. The *m*th cell on the top row sends a signal s_1 in 45° direction toward (m,2m) cell. The other signal s_2 is also sent from the (1,1) cell in 45° direction toward the (2m,2m) cell. If some cell on the *i*th column accepts the signal s_1 (s_2), it then sends this signal s_1 (s_2) horizontally to the right. On the rightmost column, the cell that accepts signal s_1 (s_2) propagates the input symbol b (b'), which came from the left, vertically toward the bottom. At position (2m,2m), the accepting cell enters an accepting state iff the input symbol b and b' propagated from the above are different. Note that the guess for the center position m can be checked from the signal s_1 and a signal from the (1,1) cell toward the (m,2m) cell. It is clear that $T(M)=T_1$.■

PARSING TREE ADJOINING GRAMMARS

Aravind K. Joshi
Dept. of Computer & Information Science
University of Pennsylvania
Philadelphia, PA 19104
USA

K. Vijay-Shanker
Dept. of Computer Science
University of Delaware
Newark, DE 19716
USA

Abstract

Tree Adjoining Grammar (TAG) is a formalism for natural language grammars. In this paper, we have described a parsing algorithm (CYK type) for TAG and shown that the parsing complexity is n^6, where n is the length of the input string.

1 TREE ADJOINING GRAMMARS

A *tree adjoining grammar (TAG)* $G = (I, A)$ where I and A are finite sets of *elementary trees*. The trees in I will be called the *initial trees* and the trees in A, the *auxiliary trees*. A tree α is an initial tree if it is of the form in (1):

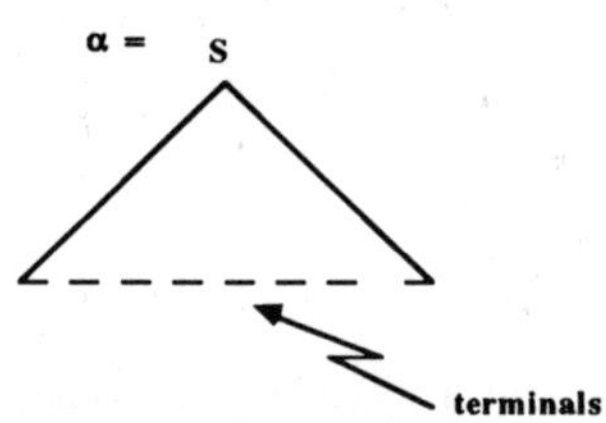

That is, the root node of α is labelled S and the frontier nodes are all terminals. A tree β is an auxiliary tree if it is of the form in (2):

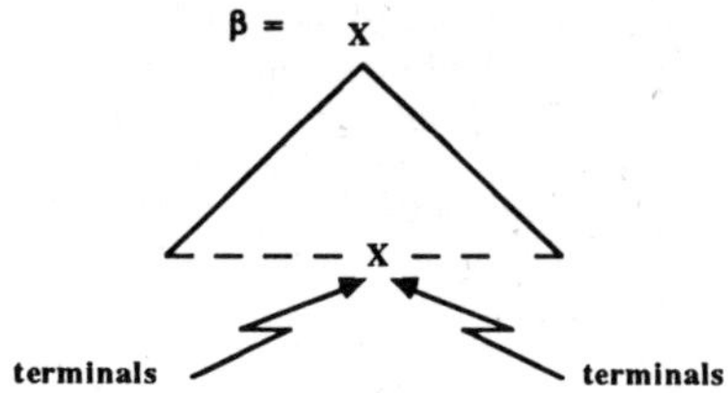

That is, the root node of β is labelled X where X is a non-terminal and the frontier nodes are all terminals except one which is labelled X, the same label as that of the root. The node labelled X on the frontier will be called the foot node of β. The internal nodes are non-terminals. The initial and the auxiliary trees are not constrained in any manner other than as indicated above. The idea, however, is that both the initial and auxiliary trees will be *minimal* in some sense. An initial tree will correspond to a *minimal* sentential tree (i.e., without recursing on any non-terminal) and an auxiliary tree, with root and foot node labelled X, will correspond to a *minimal* recursive structure that must be brought into the derivation, if one recurses on X.

We will now define a composition operation called *adjoining* (or *adjunction*), which composes an auxiliary tree β with a tree γ. Let γ be a tree containing a node n bearing the label X and let β be an auxiliary tree whose root node is also labelled X. (Note that β must have, by definition, a node (and only one such) labelled X on the frontier.) Then the adjunction of β to γ at node n will be the tree γ' that results when the following operations are carried out: 1) The sub-tree of γ dominated by n, call it t, is excised; 2) The auxiliary tree β is attached at n and its root node is identified with n; 3) The sub-tree t is attached to the foot node of β and the root node n of t is identified with the foot node of β.

Figure 1 below illustrates this operation.

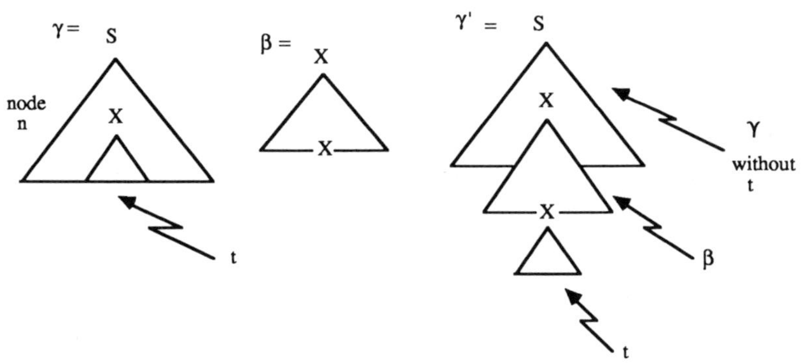

Figure 1:

The intuition underlying the adjoining operation is a simple one but the operation is distinct from other operations on trees that have been discussed in the literature. In particular, we want to emphasize that adjoining is not a substitution operation in the usual sense.

The definition of adjunction allows more complex constraints to be placed on adjoining. Associated with each node is a *selective adjoining (SA)* constraint specifying the subset of auxiliary trees which can be adjoined at this node. Trees can only be included in the SA constraint associated with a particular node if their root and foot are labelledwith the same nonterminal that labels the node. A mechanism is provided for ensuring that adjunction is performed at a node. This is done by associating an *obligatory adjoining (OA)* constraint with that node.

We should note that the SA and OA constraints are more than mere notational convenience, since they increase the generative power of the formalism. If the SA constraint specifies an empty subset of trees, then adjunction cannot be performed at this node—we call this constraint the *null adjoining (NA)* constraint.

Let us now define two auxiliary notions, the tree set of a TAG grammar and the string language of a TAG. Suppose G=(I,A) is a TAG with a finite set of initial trees, a finite set of auxiliary trees, and the ***adjoining*** operation, as above. Then we define the ***tree set*** of a TAG G, $T(G)$, to be the set of all trees derived in G starting from initial trees in I. We further define the ***string language*** (or ***language***) of G to be the set of all terminal strings of the trees in $T(G)$. The relationship between TAGs, context-free grammars, and the corresponding string languages can then be summarized in the following theorems Joshi, Levy, and Takahashi (1975), Joshi (1985): 1) For every context-free grammar, G', there is a TAG, G, which is both weakly and strongly equivalent to G'. In other words, $L(G) = L(G')$ and $T(G) = T(G')$; 2) There exists a non-empty set of TAG grammars G_1 such that for every $G \in G_1$, $L(G)$ is context-free but there is no CFG G' such that $T(G') = T(G)$, i.e., TAGs are capable of providing structural descriptions for context-free languages that are not obtainable by a context-free grammar; 3) There exists a non-empty set of TAG grammars G_2 such that for every $G \in G_2$, $L(G)$ is strictly context sensitive; that is, there is no CFG grammar G' such that $L(G) = L(G')$, i.e., TAGs are strictly more powerful than CFGs; 4) There exist context-sensitive languages for which there are no equivalent TAGs, i.e., TAGs are properly contained in context-sensitive languages; 5) TAGs are semi-linear and hence have the constant growth property; 6) TAGs can capture only certain limited kinds of crossed dependencies. This follows from the nature of the automaton that corresponds to a TAG, called an embedded push-down automaton (EPDA), which is a generalization of the push-down automaton (PDA); 7) TAGs can be parsed in polynomial time, in fact, with a time based Kn^6, where n is the length of the string and K is a constant depending on the grammar. (The linguistic significance of TAG has been discussed by Kroch and Joshi (1985)).

1.1 Some Examples of Formal Languages

Example 1.1 Let $G = (I, A)$ be a TAG with local constraints where

I: α_1 =

A: β =

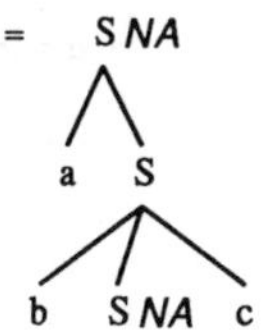

There are no constraints in α_1. In β no auxiliary trees are adjoinable at the root node and the foot node and for the center S node there are no constraints.

Starting with α_1 and adjoining β to α_1 at the root node we obtain

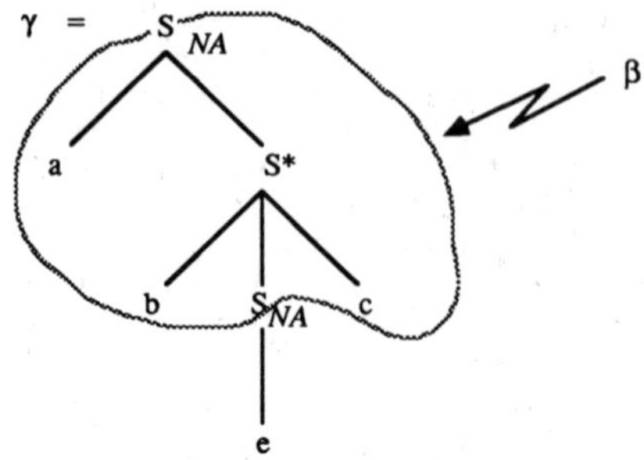

Adjoining β to the center S node (the only node at which adjunction can occur) we have

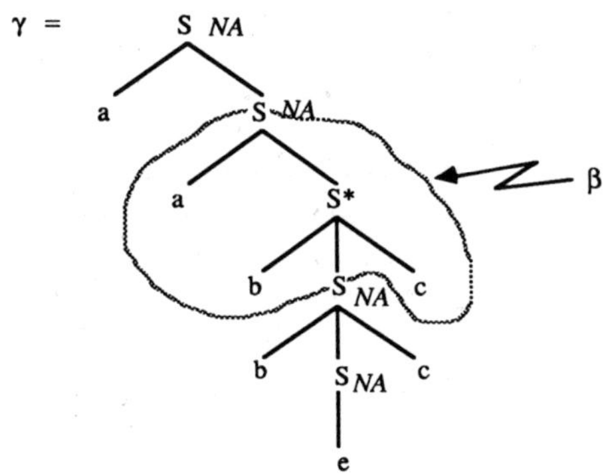

It is easy to see that G generates the string language

$$L = \{a^n b^n e c^n / n \geq 0\}$$

Example 1.2 Let G' be a TAG similar to G in Example 1.1, except that in G' there are no constaints in β. G' generates

$$L = \{wec^n / n \geq 0,\ \#\ a\text{'s in } w = \#\ b\text{'s in } w = n, \text{ and for any proper initial string } u \text{ of } w,\ \#\ a\text{'s in } u \geq \#\ b\text{'s in } u.\}$$

This language is closely related to the context-sensitive language (discussed in the linguistic literature), which can also be shown to be a TAG language.

Example 1.3 Let $G = (I, A)$ be a TAG with local constraints where

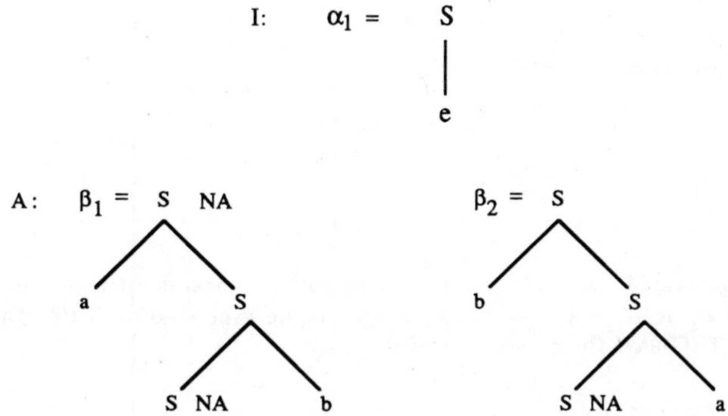

G generates the language

$$L = \{wew/w \in \{a,b\}^*\}$$

Example 1.4 Let G' be a TAG which is the same as G in Example 1.3 but without any local constraints. The corresponding language is

$$L = \{wew'/w, w' \in \{a,b\}^*, |w| = |w'| = 2n, \\ \#\ a\text{'s in } w = \#\ a\text{'s in } w' = \#\ b\text{'s} \\ \text{in } w = \#\ b\text{'s in } w' = n\}$$

This language is related to Swiss-German, discussed in the linguistic literature.

Example 1.5 Let $G = (I, A)$ be a TAG with local constraints where

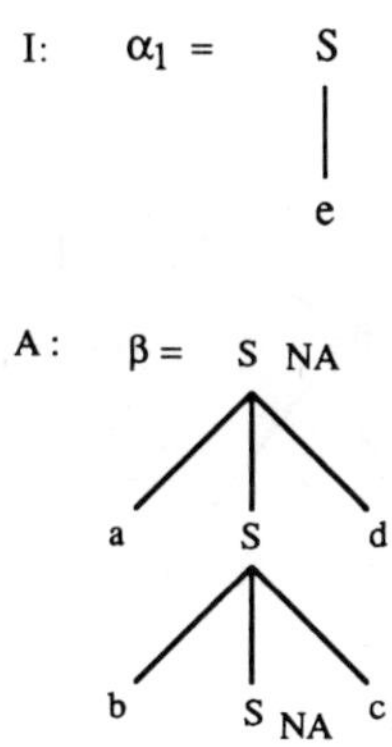

G generates

$$L = \{a^n b^n e c^n d^n / n \geq 1\}$$

Note that it can be shown that languages

$$L^1 = \{a^n b^n c^n d^n e^n / n \geq 1\}$$

and

$$L^2 = \{www / w \in \{a, b\}^*\}$$

cannot be generated by TAGs either with or without local constraints (Joshi 1985). Other languages such as $L' = \{a^{n^2} | n \geq 1\}$ also cannot be generated by TAG. This is because the strings of a TAG have the constant growth property.

1.2 Derivation in a TAG

We will not describe formally the notion of derivation in a TAG, however we will give an informal discussion which will make the notion of derivation in TAG precise enough for our purpose. Adjoining is an operation defined on an elementary tree, say γ, an auxiliary tree, say β, and a node (i.e., an address) in γ, say **n**. Thus, every instance of adjunction is of the form "β is adjoined to γ at **n**," and this adjunction is always and only subject to the local constraints associated with **n**. Although we very often speak of adjoining a tree to a node in a complex structure, we do so only for convenience. Strictly speaking, adjoining is always at a node in an elementary tree; and, therefore, it is more precise to talk about adjoining at an address in an elementary tree. More than one auxiliary tree can be adjoined to an elementary tree as long as each tree is adjoined at a distinct node. After these auxiliary trees are adjoined to the elementary tree, only nodes in the auxiliary trees are available for further adjunction.

Now suppose that α is an initial tree and that $\beta_1, \beta_2, \ldots$ are auxiliary trees in a TAG, G. Then the derivation structure corresponding to the generation of a particular string in L(G) might look as follows:

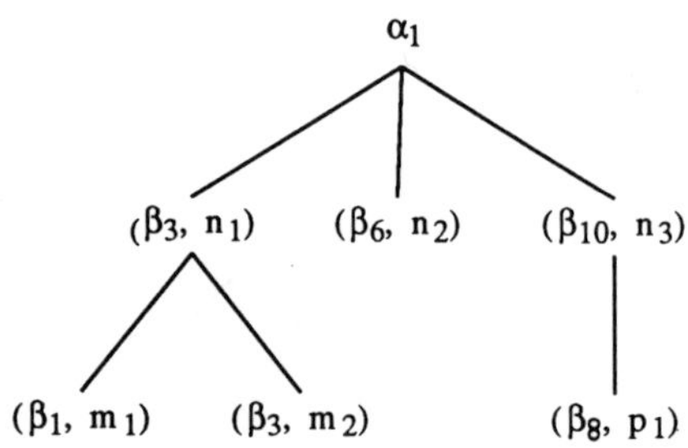

α_1 is an initial tree. β_3, β_6 and β_{10} are adjoined at nodes n_1, n_2, and n_3 respectively in α_1, where n_1, n_2, and n_3 are all distinct nodes. β_1 and β_3 are adjoined to β_3 at nodes m_1 and m_2 respectively. Again, m_1 and m_2 are distinct. β_6 has no further adjunctions but β_8 is adjoined to β_{10} at node p_1. Note that the derivation structure D implicitly characterizes the 'surface' tree that is generated by it. In this way the derivation structure can be seen as the basic formal object constructed in the course of sentence. Associated with it will be two mappings, one to a surface syntactic tree and the other to a semantic interpretation, as below.

$$\text{surface tree} \longleftarrow \text{derivation structure} \longrightarrow \text{semantic interpretation}$$

In a CFG, the derivation structure is the same as the surface structure. In a TAG this is not the case. Several of the formalisms that we have shown equivalent are comparable at the level of the derivation structures.

2 PARSING TREE ADJOINING GRAMMARS

2.1 Definitions

We will give a few additional definitions. These are not necessary for defining derivations in a TAG as defined in Section 1. However, they are introduced to help explain the parsing algorithm and the proofs for some of the closure properties of TAL's.

Definition 2.1 Let γ, γ' be two trees. We say $\gamma \vdash \gamma'$ if in γ we adjoin an auxiliary tree to obtain γ'.

$\vdash^*$ is the reflexive, transitive closure of $\vdash$.

Definition 2.2 γ' is called a derived tree if $\gamma \vdash^* \gamma'$ for some elementary tree γ.

We then say $\gamma' \in D(\gamma)$.

The frontier of any derived tree γ belongs to either Σ^* N $\Sigma^+ \cup \Sigma^+$ N Σ^* if $\gamma \in D(\beta)$ for some auxiliary tree β, or to Σ^* if $\gamma \in D(\alpha)$ for some initial tree α. Note if $\gamma \in D(\alpha)$ for some initial tree α, then γ is also a sentential tree.

If β is an auxiliary tree, $\gamma \in D(\beta)$ and the frontier of γ is w_1 X w_2 (X is a nonterminal, $w_1, w_2 \in \Sigma^*$) then the leaf node having this non-terminal symbol X at the frontier is called the foot of γ.

Sometimes we will be loosely using the phrase 'adjoining with a derived tree' $\gamma \in D(\beta)$ for some auxiliary tree β. What we mean is that suppose we adjoin β at some node and then adjoin within β and so on, we can also derive the desired derived tree $\in D(\beta)$ which uses the same adjoining sequence and use this resulting tree to 'adjoin' at the original node.

2.2 The Parsing Algorithm

The algorithm we present here to parse Tree-Adjoining Languages (TALs), is a modification of the CYK algorithm, which uses a dynamic programming technique to parse CFLs. For the sake of making our description of the parsing algorithm simpler, we shall present the algorithm for parsing without considering local constraints. We will later show how to handle local constraints.

We shall assume that any node in the elementary trees in the grammar has at most two children. This assumption can be made without a loss of generality, because it can be easily shown that for any TAG G there is an equivalent TAG G_1 such that any node in any elementary tree in G_1 has at most two children. A similar assumption is made in the CYK algorithm. We use the terms ancestor and descendant throughout the paper as a transitive and reflexive relation, for example, the foot node may be called the ancestor of the foot node.

The algorithm works as follows. Let $a_1 \ldots a_n$ be the input to be parsed. We use a four-dimensional array A; each element of the array contains a subset of the nodes of derived trees. We say a node X of a derived tree γ belongs to $A[i,j,k,l]$ if X dominates a sub-tree of γ whose frontier is given by either $a_{i+1} \ldots a_j \ Y \ a_{k+1} \ldots a_n$ (where the foot node of γ is labelled by Y) or $a_{i+1} \ldots a_n$ (i.e., $j = k$. This corresponds to the case when γ is a sentential tree). The indices (i,j,k,l) refer to the positions between the input symbols and range over 0 through n. If $i = 5$, say, then it refers to the gap between a_5 and a_6.

Initially, we fill $A[i, i+1, i+1, i+1]$ with those nodes in the frontier of the elementary trees whose label is the same as the input a_{i+1} for $0 \leq i \leq n-1$. The foot nodes of auxiliary trees will belong to all $A[i,i,j,j]$, such that $i \leq j$.

We are now in a position to fill in all the elements of the array A. There are five cases to be considered.

Case 1 We know that if a node X in a derived tree is the ancestor of the foot node, and node Y is its right sibling, such that $X \in A[i,j,k,l]$ and $Y \in A[l,m,m,n]$, then their parent, say, Z should belong to $A[i,j,k,n]$, see Fig 2a.

Case 2 If the right sibling Y is the ancestor of the foot node such that it belongs to $A[l,m,n,p]$ and its left sibling X belongs to $A[i,j,j,l]$, then we know that the parent Z of X and Y belongs to $A[i,m,n,p]$, see Fig 2b.

Case 3 If neither X nor its right sibling Y are the ancestors of the foot node (or if there is no foot node) then if $X \in A[i,j,j,l]$ and $Y \in A[l,m,m,n]$ then their parent Z belongs to $A[i,j,j,n]$.

Case 4 If a node Z has only one child X, and if $X \in A[i,j,k,l]$, then obviously $Z \in A[i,j,k,l]$.

Case 5 If a node $X \in A[i,j,k,l]$, and the root Y of a derived tree γ having the same label as that of X, belongs to $A[m,i,l,n]$, then adjoining γ at X makes the resulting node to be in $A[m,j,k,n]$, see Fig 2c.

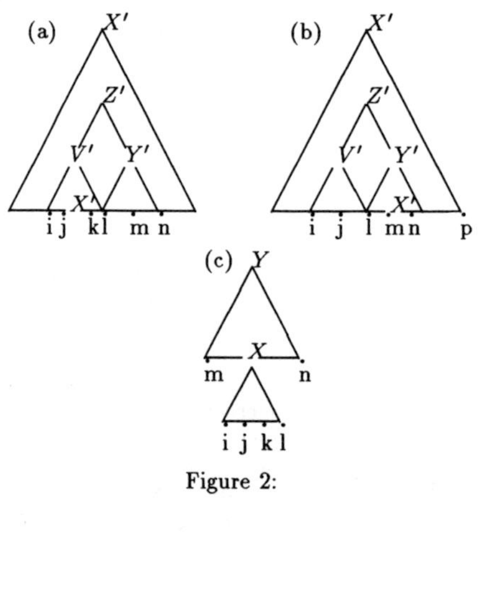

Figure 2:

Although we have stated that the elements of the array contain a subset of the nodes of derived trees, what the array really contains are the addresses of nodes in the elementary trees. Thus the size of any set is bounded by a constant, determined by the grammar. It is hoped that the presentation of the algorithm below will make it clear why we do so.

2.3 The Algorithm

The complete algorithm is given below:

Step 1	For $i = 0$ to $n-1$ step 1 do
Step 2	Put all nodes in the frontier of elementary trees whose label is a_{i+1} in $A[i, i+1, i+1, i+1]$.
Step 3	For $i = 0$ to $n-1$ step 1 do
Step 4	For $j = i$ to $n-1$ step 1 do
Step 5	Put foot nodes of all auxiliary trees in $A[i, i, j, j]$
Step 6	For $l = 0$ to n step 1 do
Step 7	For $i = l$ to 0 step -1 do
Step 8	For $j = i$ to l step 1 do
Step 9	For $k = l$ to j step -1 do
Step 10	Do Case 1
Step 11	Do Case 2
Step 12	Do Case 3
Step 13	Do Case 5
Step 14	Do Case 4
Step 15	Accept if root of some initial tree $\in A[0, j, j, n]$, $0 \le j \le n$

where,

1. Case 1 corresponds to situation where the left sibling is the ancestor of the foot node. The parent is put in $A[i, j, k, l]$ if the left sibling is in $A[i, j, k, m]$ and the right sibling is in $A[m, p, p, l]$, where $k \le m < l$, $m \le p$, $p \le l$. Therefore Case 1 is written as

   For $m = k$ to $l-1$ step 1 do

   for $p = m$ to l step 1 do

   if there is a left sibling in $A[i, j, k, m]$ and the right sibling in $A[m, p, p, l]$ satisfying appropriate restrictions then put their parent in $A[i, j, k, l]$.

2. Case 2 corresponds to the case where the right sibling is the ancestor of the foot node. If the left sibling is in $A[i, m, m, p]$ and the right sibling is in $A[p, j, k, l]$, $i \le m < p$ and $p \le j$, then we put their parent in $A[i, j, k, l]$. This may be written as

   For $m = i$ to $j-1$ step 1 do

   For $p = m+1$ to j step 1 do

   for all left siblings in $A[i, m, m, p]$ and right siblings in $A[p, j, k, l]$ satisfying appropriate restrictions put their parents in $A[i, j, k, l]$.

3. Case 3 corresponds to the case where neither children are ancestors of the foot node. If the left sibling $\in A[i, j, j, m]$ and the right sibling $\in A[m, p, p, l]$ then we can put the parent in $A[i, j, j, l]$ if it is the case that ($i < j \le m$ or $i \le j < m$) and ($m < p \le l$ or $m \le p < l$). This may be written as

   for $m = j$ to $l-1$ step 1 do

for $p = j$ to l step 1 do

for all left siblings in $A[i, j, j, m]$ and

right siblings in $A[m, p, p, l]$ satisfying the appropriate restrictions put their parent in $A[i, j, j, l]$.

4. Case 5 corresponds to adjoining. If X is a node in $A[m, j, k, p]$ and Y is the root of a auxiliary tree with same symbol as that of X, such that Y is in $A[i, m, p, l]$ (($i \leq m \leq p < l$ or $i < m \leq p \leq l$) and ($m < j \leq k \leq p$ or $m \leq j \leq k < p$)). This may be written as

   for $m = i$ to j step 1 do

   for $p = m$ to l step 1 do

   if a node $X \in A[m, j, k, p]$ and the root of auxiliary tree is in $A[i, m, p, l]$ then put X in $A[i, j, k, l]$

   Case 4 corresponds to the case where a node Y has only one child X. If $X \in A[i, j, k, l]$ then put Y in $A[i, j, k, l]$. Repeat Case 4 again if Y has no siblings.

2.4 Complexity of the Algorithm

It is obvious that steps 10 through 15 (cases 1-5) are completed in $O(n^2)$, because the different cases have at most two nested for loop statements, the iterating variables taking values in the range 0 through n. They are repeated at most $O(n^4)$ times, because of the four loop statements in steps 6 through 9. The initialization phase (steps 1 through 5) has a time complexity of $O(n+n^2) = O(n^2)$. Step 15 is completed in $O(n)$. Therefore, the time complexity of the parsing algorithm is $O(n^6)$.

2.5 Correctness of the Algorithm

The main issue in proving the algorithm correct is to show that while computing the contents of an element of the array A, we must have already determined the contents of other elements of the array needed to correctly complete this entry. We can show this inductively by considering each case individually. We give an informal argument below.

Case 1: We need to know the contents of $A[i, j, k, m]$, $A[m, p, p, l]$ where $m < l$, $i < m$, when we are trying to compute the contents of $A[i, j, k, l]$. Since l is the variable itererated in the outermost loop (step 6), we can assume (by induction hypothesis) that for all $m < l$ and for all p, q, r, the contents of $A[p, q, r, m]$ are already computed. Hence, the contents of $A[i, j, k, m]$ are known. Similarly, for all $m > i$, and for all p, q, and $r \leq l$, $A[m, p, q, r]$ would have been computed. Thus, $A[m, p, p, l]$ would also have been computed.

Case 2: By a similar reasoning, the contents of $A[i, m, m, p]$ and $A[p, j, k, l]$ are known since $p < l$ and $p > i$.

Case 3: When we are trying to compute the contents of some $A[i, j, j, l]$, we need to know the nodes in $A[i, j, j, p]$ and $A[p, q, q, l]$. Note $j > i$ or $j < l$. Hence, we know that the contents of $A[i, j, j, p]$ and $A[p, q, q, l]$ would have been computed already.

Case 5: The contents of $A[i, m, p, l]$ and $A[m, j, k, p]$ must be known in order to compute $A[i, j, k, l]$, where ($i \leq m \leq p < l$ or $i < m \leq p \leq l$) and ($m \leq j \leq k < p$ or $m < j \leq k \leq p$). Since either $m > i$ or $p < l$, contents of $A[m, j, k, p]$ will be known. Similarly, since either $m < j$ or $k < p$, the contents of $A[i, m, p, l]$ would have been computed.

2.6 Parsing with Local Constraints

So far,we have assumed that the given grammar has no local constraints. If the grammar has local constraints, it is easy to modify the above algorithm to take care of them. Note that in Case 5, if an adjunction occurs at a node X, we add X again to the element of the array we are computing. This seems to be in contrast with our definition of how to associate local constraints with the nodes in a sentential tree. We should have added the root of the auxiliary tree instead to the element of the array being computed, since so far as the local constraints are concerned, this node decides the local constraints at this node in the derived tree. However, this scheme cannot be adopted in our algorithm for obvious reasons. We let pairs of the form (X, C) belong to elements of the array, where X is as before and C represents the local constraints to be associated with this node.

We then alter the algorithm as follows. If (X, C_1) refers to a node at which we attempt to adjoin with an auxiliary tree (whose root is denoted by (Y, C_2)), then adjunction would determined by C_1. If adjunction is allowed, then we can add (X, C_2) in the corresponding element of the array. In cases 1 through 4, we do not attempt to add a new element if any one of the children has an obligatory constraint.

Once it has been determined that the given string belongs to the language, we can find the parse in a way similar to the scheme adopted in CYK algorithm. To make this process simpler and more efficient, we can use pointers from the new element added to the elements which caused it to be put there. For example, consider Case 1 of the algorithm (step 10). If we add a node Z to $A[i, j, k, l]$, because of the presence of its children X and Y in $A[i, j, k, m]$ and $A[m, p, p, l]$ respectively, then we add pointers from this node Z in $A[i, j, k, l]$ to the nodes X, Y in $A[i, j, k, m]$ and $A[m, p, p, l]$. Once this has been done, the parse can be found by traversing the tree formed by these pointers.

A parser based on the techniques described above has been implemented. More recently, an Early-type parser for TAG has been designed and implemented (Schabes and Joshi, 1988).

References

[1] Joshi, A.K., How much context-sensitivity is necessary for charecterizing structural descriptions — tree adjoining grammars. In *Natural Language Processing — Theoretical, Computational, and Psychological Perspectives*, (D. Dowty, L. Karttunen, A. Zwicky, Eds.), Cambridge University Press, New York, 1985. Originally presented in May 1983 at the Workshop on Natural Language Parsing at the Ohio State University.

[2] Joshi, A.K. An introduction to tree adjoining grammars. In (A. Manaster-Ramer, Ed.), *Mathematics of Language*, John Benjamins, Amsterdam, 1987.

[3] Joshi, A.K., Levy, L.S., and Takahashi, M., Tree adjunct grammars. *Journal of Computer Systems and Sciences*, 10(1), 1975.

[4] Kroch, T., and Joshi, A.K., Linguistic relevance of tree adjoining grammars. *Technical Report, MS-CIS-85-18, Dept. of Computer and Information Science, University of Pennsylvania*, April 1985. (A revised version will appear in *Linguistics and Philosophy*).

[5] Schabes, Y. and Joshi, A.K. An Earley-type parsing algorithm for tree adjoining grammars. In *Proceedings of the 26th Meeting of the Association for Computational Linguistics*, 1988.

DISCRETE LOGARITHMS AND DISCREET CURVES

Neal Koblitz, Department of Mathematics GN-50,
University of Washington, Seattle WA 98195, U.S.A.

The jacobian of an algebraic curve defined over a finite field can be used in public key cryptography provided that its cardinality is divisible by a large prime. Examples are given.

1. INTRODUCTION: PUBLIC KEY AND DISCRETE LOG

In recent years the algebraic geometry of curves over finite fields has found practical application in the study of error-correcting codes and in public key cryptography. The two main applications in cryptography are to the factorization of large integers (see [1] and [16]) and to the design of public key cryptosystems based on the discrete logarithm problem (see [10], [12], [13], [19]). This paper is devoted to the latter application.

Public key cryptography is based on the presumed existence of one-way (or trapdoor) functions - functions that are relatively easy to compute but computationally very difficult to invert. One basic source of such functions is the discrete logarithm problem. In Section 2 we will describe a public key cryptosystem based on discrete logs. We now define the discrete logarithm problem in the general context of an arbitrary finite group.

Let G be a finite group, in which the group operation may be written multiplicatively or (if G is abelian) additively. Let g be a fixed element of G. The discrete logarithm problem is as follows: given an element $a \in \mathbf{G}$, determine whether a is in the cyclic subgroup generated by g, and if so, find $k \in \mathbf{Z}$ which solves the equation $kg = a$. In the case of a group written multiplicatively - such as the multiplicative group of a finite field - the latter equation is written $g^k = a$, i.e., we are looking for the discrete analogue of the logarithm of a to the base g.

In the case of the classical logarithm, computing logarithms to a prescribed accuracy is computationally no harder than raising to powers. However, this is not the case in the discrete context.

The first examples of G that were considered were the multiplicative groups of finite fields $\mathbf{F}_q$. However, special techniques are available in that situation, and in the important special case when q is a power of 2, especially efficient algorithms were found by Coppersmith (see [20] for a detailed survey of discrete logs on $\mathbf{F}_q^x$).

However, the algorithm that is available for an arbitrary group G - due to Silver-Pohlig-Hellman - is much slower. The number of operations in this general-purpose algorithm in fact is of the order $\sqrt{p}$, where p is the largest prime dividing #G. In the case of the groups discussed below that arise from algebraic curves, at the present time there is no quicker algorithm known.

2. KEY EXCHANGE AND MESSAGE TRANSMISSION

Suppose we have a group G and a fixed element $g \in G$ such that the discrete logarithm problem is computationally unfeasible in G (more precisely, in the cyclic subgroup of G generated by g). We now describe how two users A and B can either (1) agree upon a secret key for use in a traditional (non-public-key) cryptosystem, using uncoded publicly accessible communication; or else (2) send each other encrypted messages, again with all of their communication occurring in the open.

We shall suppose that a "key" is a random element of a (large) finite field $\mathbf{F}_q$, and a "message" is made up of a string of elements of $\mathbf{F}_q$. We further suppose that we have an easily constructed map from G to $\mathbf{F}_q$. For example, if G is a subset of the xy-plane over $\mathbf{F}_q$, then we might use the map $x : G \longrightarrow \mathbf{F}_q$ that sends a point to its x-coordinate. With this example in mind, in the general context we shall also let x denote our map from G to $\mathbf{F}_q$.

We must assume that the group G (as a set with an algorithm for the group operation), the element $g \in G$, the value of q, and the map $x : G \longrightarrow \mathbf{F}_q$ are all publicly known. However, we assume that no one has the computational capability of determining $k \in \mathbf{Z}$ from knowledge of the element $kg \in G$ (if G is written additively; g^k if G is written multiplicatively).

(1) (Due to Diffie-Hellman [4].) Suppose that users A and B wish to exchange (i.e., agree upon) a random element of $\mathbf{F}_q$. Here is the procedure. Each user chooses a random natural number k in a suitable range (of order of magnitude #G, or perhaps the order of the element g, if this is known). Suppose A chooses k_A and B chooses k_B. Next, A computes $k_A g$ and sends it to B; meanwhile, B computes $k_B g$ and sends it to A. The secret key they use is then

$$x(k_A k_B g).$$

Notice that A can determine this by multiplying the element $k_B g$ (which A received from B) by his/her secret k_A and then applying the map x; and B can determine $x(k_A k_B g)$ analogously by applying x to $k_B(k_A g)$.

(2) (Based on a suggestion of C.Vanstone.) Now suppose that A wants to send B a message unit $m \in \mathbf{F}_q$. The procedure is much the same as in (1). Again B chooses a secret natural number k_B and sends $k_B g$ to A. User A chooses a secret k_A (which should be chosen over again for each message unit m, in order to avoid making it relatively easy to break the code). Then A sends both

$$k_A g \in G \qquad \text{and} \qquad m + x(k_A k_B g) \in \mathbf{F}_q$$

to B, who can recover m by subtracting $x(k_B(k_A g))$ from the received element of $\mathbf{F}_q$. All we are doing is using a shift encryption in $\mathbf{F}_q$, but with the amount of the shift determined by a key which is exchanged as in (1) and which varies from one message unit to the next.

3. JACOBIANS OF HYPERELLIPTIC CURVES

We consider the hyperelliptic curve $v^2 + hv = f(u)$ defined over the field $\mathbf{F}_q$ of q elements. Here $f(u) \in \mathbf{F}_q[u]$ is a monic polynomial of degree 2g + 1 (the integer g is called the genus); h in general may be a polynomial in u, but for us it will always be either the constant 0 or 1. We require that the curve have no singular points, i.e., there is no common solution of the equations $2v + h = 0$ and $f'(u) = 0$. In addition to the affine points (x,y), $x,y \in \mathbf{F}_q$, for which u = x and v = satisfy the equation, the curve also contains a single point at infinity with homogeneous coordinates (x,y,z) = (0,1,0).

We now define the jacobian **J** of the curve. From an abstract point of view, we start with the notion of divisor, which is a finite formal sum $D = \Sigma m_i P_i$ of points on the curve with coordinates in the algebraic closure of $\mathbf{F}_q$ which is fixed by the q-th power map on the coordinates (i.e., that map causes the P_i in the sum to be permuted). The degree is Σm_i. The jacobian **J** is the quotient of the group of divisors of degree zero by the subgroup of divisors of rational functions (defined over $\mathbf{F}_q$) on the curve. An element of **J** is called a divisor class.

From a more concrete point of view, in the case of a hyperelliptic curve we can view divisor classes as follows. Every element $D \in \mathbf{J}$ is uniquely associated to a pair of functions $a,b \in \mathbf{F}_q[u]$ for which $\deg a \leq g$, $\deg b < \deg a$, and $b(u)^2 + hb(u) - f(u)$ is divisible by $a(u)$; namely, D is the equivalence class of the g.c.d. of the divisors of the functions $a(u)$ and $b(u) - v$. The element D of **J** is then denoted div(a,b). For more details, see [12] and [3].

To add two elements $\mathrm{div}(a_1,b_1)$, $\mathrm{div}(a_2,b_2) \in \mathbf{J}$, one proceeds in two stages. First, let $d = d(u)$ be the g.c.d. of the three polynomials $a_1(u)$, $a_2(u)$ and $b_1(u) + b_2(u) + h$; and choose $s_1(u)$, $s_2(u)$ and $s_3(u)$ to be polynomials in u such that $d = s_1a_1 + s_2a_2 + s_3(b_1 + b_2 + h)$. Next, set $a = a_1a_2/d^2$ and

$$b(u)=(s_1(u)a_1(u)b_2(u)+s_2(u)a_2(u)b_1(u)+s_3(u)(b_1(u)b_2(u) +f(u)))/d(u) \pmod{a(u)}.$$

(The notation (mod a(u)) means the remainder after division by a(u).)

In stage 2, if $\deg a > g$, we replace the pair (a,b) by the equivalent pair (a',b') defined by setting

$a'(u) = (f(u) - b(u)^2 - hb(u))/a(u)$ and $b'(u) = -b(u) - h \pmod{a'(u)}$. Since $\deg a' < \deg a$, successive application of this procedure leads to a pair $\mathrm{div}(a'',b'')$ with $\deg a'' \le g$ such that $\mathrm{div}(a'',b'') = \mathrm{div}(a_1,b_1) + \mathrm{div}(a_2,b_2)$. This concludes the description of the group law in **J**.

Remark. The abstract definition of the jacobian applies to any curve. However, the concrete realization of the group law is more complicated when the curve is not hyperelliptic. The reason for the relatively simple algorithm for the group law in the case of a hyperelliptic curve is that hyperelliptic curves are analogous to quadratic field extensions of the rational numbers: such a curve is a degree-two covering of the projective line, obtained by "adjoining" the square root of $f(u)$ (in the case $h = 0$, i.e., $v^2 = f(u)$). Because of this analogy, the algorithm for adding divisor classes in **J** is similar to the classical procedure for composing classes of quadratic forms (see Chapter VI of [18]).

Special cases. 1. When $g = 1$, the curve is an elliptic curve. In that case there is a natural 1-to-1 correspondence between divisor classes and points on the curve, and the group law on **J** described above is easily seen to reduce to the usual formulas for the addition of points on an elliptic curve (see, for example, [8]).

2. When computing a large multiple of an element in a finite group (raising an element to a high power, if the group is written multiplicatively), one usually uses the "repeated doubling" (or "squaring") method. That is, to compute kg, where $k = \varepsilon_o + 2\,\varepsilon_1 + \ldots + 2^l\,\varepsilon_l$, $\varepsilon_i \in \{0,1\}$, one successively computes $2^i g = 2(2^{i-1}g)$ and

$$k_i g = (\varepsilon_o + \ldots + 2^i \varepsilon_i) g = \begin{cases} k_{i-1}g, & \text{if } \varepsilon_i = 0, \\ 2^i g + k_{i-1}g, & \text{if } \varepsilon_i = 1. \end{cases}$$

In the special case of doubling an element of **J**, the above algorithm becomes simpler. For example, if q is a power of 2 and h = 1, then in stage 1 one obtains $a(u) = a_1(u)^2$, $b(u) = b_1(u)^2 + f(u) \pmod{a(u)}$.

A particularly simple example is the elliptic curve $v^2 + v = u^3$ over the field $\mathbf{F}_q$ with q a power of 2. Then for any point P = (x,y) we have $2P = (x^4, y^4 + 1)$.

4. FINDING DISCREET CURVES

Recall that in order for **J** to be suitable for cryptographic applications, we want #**J** to be divisible by a large prime factor. If the equation $v^2 + hv = f(u)$ of a hyperelliptic curve C defined over the field $\mathbf{F}_q$ (where we let the coordinates take values) is chosen so that the corresponding jacobian has this property, then we shall call C a discreet curve. The word "discreet" has the meaning "can be trusted to keep a secret," and has nothing to do with the word "discrete," as in "discrete logarithms." More precisely, we shall say that a curve C defined over $\mathbf{F}_q$ is B-discreet if #**J** is divisible by a prime factor $p \geq \#\mathbf{J}/B$.

We now recall what is known about the number of elements in the jacobian of a curve of genus g. To do this we suppose that our curve C defined over $\mathbf{F}_q$ is fixed, but that we may want to consider the same curve over an extension field $\mathbf{F}_{q^n}$. We shall let $\tilde{M}_n$ denote the number of points on C considered over that larger field. Here we include the points at infinity in our count (of which there is exactly one in the case of hyperelliptic C). We further define M_n to be the difference between $\tilde{M}_n$ and the number of points on a projective line, i.e., $M_n = \tilde{M}_n - q^n - 1$, and we define N_n to be the number of elements in $\mathbf{J}(\mathbf{F}_{q^n})$, i.e., the number of divisor classes of the curve considered over the field $\mathbf{F}_{q^n}$:

$$N_n = \#(\mathbf{J}(\mathbf{F}_{q^n})).$$

A basic fact about the N_n is that there is a simple method for determining the sequence $N_1, N_2, \ldots$ by counting the number of $\mathbf{F}_{q^n}$-solutions of the equation of C for the first g values $n = 1, \ldots, g$. We now describe this method.

Associated with the curve C is a polynomial Z(T) (the zeta-polynomial) of degree 2g with integer coefficients having the form

$$\begin{aligned} Z(T) &= T^{2g} + a_1T^{2g-1} + \ldots + a_{g-1}T^{g+1} + a_gT^g + \\ &\qquad qa_{g-1}T^{g-1} + q^2a_{g-2}T^{g-2} + \ldots + q^{g-1}a_1T + q^g \\ &= \prod_{j=1}^{g} ((T - \alpha_j)(T - \overline{\alpha_j})), \end{aligned}$$

where $a_1, \ldots, a_g \in \mathbf{Z}$ and where $\overline{\alpha_j} = q/\alpha_j$ (i.e., the roots are complex numbers of absolute value $\sqrt{q}$). The relationship between Z(T) and $\{M_n\}$ is the following power series identity, where $\tilde{Z}(T)$ denotes the reciprocal polynomial $T^{2g}Z(1/T)$:

$$\log(\tilde{Z}(T)) = \sum_{n=1}^{\infty} \frac{M_n}{n} T^n.$$

Note that the first g values $M_1, \ldots, M_g$ are enough to determine the coefficients of Z(T).

Once Z(T) has been found, N_n can be determined from the formula

$$N_n = \prod_{j=1}^{g} |1 - \alpha_j^n|^2, \tag{1}$$

where $|\ |$ denotes the usual complex absolute value. In particular, $N_1 = Z(1)$.

Remarks. 1. Observe from (1) that $(q^{n/2} - 1)^{2g} \le N_n \le (q^{n/2} + 1)^{2g}$, i.e., N_n is asymptotically of magnitude q^{ng}.

2. In the simplest case, when $g = 1$, we have $N_n = |1 - \alpha^n|^2$, where α is a root of $T^2 + M_1T + q$.

3. If n is composite, d/n, then N_d/N_n. Suppose that n is prime. By (1), we have

$$N_n/N_1 = \prod_{j=1}^{g} |(1 - \alpha_j^n)/(1 - \alpha_j)|^2. \tag{2}$$

If the α_j are not all conjugates, i.e., if the polynomial Z(T) factors over the rationals, then even for n prime the value N_n/N_1 in (2) has a corresponding factorization.

Example. For C given by $v^2 + v = u^5$ over $\mathbf{F}_2$, $g = 2$, we have $Z(T) = T^4 + 4 = (T^2 + 2T + 2)(T^2 - 2T + 2)$ with roots $\pm 1 \pm i$; for n odd, N_n is given by
$N_n = (2^n + 2^{(n+1)/2} + 1)(2^n - 2^{(n+1)/2} + 1)$.

On the other hand, if all of the α_j are conjugates, then $N_n/N_1 = \mathbf{N}((\alpha_1^n - 1)/(\alpha_1 - 1))$, where $\mathbf{N}$ denotes the absolute norm of an algebraic number. The question of primality of these norms is a natural generalization of the general Mersenne problem, which concerns primality of numbers of the form $(a^n - 1)/(a - 1)$ (n prime) (see [2] and [21]).

In searching for "discreet" curves over $\mathbf{F}_{p^n}$, one can take several points of view.

(a) One can fix the genus g and the field (i.e., p and n), and let the coefficients of the curve's equation vary. One expects, roughly speaking, that as these coefficients vary the number of points on the jacobian will be nearly uniformly distributed in an interval of the form $(p^{gn} - cp^{(g-1/2)n}, p^{gn} + cp^{(g-1/2)n})$. This has been studied in detail in the cases g = 1, n = 1, p large (see [16]) and g = 2, n = 1, p large (see [1]).

(b) One can fix a curve with rational coefficients, and consider the jacobian of its reduction modulo p (i.e., over $\mathbf{F}_p$) as p varies. In the case g = 1, conjectural formulas for the probability that the corresponding elliptic curve has a prime number of points (i.e., that it is 1-discreet) are given in [11].

(c) One can fix $\mathbf{F}_p$ (or a finite extension of $\mathbf{F}_p$) and also fix a curve C with coefficients in that field. One then considers $\mathbf{J}(\mathbf{F}_{p^n})$, i.e., the jacobian $\mathbf{J}$ of the curve considered over the extension field $\mathbf{F}_{p^n}$. Here n is chosen so that $C(\mathbf{F}_{p^n})$ is discreet, i.e., the number of elements in the corresponding $\mathbf{J}$ is divisible by a large prime.

In Remark 3 we saw that for this, the curve must have been chosen so that its zeta-polynomial $Z(T) = \Pi_{j=1}^{2g} (T - \alpha_j)$ is irreducible over $\mathbf{Q}$, i.e., all of the α_j are conjugates of $\alpha = \alpha_1$. When n is prime, one can then hope for primality (or "near primality") of the norm of the algebraic integer $(\alpha^n - 1)/(\alpha - 1)$. In this generalization of the Mersenne prime problem, most likely the frequency of occurrence of prime values is predicted by a heuristic estimate of the same form as in the classical Mersenne case (see [23]).

(d) One can fix the field of definition $\mathbf{F}_{p^n}$ and examine a family of curves of varying genus. Even if p^n is small, the size of the group of points will grow rapidly with the genus, since it is of order p^{gn}. If one wants $\#\mathbf{J}$ to be a prime number or the product of a large prime and a small factor, then a necessary condition is that the zeta-polynomial be irreducible.

One advantage of point of view (d), in addition to the possible desirability of having one more parameter to vary (the genus g), is that one can limit oneself to curves with special symmetry properties. This often makes it possible to compute the number of points much more rapidly (and also carry out the algorithm for finding multiples of points somewhat faster) than in the case of a general curve. A particularly nice family of curves is given by: $v^2 + v = u^d$, $d = 2g + 1$.

5. TWISTED HYPERELLIPTIC CURVES

Given a hyperelliptic curve C of the form (i) $v^2 = f(u)$ over a field $\mathbf{F}_q$ of odd characteristic, or of the form (ii) $v^2 + v = f(u)$ over a finite field of characteristic 2, we define its twist $\tilde{C}$ to be

(i) the curve $v^2 = \eta f(u)$, where η is any element of $\mathbf{F}_q$ which is not a square in $\mathbf{F}_q$ (equivalently, $\eta^{(q-1)/2} = -1$);

(ii) the curve $v^2 + v = f(u) + \eta$, where η is any element of $\mathbf{F}_q$ which cannot be represented in the form $\xi^2 + \xi$ for $\xi \in \mathbf{F}_q$ (equivalently, η has absolute trace 1).

It is easy to see that $\tilde{C}$ is well-defined upto a linear change of variables over $\mathbf{F}_q$, independently of the choice of η. Moreover, an elementary argument shows that

$$\#(C(\mathbf{F}_{q^n})) = \#(\tilde{C}(\mathbf{F}_{q^n})), \qquad n \text{ even};$$

$$\#(C(\mathbf{F}_{q^n})) + \#(\tilde{C}(\mathbf{F}_{q^n})) = 2(q^n + 1), \qquad n \text{ odd}.$$

As a consequence of this, the roots $\tilde{\alpha}_j$ of the zeta-polynomial of $\tilde{C}$ are the negatives of the roots of the zeta-polynomial of C:

$$\tilde{\alpha}_j = -\alpha_j, \qquad j = 1,\ldots,g.$$

6. AN EXAMPLE

Let C_d be the curve over $\mathbf{F}_2$ given by the equation $v^2 + v = u^d$, and let $\tilde{C}_d$ be given by the equation $v^2 + v = u^d + 1$, where $d = 2g + 1$ is a prime number congruent to -1 modulo 8 such that 2 has multiplicative order g modulo d. In that case it can be shown that

$$Z(C_d;T) = \frac{(1 - \alpha T^g)(1 - \bar{\alpha} T^g)}{(1 - T)(1 - 2T)};$$

$$Z(\tilde{C}_d;T) = \frac{(1 + \alpha T^g)(1 + \bar{\alpha} T^g)}{(1 - T)(1 - 2T)},$$

where

$$\alpha = 2^{(g-h-2)/2}(a + b\sqrt{-d}\,),$$

in which h is the class number of $\mathbf{Q}(\sqrt{-d}\,)$ and a,b are odd integers such that $a^2 + db^2 = 2^{h+2}$. Here a and b are unique upto a choice of sign; the sign of a is determined by the congruence $2^{(g-h-2)/2}a \equiv 1 \pmod{d}$ (and the sign of b is arbitrary, since changing its sign merely interchanges α and $\bar{\alpha}$).

The number of $\mathbf{F}_2$-points on the jacobian of C_d is always divisible by d; however, the number of points on the jacobian of the twisted curve $\tilde{C}_d$ is not. Thus, it is a priori possible for the number of points on the latter jacobian to be a prime number or a small factor times a large prime. For example, if we take d = 383, then we have:

$$g = 191, \quad h = h(\mathbf{Q}(\sqrt{-383}\,)) = 17, \quad \alpha = 2^{86}(-711 + 7\sqrt{-383}),$$

$$\#(\mathbf{J}(\tilde{C}_{383})(\mathbf{F}_2)) = 3P,$$

where P is a 58-digit prime (its primality was kindly verified for me by A. Odlyzko).
Explicitly,

$$\begin{aligned} P &= ((1 - 711 \cdot 2^{86})^2 + 49 \cdot 383 \cdot 2^{172})/3 \\ &= 1046183622564446793972631570497937095686563183433452530347. \end{aligned}$$

Thus, the curve $v^2 + v = u^{383} + 1$ over $\mathbf{F}_2$ is 3-discreet.

REFERENCES

[1] Adleman, L.M. and Ming-Deh A. Huang, "Recognizing primes in random polynomial time," Proceedings 19th ACM Symp. Theory Comp., New York: ACM, 462-469 (1987).

[2] Brillhart, J., Lehmer, D.H., Selfridge, J.L., Tuckerman, B. and Wagstaff, S.S., Jr., Factorization of $b^n \pm 1$, b = 2,3,5,6,7,10,11,12 up to High Powers, Amer. Math. Society, 1983.

[3] Cantor, D., "Computing in the jacobian of a hyperelliptic curve," Math. of Computation, **48**, 95-101 (1987).

[4] Diffie, W. and Hellman, M., "New directions in cryptography, " IEEE Trans. Inform. Theory, **22**, 644- 654 (1976).

[5] Fulton, W., Algebraic Curves, Benjamin, New York (1969).

[6] ElGamal, T., "A public key cryptosystem and a signature scheme based on discrete logarithms," IEEE Trans. Inform. Theory, **31**, 469-472 (1985).

[7] Ireland, K. and Rosen, M., A Classical Introduction to Modern Number Theory, Springer-Verlag, New York (1982).

[8] Koblitz, N., Introduction to Elliptic Curves and Modular Forms, Springer-Verlag, New York, (1984).

[9] Koblitz, N., A Course in Number Theory and Cryptography, Springer-Verlag, New York (1987).

[10] Koblitz, N., "Elliptic curve cryptosystems," Math. of Computation, **48**, 203-209 (1987).

[11] Koblitz, N., "Primality of the number of points on an elliptic curve over a finite field," Pacific J. Math., **131**, 157-165 (1988).

[12] Koblitz, N., "Hyperelliptic cryptosystems," to appear in Journal of Cryptology.

[13] Koblitz, N., "A family of jacobians suitable for discrete log cryptosystems,", to appear in Proceedings of Crypto '88.

[14] Koblitz, N. and Rohrlich, D., "Simple factors in the jacobian of a Fermat curve," Can. J. Math., **30**, 1183-1205 (1978).

[15] Lang, S., Introduction to Algebraic Geometry, Inter science, New York (1958).

[16] Lenstra, H.W.,Jr., "Factoring integers with elliptic curves," Report 86-18, Mathematisch Instituut, Universiteit van Amsterdam (1986).

[17] Lidl, R. and Niederreiter, H., Finite Fields, Addison-Wesley, Reading, Mass. (1983).

[18] Mathews, G.B., Theory of Numbers, 2nd ed., Chelsea Publ. Co., New York (1961).

[19] Miller, V., "Use of elliptic curves in cryptography," Advances in Cryptology - Crypto '85, Springer-Verlag, New York, 417-426 (1986).

[20] Odlyzko, A.M., "Discrete logarithms and their cryptographic significance," Advances in Cryptography: Proceedings of Eurocrypt 84, Springer-Verlag, New York, 224-314 (1985).

[21] Seah, E. and Williams, H.C., "Some primes of the form $(a^n - 1)/(a - 1)$," Math. of Computation, **33**, 1337-1342 (1979).

[22] Shanks, D., Solved and Unsolved Problems in Number Thoery, 3rd ed., Chelsea Publ. Co., New York (1985).

[23] Wagstaff, S.S.,Jr., "Divisors of Mersenne numbers," Math. of Computation, **40**, 385-397 (1983).

[24] Waterhouse, W.C., "Abelian varieties over finite fields," Ann. Sci. Ecole Norm. Sup. (4), **2**, 521-560 (1969).

[25] Weil, A., "Numbers of solutions of equations in finite fields," Bull. Amer. Math. Soc., **55**, 497-508 (1949).

Deterministic Indian Parallel Systems

Manfred Kudlek
Fachbereich Informatik, Universitat Hamburg
D—2000 Hamburg 13, FRG

Abstract

The deterministic version of Indian parallel systems is studied. In the context-independent case the application of homomorphisms is more powerful than the use of a terminal subalphabet, both for systems with one or finitely many tables. The effect of one or finitely many axioms, erasing in the productions, and of applying codings, weak codings, non-erasing or arbitrary homomorphisms is considered, and a (not yet) complete hierarchy of language families obtained by such methods is presented, including also the relations to context-free and $ETOL$ languages. Some results in the context-dependent case are given too.

1 Introduction

In [10,11,12] a special class of parallel rewriting systems has been considered, the so called Indian parallel systems, named after the authors of [11]. According to the form of rewriting these systems are situated somehow between (sequential) Chomsky type grammars (or Semi Thue systems) and (completely parallel) Lindenmayer systems. In one step of rewriting one symbol is rewritten at every place of its occurrence whereas the other symbols remain unchanged. This definition is a slight generalization of the original more strict version introduced in [11]. In this original version rewriting is done by using only one production. Thus the original version is just the deterministic case of the general one defined in [5] or in this paper.

To use a short but general and convenient notation for such systems and their corresponding language families the framework having been introduced for Lindenmayer systems is adopted, with the addition of the letter B for Indian parallel systems, standing for the Sanskrit name of India, Bharat.

Thus the original Indian parallel systems are denoted by $EDTOB$, and the $ETOL_{[1]}$ systems considered in [8,9] by $ETOB$.

Nondeterministic Indian parallel systems have been considered in [4,5]. In this paper the deterministic case is studied.

2 Definitions

An Indian parallel system is a triple $G = (V, A, P)$ where V is a finite set of symbols (alphabet), $A \subseteq V^*$ a finite set of starting words (axioms), and P a finite set of productions.

For context-independent systems $P \subseteq V \times V^*$, and the one step derivation relation $\rightarrow$ is defined by

$$\begin{aligned} & u_0xu_1\cdots u_{k-1}xu_k \to u_0b_1u_1\cdots u_{k-1}b_ku_k \\ \Leftrightarrow\ & (u_0u_1\cdots u_k \in (V-\{x\})^* \wedge \forall i \in \{1,\cdots,k\} : (x,b_i) \in P). \end{aligned}$$

For context-dependent systems $P \subseteq (((\lambda \cup \$)V^* \times V \times V^*(\lambda \cup \$))) \times V^*$, where $\$ \notin V$ is a dummy symbol denoting the fact that the context may occur at the end of words to be rewritten. In this case the one step derivation relation $\to$ is defined by

$$\begin{aligned} & u_0xu_1\cdots u_{k-1}xu_k \to u_0b_1u_1\cdots u_{k-1}b_ku_k \\ \Leftrightarrow\ & (u_0u_1\cdots u_k \in (V-\{x\})^* \wedge \forall i \in \{1,\cdots,k\} : \\ & (\exists(l_i,x,r_i,b_i) \in P : ((u_{i-1} = u'_{i-1}l_i \vee \$u_{i-1} = l_i) \wedge (u_i = r_iu'_i \vee u_i\$ = r_i)) \vee \\ & (\neg\exists(l_i,x,r_i,b_i) \in P : ((u_{i-1} = u'_{i-1}l_i \vee \$u_{i-1} = l_i) \wedge (u_i = r_iu'_i \vee u_i\$ = r_i)) \wedge \\ & b_i = x))) \end{aligned}$$

where l_i (r_i) is a left (right) context of the ith x in the word $\$u_0xu_1\cdots u_k\$$.

Thus, for context-dependent systems it is possible that at some positions in the word to be rewritten there is no proper context for x. In this case x has to be rewritten only at such positions where there exists a proper context. At the other positions x remains unchanged.

As usual, $\xrightarrow{*}$ will denote the reflexive and transitive closure of $\to$.

The letter B will be used to denote Indian parallel systems, reminding to the Sanskrit name of India, *Bharat*.

The letter O will be used for no interaction, i.e. context-independent (context-free) systems. Otherwise the letter I for interaction is used, denoting context-dependent (context-sensitive) systems. This gives FOB and FIB systems, where the letter F stands for finite set of axioms. Note, that also $A = \emptyset$ and $A = \{\lambda\}$ are allowed, λ denoting the empty word.

If $card(A) = 1$, i.e. there is only one axiom, the letter F is omitted, giving OB and IB systems.

If all productions $(x,b) \in P$ ($(l,x,r,b) \in P$) are monotone (propagating), i.e. if $1 \leq lg(b)$, then the letter P for propagating is used, giving $PFOB$, POB, $PFIB$, and PIB systems.

An Indian parallel system is called deterministic if in the context-independent case

$$((x,b_1) \in P \wedge (x,b_2) \in P) \ \Rightarrow\ b_1 = b_2$$

and in the context-dependent case

$$\begin{aligned} & ((l_1,x,r_1,b_1) \in P \wedge (l_2,x,r_2,b_2) \in P \wedge \\ & (l_2 = l'_2l_1 \vee l_1 = l'_1l_2 \vee r_2 = r_1r'_2 \vee r_1 = r_2r'_1) \\ \Rightarrow\ & (l_1 = l_2 \wedge r_1 = r_2 \wedge b_1 = b_2). \end{aligned}$$

Thus, in context-independent Indian parallel systems there is at most one production for every $x \in V$. In context-dependent systems there may be several productions for some x with different contexts, but the rewriting of x at every position is unique.

The letter D is used for such deterministic systems, giving e.g. $PDFOB$, or DIB systems.

In parallel rewriting it is possible to change the set of productions from one derivation step to another. In other words, triples $G = (V, A, \underline{T})$ with $\underline{T} = \{P_1, \cdots, P_m\}$ and not necessarily $P_i \cap P_j = \emptyset$ for $i \neq j$ may be considered. Such sets P_i are called tables, and therefore the letter T will be used for such systems. In each derivation step productions only from one table can be used. If the productions of all tables are propagating (deterministic), the letter P (D) is used again. Thus e.g. TOB, $PTFOB$, or $PDTFIB$ systems are obtained.

The sentential form language generated by a system G is defined by the following set $S(G) := \{w \in V^* \mid \exists u \in A : u \overset{*}{\Rightarrow} w\}$.

Families of languages belonging to the corresponding families of rewriting systems are denoted by underlining, e.g. $\underline{OB}$, $\underline{PDOB}$, $\underline{DFIB}$, $\underline{DFIB}$, or $\underline{PDTFIB}$.

If a subalphabet $V_T \subseteq V$ of terminal symbols is specified, indicated by writing the quadruple $G = (V, V_T, A, P)$, another kind of languages may be defined, namely by the set $L(G) := S(G) \cup V_T^*$.

In this case the letter E for extension (from the subalphabet) will be attached in front and underlined, giving e.g. $\underline{EOB}$, $\underline{EDTOB}$, $\underline{EPDTFOB}$, or $\underline{EPIB}$.

If $\underline{X}$ is any language family, and $\hat{H}$, H, $\hat{C}$, C denote, respectively, the classes of arbitrary homomorphisms, non-erasing homomorphisms ($lg(h(x)) \geq 1$), weak codings (literal homomorphisms with $lg(h(x)) \leq 1$), and codings (literal homomorphisms with $lg(h(x)) = 1$), the corresponding language families $\{h(L) \mid h \in \hat{H}, L \in \underline{X}\}$ etc. will be denoted by $\underline{\hat{H}X}$ etc.. By this $\underline{\hat{H}OB}$, $\underline{CPDTOB}$, or $\underline{\hat{C}EDTFOB}$ is obtained e.g..

It is a trivial fact that the operators $\hat{H}$, H, $\hat{C}$, C on the one hand, and the operator E on the other hand, commute, i.e. $\underline{\hat{H}EX} = \underline{E\hat{H}X}$ etc. for any language family $\underline{X}$.

If L is any language, then let $L^{\triangle} := L - \{\lambda\}$.

For any language family X define $\underline{X}^{\triangle} := \{L^{\triangle} \mid L \in \underline{X}\}$ and $\underline{X}^{\blacktriangle} := \underline{X}^{\triangle} \cup \{\{\lambda\}\}$. It is easy to show that $\underline{X}^{\blacktriangle\blacktriangle} = \underline{X}^{\blacktriangle}$.

Finally, let $\underline{REG}$, $\underline{CF}$, $\underline{CS}$, $\underline{RE}$, and $\underline{ETOL}$ denote the classes of regular, context-free, context-sensitive, recursively enumerable, and $ETOL$ languages, respectively.

3 Context-independent Systems

The results in this section are for context-independent Indian parallel systems. The first lemmas state some indentities concerning finitely many axioms and monotone productions. Thus, for extension and homomorphisms one axiom suffices or essentially suffices for TOB systems.

Lemma 1 : $\underline{EDTOB} = \underline{EDTFOB}$.

Proof: Let $G = (V, A, \underline{T}) \in EDTFOB$. Choose some $S \notin V$, $\{S\}$ as new set of axioms, and add the new tables $\{\{(S, u)\} \mid u \in A\}$. □

Lemma 2 : $\underline{EPDTOB} = \underline{EPDTFOB}^{\blacktriangle} \subset \underline{EPDTFOB}$.

Proof : It is trivial to show : $\lambda \in L \in \underline{EPDTFOB} \Leftrightarrow \lambda \in A$. As in Lemma 1 choose $S \notin V$, $\{S\}$, and add new tables $\{\{(S, u)\} \mid u \in A^{\triangle}\}$. The strict inclusion is trivial. □

Lemma 3 : $\underline{HDTOB} = \underline{HDTFOB}$, $\underline{\hat{H}DTOB} = \underline{\hat{H}DTFOB}$.

Proof : Again, choose $S \notin V$, $\{S\}$, and add the new tables $\{\{(S,u)\} \mid u \in A\}$. Define the new homomorphism h' by $h'(x) = h(x)$ if $x \in V$, $h'(S) = h(u)$ for some $u \in A$ with $u \neq \lambda$. □

Lemma 4 : $\underline{HPDTOB} = \underline{HPDTFOB}^{\blacktriangle} \subset \underline{HPDTFOB}$.

Proof : As in Lemma 2, $\lambda \in L \in \underline{HPDTFOB} \Leftrightarrow \lambda \in A$. As in Lemma 3 choose $S \notin V$, $\{S\}$, and add new tables $\{\{(S,u)\} \mid u \in A^{\triangle}\}$, and define h' in the same way. □

The next lemma states that monotone productions suffice if erasing homomorphisms or weak codings are applied.

Lemma 5 : $\underline{\hat{C}PDOB} = \underline{\hat{C}DOB}$, $\underline{\hat{C}PDFOB} = \underline{\hat{C}DFOB}$, $\underline{\hat{C}PDTOB} = \underline{\hat{C}DTOB}$, $\underline{\hat{C}PDTFOB} = \underline{\hat{C}DTFOB}$, $\underline{\hat{H}PDOB} = \underline{\hat{H}DOB}$, $\underline{\hat{H}PDFOB} = \underline{\hat{H}DFOB}$, $\underline{\hat{H}PDTOB} = \underline{\hat{H}DTOB}$, $\underline{\hat{H}PDTFOB} = \underline{\hat{H}DTFOB}$.

Proof : By the padding technique, i.e. using a new symbol $\$ \notin V$, replacing each production $(x,\lambda) \in P$ by $(x,\$)$, and defining h' by $h'(x) = x$ for $x \in V$ and $h'(\$) = \lambda$. □

The next lemmas are trivial consequences from the preceding ones.

Lemma 6 : $\underline{CEPDTOB} = \underline{CEPDTFOB}^{\blacktriangle} \subset \underline{CEPDTFOB}$.

Proof : As in Lemmas 2 and 4. □

Lemma 7 : $\underline{CEDTOB} = \underline{CEDTFOB}$, $\underline{\hat{C}EPDOB} = \underline{\hat{C}EDOB}$, $\underline{\hat{C}EPDFOB} = \underline{\hat{C}EDFOB}$, $\underline{\hat{C}EPDTOB} = \underline{\hat{C}EDTOB} = \underline{\hat{C}EPDTFOB} = \underline{\hat{C}EDTFOB}$.

Proof : This follows from Lemmas 1 and 5. □

The relation of deterministic Indian parallel systems to L systems is given in the following lemma.

Lemma 8 : $\underline{XDTOB} \subseteq \underline{XDTOL}$, $\underline{XDTFOB} \subseteq \underline{XDTFOL}$ *for any prefix* X *formed from the set* $\{\lambda, D, P, E, C, \hat{C}, H, \hat{H}\}$.

Proof : Let $G = (V, A, \underline{T})$ with $\underline{T} = \{P_1, \ldots, P_m\}$. Just split each P_i into the tables $P_i(x) = \{(x,u) \in P_i\}$, and extend each $P_i(x)$ to a L table $P_i'(x) = P_i \cup \{(y,y) \mid y \neq x\}$. □

As in the nondeterministic case the use of homomorphisms is at least as powerful as the use of extension.

Lemma 9 : $\underline{EPDOB} \subseteq \underline{HPDOB}$, $\underline{EPDFOB} \subseteq \underline{HPDFOB}$, $\underline{EDOB} \subseteq \underline{HDOB}$, $\underline{EDFOB} \subseteq \underline{HDFOB}$, $\underline{EPDTOB} \subseteq \underline{HPDTOB}$, $\underline{EPDTFOB} \subseteq \underline{HPDTFOB}$, $\underline{EDTOB} \subseteq \underline{HDTOB}$.

Proof : Let $G = (V, V_T, A, \underline{T})$, and define $G_x := (V, \{x\}, \underline{T})$. Since the emptiness problem for $\underline{ETOL}$ is decidable, by Lemma 8 it is decidable for any $x \in V$ whether $L(G_x) = \emptyset$. Reduce G to a system G' without such x for which $L(G_x) = \emptyset$. Clearly, $L(G'_x) = L(G_x)$. Moreover, $L(G_x) = \{\lambda\}$ is decidable too (since $\underline{ETOL}$ is closed under intersection with regular sets decide $L \cap V_T^+ = \emptyset$). Construct from G' a system G'' by erasing all $x \in V - V_T$ with $L(G_x) = \{\lambda\}$ on the right hand side of productions, and in the axioms. Clearly again, $L(G''_x) = L(G_x)$, and $L(G'') = L(G)$.

For such $x \in V - V_T$ with $L(G_x) \neq \emptyset$ and $L(G_x) \neq \{\lambda\}$ it is possible to find effectively a $w(x) \in L(G_x)$ with $w(x) \neq \lambda$ in whose derivation tree no $y \in V$ occurs twice on a path (i.e. there are no loops for y). This can be done by ordering the symbols $x \in V - V_T$ and constructing succesively derivation trees using already known ones (nondeterminism is only posssible by using different tables). The $w(x)$ are 'first' cuts through such a tree. Define the homomorphism h by $h(x) = w(x)$ for $x \in V - V_T$, $h(x) = x$ for $x \in V_T$, and consider $S(G'')$. Then $h(S(G'')) = L(G)$. □

From this the following corollary is an obvious consequence.

Corollary 1 : $\underline{CEPDOB} \subseteq \underline{HPDOB}$, $\underline{CEPDFOB} \subseteq \underline{HPDFOB}$,
$\underline{CEDOB} \subseteq \underline{HDOB}$, $\underline{CEDFOB} \subseteq \underline{HDFOB}$,
$\underline{CEPDTOB} \subseteq \underline{HPDTOB}$, $\underline{CEPDTFOB} \subseteq \underline{HPDTFOB}$,
$\underline{CEDTOB} \subseteq \underline{HDTOB}$,
$\underline{\hat{C}EDOB} \subseteq \underline{\hat{H}DOB}$, $\underline{\hat{C}EDFOB} \subseteq \underline{\hat{H}DFOB}$,
$\underline{\hat{C}EDTOB} \subseteq \underline{\hat{H}DTOB}$.

So far identities and inclusions have been presented. In the following lemmas non-inclusion results will be given. A number of them have been shown in [5] already.

Lemma 10 : $\underline{CPDOB} \not\subseteq \underline{TFOB}$.

Proof : Consider the language $L = \{a^n b^n \mid 1 \leq n\}$. Obviously, $L \in \underline{CPDOB}$ by the system $G = (\{a, b, c\}, \{cb\}, \{(c, acb)\})$, and h defined by $h(a) = h(c) = a$, $h(b) = b$. But $L \notin \underline{TFOB}$ by [5], L13. □

Lemma 11 : $\underline{DOB} \not\subseteq \underline{CPFOB}$.

Proof : Consider $L = \{b^k c((ab)^{2^m-1}a)^{2^n} \mid 0 \leq k, m, n\}$. $L \in \underline{DOB}$ by the system $G = (\{a, b, c\}, \{ca\}, \{(a, aba), (b, \lambda), (c, bc)\})$, but $L \notin \underline{CPFOB}$ by considering all possible productions for symbols from $h^{-1}(x)$ if $x \in \{a, b, c\}$ and $L = h(S(G'))$ with $G' = (V', A', P') \in PFOB$, and proving that A' has to be infinite.

(Unfortunately, $\hat{C}PTFOB$ has been written in [5], L14 instead of $\hat{C}PFOB$). □

Lemma 12 : $\underline{DOB} \not\subseteq \underline{PTFOB}$.

Proof : Consider L from Lemma 11. Assume $L = L(G)$ for some $G \in PTFOB$. It can be shown that the only possible productions are (a, a), (a, aba), (b, b), and $(c, b^j c)$ for some j. But then only finitely many words a^n can be generated. Thus $L \notin \underline{PTFOB}$. □

Lemma 13 : $\underline{DOB} \not\subseteq \underline{CEPDOB}$.

Proof : Consider $L = \{a, b, ac, bc, bcc\}$. Obviously, $L \in \underline{DOB}$ by the DOB system $G = (\{a,b,c\}, \{ac\}, \{(a,bc),(b,b),(c,\lambda)\})$. But $L \notin \underline{CEPDOB}$ by showing that any system producing all $w \in L$ will also produce acc. □

Lemma 14 : $\underline{HPDOB} \not\subseteq \underline{\hat{C}TFOB}$.

Proof : Consider $L = \{a^n bcd^n \mid 0 \leq n\}$. Clearly, $L \in \underline{HPDOB}$ by the system $G = (\{a,d,e\}, \{e\}, \{(e, aed)\})$ with $h(e) = bc$, $h(a) = a$, $h(d) = d$. But $L \notin \underline{\hat{C}TFOB}$ by [5], L16. □

Lemma 15 : $\underline{PDFOB} \not\subseteq \underline{\hat{C}TOB}$.

Proof : Consider $L = \{ab, cd\}$. Trivially, $L \in \underline{PDFOB}$, but $L \notin \underline{\hat{C}TOB}$ by [5], L15. □

Lemma 16 : $\underline{PDFOB} \not\subseteq \underline{\hat{H}DOB}$.

Proof : Consider $L = \{ab^{2^n}, b^{2^n}a \mid 0 \leq n\}$. $L \in \underline{PDFOB}$ by the PDFOB system $G = (\{a,b\}, \{ab, ba\}, \{(b, b^2)\}$. Assume $L = h(S(G')) \in \underline{\hat{H}DOB}$ with the new system $G' = (V', \{u_0\}, P')$. Let $w = v_0 x v_1 y v_2 \in S(G')$ with $h(v_0) = h(v_2) = \lambda$, $h(x) = ab^k$, $h(v_1) = b^l$, $h(y) = b^m$, and $k + l + m = 2^n$. Obviously, x can occur only once in w. If it is rewritten this can be done only by a production (x, s) with $h(s) = ab^i$. y and any symbol z in v_1 can be rewritten only by a production (y, t) or (z, t) with $h(t) = b^j$. Hence, any rewriting of w into w' always gives $h(w') = ab^{n'}$. By symmetry, it follows that $L \notin \underline{\hat{H}DOB}$. □

Lemma 17 : $\underline{EPDOB} \not\subseteq \underline{DTFOB}$.

Proof: Consider $L = \{a(b^3d)^k(b^2c^2d)^l(c^6d)^m \mid 0 \leq k+l+m\}$. $L \in \underline{EPDOB}$ by the system $G = (\{S, A, a, b, c, d\}, \{a, b, c, d\}, \{a\}, \{(S, Ab), (A, b^2), (a, aSd), (b, c^2), (c, c), (d, d)\})$. It is obvious that $L \subseteq L(G)$. The inverse inclusion $L(G) \subseteq L$ can be seen by induction on the words $u \in S(G)$.

Assume $L \in \underline{DTFOB}$ and consider any $w \in L$. Then it follows that for $x \in \{b, c, d\}$ only trivial productions (x, x) are possible, and for a only productions $(a, a(b^3d)^n)$. But then the production of new b^2c^2d or c^6d is impossible. □

Lemma 18 : $\underline{CPDOB} \not\subseteq \underline{EFOB}$.

Proof : Consider the language $L = \{a^{2^n+1} \mid 0 \leq n\}$. Trivially, $L \in \underline{CPDOB}$ by $G = (\{b,a\}, \{ba\}, \{(a, a^2), (b, b)\})$ and $h(a) = h(b) = a$. But $L \notin \underline{EFOB}$ by [5], L23. □

Lemma 19 : $\underline{EPDOB} \not\subseteq \underline{\hat{C}TOB}$.

Proof : Consider $L = \{b^3, b^2c^2, c^6\}$. Clearly, $L \in \underline{EPDOB}$ by the EPDOB system $G = (\{A, b, c\}, \{b, c\}, \{Ab\}, \{(A, b^2), (b, c^2), (c, c)\})$. But by considering all possibilities for the axiom and the productions of some $G' \in \underline{TOB}$ it follows that $L \notin \underline{\hat{C}TOB}$. □

Lemma 20 : $\underline{HDOB} \not\subseteq \underline{HPDTOB}$.

Proof : Consider $L = \{\lambda, ab, cd\}$. Obviously, $L \in \underline{HDOB}$ by the DOB system $G = (\{A, B\}, \{A\}, \{(A, B), (B, \lambda)\})$ and $h(A) = ab$, $h(B) = cd$. But $L \notin \underline{HPDTOB}$, since $\lambda \in L \in \underline{HPDTFOB} \Leftrightarrow \lambda \in A$. □

Lemma 21 : $\underline{\hat{C}DOB} \not\subseteq \underline{CTOB}$.

Proof : Consider $L = \{a^{2^n}a^{2^n}, a^{2^n}bca^{2^n} \mid 0 \le n\}$. It is obvious that $L \in \underline{\hat{C}DOB}$ by the system $G = (\{a,b,c,d\}, \{ada\}, \{(a,aa),(b,b),(c,c),(d,bc)\})$ with $h(x) = x$ for $x \in \{a,b,c\}$, and $h(d) = \lambda$. But $L \notin \underline{CTOB}$ by showing that from the axiom either only words $a^{2^n}a^{2^n}$ or $a^{2^n}bca^{2^n}$ can be generated without yielding additional words. □

As a consequence from the previous lemmas it follows that all results known so far in the context-independent case with one table can be summarized by

Theorem 1 : *The relations holding between different variations of deterministic context-independent Indian parallel systems with one table are given by the (not yet complete) mixed diagram 1 where the arrows connecting X with Y (omitting the underlining of language families) have the meanings :*

—— : $\underline{X} \subseteq \underline{Y}$, ⟶ : $\underline{X} \subset \underline{Y} \wedge \underline{X}^{\blacktriangle} \neq \underline{Y}^{\blacktriangle}$, - - - → : $\underline{X} \subset \underline{Y} \wedge \underline{X}^{\blacktriangle} = \underline{Y}^{\blacktriangle}$

Diagram 1 :

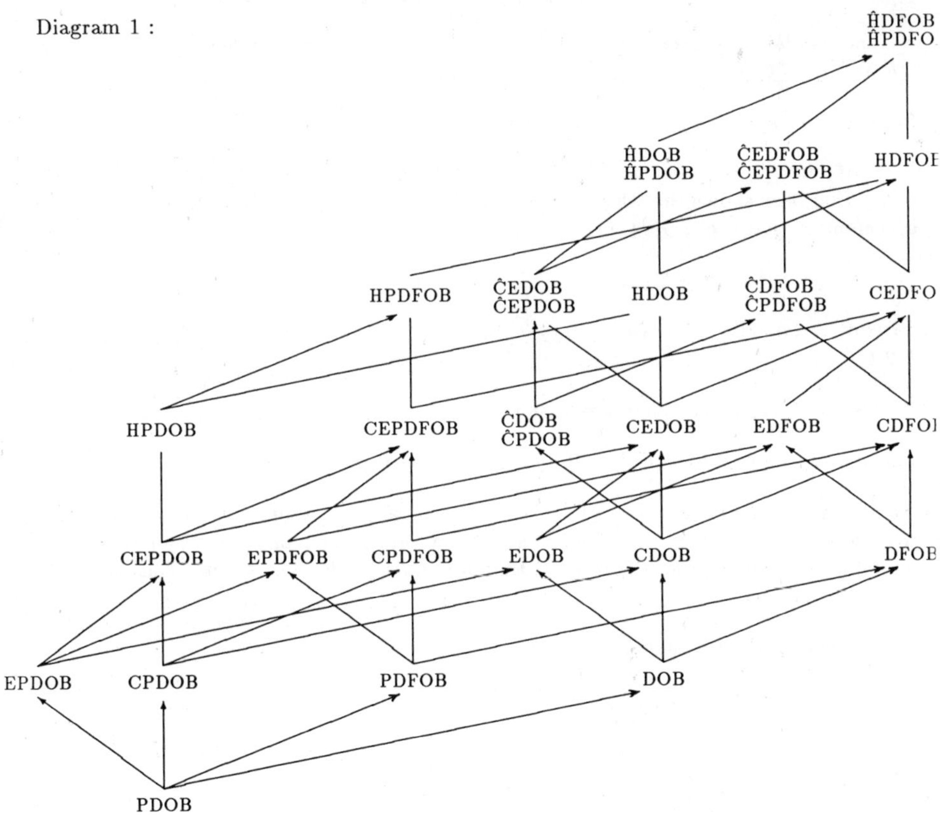

For systems with several tables the following lemmas hold. The first one states the relation between systems with one and several tables.

Lemma 22 : $\underline{PDTOB} \not\subseteq \underline{\hat{H}FOB}$.

Proof : Consider $L = \{a^{2^m 3^n} \mid 0 \leq m, n\}$. Obviously, $L \in \underline{PDTOB}$ by the system $G = (\{a\}, \{a\}, \{\{(a, a^2)\}, \{(a, a^3)\}\}$. But $L \notin \underline{\hat{H}FOB}$ by [5], L24. □

Lemma 23 : $\underline{EPDTOB} \not\subseteq \underline{\hat{C}TFOB}$.

Proof : Consider $L = \{a^n bcd^n \mid 0 \leq n\}$. Obviously, $L \in \underline{EPDTOB}$ by the system $G = (\{S, a, b, c, d\}, \{a, b, c, d\}, \{S\}, \{\{(S, bc)\}, \{(S, aSd)\}\})$, but $L \notin \underline{\hat{C}TFOB}$ as in Lemma 14. □

Lemma 24 : $\underline{\hat{C}DTOB} \not\subseteq \underline{CTOB}$.

Proof : Consider $L = \{\lambda, ab, cd\}$. Trivially, $L \in \underline{\hat{C}DTOB}$ by the $DTOB$ system $G = (\{a, b, c, d, e\}, \{e\}, \{\{(e, ab)\}, \{(e, cd)\}\})$ with the homomorphism h defined by $h(e) = \lambda$, and $h(x) = x$ for $x \in \{a, b, c, d\}$. But $L \notin \underline{CTOB}$ by [5], L17. □

The relation to context-free languages is given by the following lemmas, stating that $\underline{CF}$ and $\underline{\hat{H}DTOB}$ are incomparable.

Lemma 25 : $\underline{CF} \not\subseteq \underline{\hat{H}DTOB}$.

Proof: In [7] it is shown that $\underline{EDTOL} = \underline{CDTOL} = \underline{\hat{C}DTOL} = \underline{HDTOL} = \underline{\hat{H}DTOL}$. In [1] it has been shown that there exist $\underline{CF}$ languages not in $\underline{EDTOL}$. Therefore it follows by Lemma 8 that $\underline{CF} \not\subseteq \underline{\hat{H}DTOB}$. □

Lemma 26 : $\underline{PDOB} \not\subseteq \underline{CF}$.

Proof : Trivially, $L = \{a^{2^n} \mid 0 \leq n\} \in \underline{PDOB}$ by $G = (\{a\}, \{a\}, \{(a, aa)\})$. But $L \notin \underline{CF}$. □

The place of regular languages is shown by

Lemma 27 : $\underline{REG}^{\triangle} \subset \underline{EPDTOB}$, $\underline{REG} \subset \underline{EPDTFOB}$.

Proof : Any language $L \in \underline{REG}^{\blacktriangle}$ can be generated by a one-sided linear grammar $G = (V, V_T, \{S\}, P)$ with productions only of the form $A \rightarrow Bx$ or $A \rightarrow x$. By putting each production into one table it is obvious that $L \in \underline{EPDTOB}$. The strict inclusions follow from Lemma 26. □

The relation to L systems is given by

Lemma 28 : $\underline{PDOL} \not\subseteq \underline{\hat{H}TOB}$.

Proof : Consider $L = \{a^{2^n} bc^{2^n} \mid 0 \leq n\}$. Clearly, $L \in \underline{PDOL}$ by the $PDOL$ system $G = (\{a, b, c\}, \{abc\}, \{(a, aa), (b, b), (c, cc)\})$. But $L \notin \underline{\hat{H}TOB}$ by [5]. □

From the fact $\underline{EPDTOL} = \underline{EPDTFOL}^{\blacktriangle} \subset \underline{EPDTFOL} = \underline{EDTOL} = \underline{EDTFOL}$ (see e.g. [9]) and the lemmas presented, the results known so far for the context-independent case with several tables can be summarized by

Theorem 2 : *The relations holding between different variations of deterministic context-independent Indian parallel systems with several tables are given by the (not yet complete) mixed diagram 2, with the same meanings of the arrows as in Theorem 1.*

Diagram 2 :

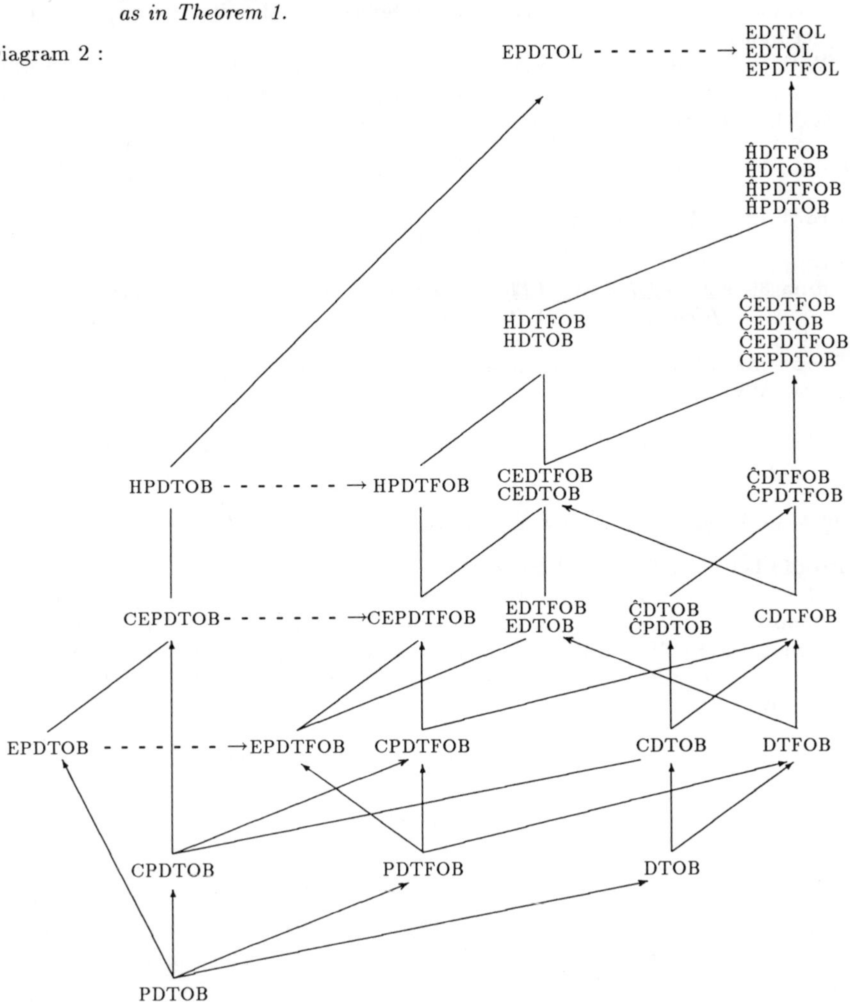

4 Context-dependent Systems

In this section some results for deterministic context-dependent Indian parallel systems are presented, mainly that the context-sensitive and recursively enumerable languages can also be characterized by such systems.

The definition of context-dependent systems can be formulated in an alternative way equivalent to the definition above. This definition uses a context of fixed size (m, n) for all productions (m to the left and n to the right), such that any production has the form (l, x, r, b) with $u \in \{\$\}^*V^*$, $r \in V^*\{\$\}^*$ and $lg(l) = m$, $lg(r) = n$.

By filling up each context of the original definition to a maximal length and defining productions for any such context it is easy to see that both definitions are equivalent with respect to derivation.

With the new definition determinism can be defined in another way equivalent to the one above : $((l, x, r, b_1) \in P \wedge (l, x, r, b_2) \in P) \Rightarrow b_1 = b_2$, which holds both for the context-independent as well as for the context-dependent case.

Lemma 29 : $\underline{EPDTIB} = \underline{EPDTFIB}^{\blacktriangle} \subset \underline{EPDTFIB}$, , $\underline{EPDTIB} = \underline{EDTFIB}$.

Proof : As in Lemmas 1 and 2. □

Lemma 30 : $\underline{XDTIB} \subseteq \underline{XDTIL}$, $\underline{XDTFIB} \subseteq \underline{XDTFIL}$ *for any prefix* X *formed from the set* $\{\lambda, D, P, E, C, \hat{C}, H, \hat{H}\}$.

Proof : As in Lemma 8, but extending each $P_i(x)$ by adding all other contexts (l, y, r, y) of sufficiently large size to P_i'. □

The next result states that the recursively enumerable languages are just the $EDIB$ languages.

Theorem 3 : $\underline{RE} = \underline{EDIB} = \underline{EDFIB} = \underline{EDTIB} = \underline{EDTFIB}$.

Proof : Let $L \in \underline{RE}$. Then there exists a grammar $G = (V, V_T, \{S\}, P)$ with productions $P = \{r_1, \cdots, r_n\}$ and $L = L(G)$. It can be assumed that any $r_j = u_j \rightarrow v_j \in P$ has one of the forms $a_j b_j \rightarrow c_j d_j$, $a_j \rightarrow b_j c_j$, $a_j \rightarrow x_j$, or $a_j \rightarrow \lambda$, with $\{a_j, b_j, c_j, d_j\} \subseteq V$ and $x_j \in V_T$.

From G an $EDIS$ system (deterministic Semi-Thue system with extension, see [6]) $G' = (V', V_T, \{ASB_0\}, P')$ with $L(G') = L$ can be constructed. The set of productions is given by :

$$\begin{aligned} P' \;=\; \{ & AB_0 \rightarrow \lambda, xK \rightarrow Kx, CK \rightarrow L, Lx \rightarrow xL, LB_0 \rightarrow \lambda, Ay \rightarrow CTy, Ty \rightarrow yT, \\ & TB_0 \rightarrow KB_0, yB_0 \rightarrow yB_1, yB_i \rightarrow yR_iB_{i+1}, yB_n \rightarrow yR_nB_0, yR_j \rightarrow R_jy, \\ & R_iR_j \rightarrow R_j, TR_ju_j \rightarrow Dv_jE, yD \rightarrow Dy, CD \rightarrow A, Ey \rightarrow yE, ER_j \rightarrow E, \\ & EB_0 \rightarrow B_0, EB_j \rightarrow B_0 \mid \\ & x \in V_T, y \in V, 1 \leq i < n, 1 \leq j \leq n, r_j = u_j \rightarrow v_j \in P\} \end{aligned}$$

This system works by sending signals T from the left to find a position for rewriting, and producing and sending signals R_j from the right for applying productions r_j. If L arrives at the right end a signal K is sent to the left checking the word w for $w \in V_T^*$ and producing it.

The productions $TR_ju_j \rightarrow Dv_jE$ can be replaced by a number of productions according to the form of r_j in the following way, still yielding an equivalent $EDIS$ system G_1' :

$$\begin{aligned} r_j = a_jb_j \rightarrow c_jd_j \;&:\; \{TR_j \rightarrow F_j, F_ja_j \rightarrow G_j, G_jb_j \rightarrow Dc_jd_jE\} \\ r_j = a_j \rightarrow b_jc_j \;&:\; \{TR_j \rightarrow F_j, F_ja_j \rightarrow Db_jc_jE\} \\ r_j = a_j \rightarrow x_j \;&:\; \{TR_j \rightarrow F_j, F_ja_j \rightarrow Dx_jE\} \\ r_j = a_j \rightarrow \lambda \;&:\; \{TR_j \rightarrow F_j, F_ja_j \rightarrow ED\} \end{aligned}$$

From this system an equivalent $EDIB$ system G'' will be constructed. This is done by constructing for each production from G'_1 a number of productions from G'' in the following way where $x, x', x'' \in V_T$, $y, y', y'' \in V$, $1 \leq i < n$ and $1 \leq j \leq n$:

$$
\begin{aligned}
P'' \ = \ & \{(\$, A, B_0, \lambda), (\$, B_0, \$, \lambda), (x, K, B_0, [x,K]), (x, K, x'', [x,K]), (C, x, [x,K]), \\
& (x', x, [x,K], K), (K, [x,K], B_0, x), (K, [x,K], x'', x), (\$, C, K, \lambda), \\
& (\$, K, x, L), (\$, L, x, [x,L]), (x', L, x, [x,L]), ([x,L], x, x'', L), \\
& ([x,L], x, B_0, L), (\$, [x,L], L, x), (x', [x,L], L, x), (L, B_0, \$, \lambda), (x, L, \$, \lambda), \\
& (\$, A, y, CT), (C, T, y, [y,T]), (y'', T, y, [y,T]), ([y,T], y, y', T), \\
& ([y,T], y, R_j, T), ([y,T], y, B_0, T), (C, [y,T], T, y), (y'', [y,T], T, y), \\
& (x, T, B_0, K), (y, B_0, \$, B_1), (y, B_i, \$, R_i B_{i+1}), (y, B_n, \$, R_n B_0), \\
& (y, R_i, B_{i+1}, [x,i]), (y, R_j, y'', [x,j]), (y, R_n, B_0, [y,n]), (y', y, [y,j], R_j), \\
& (R_i, y, [y,j], R_j), (T, y, [y,j], R_j), (R_j, [y,j], B_{j+1}, y), (R_j, [y,j], y'', y), \\
& (T, R_i, R_j, \lambda), (y, R_i, R_j, \lambda), (y, D, y', [y,D]), (y, D, E, [y,D]), \\
& (C, y, [y,D], D), (y'', y, [y,D], D), (D, [y,D], y', y), (D, [y,D], E, y), \\
& (\$, C, D, \lambda), (\$, D, y, A), (\$, D, E, A), (D, E, y, [y,E]), (y', E, y, [y,E]), \\
& ([y,E], y, y'', E), ([y,E], y, B_j, E), ([y,E], y, B_0, E), (D, [y,E], E, y), \\
& (y', [y,E], E, y), (E, R_j, y, \lambda), (E, R_i, B_{i+1}, \lambda), (E, R_n, B_0, \lambda), (E, B_j, \$, B_0), \\
& (y, E, B_0, \lambda), (A, E, B_0, \lambda), (T, R_j, D, \lambda), (C, T, D, \lambda), (y, T, D, \lambda)\} \\
\cup \ & \{(R_j, a_j, b_j, F_j), (F_j, b_j, y', D c_j d_j E), (F_j, b_j, R_k, D c_j d_j E), \\
& (F_j, b_j, B_{j+1}, D c_j d_j E), (T, R_j, F_j, \lambda), (R_j, F_j, D, \lambda) \mid a_j b_j \rightarrow c_j d_j \in P\} \\
\cup \ & \{(R_j, a_j, y', D b_j c_j E), (R_j, a_j, R_k, D b_j c_j E), (R_j, a_j, B_{j+1}, D b_j c_j E) \mid \\
& a_j \rightarrow b_j c_j \in P\} \\
\cup \ & \{(R_j, a_j, y', D x_j E), (R_j, a_j, R_k, D x_j E), (R_j, a_j, B_{j+1}, D x_j E) \mid a_j \rightarrow x_j \in P\} \\
\cup \ & \{(R_j, a_j, y', DE), (R_j, a_j, R_k, DE), (R_j, a_j, B_{j+1}, DE) \mid a_j \rightarrow \lambda \in P\} \\
\cup \ & \{(X, Y, Z, Y) \mid else\}
\end{aligned}
$$

The $[y, u]$ are new symbols. G'' simulates the derivations of G'_1 and generates the same language L. Note that all productions of G'' are of the size $(1,1)$.

Thus $\underline{RE} \subseteq \underline{EDIB}$. Since the inverse inclusion $\underline{EDIB} \subseteq \underline{RE}$ is obvious, it follows that $\underline{RE} = \underline{EDIB}$. □

The following result shows the relation to context-sensitive languages.

Theorem 4 : $\underline{CS} = \underline{EPDFIB} = \underline{EPDTFIB}$, $\underline{CS}^{\blacktriangle} = \underline{EPDTIB}$.

Proof : $\underline{EPDTFIB} \subseteq \underline{CS}$ follows from $\underline{EPDTFIB} \subseteq \underline{EPDTFIL} = \underline{CS}$ by [13].

$\underline{CS} \subseteq \underline{EPDFIB}$ can be shown by a technique similar to that of Theorem 3. This is achieved by first constructing for $G \in CS$, which can be assumed to have only productions of the forms $a_j b_j \rightarrow c_j d_j$, $a_j \rightarrow b_j c_j$ or $a_j \rightarrow x_j$, an equivalent $EPDFIS$ system $G' = (V', V_T, A', P')$. If all $w \in L(G)$ with $lg(w) < 3$ are put into A' it can be assumed that G has only productions of the form $a_j b_j \rightarrow c_j d_j$. With $x, x' \in V_T$ and $y, y' \in V$ the set of productions P' is defined by :

$$\begin{aligned}
P' \;=\; & \{x[x',K]\rightarrow[x,K]x', [x,C][x',K]\rightarrow x[x',L], [x,L]x'\rightarrow x[x',L], \\
& [x,L][x',B_0]\rightarrow xx', [y,A]y'\rightarrow[y,CT]y', [y,CT]y'\rightarrow[y,C][y',T], \\
& [y,T]y'\rightarrow y[y',T], [y,T][y',B_0]\rightarrow y[y',TB_0], x[x',TB_0]\rightarrow[x,K][x',B_0], \\
& y[y',TB_i]\rightarrow y[y',TR_iB_{i+1}], y[y',B_0]\rightarrow y[y',B_1], y[y',B_i]\rightarrow y[y',R_iB_{i+1}], \\
& y[y',B_n]\rightarrow y[y',R_nB_0], y[y',R_iB_{i+1}]\rightarrow[y,R_i][y',B_{i+1}], \\
& y[y',R_nB_0]\rightarrow[y,R_n][y',B_0], y[y',R_j]\rightarrow[y,R_j]y', [y,R_i][y',R_j]\rightarrow[y,R_j]y', \\
& [y,T][y',R_j]\rightarrow[y,TR_j]y', [y,CT][y',R_j]\rightarrow[y,CTR_j]y', y[y',D]\rightarrow[y,D]y', \\
& [y,C][y',D]\rightarrow[y,A]y', [y,E]y'\rightarrow y[y',E], [y,E][y',R_j]\rightarrow y[y',E], \\
& [y,E][y',R_iB_{i+1}]\rightarrow y[y',B_0], [y,E][y',R_nB_0]\rightarrow y[y',B_0]\} \\
\cup \; & \{[a_j,CTR_j]b_j\rightarrow[c_j,A][d_j,E], [a_j,TR_j]b_j\rightarrow[c_j,D][d_j,E], \\
& [a_i,TR_i][b_i,B_{i+1}]\rightarrow[c_i,D][d_i,B_0] \mid a_jb_j\rightarrow c_jd_j \in P\}
\end{aligned}$$

Again, $[y,u]$ are new symbols. G' works similar to G'_1 of Theorem 3, with the difference that the signals are not separate symbols but are attached to the $y \in V$.

From G' an equivalent $EPDFIB$ system can be constructed, with all productions of size $(1,1)$, using the same method as in Theorem 3.

Therefore $\underline{CS} = \underline{EPDFIB} = \underline{EPDTFIB}$ by Lemmas 29 and 30. □

The situation for deterministic context-dependent Indian parallel systems differs somehow from that of deterministic context-dependent Lindenmayer systems since (see [13]) $\underline{RE} = \underline{EDIL} = \underline{EDFIL} = \underline{EDTIL} = \underline{EDTFIL}$ and $\underline{CS} = \underline{EPDTIL} = \underline{EPDTFIL}$, but $\underline{DLBA} = \underline{EPDFIL}$.

The reason for this difference seems to originate from the fact that in $EPDFIL$ systems every symbol has to be rewritten whereas in $EPDFIB$ systems only one symbol at every position.

References

[1] Ehrenfeucht, A., Rozenberg, G. : *On some context free languages that are not deterministic ETOL languages.* RAIRO 11, pp 273-291, 1977.

[2] Kleijn, H. C. M., Rozenberg, G. : *A Study of Parallel Rewriting Systems.* IC 44, pp 134-163, 1980.

[3] Kudlek, M. : *Comparing Several Ways of Context-independent Parallel Rewriting.* LNCS 28, pp 122-130, 1975.

[4] Kudlek, M. : *Indian Parallel Systems.* Records of the 2nd Conference on FST and TCS, pp 283-289, 1982.

[5] Kudlek, M. : *Languages Defined by Indian Parallel Systems.* in : *The Book of L*, pp 233-243, Springer, 1986.

[6] Kudlek, M. : *Languages Defined by Deterministic Semi-Thue Systems.* Topics in the Theoretical Bases and Applications of Computer Science, Proceedings Fourth Hungarian Computer Science Conference, pp 41-52, Akadémiai Kiadó, 1986.

[7] Nielsen, M., Rozenberg, G., Salomaa, A., Skyum, S. : *Nonterminals, Homomorphisms and Codings in Different Variations of OL-Systems I : Deterministic Systems.* AI 4, pp 87-106, 1974.

[8] Rozenberg, G. : *A Survey of Results and Open Problems in the Mathematical Theory of L Systems.* in : Book, R. : *Formal Language Theory - Perspectives and Problems.* Academic Press, 1980.

[9] Rozenberg, G., Salomaa, A. : *The Mathematical Theory of L Systems.* Academic Press, 1980.

[10] Salomaa, A. : *Parallelism in Rewriting Systems.* LNCS 14, pp 523-533, 1974.

[11] Siromoney, R., Krithivasan, K. : *Parallel Context-free Languages.* IC 24, pp 155-162, 1974.

[12] Skyum, S. : *Parallel Context-free Languages.* IC 26, pp 280-285, 1974.

[13] Vitányi, P. M. B. : *Lindenmayer Systems : Structure, Languages, and Growth Functions.* Mathematisch Centrum, Amsterdam, 1978.

HEXAGONAL CELLULAR AUTOMATA

MEENA MAHAJAN

and

KAMALA KRITHIVASAN

Department of Computer Science and Engineering

I.I.T., MADRAS, 600036, INDIA.

ABSTRACT

Hexagonal Cellular Automata (HCA) are defined as a variation of the rectangular 2-D cellular automata (RCA) studied in the literature. Equivalence of HCA and RCA is shown. Some algorithms for manipulation of patterns on the HCA are presented. The application of HCA to generating and parsing languages over hexagonal arrays, as described by the grammatical models proposed by Siromoney and Siromoney[15], is discussed.

1. INTRODUCTION

Hexagonal arrays and hexagonal patterns are found in the literature on picture processing and scene analysis[7,8,9]. These arrays have been studied as formal models[15], where the authors introduce array grammars to generate languages of hexagonal arrays. They also indicate the application of such models to 2-D representations of 3-D scenes composed of rectangular parallelepipeds, and to the problem of recognition of perceptual twins[10].

Cellular automata as acceptors for string languages have been studied extensively[17,18,19]. Systolic pyramid automata[4], which are in some sense equivalent to 2-D cellular automata, have been studied with respect to recognition of matrix and array grammars[11,12,13]. In this paper we introduce hexagonal cellular automata (cells placed on a triangular grid), and study their relation to the formal models for hexagonal arrays[15].

Section 2 introduces hexagonal cellular automata, gives definitions, shows equivalence to Turing machines, and gives two examples to illustrate basic algorithms for pattern manipulation. Sections 3 and 4 study the relation of these automata to hexagonal kolam array languages and controlled table L-array languages respectively, the two models proposed in (15). Generators and acceptors for these languages are described.

2. HEXAGONAL CELLULAR AUTOMATA

In the 2-D cellular automata discussed in the literature[(1)], cells are arranged on a square lattice, i.e., in a one- to-one correspondence with $I \times I$ (I is the set of integers.). Each cell is directly connected to its two adjacent vertical neighbours and two horizontal neighbours. The underlying interconnection structure is a rectangular grid; so henceforth we shall refer to these cellular automata as RCA (rectangular CA). Hexagonal cellular automata (HCA) are defined as a direct extension of RCA. In these CA, the underlying interconnection structure is the equiangular triangular grid. Thus each cell has six neighbours, arranged in a regular hexagon with itself at the centre (fig. 1); hence the name.

The operation of the HCA is exactly like the operation of the RCA. There is a finite set of states Q; each cell is in some state $q \in Q$ at every time instant; at successive time instants all cells synchronously change state depending on their current state and the current states of their six neighbours. The transition function at each cell is identical; it is as if multiple copies of the same finite state automaton are placed at each cell. We assume the existence of a special state, q_0, called the quiescent state, and, as in the case of RCA, stipulate that at any time instant only a finite number of cells are non-quiescent. Further, a cell with a quiescent neighbourhood remains quiescent (neighbourhood of a cell = itself and its six neighbours).

Formally, an HCA is a 3-tuple $H = (Q, q_0, \delta)$ where Q is the set of states, $q_0 \in Q$ is the quiescent state, and $\delta : Q \times Q^6 \rightarrow Q$ is the transition function subject to $\delta(q_0, q_0, q_0, q_0, q_0, q_0, q_0) = q_0$. The arguments to δ are as follows: the first argument is the state of the cell under consideration, and the next six arguments are the states of its six neighbours read in clockwise order starting from the top. The function value gives the new state of the cell under consideration. Rather than write $\delta(x,a,b,c,d,e,f) = y$, we write this pictorially as

$$\delta\begin{pmatrix} & a & \\ f & & b \\ & x & \\ e & & c \\ & d & \end{pmatrix} = y.$$

A configuration of the HCA is an assignment of states to cells on the triangular grid, such that at most a finite number of cells are non-quiescent. At each time instant, each cell simultaneously changes state as per the transition function, giving rise to a new configuration.

In sections 3 and 4 we shall consider languages of hexagonal arrays(15), and see how HCA relate to these classes of languages. Two models will be considered: a) the generator model, and b) the recogniser model. In the generator model, the HCA starts from an initial configuration and generates all the arrays belonging to a language L. Clearly, it may not be possible to generate these arrays at successive time steps; intermediate transitions may be required. Let $H_1, H_2, .. , H_i, ...$ be an enumeration of all arrays in L. Then whenever the HCA enters a configuration equal to H_i, it should indicate this. For this we adopt the convention that whenever an H_i is generated, the bottommost cell of H_i, cell 'D', will enter a special state. Thus intermediate configurations of the HCA are either not convex hexagons at all, or ones in which the cell 'D' is not in a special state.

For the recogniser model, the initial configuration is the input array, i.e., a convex hexagon. Its bottommost cell is now considered to be the distinguished cell 'D'. At any time t, if cell 'D' goes into an 'accept' state, then the input array belongs to the language L. Thus the notion of acceptance by an HCA can be defined for hexagonal array languages. If the input hexagon H does not belong to the language, the behaviour of the acceptor can be anything. However, if we can define an acceptor which also goes to a prespecified reject state when H is not in the language, then we have a stronger notion of acceptance, termed recognition[18].

In an HCA, the interconnection graph is an equiangular triangular grid. It consists of 3 families of parallel lines, with orientations |, /, and \ respectively. Removing any one family leaves a graph isomorphic to the rectangular grid, as shown in fig. 2. Clearly, an HCA has all the connections of the RCA, and more. A mapping between the two CA may be defined as follows:

In an HCA, each cell x has 6 neighbours, whose positions are as indicated. In an RCA, a cell X has 4 neighbours - left(L), up(U), right(R), and down(D) as shown below.

```
        a                    U
    f       b
        x               L    X    R
    e       c
        d                    D
```

If a cell x of an HCA is to be mapped onto cell X of an RCA, consider the 4 neighbours resulting when the family of vertical lines of the HCA is deleted. i.e.,

```
    f       b
        x
    e       c
```

These may be mapped to the 4 neighbours of X as follows:

$$f(x) = L(X), \quad b(x) = U(X),$$
$$c(x) = R(X), \quad e(x) = D(X). \tag{1}$$

Doing a similar mapping for the neighbours of b and e, we get

$$a(x) = L(U(X)), \; d(x) = D(R(X)). \tag{2}$$

The mapping is shown in fig. 3. The neighbourhood of cell x, as represented in the RCA, is highlighted. The missing vertical lines of the HCA are the dotted left-to-right diagonals of the RCA. It is also clear how an RCA can be mapped onto an HCA; for cell X of the RCA mapped onto cell x of the HCA, equation 1 gives the relationship between the neighbours of X and the neighbours of x.

The transitions of the RCA (Q, q_0, δ_R) can be simulated by the HCA (Q, q_0, δ_H) in one step as follows:

$$\delta_H \begin{pmatrix} & a & \\ f & & b \\ & x & \\ e & & c \\ & d & \end{pmatrix} = \delta_R \begin{pmatrix} & b & \\ f & x & c \\ & e & \end{pmatrix}$$

The transitions of the HCA can be simulated by the RCA at half-speed; i.e., for each transition of the HCA, the RCA goes through 2 transitions as follows:

$$\delta_R \begin{pmatrix} & c & \\ g & h & i \\ & m & \end{pmatrix} = ghi,$$

a -- b -- c -- d -- e
f -- g -- h -- i -- j
k -- l -- m -- n -- o

giving rise to the intermediate configuration, and

abc bcd cde
fgh ghi hij
klm lmn mno

$$\delta_R \begin{pmatrix} & bcd & \\ fgh & ghi & hij \\ & lmn & \end{pmatrix} = \delta_H \begin{pmatrix} & b & \\ g & & c \\ & h & \\ m & & i \\ & n & \end{pmatrix}$$

Thus we have the following theorem:

Theorem 2.1 : Every HCA can be simulated by an RCA and vice versa; i.e., HCA and RCA are equivalent in power.

From this it follows that the sequential machine characterisation of an RCA can also be used for the HCA.

An RCA R can be simulated by a Turing machine M with a 2-D worktape T which stores in its cells the configuration of the RCA. For a single transition of the RCA, M will go through a series of transitions, sequentially updating the states of all cells with a non-quiescent neighbourhood. Thus a Turing machine can simulate any RCA and hence any HCA.Conversely, a HCA or RCA can simulate any Turing machine, because it contains an unbounded 1-D CA within it, and 1-D CAs have been shown to simulate Turing machines[(1)]. Thus we have the following result:

Theorem 2.2 : Hexagonal Cellular Automata and Turing machines are exactly equivalent in computing power.

Similar to the one-way 1-D and 2-D CA, we can define one-way HCA, OHCA, where a cell gets input only from neighbours in positions e, d, c, and gives output only to neighbours in positions f, a, b. The OHCA can be shown to be equivalent to the one-way RCA and thus also equivalent to the trellis defined in (3).

If the states of a CA are mapped onto integers, then the CA is said to be totalistic if the transition function depends only on the sum of the states of all cells in the neighbourhood of a given cell. For every HCA, an equivalent totalistic HCA which simulates it in real time can be constructed. The construction is based on giving a suitable colouring for the underlying graph and then applying the technique described in (2).

The interconnection structure for the HCA is the equiangular triangular grid. Thus any convex hexagon represented on the HCA is equiangular and has opposite sides parallel. It can be shown that if the lengths of the sides of the hexagon, taken in clockwise order, are p, q, r, s, t, u, (see fig. 4) then $s = p + k$, $t = q - k$ and $u = r + k$, for some k. If $k = 0$, then the opposite sides of the hexagon are parallel and equal;

such hexagons are referred to as b-hexagons[15]. If k = 0, we have a non-b hexagon. A b-hexagon with p = q = r has opposite sides parallel and all sides equal; it is a regular hexagon.

Several pattern transforms can be defined for convex hexagons; typical examples are rotation through multiples of 60° and mirror reflection about an edge. Similarly, property checking for convex hexagons is of interest for properties like regularity, 60° rotation symmetry, 120° rotation symmetry and so on. Algorithms on the HCA for some of the above problems have been presented in (5). For illustration, two of them are given below. The convex hexagon is represented on the HCA by having cells within the hexagon in some non-quiescent state and all other cells in quiescent state. Some observations which are often used in the algorithms are given below.

(i) In a convex hexagon, cells along the border 'know' that they are on the border. This is so because cells on vertices of the hexagon have exactly 3 quiescent neighbours, while cells along an edge have exactly 2 quiescent neighbours.

(ii) If cells along a continuous non-self-intersecting path on the HCA are marked, then they can operate in conjunction as a 1-D CA, even though they may not be in a straight line. This follows from the fact that along the path, each cell knows its predecessor and successor (this information must be imparted at the time of marking the path). See fig. 5.

(iii) Each cell affects the change of state of every cell in its neighbourhood. This can be viewed as the sending of signals by a cell to all its neighbours. The algorithms presented below will thus talk of signals being sent across the HCA, rather than state changes at cells.

Algorithms:

(1) Firing Squad problem for a regular hexagon :

Given a regular hexagon as the initial configuration, with the distinguished cell D (bottommost vertex) in state \$ and all other cells in state @, we wish to achieve, at some time t, a configuration where all cells of the hexagon are in state #, such that no cell of the hexagon enters state # prior to t.

The firing squad problem for linear arrays (initial configuration $\$@^{n-1}$, final configuration $\#^n$) has been solved in various ways[4]. The time taken for this algorithm, L(n), has been shown to be at least 2n-2. This algorithm can be easily extended to RCA as follows. Let the topleft cell of the mxn rectangle be in state \$. In time L(n), all cells in the topmost row can be brought simultaneously into an intermediate state #'. At this time, each cell c_{1j} of the topmost row can initiate a firing squad algorithm on the jth column; so in another L(m) time units all cell in each column go to state # (denoted as 'fired'), i.e., all cells in the entire rectangle fire at time L(n) + L(m).

For a regular hexagon H, the trick lies in dividing the hexagon into rectangles which can fire simultaneously. To do this, D sends signals S_F, S_B and S_E to cells F, B, E respectively. See fig. 6. S_E returns to D from E. Thus S_F, S_B and S_E reach F, B and D at the same time instant 2n (where n is the length of a side). Cells B, D, F are the corner vertices of rectangles BCOA, DEOC and FAOE respectively. They can run RCA firing squad algorithms on these rectangles, firing all cells of H after a total time of 2n + 2L(n). Note that the cells along the radii OA, OC and OE must be able to keep track of signals for 2 distinct RCA algorithms, since they participate in the firing squad algorithms of both rectangles adjacent to them.

(2) To move a convex hexagon parallel to an edge until the edge reaches a prespecified boundary.

Without loss of generality, assume that the edge is vertical (edge BC of fig. 4) and the desired movement is to the right. A boundary GG′ to the right of edge BC and parallel to it is premarked as the edge along which edge BC of the shifted hexagon must finally reside. Note that there is no straight line path for right movement. So a q-pulse must travel right in a zigzag fashion, moving to the neighbour at position b at odd time instants and to the neighbour at position c at even time instants. So the pulse travels as a tuple (q, up) or (q, down) indicating whether it will move to neighbour b next (and become (q, down) there) or to neighbour c (and change to (q, up)). Positions of neighbours of a cell are shown in figure 1.

The rightmost column of the hexagon H sends pulses, travelling right at unit speed, at time t = 1. The next column sends out pulses at t = 2, the third rightmost column at t = 3 and so on. Effectively, a column sends pulses right one time unit after the column to its right has done so. When the rightmost column pulses reach GG′, they stop moving and 'stabilise'; i.e., they revert from tuples (q,up) or (q,down) to singletons q. The pulses from other columns stabilise when they find that the pulses to their right have stabilised; i.e., they halt one column before the previous column. Thus if GG′ is m columns away from BC, then the rightmost column stabilises at time t = m, the next at t = m+1, and so on. See fig. 7. If the width of H along the direction normal to GG′ is w, then this algorithm requires m+w-1 units of time.

3. GENERATING AND RECOGNISING HEXAGONAL KOLAM ARRAY LANGUAGES

The main motivation for studying HCA has been to study its relationship to the languages of hexagonal arrays[15]. In (15), formal grammatical models for generating such arrays have been discussed. The main point to be noted is that unlike strings, hexagons cannot be concatenated to give hexagons. So the grammatical models use arrowhead concatenation, which is illustrated in fig. 8.

A hexagonal kolam array grammar has 3 disjoint sets of alphabets - nonterminals, intermediates and terminals. There are 3 types of rewriting rules : (i) In the first type, called non-terminal rules, the left hand side (l.h.s) has one non-terminal and the right hand side (r.h.s) has exactly one non-terminal along with zero or more intermediates. Treating the intermediates as terminals, these rules are either left linear or linear. (ii) The second type has a single terminal rule with a non-terminal on the l.h.s and a hexagonal array of terminals on the r.h.s.. (iii) In the third type, comprising of intermediate rules, usually the intermediate languages are specified rather than enumerating the intermediate rules. These languages consist of arrowheads made up of terminal symbols.

Derivation proceeds as follows:

Initially, non-terminal rules are applied in sequence, with arrows indicating direction of concatenation, and parentheses inserted at each step. This results in a string with intermediates and one non-terminal. In the second phase, the non-terminal is replaced by a hexagonal array of terminals, using the terminal rule. In the last phase, starting from the innermost parenthesis, each intermediate is replaced by an arrowhead of appropriate size (appropriate with respect to concatenation) from the corresponding language. This arrowhead is concatenated to the existing hexagon to get a new hexagon.

The grammar is called regular (R) or linear (L) according as the first phase (applying non-terminal rules) is left linear or linear. (Note : In this context, a linear rule is one which involves arrowheads of opposite directions, like $S \rightarrow ((S' \uparrow a) \downarrow b)$. This parallels the linear rule $S \rightarrow aS'b$ of string grammars.) Further, a regular grammar may be R:R or R:CF or R:CS according as all intermediate languages are regular, or all are context-free and at least one is not regular, or all are context-sensitive and at least one is not context-free. Similarly, we have (L:R), (L:CF) and (L:CS) grammars.

<u>example 3.1</u> G_1 is an R:R grammar.

$G_1 = (V, I, P, S, \mathcal{L})$

$V = V_1 \cup V_2$

$V_1 = \{S, S_1\}$ non-terminals

$V_2 = \{a,b,c,x,y,z\}$ intermediates

$I = \{G, Y\}$ terminals

$P = P_1 \cup P_2$

$P_1 = \{S \rightarrow (((S_1 \nearrow a) \nwarrow b) \downarrow c),\ S_1 \rightarrow (((S \nearrow x) \nwarrow y) \downarrow z)\}$

non-terminal rules

```
                 G
             G       G
P2 = {S →        G       }        terminal rule
             G       G
                 G
```

$\mathcal{L} = \{L_a, L_b, L_c, L_x, L_y, L_z\}$ set of intermediate languages

$L_a = L_c = \{G^n \langle G \rangle G^n\}$ where the letters of the arrowhead are written clockwise and the letter within $\langle\ \rangle$ appears at the vertex of the arrowhead.

$L_b = \{G^n \langle G \rangle G^{n+1}\}$, $L_y = \{Y^n \langle Y \rangle Y^{n+1}\}$

$L_x = L_z = \{Y^n \langle Y \rangle Y^n\}$

A typical derivation is shown below:

<u>Phase 1</u> $S \Rightarrow (((S_1 \nearrow a) \nwarrow b) \downarrow c)$

$\Rightarrow ((([[[S \nearrow x] \nwarrow y] \downarrow z] \nearrow a) \nwarrow b) \downarrow c)$

```
                        G
                    G       G
Phase 2   ⇒ ((([[[      G       ↗ x] ↖ y] ↓ z] ↗ a) ↖ b) ↓ c)
                    G       G
                        G
```

<u>Phase 3</u>

```
                          Y
                      G       Y
                  G       G
        ⇒ ((([[       G       Y  ↖ y] ↓ z] ↗ a) ↖ b) ↓ c)
                  G       G
                      G
```

```
               Y
          Y         Y
     Y         G         Y
          G         G
⇒ ((([ Y        G         Y   ↓ z] ↗ a) ↖ b) ↓ c)
          G         G
               G
```

```
               Y
          Y         Y
     Y         G         Y
          G         G
⇒ (((  Y        G         Y    ↗ a) ↖ b) ↓ c)
          G         G
     Y         G         Y
          Y         Y
               Y
```

```
                    G
               G         G
          G         Y         G
     G         Y         Y         G
          Y         G         Y
     G         G         G         G
 *⇒       Y         G         Y
     G         G         G         G
          Y         G         Y
     G         Y         Y         G
          G         Y         G
               G         G
                    G
```

Consider the generator model HCA for $L_1 = L(G_1)$. The HCA should start off in some specified initial configuration H_0, and generate all hexagonal arrays belonging to L_1. A natural choice for H_0 is the r.h.s of the terminal rule. The arrays of L_1, say H_0, H_1, ..., H_i, ... are such that H_i has i concentric hexagons of Y's. So the HCA can generate H_{i+1} from H_i in a very natural way, in 2 steps, as described by the transition function below.

$\delta(Y) = \overline{Y}$, $\delta(G) = \overline{G}$, $\delta(\overline{Y}) = Y$, $\delta(\overline{G}) = G$

(where $\delta(x) = y$ means that a cell in state x goes to state y independent of the states of its neighbours.)

$$\delta\begin{pmatrix} & a & \\ f & & b \\ & q_0 & \\ e & & c \\ & d & \end{pmatrix} = q_0 \text{ if } a,b,c,d,e,f = q_0$$

$= \overline{Y}$ if exactly 1, or 2 adjacent neighbours, are in state G (i.e., the cell borders an H_i.)

$= G$ if exactly 1, or 2 adjacent neighbours, are in state $\overline{Y}$, (i.e., the cell is on an edge of H_{i+1}.)

Clearly, this HCA goes through a series of configurations C_0, C_1, ..., C_i, ... where every C_{2i} belongs to the language and every C_{2i+1} does not. As per the convention adopted in section 2, if C_i is a hexagon belonging to the language, then the bottommost cell D of C_i should go into a special state to indicate this. So we can modify the transition function such that

$$\delta\begin{pmatrix} & a & \\ f & & b \\ & q_0 & \\ e & & c \\ & d & \end{pmatrix} = (G,\#) \text{ if } a = \overline{Y} \text{ and } b,c,d,e,f = q_0,$$

and keep the rest of the function unaltered. Also, the initial configuration is changed to

```
       G
   G       G
       G
   G       G
     (G,#)
```

The first 3 configurations this HCA goes through are shown in fig. 9.

Now, it is clear why the distinguished cell is allowed to change with time; it is visually more appealing. This is merely a matter of convenience; it is possible to fix the distinguished cell a priori and to send signals to it when it must enter a special state.

Another point to note is that in the above example, the concatenation of three arrowheads (a,b,c or x,y,z) is simulated simultaneously in one transition by the HCA; all boundaries of the hexagon expand simultaneously. This is possible because of symmetry in the resulting hexagons.

<u>example 3.2</u> G_2 is a R:CF grammar

$G_2 = (V, I, P, S, \mathcal{L})$

$V = V_1 \cup V_2,\ V_1 = \{S\},\ V_2 = \{x,y,z\}$

$I = \{O, B\}$,

$P = P_1 \cup P_2,\ P_1 = \{S \rightarrow (((S \nearrow x) \nwarrow y) \downarrow z)$

```
                    B
                 B     B
P2 = {S →           B      }
                 B     B
                    B
```

$\mathcal{L} = \{L_x, L_y, L_z\},\ L_x = \{O^n\langle B\rangle O^n\}$

$L_y = \{O^n\langle B\rangle O^nB\},\quad L_z = \{BO^n\langle B\rangle O^nB\}$

The first three members of $L(G_2)$ are shown in fig. 10.

In this grammar, again, successive hexagons H_1, ..., H_i, ... can be generated by padding the previous hexagon with an outer border. Thus a generator model HCA for $L_2 = L(G_2)$ starts with initial configuration

$$\begin{array}{ccc} & B & \\ B & & B \\ & B & \\ B & & B \\ & (B,\#) & \end{array}$$

Let H_0, H_1, ..., H_i, ... be an enumeration of the hexagons in L_2. The HCA goes through a sequence of transitions such that at time $t = i$, the configuration of the HCA is H_i, with node D indicating membership in L_2 by symbol #. The transition function can be given as follows:

$\delta(B) = B$, $\delta(O) = O$, $\delta([B,\#]) = B$,

$\delta(q_0) = O$ if q_0 is on the border but not a vertex,

$= B$ if q_0 is a new vertex adjacent to B,

$= [B,\#]$ if q_0 is a new vertex adjacent to $[B,\#]$.

$= q_0$ otherwise

In general, for any hexagonal kolam array grammar (HKAG), a generator model HCA can be designed by examining the production rules present in the grammar. Let G be an HKAG $G = (V, I, P, S, \mathcal{L})$

$V = V_1 \cup V_2$, V_1 = non-terminals

V_2 = intermediates

$P = P_1 \cup P_2$

$\mathcal{L}$ = set of intermediate languages

I = set of terminals

P_1 has rules of the type $S_1 \rightarrow S_2 \nearrow a \mid S_2 \nwarrow b \mid S_2 \downarrow c$

where $S_1, S_2 \in V_1$, $a, b, c \in V_2$,

P_2 has a terminal rule $S_1 \rightarrow H$,

where $S_1 \in V_1$, H is a hexagonal array.

Following the pattern along which derivation proceeds, the HCA should generate strings over $S_1V_2^*$ using rules from P_1, where S_1 occurs on the l.h.s of the rule in P_2. It should then construct H, and concatenate arrowheads according to the string generated. A deterministic HCA would thus work as follows: The initial configuration is H, with cell D marked as the distinguished node. D can be viewed as the topmost cell of a 1-D CA with cells arranged vertically rather than horizontally. This CA can simulate a Turing machine which enumerates all strings generated using P_1. Such an enumeration is possible because these strings belong to a regular or linear language and hence form a recursive set. Whenever the CA enumerates a new string $S_1 \alpha$, the enumeration process is suspended. Initially H exists in the configuration; at later stages it will have to be reconstructed. Since H is finite, its description can be included within the state of D, and H can be constructed. α is a string of intermediates, say, $a_1a_2...a_n$. After H has been constructed, D sequentially examines a_i, i = 1 to n. Each a_i has, associated with it, a direction of concatenation, $\nearrow$ or $\nwarrow$ or $\downarrow$. Let $\nearrow$ be the direction of concatenation. Then D sends a signal to vertex B, signifying that an arrowhead from language L_{a_i} is to be appended to the two edges adjacent at B. To make all cells on these edges react simultaneously, B must initiate a firing squad algorithm on the edges. Then the cells again participate in simulating a Turing machine to enumerate the strings of L_{a_i}. When a string of appropriate length (with respect to concatenation) is generated, enumeration stops and the string is concatenated to the arrowhead. B now sends a signal to D to indicate that the concatenation is complete and the next symbol a_{i+1} may be scanned. Note that if the arrowhead is to be appended at D itself, then after concatenation, the new distinguished cell as well as the 1-D vertical CA below it are shifted one unit downwards. When D has finished processing all a_i, the resulting hexagon above D (i.e., ignoring the vertical string below D) is one which belongs to the language. So for one time unit, D enters a special state to indicate membership in L. It then erases the hexagon (to avoid overlap with the next one) and resumes the suspended process of enumerating strings over $S_1V_2^*$ as per P_1. Thus the HCA systematically generates all hexagons in L(G).

For accepting the language L = L(G) where G is an HKAG, the initial configuration of the HCA will be some convex hexagon H′, with the bottommost cell D marked as the distinguished node. The HCA has to decide whether $H' \in L(G)$. First consider some simple examples.

<u>example 3.3</u> Consider G_1,the grammar defined in example 3.1. H′ is the input (initial configuration) of the acceptor HCA. The acceptor can merely reverse the steps of the generator, and, after every alternate step, check whether the hexagon remaining is H_0. This can be done as follows: All border cells in state G (or Y) with non-boundary adjacent cells in state Y (or G) go to state BG (or BY). For testing whether a cell is on the boundary, states BG and BY are considered equivalent to q_0. When a boundary cell is unable to make a transition, it sends a signal to D. (Signal travels vertically down and then along the edge to D.) When D gets such a signal, it initiates a checking algorithm which determines (i) whether the non-quiescent non-BG/BY cells form a convex hexagon, and, if yes, (ii) whether this convex hexagon is equal to H_0. If the answer to either (i) or (ii) is No, $H' \notin L(G_1)$, else $H' \in L(G_1)$. Since H′ is finite, the checks in (i) and (ii) run in finite time. Thus $L(G_1)$ can be accepted. In fact, rejection is also done, so the HCA described above is a recogniser for L_1.

In the general case, acceptance becomes more difficult. The technique used for the generator HCA can be used here also; i.e., generate strings $S_1\alpha$, $\alpha \in V_2^*$, using P_1, and now delete rather than append arrowheads according to α. If at any stage deletion fails because the arrowhead present is not a member of the intermediate language, then string $S_1\alpha$ is discarded and a new string $S_1\alpha'$ is generated. Also, if after all arrowheads corresponding to α have been deleted, the hexagon left behind is not H, the r.h.s. of the terminal rule in G, then $S_1\alpha$ is discarded and a new $S_1\alpha$ is generated. The input must be available for testing the new string, so the preceding deletes should be only logical, i.e., it must be possible to recover the input configuration. However, if for a $S_1\alpha$ generated using P_1, deleting arrowheads corresponding to α leaves behind H, then clearly the input H' belongs to L(G). So D goes into an accept state. This means that through this mode of acceptance, rejection may take infinite time; i.e., recognition may not always be possible.

Another method of acceptance is to use the generator model HCA as a subroutine to generate hexagons belonging to L(G). Every hexagon so generated can be shifted so that its edges AB and BC are aligned with those of the input H' (using algorithm 2). Then at each cell the two hexagons are compared. If no cell sends a reject value to D, then D accepts the input. Else the generator is resumed to generate further hexagons.

A parser for the language will not only determine membership of the input, but further, if the input belongs to the language, it will produce a sequence of rules of G, which, when applied in that order starting from the start symbol, derive the input. The acceptors described above can be modified to restricted parsers in the sense that recognition may take infinite time, but if the input is accepted, the corresponding sequence of rules is also generated. To do this, consider the first model. Strings $S_1\alpha$ are generated and tested. Along with the string, the rules used to generate it can also be stored. Then, if a string leads to success, the set of rules is already stored within the cellular array. In the second model, the generator HCA is used. This HCA can store, in the vertical 1-D array below its distinguished node, the rules used to generate the hexagonal array. Then in case the two hexagons match, the parsing sequence is again stored within the cellular array.

Both the accepting methods discussed above are slow and inefficient. However for most specific examples, efficient acceptors can be designed after an ad hoc examination of the production rules present.

4. GENERATING AND RECOGNISING CONTROLLED TABLE HEXAGONAL L-ARRAY LANGUAGES

L-systems were originally defined for string languages to describe the growth of biological systems. These systems have been extended to rectangular arrays[16], circular patterns[14], and hexagonal arrays[15]. In this section we will study the latter and their relation to HCA.

The controlled table hexagonal arrays[15] are either 0-L (context independent) or 1-L (context dependent, dependence on one neighbour). The starting point (axiom) is a hexagon, and there are three types of tables corresponding to the three directions of concatenation $\nearrow$, $\nwarrow$, and $\downarrow$. (6 directions may also be considered.) Each table consists of 0-L rules in normal form a $\rightarrow$ bc or 1-L rules in normal form ab $\rightarrow$ acd with neighbourhood context. Application of a table means that the set of rules in the table acts in parallel along the entire edge defined by the arrowhead. The sequence of application of tables in the arrowhead directions is controlled by regular, context-free or context-sensitive languages. Consider the example given below.

example 4.1 $G_3 = (V, H_0, \rho, C)$

$V = \{O, X\}$ is the set of terminals,

$$H = \begin{array}{cccc} & & X & \\ & X & & X \\ X & & O & \\ & O & & X \\ X & & O & \\ & X & & X \\ & & X & \end{array} \quad \text{is the axiom,}$$

$\rho = \{T_1, T_2, T_3\}$ is the set of tables, and

$C = \{(T_1T_2T_3)^n \mid n \geqslant 0\}$ is the control language regulating the application of tables.

$T_1 = \{ \text{OX} \nearrow \text{OOX}, \ \text{XX} \nearrow \text{XXX} \}$

$T_2 = \{ \text{XO} \nwarrow \text{XOO}, \ \text{XX} \nwarrow \text{XXX} \}$

$$T_3 = \left\{ \begin{array}{c} \text{O} \\ \text{X} \end{array} \downarrow \begin{array}{c} \text{O} \\ \text{O} \\ \text{X} \end{array}, \quad \begin{array}{c} \text{X} \\ \text{X} \end{array} \downarrow \begin{array}{c} \text{X} \\ \text{X} \\ \text{X} \end{array} \right\}$$

The first three members of this language are shown in fig. 11. The sequence of application of tables for generating H_1 is shown in fig. 12.

To give a generator HCA for this language, note that an HCA can incorporate the effect of a control string $T_1T_2T_3$ in one step, whereby all border cells change state from X to O, and all quiescent cells change state to X if they have a neighbour in state X. Thus, starting with the axiom H_0 as the initial configuration (bottommost cell in state [X,#] rather than X), the HCA generates all hexagons belonging to the language through the following transitions :

$\delta(\text{O}) = \text{O}, \quad \delta(\text{X}) = \text{O}, \quad \delta([\text{X},\#]) = \text{O},$

$\delta(q_0)$ = X if all non-quiescent neighbours are in state X,

= [X,#] if there is only one non-quiescent neighbour, in state [X,#]

= q_0 otherwise.

<u>example 4.2</u> $G_4 = (V, H_0, \rho, C)$ where

$V = \{\text{O, B, P, X}\}$

$$H_0 = \begin{array}{ccc} & \text{X} & \\ \text{X} & & \text{X} \\ & \text{X} & \\ \text{X} & & \text{X} \\ & \text{X} & \end{array}$$

$\rho = \{T_1, T_2, T_3\},$

T_1 = {B ↗ BO, O ↗ OO, P ↗ PO, X ↗ XO}
T_2 = {B ↖ BB, O ↖ BO, P ↖ BP, X ↖ BX}
T_3 = {B ↓ B, O ↓ O, P ↓ P, X ↓ X}
P P P P

Here T_1 has the effect of appending an arrowhead with all Os, T_2 appends arrowheads with all Bs, and T_3 appends arrowheads with all Ps. This is an example of a grammar where control $\{T_1^nT_2^nT_3^n \mid n \geqslant 0\}$ gives a language different from that obtained with control $\{(T_1T_2T_3)^n \mid n \geqslant 0\}$. Let C be the former control, i.e., a context-sensitive control. To generate $L_4 = L(G_4)$, an HCA must start with initial configuration H_0, and revert to it after generating each H_i, because H_{i+1} cannot be directly generated from H_i. To achieve this, let the configuration be H_i, $i > 0$ (obtained through control $T_1^iT_2^iT_3^i$), and let D_i (the distinguished cell of H_i) be in state [P,#]. D_i sends a signal to all quiescent cells bordering H_i, to change to a special state \$. D_i then fires all edges which delete symbols P, B, O and then pass the delete signal inwards. So in i time steps the configuration changes to one with axiom H_0, markers \$ along the boundary positions of H_{i+1} (to be constructed), and special state S at cell D_i of H_i. See fig. 13. D_i now sends a signal to B which fires off edge ABC for applications of table T_1. With each application of T_1, edge ABC advances towards the \$'s. When it reaches the \$ edge, application of T_1 is stopped and a signal is sent to F. The process is repeated on edge EFA, applying T_2, until \$'s are reached, and then on edge CDE, with table T_3. At this stage, D_i reverts to state P, D_{i+1} enters state [P,#], and the process of generating H_{i+2} begins. (H_1 is generated from H_0 by a slight modification of the above.) Thus all hexagons belonging to L_4 are generated.

For the general case, let G = (V, H_0, ρ , C) be a controlled table hexagonal L-array grammar. To generate L(G), the HCA begins in the initial configuration H_0. As in the case of HKAG, the 1-D CA vertically below D systematically generates all strings in C. (C may be regular, CF or CS.) For every such string α generated, the HCA constructs axiom H_0 (which may have been overwritten for the previous string), and, by sending signals to appropriate vertices, applies tables in the sequence defined by α.

The process is similar to that of appending arrowheads in an HKAG generator. One point of difference is that in a 1-L system, the quiescent boundary cells have to change state depending on not only the boundary cells but also cells one unit inside the boundary. This requires an intermediate step. For instance, along the $\nearrow$ direction, to implement a rule ex $\rightarrow$ egh, the quiescent cell does not know state e directly. So the intermediate step brings information outwards as follows:

$$\delta\begin{pmatrix} & a & \\ f & & b \\ & x & \\ e & & c \\ & d & \end{pmatrix} = [ex].$$

In the next step, the e and x cells are in states ye, ex for some y. So the quiescent cell (in position b) now knows both e and x directly from its neighbour and can accordingly change state. Such intermediate transitions must be defined for all directions.

Recognising such languages follows the method described in section 3: generate-and-compare. So it is not discussed here. In both types of languages, this recognition method will be inefficient, and it will be of interest to investigate efficient recognition algorithms for the HCA.

5. CONCLUSION

In this paper, hexagonal cellular automata have been introduced as a variation of the 2-D RCA, and their relationship to hexagonal array languages has been investigated. One of the applications of hexagonal arrays is to the 2-D representation of 3-D scenes composed of rectangular parallelepipeds. Manipulating (rotation, translation and scaling) such scenes is an important part of computer graphics software. It would be very useful if efficient parallel algorithms for these, running on 2-D or even 3-D cellular processors, could be devised. Also, it is of interest to find more efficient ways of accepting hexagonal array languages. This could assist in pattern recognition where the patterns are types of blocks.

FIGURES

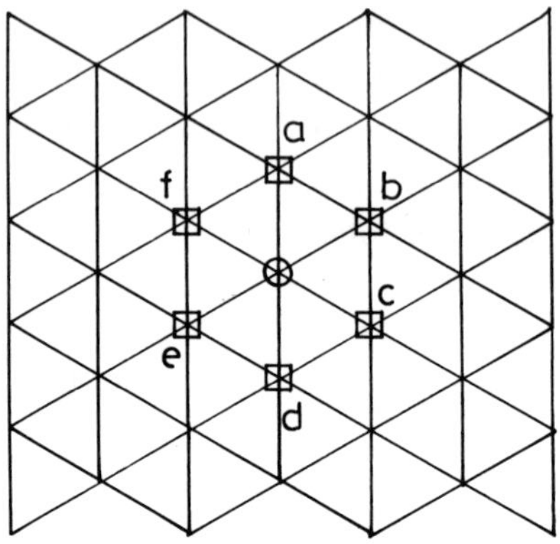

○ : cell in HCA

□ : its neighbour

Figure. 1.
Neighbourhoods in HCA

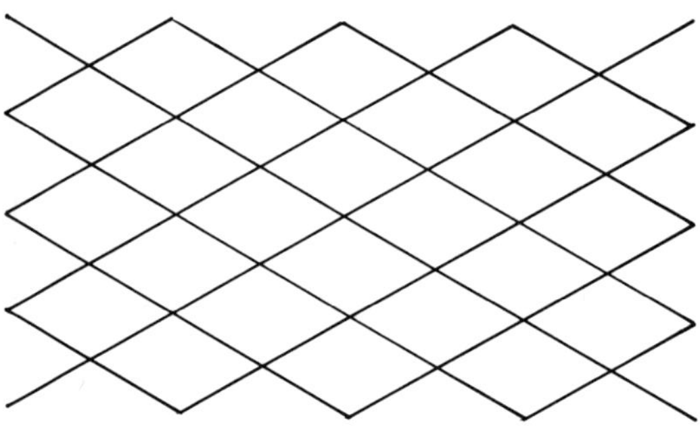

Figure. 2.
HCA with family of vertical lines missing.

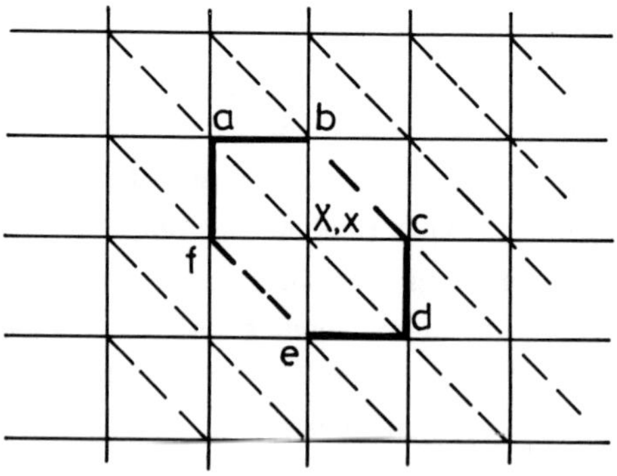

Figure. 3.
HCA embedded on RCA

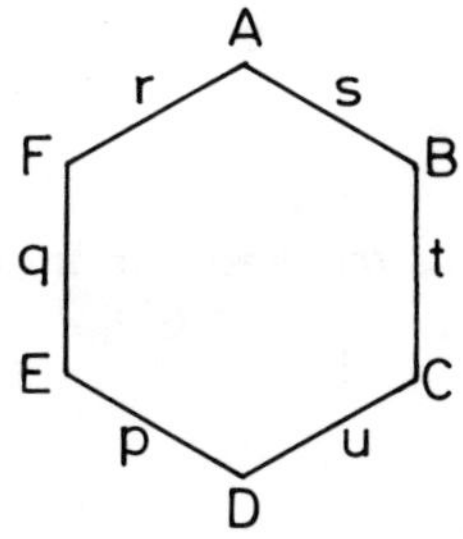

Figure. 4.
Lengths of sides of a convex hexagon.

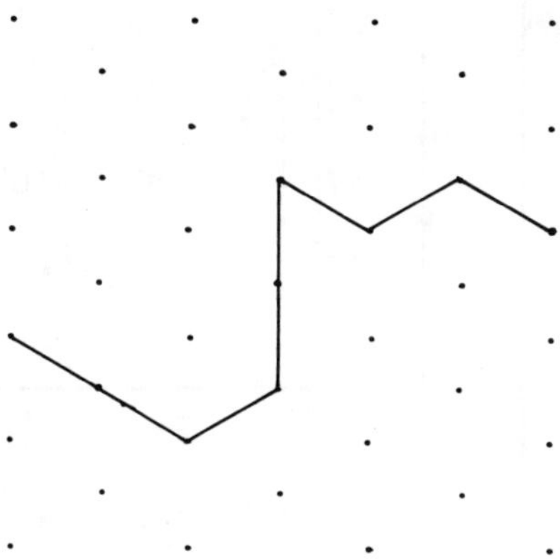

Figure. 5.
1-D CA embedded in HCA configuration

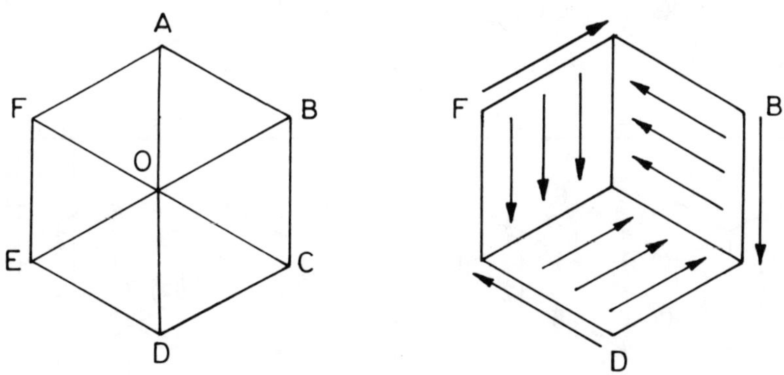

Figure. 6. Firing Squad Algorithm

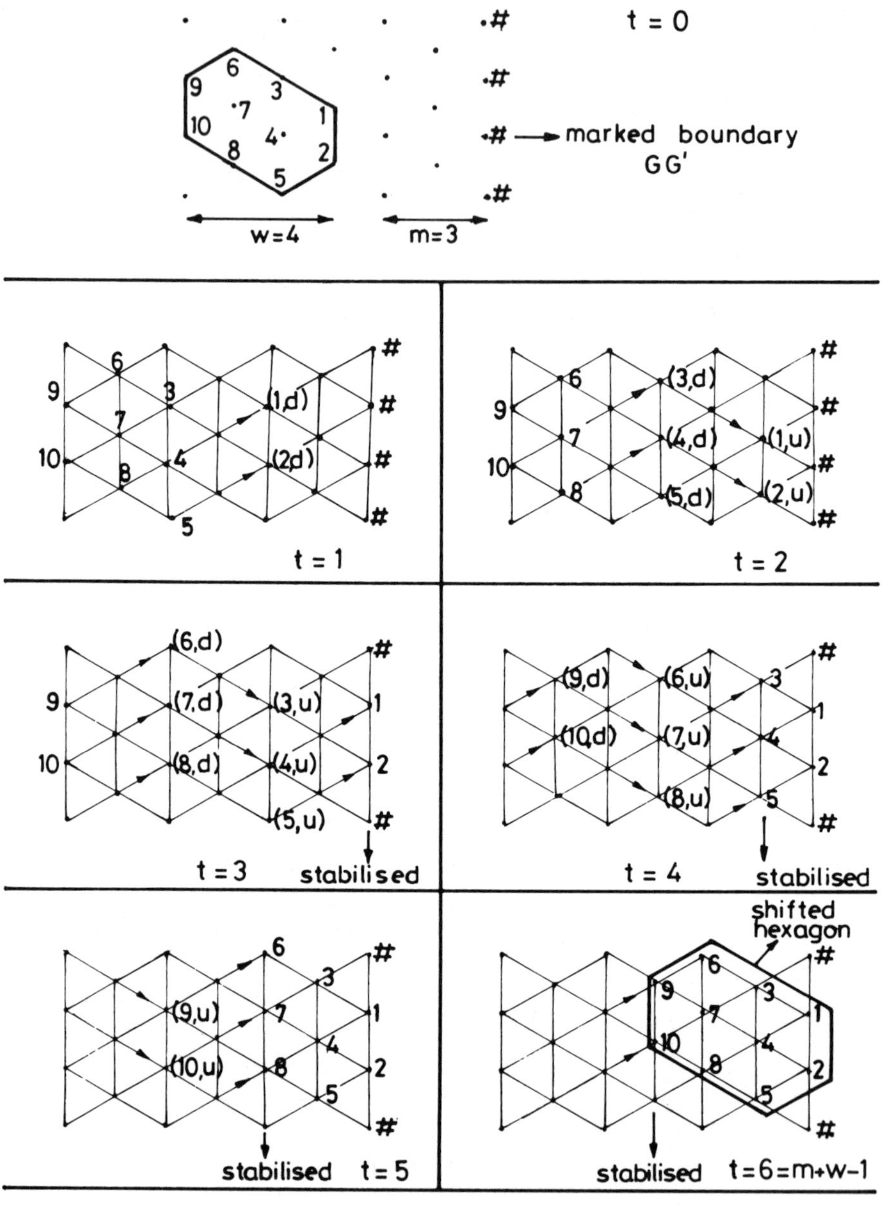

Figure. 7. Algorithm 6 illustrated

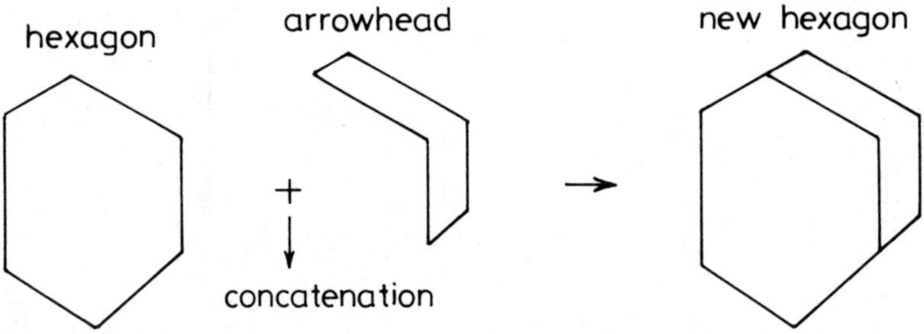

Figure. 8. Arrowhead concatenation

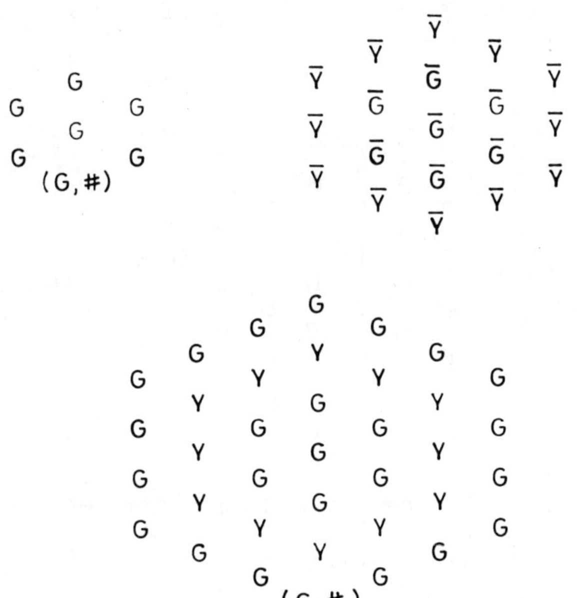

Figure. 9. The first 3 configurations of generator HCA.

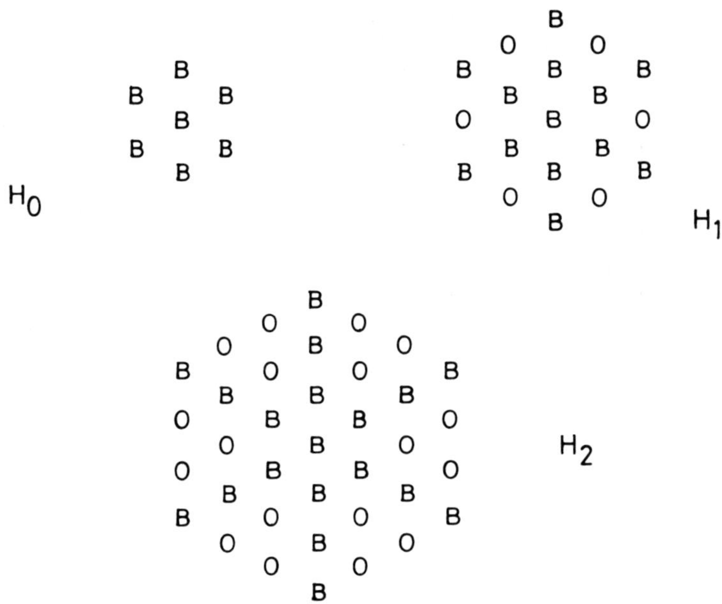

Figure. 10. The first three members of $L(G_1)$

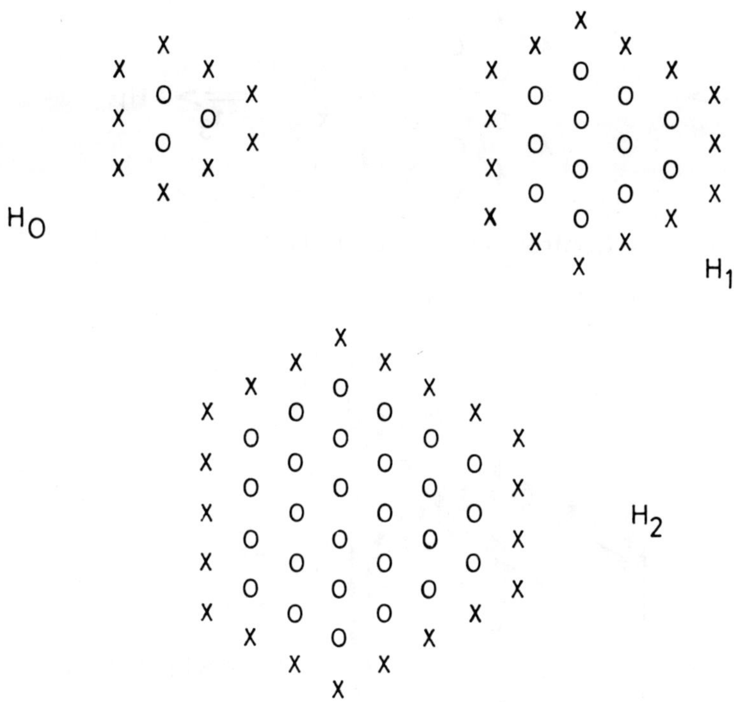

Figure. 11. The first three members of $L(G_3)$.

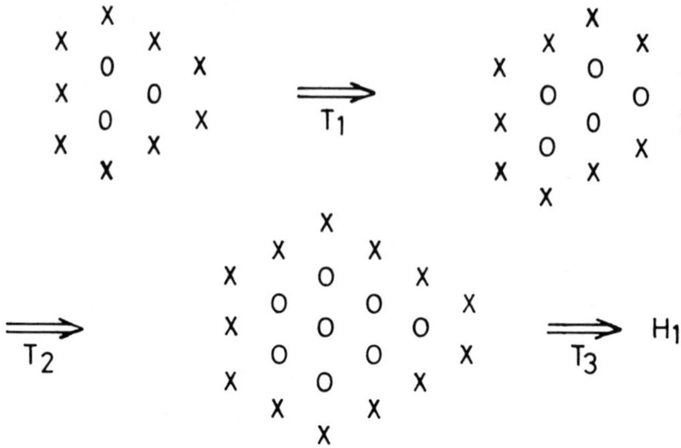

Control string = $T_1 T_2 T_3$

Figure. 12 Derivation of H_1 in $L(G_3)$

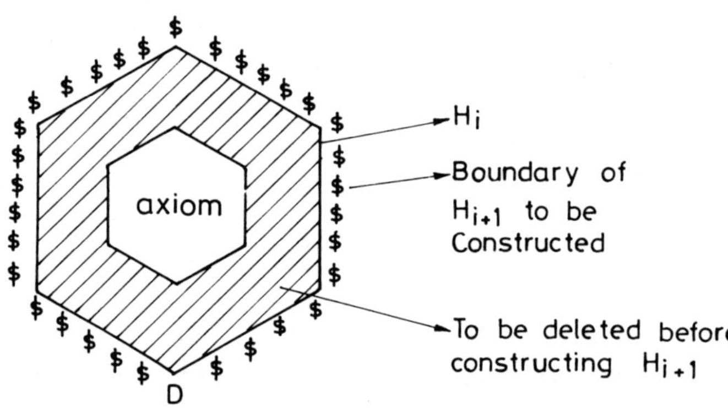

Figure. 13. Generator HCA for $L(G_4)$

References

1. Codd, E. F., "Cellular Automata", ACM Monograph Series(1968).

2. Culik, K., III, and Karhumaki, J., "On totalistic systolic networks", Information Processing Letters 26, 231-236 (1987/88).

3. Ibarra, O. H., Kim, S. M., and Moran, S., "Sequential Machine characterizations of trellis and cellular automata and applications" SIAM Journal of Computing 14, 426-447 (1985).

4. Krithivasan, K., Thulasiraman, K., and Swamy, M. N. S., "Systolic pyramid automata - properties and characterizations", submitted for publication.

5. Krithivasan, K., and Mahajan, M., "Hexagonal cellular automata", Technical Report, Dept. of Computer Science and Engg., I.I.T., Madras (November 1988).

6. Minsky, M., "Computation : Finite and Infinite Machines", Englewood Cliffs, N.J., Prentice Hall (1967).

7. Narasimhan, R., and Reddy, V. S. N., in "Some experiments in scene generation using COMPAX in Graphics Languages" (F. Nake and A. Rosenfeld, Eds.), pp. 111-120, Amsterdam, North-Holland (1972).

8. Preston, K., Jr., "Applications of cellular automata in biomedical image processing", in 'Computer Techniques in Biomedicine and Medicine' (Enoch Haga, Ed.), Auerbach, Philadelphia (1973).

9. Rosenfeld, A., and Pfaltz, J. L., "Distance functions on digital pictures", Pattern Recognition 1, 33-61 (1968).

10. Sankar, P. V., "A vertex coding scheme for interpreting ambiguous

trihedral solids", TR 127, Tata Institute of Fundamental Research, Bombay (November 1974).

11. Siromoney, G., Siromoney, R., and Krithivasan, K., "Abstract families of matrices and picture languages", Computer Graphics and Image Processing 1, 284-307 (1972).

12. Siromoney, G., Siromoney, R., and Krithivasan, K., "Picture languages with array rewriting rules", Information Control 22, 447-470 (1973).

13. Siromoney, G., Siromoney, R., and Krithivasan, K., "Array grammars and kolam", Computer Graphics and Image Processing 3, 63-82 (1974).

14. Siromoney, G., and Siromoney, R., "Radial grammars and radial L-systems", Computer Graphics and Image Processing 4, 361-374 (1975).

15. Siromoney, G., and Siromoney, R., "Hexagonal arrays and rectangular blocks", Computer Graphics and Image Processing 5, 353-381 (1976).

16. Siromoney, R., and Siromoney, G., "Extended controlled table arrays", TR-304, Computer Science Centre, University of Maryland (May 1974).

17. Smith, A. R., III, "Cellular automata and formal languages", in Proceedings, 11th SWAT, pp. 216-224 (1970).

18. Smith, A. R., III, "Real-time language recognition by one-dimensional cellular automata", JCSS 6, 233-253 (1972).

19. Sommerhalder, R., and van Westrhenen, S. C., "Parallel language recognition in constant time by cellular automata", Acta Informatica 19, 397-407 (1983).

A Petri Net Model of Asynchronously Communicating Sequential Processes

Madhavan Mukund and P. S. Thiagarajan
The Institute of Mathematical Sciences,
Madras 600 113, INDIA

ABSTRACT

We propose a net-based model called Asynchronously Communicating Sequential Systems (ACSSs) to study asynchronous communication. We restrict ourselves to systems consisting of a finite number of sequential agents that communicate with each other via messages sent along one-way "process-to-process" channels whose capacity can be, in general, unbounded. In this model, a sequential agent is denoted by a restricted type of Petri net called a safe S-net, in which no two transitions can ever occur concurrently. The channels are modelled by ordinary Petri net places. We show that the theory of trace languages can be extended to capture the non-sequential behaviour of an ACSS. We also show that our trace semantics leads in a smooth fashion to an event structure semantics of ACSSs. In some sense, both the theory of traces and the theory of event structures have so far "worked" only for safe Petri nets. Hence our results identify a (much) larger class of Petri nets — with a nice interpretation — to which these two theories can be applied.

0. INTRODUCTION

Asynchronous communication is one of the popular means of achieving coordination between the components of a distributed system. When the components are located at a considerable physical distance from each other, "message passing" is the only means for achieving coordination.

In this paper we put forward a simple model of distributed systems where the system is assumed to be composed out of a finite number of sequential components which communicate asynchronously with each other (i.e. they pass messages to each other). By a sequential component we mean a subsystem which does not exhibit any concurrency in its behaviour, even if run autonomously. Our major aim is to demonstrate that a non-interleaved behavioural description of such a system can be given using standard techniques that have traditionally been applied to capture the behaviour of synchronously communicating distributed systems.

To be specific, our model is called Asynchronously Communicating Sequential Systems (ACSSs, for short). It is based on a class of Petri nets. We start with purely sequential behavioural descriptions of an ACSS called <u>firing sequences</u>. We then show how the theory of traces initiated by Mazurkiewicz [M] can be generalized to recover information concerning concurrency from the firing sequences. We first partition the set of firing sequences with the help of an equivalence relation. Next, we impose a standard ordering relation over the equivalence classes of firing sequences. We then prove that the resulting poset is of a kind that lets us recover a labelled event structure from it in a canonical fashion. Event structures are a poset-based model of distributed systems and processes. In an event structure the three fundamental phenomena of causality, concurrency and indeterminacy (also called choice or conflict) are clearly separated from each other. Event structures have an extensive theory [W2]. This theory has strong connections to net theory [NPW,T1], the theory of trace languages [RoT] and Domain theory [W2]. The event structure formalism has been successfully applied to provide the non-interleaved denotational semantics of CCS-like languages [W1].

In Section 1, we formulate the ACSS model. Our model is, in some sense, an extended version of a model studied by Reisig [R], where the main aim was to characterize freedom from deadlock. The ACSS model is a simplified version of the so-called FIFO nets [FM]. An ACSS can also be viewed as a formal and "pure" (i.e. uninterpreted) version of a model that has been used by various researchers in the study of distributed algorithms [DS,CM1,CM2,CL].

In Section 2, we provide a brief introduction to the theory of event structures. In particular, we characterize those posets that permit an event structure to be extracted from them in a canonical manner.

In Section 3, we define an equivalence relation over the firing sequences of an ACSS. The notion of firing sequences is the standard one taken from net theory [RT]. Our choice of the equivalence relation has been strongly guided by the theory of trace languages. It may be viewed as a non-trivial generalization of the basic idea underlying the theory of trace languages. We then impose an ordering relation over the equivalence classes of firing sequences. The rest of the section is devoted to establishing some basic properties of the resulting poset.

In Section 4, we demonstrate that this poset of equivalence classes of firing sequences falls in the class characterized in Section 1. As a result, we obtain an event structure representation of the behaviour of an ACSS. The intermediate lemmas stated in this section have exact counterparts in [RoT]. Hence, in order to save space, we do not give detailed proofs here.

In the final section, we summarize the contents of the paper and point to some more related literature.

1. THE MODEL

An ACSS will be modelled as a special kind of marked net. Hence, we shall begin with a rapid introduction to marked nets and related terminology. For more details concerning the theory of marked nets, the reader is referred to [P,R,RT].

Definition 1.1

A net is a triple $N = (S,T,F)$ where

i) S and T are sets such that $S \cap T = \emptyset$ and $S \cup T \neq \emptyset$.

ii) $F \subseteq (S \times T) \cup (T \times S)$ such that

$$\text{domain}(F) \cup \text{range}(F) = S \cup T, \text{ where}$$

$$\text{domain}(F) = \{ x \mid \exists y.\ (x,y) \in F \} \text{ and}$$

$$\text{range}(F) = \{ y \mid \exists x.\ (x,y) \in F \}. \qquad \square$$

S is the set of S-elements, T is the set of T-elements and F is the flow relation. In diagrams, the S-elements will be drawn as circles, the T-elements will be drawn as boxes and the flow relation will be represented through directed arcs. Figure 1.1 is an example of a net.

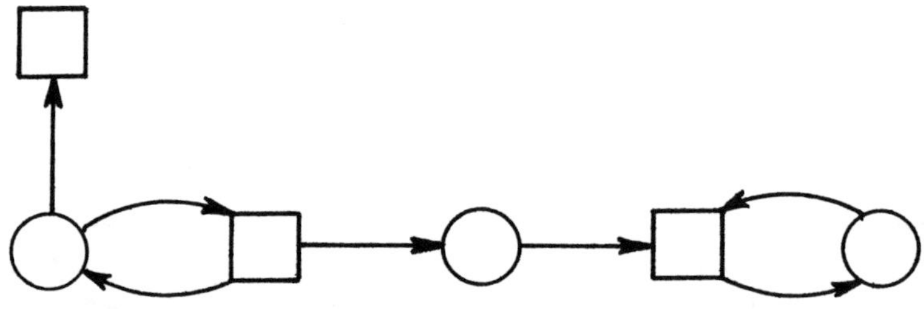

Figure 1.1

It is clear that a net may be viewed as a directed bipartite graph. Hence, we shall apply standard graph theoretic terminology in talking about nets without bothering to nail down the formal details.

Let $N = (S,T,F)$ be a net. Then $X = S \cup T$ is the set of elements of N. The notation we now introduce to talk about the neighbourhood of a net element will be used extensively in this paper.

Let $x \in X$. Then $^{\bullet}x = \{ y \mid (y,x) \in F \}$ and

$x^{\bullet} = \{ y \mid (x,y) \in F \}$.

This "dot" notation is extended to a subset of elements in the obvious way. In this paper, we shall often refer to the S-elements as <u>places</u> and the T-elements as <u>transitions</u>. If t is a transition in the net $N = (S,T,F)$ then $^{\bullet}t$ will be called the set of <u>input places</u> of t and $t^{\bullet}$ will be called the set of <u>output places</u> of t.

A <u>marking</u> of the net $N = (S,T,F)$ is a function $M : S \to \mathbb{N}_0 = \{0,1,2,...\}$. The transition t is said to be <u>enabled</u> at the marking M if $M(s) \geq 1$ for every $s \in {}^{\bullet}t$. This is denoted by $M[t>$. A transition may <u>occur</u> at a marking only if it is enabled at that marking. When t occurs at M, a new marking M′ is obtained which is given by:

$$\forall s \in S. \quad M'(s) = \begin{cases} M(s) - 1, & \text{if } s \in {}^{\bullet}t - t^{\bullet} \\ M(s) + 1, & \text{if } s \in t^{\bullet} - {}^{\bullet}t \\ M(s) & \text{otherwise.} \end{cases}$$

The transformation of M into M′ by the occurrence of t at M will be denoted as $M[t>M'$. It will be convenient to extend this idea to a sequence of transitions. We shall say that $t_0 t_1 \ldots t_n$ is a <u>firing sequence</u> at the marking M, if there exists a sequence of markings $M_0, M_1, \ldots, M_{n+1}$ with $M = M_0$ such that for $0 \leq i \leq n$, $M_i[t_i>M_{i+1}$. The transformation of M_0 into M_{n+1} by the occurrence of $t_0 t_1 \ldots t_n$ starting at M will be denoted as $M[t_0 t_1 \ldots t_{n+1}>M_{n+1}$. By convention, $M[\lambda>M$ for every marking M. Here and elsewhere, λ will represent the null sequence.

<u>Definition 1.2</u>

A <u>marked net</u> is a quadruple $MN = (S,T,F,M_{in})$ where $N_{MN} = (S,T,F)$ is a net called the <u>underlying net</u> of MN and M_{in} is a marking of N_{MN} called the <u>initial marking</u> of MN.

□

FS_{MN} will denote the set of firing sequences of N_{MN} at M_{in}. We will often refer to this set as the set of firing sequences of MN. In diagrams, a marking will be shown by placing M(s) "tokens" (small darkened circles) within the circle representing s. Figure 1.2 is an example of a marked net.

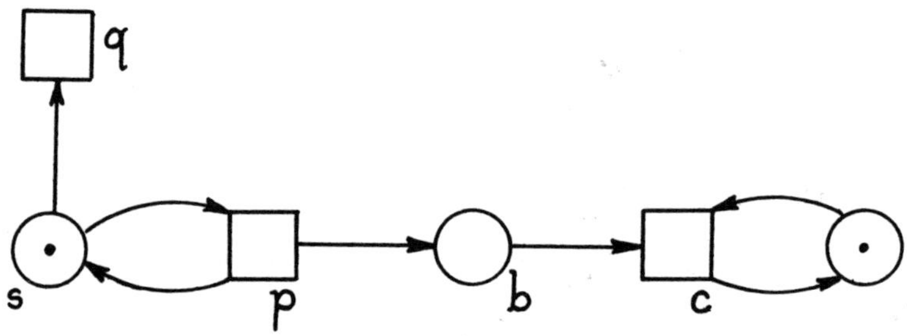

Figure 1.2

ppq, *ppcc* and *ppqc* are some of the firing sequences of this marked net.

The structure of a sequential component in an ACSS can be captured with the help of a restricted kind of net called an S-net.

An <u>S-net</u> is a net N = (S,T,F) such that $\forall t \in T$, $|{}^{\cdot}t| \le 1$ and $|t^{\cdot}| \le 1$. In this paper we shall in fact assume that for every S-net N = (S,T,F) we consider, it is the case that $|{}^{\cdot}t| = 1$ and $|t^{\cdot}| = 1$ for every $t \in T$.

Let N = (S,T,F) be a finite (i.e. $S \cup T$ is a finite set) and connected S-net and let M be a marking such that $\sum_{s \in S} M(s) = 1$. It is easy to see that the marked net (S,T,F,M) represents a sequential state machine (which, in general, will be incompletely specified). In particular, the set of firing sequences of (S,T,F,M) will be a regular subset of T^*. With this in mind we are now prepared to define our model. As a part of the definition we will also introduce a number of notations that will be used through the rest of the paper.

<u>Definition 1.3</u>

An Asynchronously Communicating Sequential System (ACSS) is a structure $\mathcal{S} = (N_1, N_2, \ldots N_n, B, L, M_{in})$ which satisfies the following conditions.

i) $n \geq 1$ and we let i, j and k range over $\{1,2,\ldots n\}$.

ii) Each N_i is a finite connected S-net with $N_i = (S_i, T_i, F_i)$. We set $X_i = S_i \cup T_i$, $S = \bigcup_{i=1}^{n} S_i$, $T = \bigcup_{i=1}^{n} T_i$, $X = S \cup T$ and $F = \bigcup_{i=1}^{n} F_i$.

iii) If $i \neq j$ then $X_i \cap X_j = \emptyset$.

iv) B is a finite set of <u>buffers</u> such that $B \cap X = \emptyset$.

v) $L \subseteq (B \times T) \cup (T \times B)$ is the <u>communication relation</u> and we set ${}^{\bullet}b = \{t \mid (t,b) \in L\}$ and $b^{\bullet} = \{t \mid (b,t) \in L\}$ for every $b \in B$.

vi) L is such that for each $b \in B$ there exist <u>distinct</u> i and j such that ${}^{\bullet}b \subseteq T_i$ and $b^{\bullet} \subseteq T_j$.

vii) $M_{in} : S \cup B \rightarrow \mathbb{N}_0$ is the <u>initial marking</u> and it satisfies

$$\sum_{s \in S_i} M_{in}(s) = 1 \text{ for every } i$$

□

The first three clauses together with the last clause say that there are n sequential components (i.e. <u>agents</u>) that are pair-wise disjoint. They communicate with each other via buffers, as specified by the communication relation. The communication is point-to-point and unidirectional, and no agent communicates directly with itself. The communication conditions are captured by clauses iv to vi.

The marked net shown in Figure 1.2 may be viewed as an ACSS consisting of two agents. The first agent (which may be termed the producer) is represented by the S-net ({s},{p,q},{(s,p),(p,s),(s,q)}). The producer communicates with the second agent, which may be called the consumer , via the buffer b. The communication relation for this system is {(p,b),(b,c)}.

Given an ACSS $\mathcal{S} = \{N_1, N_2, . . . N_n, B, L, M_{in}\}$ we can associate with $\mathcal{S}$ the marked net $\hat{\mathcal{S}} = (\hat{S}, \hat{T}, \hat{F}, \hat{M}_{in})$, where $\hat{S} = S \cup B$, $\hat{T} = T$, $\hat{F} = F \cup L$ and $\hat{M}_{in} = M_{in}$ (recall the notations introduced in Definition 2.3). Consequently, the notions we have introduced for marked nets can be carried over to ACSSs in a smooth fashion. In what follows we will often not distinguish between the ACSS $\mathcal{S}$ and the associated marked net $\hat{\mathcal{S}}$. This should cause no confusion.

As noted earlier, the autonomous behaviour of an individual agent in an ACSS will be regular. This is due to the fact that the underlying net is a finite connected S-net carrying only one token at the initial marking. However, once the agents start to communicate with each other, their individual behaviours might no longer be regular. We can bring this out in an informal fashion through an example, shown in Figure 1.3.

In this ACSS, the autonomous behaviour of the agent A_1 is the prefix closure of the set a^*bc^* which is a regular subset of $\{a,b,c\}^*$. However, if we project the set of

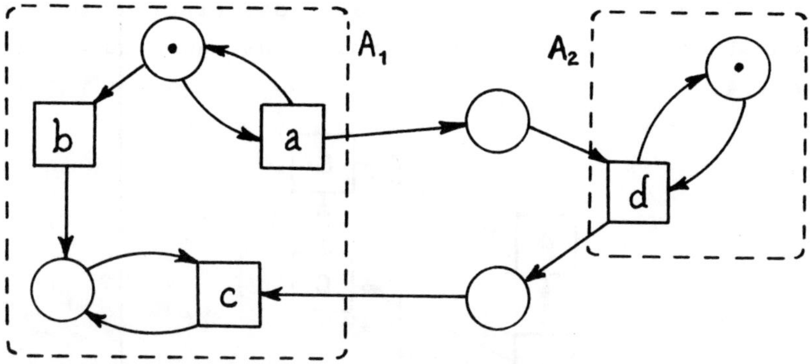

Figure 1.3

firing sequences of the entire ACSS onto A_1 (i.e. we erase all occurrences of d) then we get the prefix closure of the set $\{ a^m bc^n | m \le n \ge 0 \}$ which is not a regular subset of $\{a,b,c\}^*$.

It is also easy to observe that the set of firing sequences of an ACSS, in general, is <u>not</u> a regular subset of the free monoid generated by its set of transitions. This follows from the two examples we have shown so far.

We now turn to the main task of the paper. Our aim is to find a behavioural description of an ACSS which clearly represents the causality, concurrency and indeterminacy contained in the behaviour of the system. It is not difficult to see that the set of firing sequences of an ACSS is merely a good <u>starting</u> point for working out such a behavioural description. This is because the firing sequence representation "loses", in some sense, information concerning concurrency (i.e non-sequentiality) and conflict.

To see this, consider the ACSS shown in Figure 1.2. The firing sequences *ppcc* and *pcpc* both represent the <u>same</u>

stretch of behaviour. An adequate description of this stretch of behaviour would be through the labelled poset in Figure 1.4.

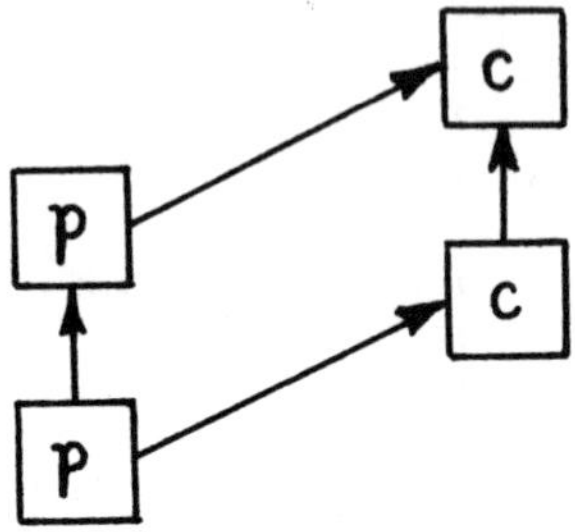

Figure 1.4

On the other hand, the firing sequences *pq* and *ppq* represent two stretches of behaviour that are mutually exclusive. These two behavioural possibilities are best represented together as a labelled tree, as in Figure 1.5.

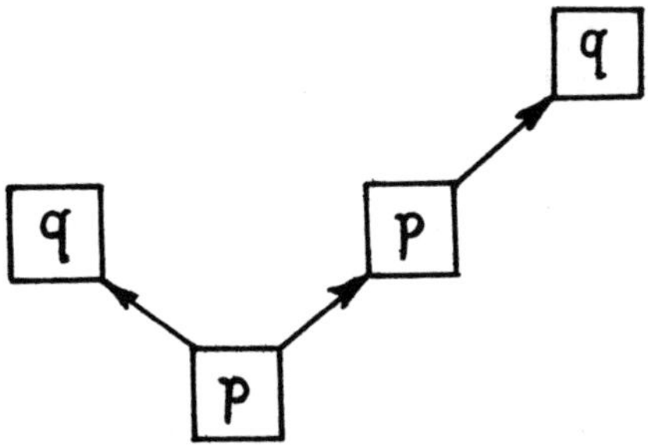

Figure 1.5

With both concurrency and indeterminacy present, firing sequences hide a lot of important information. We propose to extract this information by generalizing the trace theory approach of [M]. Our final target is a labelled event structure representation of the behaviour of an ACSS in which all information concerning causality, concurrency and conflict is made available explicitly.

2. EVENT STRUCTURES

An event structure represents the behaviour of a distributed system through a set of event occurrences, a causality relation that partially orders the event occurrences and a conflict relation which reflects the choices available to the system.

Definition 2.1

An event structure is a triple ES = (E, ≤, #) where

i) E is a set of events

ii) ≤ ⊆ E x E is a partial order, called the causality relation.

iii) # ⊆ E x E is an irreflexive, symmetric relation, called the conflict relation.

iv) For any e_1, e_2, e_3 in E, e_1 # e_2 and $e_2 \le e_3$ implies e_1 # e_3

□

The last clause in the definition ensures that the past of every event is "consistent", in the sense of being conflict-free. This will become clear once we introduce the notion of a configuration.

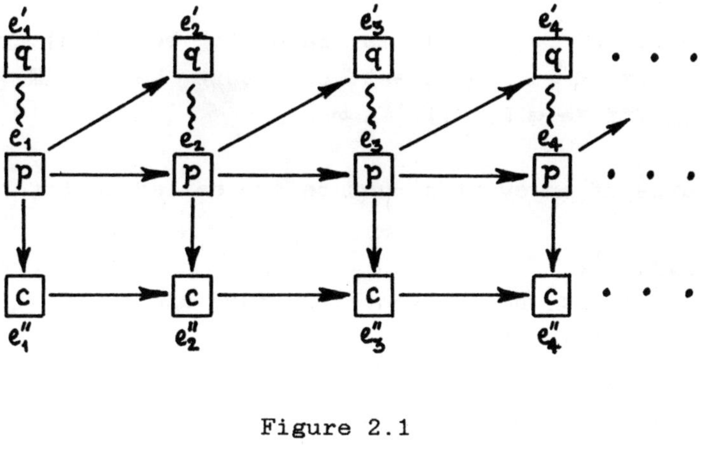

Figure 2.1

Figure 2.1 shows an example of an event structure. The events have been labelled to model the situation of Figure 1.2, where a producer communicates items via an unbounded buffer to a consumer. The producer can quit after producing zero or more items. Both the producer and the consumer are assumed to work sequentially.

For convenience, in Figure 2.1 we have shown only the "minimal" elements of the causality relation (as directed arcs) and the conflict relation (as squiggly lines). Thus, $e_1 \leq e_3$ because $e_1 \leq e_2$ and $e_2 \leq e_3$. Moreover, $e_1' \# e_2''$ since $e_1' \# e_1$ and $e_1 \leq e_2''$.

We restrict our attention to the class of finitary event structures. In this class, each event is guaranteed to have a finite past. More precisely, we have the following definitions.

Let $(X,\sqsubseteq)$ be a poset and $Y \subseteq X$. Then,

$$\downarrow Y = \{x \in X \mid \exists y \in Y.\ x \sqsubseteq y\}$$

For an event structure $ES = (E,\leq,\#)$ and a set $Y \subseteq E$, $\downarrow Y$ is defined in a similar manner with respect to $\leq$. For $Y = \{y\}$, we write $\downarrow y$ instead of $\downarrow\{y\}$.

The poset $PO = (X,\sqsubseteq)$ is said to be <u>finitary</u> iff $\forall x \in X,\ |\downarrow x| < \infty$. The event structure $ES = (E,\leq,\#)$ is <u>finitary</u> iff $\forall e \in E,\ |\downarrow e| < \infty$.

The states of an event structure are called configurations.

<u>Definition 2.2</u>

Let $ES = (E,\leq,\#)$ be an event structure and $c \subseteq E$

i) c is <u>#-free</u> iff $(c \times c) \cap \# = \emptyset$.

ii) c is <u>left-closed</u> iff $c = \downarrow c$.

iii) c is a <u>configuration</u> iff c is #-free and left-closed.

iv) C^{∞}_{ES} = {c ⊆ E | c is a configuration }

v) C_{ES} = {c ⊆ E | c is a <u>finite</u> configuration } □

For the event structure shown in Figure 2.1, $\{e_1, e_2\}$, $\{e_1, e_2, e_1''\}$ and $\{e_1, e_2, e_3, \ldots\}$ are configurations, but $\{e_1, e_1'\}$ and $\{e_1, e_2, e_2''\}$ are not.

A configuration represents a state of the system after the occurrence of a subset of events. The definition captures the intuitive notion of when such a state is "reachable" in a given system. First, an event can occur only after all the events that lie in its past have occurred. Further, two conflicting events cannot both occur in the same stretch of behaviour. Consequently, two events that are neither ordered causally nor in conflict with each other can occur concurrently.

We now make precise the statement made earlier, that the definition of an event structure ensures that the past of each event is consistent in the sense of being conflict-free.

<u>Proposition 2.3</u>

For a (finitary) event structure ES = (E,≤,#) and e ∈ E, ↓e is a (finite) configuration.

<u>Proof</u>

Follows from the definitions. □

It is possible to characterize finitary event structures in terms of their finite configurations ordered under inclusion. For this we need to introduce the notion of a finitely coherent, prime algebraic poset.

We assume the standard notion of consistency in a poset PO = (X,⊑). Given a set Y ⊆ X, we say that Y is

<u>consistent</u>, denoted $Y\uparrow$, if Y has an upper bound in X. Y is said to be <u>pairwise consistent</u> iff any two of its elements have an upper bound in X. If $Y = \{y_1, y_2\}$, we write $y_1 \uparrow y_2$ rather than $\{y_1, y_2\}\uparrow$.

As usual, for a poset PO = $(X, \sqsubseteq)$ and a set $Y \subseteq X$, we shall denote the least upper bound (l.u.b.) and greatest lower bound (g.l.b.) of Y by $\sqcup Y$ and $\sqcap Y$ respectively, whenever they exist.

The poset PO = $(X, \sqsubseteq)$ is said to be <u>(finitely) coherent</u> iff every (finite) pairwise consistent subset of X has a l.u.b. in X.

The poset shown in Figure 2.2 is <u>not</u> finitely coherent because $\{x_1, x_2, x_3\}$ is a pairwise consistent set of elements which does not have a l.u.b.

Let PO = $(X, \sqsubseteq)$ be a poset. An element $p \in X$ is said to be a <u>prime</u> iff for every $Y \subseteq X$, if $\sqcup Y$ exists and $p \sqsubseteq \sqcup Y$, then there exists $y \in Y$ such that $p \sqsubseteq y$.
PO = $(X, \sqsubseteq)$ is <u>prime algebraic</u> iff

$$\forall x \in X.\ x = \sqcup\{p \in X \mid p \text{ is a prime and } p \sqsubseteq x\}.$$

Figure 2.3 is an example of a poset which is <u>not</u> prime algebraic. We have indicated the prime elements by

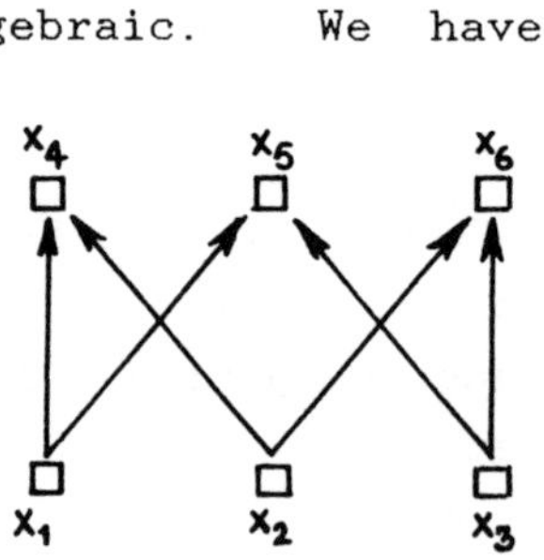

Figure 2.2

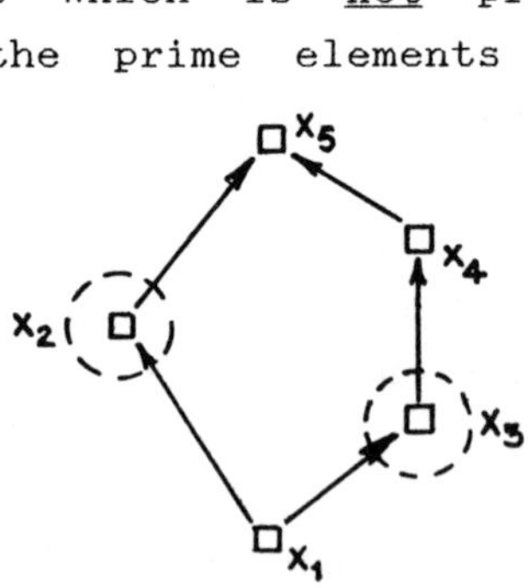

Figure 2.3

circling them. x_4 is not a prime element because $x_2 \sqcup x_3 = x_5$ and $x_4 \sqsubseteq x_5$ but neither $x_4 \sqsubseteq x_2$ nor $x_4 \sqsubseteq x_3$. This poset is not prime algebraic because x_4 is not the l.u.b. of all the primes below it.

In [NPW], a representation result is established linking event structures to coherent prime algebraic posets. Based on this result, it is easy to establish the following link between a finitary event structure ES, and the poset $(C_{ES}, \subseteq)$ of the finite configurations of ES ordered under inclusion.

<u>Theorem 2.4</u>

Let ES = $(E, \leq, \#)$ be a finitary event structure. Then $(C_{ES}, \subseteq)$ is a finitary, finitely coherent, prime algebraic poset with $\{\downarrow e \mid e \in E\}$ as its set of primes. We shall denote this poset by $\mathcal{PO}$ [ES].

□

In the converse direction, we have the following result.

<u>Theorem 2.5</u>

Let PO = $(X, \sqsubseteq)$ be a finitary, finitely coherent, prime algebraic poset. Then ES = $(P, \leq, \#)$ is an event structure, where

i) $P \subseteq X$ is the set of primes of PO.

ii) For all $p_1, p_2 \in P$, $p_1 \leq p_2$ iff $p_1 \sqsubseteq p_2$.

iii) For all $p_1, p_2 \in P$, $p_1 \# p_2$ iff not $p_1 \uparrow p_2$.

We shall denote this event structure by $\mathcal{ES}$ [PO]. □

It is a pleasant surprise that the mappings defined in Theorems 2.4 and 2.5 yield, under composition, isomorphisms over the appropriate classes of objects.

For event structures ES and ES′, we write ES $\simeq$ ES′ to indicate that ES and ES′ are isomorphic in the obvious sense. By abuse of notation, the symbol $\simeq$ will also be used to denote that a pair of posets are isomorphic.

<u>Corollary 2.6</u>
Let ES = $(E,\le,\#)$ be a finitary event structure and PO = $(X,\sqsubseteq)$ be a finitely coherent, prime algebraic poset. Then

i) $ES \simeq \mathcal{ES}[\mathcal{PO}[ES]]$

ii) $PO \simeq \mathcal{PO}[\mathcal{ES}[PO]]$

□

As a result of this corollary, we can freely move back and forth between event structures and finitely coherent prime algebraic posets.

Before concluding this section, we introduce the notion of a labelled event structure. Let Σ be a finite, non-empty alphabet set. A (Σ)-<u>labelled event structure</u> is a quadruple ES = $(E,\le,\#,\varphi)$, where $(E,\le,\#)$ is an event structure and $\varphi : E \to \Sigma$ is the <u>labelling function</u>.

Figure 2.1 may be viewed as example of a Σ-labelled event structure with $\Sigma = \{p,q,c\}$.

3. THE TRACE SEMANTICS

The aim now is to extract information concerning conflicts and concurrency from the set of firing sequences of an ACSS.

For the rest of the paper we fix an ACSS $\mathcal{A} = (N_1, N_2, \ldots, N_n, B, L, M_{in})$. As mentioned earlier, we shall often not distinguish between $\mathcal{A}$ and the associated marked net $\hat{\mathcal{A}} = (\hat{S},\hat{T},\hat{F},\hat{M}_{in})$. FS $\subseteq (\hat{T})^*$ will denote the set of firing sequences of $\mathcal{A}$, where $(\hat{T})^*$ will denote as usual the free monoid generated by $\hat{T}$. We let x,y and z with or without subscripts range over $(\hat{T})^*$. We let $\rho, \rho', \sigma, \sigma'$ with or without subscripts range over FS. We let a,b and d with or without subscripts range over $\hat{T}$. $|x|$ will denote the length of the sequence x and $\#_a(x)$ will denote the number of times a appears in x.

$[M_{in}>$ will denote the set of <u>reachable markings</u> of $\hat{\mathcal{S}}$ and is defined to be the least set of markings of $(\hat{S},\hat{T},\hat{F})$ containing M_{in} such that if $M \in [M_{in}>$ and $M[a>M'$ then $M' \in [M_{in}>$. It will be convenient to define the function $f: FS \rightarrow [M_{in}>$ given by $f(\rho) = M$ where $M_{in}[\rho>M$. To simplify notation we will always write M_ρ instead of $f(\rho)$.

We start with some simple but useful observations.

<u>Proposition 3.1</u>

i) $\forall M \in [M_{in}>. \forall i \in \{1,2,\ldots,n\}. \sum_{s \in S_i} M(s) = 1$

ii) Suppose $M_\rho[a>$ and $M_\rho[b>$ with $a \in T_i$ and $b \in T_j$ such that $i \neq j$. Then $\rho ab \in FS$ and $\rho ba \in FS$. Moreover, $M_{\rho ab} = M_{\rho ba}$.

<u>Proof</u>:

Both parts of the result follow easily from the definitions.

□

For capturing the equivalence relation we have in mind, it will be convenient to introduce one addition piece of notation. Let $X \subseteq T$. Then $x \upharpoonright X$ is the sequence obtained by erasing from x all letters that are not members of X.

Formally, $x \upharpoonright X$ is defined inductively as:

i) $\lambda \upharpoonright X = \lambda$

ii) $ya \upharpoonright X = \begin{cases} (y \upharpoonright X)a, & \text{if } a \in X \\ (y \upharpoonright X), & \text{otherwise} \end{cases}$

Definition 3.2

i) $\rho \sim \rho' \triangleq \rho\restriction T_i = \rho'\restriction T_i$ for every $i \in \{1,2,..,n\}$.

ii) $[\rho] = \{\rho' | \rho \sim \rho'\}$.

iii) $FS/\sim = \{[\rho] | \rho \in FS\}$.

□

Clearly, $\sim$ is an equivalence relation. It is important to note that $\sim$ by definition is a subset of FS x FS and not a subset of $(\hat{T})^* \times (\hat{T})^*$. Hence, whenever, we write $x \sim y$, we mean that $x \in FS$ and $y \in FS$ and $x \sim y$. For the ACSS shown in Figure 1.2, $ppcc \sim pcpc$ but $ppc \nsim pqc$. The following facts follow directly from the definition of the relation $\sim$.

Proposition 3.3

Suppose $\rho \sim \rho'$. Then $|\rho| = |\rho'|$. In fact $\#_a(\rho) = \#_a(\rho')$ for every a. Hence $M_\rho = M_{\rho'}$. □

The definition of $\sim$ is a generalization of the trace theory approach initiated in [M]. In trace theory, an irreflexive and symmetric independence relation I is associated with a set of actions Σ. Pairs of actions belonging to I can occur concurrently in all contexts and hence can be commuted whenever they appear adjacent to each other in a sequence of actions. In this manner, I induces a congruence $\simeq$ which is used to partition Σ^*.

Similarly, in our model $\sim$ captures information about concurrency and is used to partition FS into classes of "equivalent" behaviours. This will become clear as we proceed to work out the event structure representation of the behaviour of $\mathcal{A}$. However, here concurrency is "context-dependent", so one cannot capture it by means of a global independence relation on the set $\hat{T}$. It is in this sense that we generalize the trace theory approach.

The next crucial step we take is to define an ordering relation over FS/~.

Definition 3.4

$[\rho] \sqsubseteq [\rho'] \triangleq \forall \rho_1 \in [\rho].\exists \rho'_1 \in [\rho'].\ \rho_1$ is a prefix of ρ'_1 □

Clearly $\sqsubseteq$ is a partial ordering relation. Figure 3.1 shows a fragment of (FS/~,$\sqsubseteq$) for the ACSS of Figure 1.2.

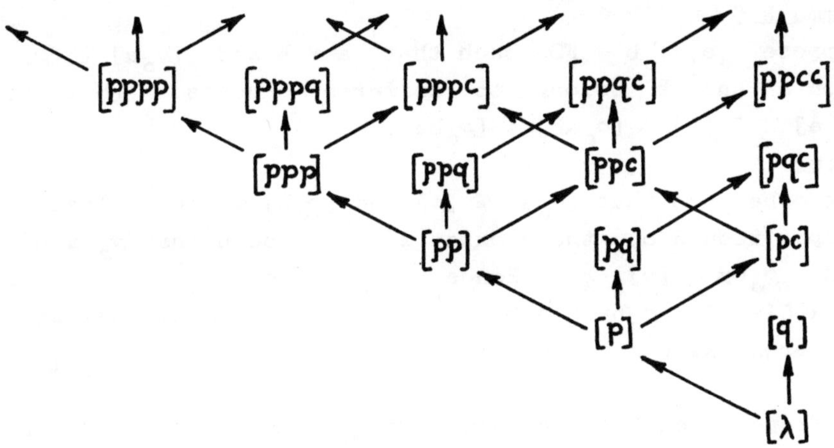

Figure 3.1

The rest of this section will be devoted to working out some basic properties of the poset (FS/~,$\sqsubseteq$). This will enable us to prove the main result in the next section.

Proposition 3.5

The following statements are equivalent

i) $[\rho] \sqsubseteq [\rho']$.

ii) There exists x such that $\rho x \in [\rho']$.

iii) There exists x such that for every $\rho_1 \in [\rho]$, it is the case that $\rho_1 x \in [\rho']$.

<u>Proof</u>:

(i) $\longrightarrow$ (ii): Trivial.

(ii) $\Longrightarrow$ (iii):

Suppose $\rho x \in [\rho']$ for some x. Consider $\rho_1 \in [\rho]$. By Proposition 3.3, $M_{\rho_1} = M_\rho$. Since x is a firing sequence at M_ρ we know that $\rho_1 x$ is also a firing sequence. Clearly, $\rho_1 x \sim \rho x$ because $\rho_1 \sim \rho$.

(iii) $\longrightarrow$ (i): Trivial. □

<u>Lemma 3.6</u>

Suppose $\rho_0 a, \rho_0 b \in FS$ such that $a \neq b$ and $[\rho_0 a] \uparrow [\rho_0 b]$. Then a and b belong to different agents. Moreover, $[\rho_0 a] \sqcup [\rho_0 b] = [\rho_0 ab] = [\rho_0 ba]$.

<u>Proof</u>:

Let ρ be such that $[\rho_0 a] \sqsubseteq [\rho]$ and $[\rho_0 b] \sqsubseteq [\rho]$. Then, by Proposition 3.5, there exist x and y such that $\rho_0 ax \in [\rho]$ and $\rho_0 by \in [\rho]$. Hence, $\rho_0 ax \sim \rho_0 by$. But $\rho_0 ax \restriction \{a,b\} \neq \rho_0 by \restriction \{a,b\}$. Hence a and b must belong to different agents.

By Proposition 3.1, we know that $\rho_0 ab, \rho_0 ba \in FS$. Clearly, $\rho_0 ab \sim \rho_0 ba$. Hence $[\rho_0 ab]$ is an upper bound for $[\rho_0 a]$ and $[\rho_0 b]$. Consider now an upper bound $[\rho]$ for $[\rho_0 a]$ and $[\rho_0 b]$. We must show that $[\rho_0 ab] \sqsubseteq [\rho]$. Once again, by Proposition 3.5, there exist x and y such that $\rho_0 ax \in [\rho]$ and $\rho_0 by \in [\rho]$. Hence, $\rho_0 ax \sim \rho_0 by$. Since $a \neq b$ it must be the case that $\#_b(x) > 0$. Therefore x can be written as $x = x_1 b x_2$ with $\#_b(x_1) = 0$.

Assume that $b \in T_i$. We first observe that $\#_d(x_1) = 0$ for every $d \in T_i$. This must be the case because otherwise $\rho_0 a x_1 b x_2 \restriction T_i \neq \rho_0 by \restriction T_i$ by virtue of the fact that $\#_b(x_1) = 0$. Now we proceed by induction on $k = |x_1|$.

<u>k = 0</u>: Then we are done.

<u>$k > 0$</u>

Let $x_1 = x_1'd$ with $d \in T_j$. We already know that $j \neq i$.

<u>Claim</u>

b is enabled at $M_{\rho_0 a x_1'}$

<u>Proof of claim</u>

If not, there exists a buffer place $s \in {}^{\cdot}b \cap d^{\cdot}$ such that $M'(s) = 0$ where $M' = M_{\rho_0 a x_1'}$. This follows from the fact that d and b belong to different agents. Let $M_0 = M_{\rho_0}$. Then $M_0(s) > 0$ because $\rho_0 b \in FS$. But this implies that $M'(s) > 0$ also because no transition belonging to T_i appears in x_1', as already observed. This completes the proof of the claim.

Returning to the main proof, we now have, by Proposition 3.1, that $\rho_0 x_1' bd \in FS$ also and hence $\rho_0 x_1' bdx_2' \in FS$. Clearly $\rho_0 x_1' bdx_2' \sim \rho$. The required result now follows from the induction hypothesis.

□

<u>Lemma 3.7</u>

Let $\rho a_1, \rho a_2, \ldots, \rho a_k \in FS$ such that $\forall\, i,j \in \{1,2,\ldots,k\}$, $i \neq j$ implies that a_i and a_j belong to different agents. Then $\rho a_{g(1)} a_{g(2)} \ldots a_{g(k)} \in FS$ for every <u>permutation</u> $g: \{1,2,\ldots,k\} \longrightarrow \{1,2,\ldots,k\}$.

Moreover, $\sqcup\{\rho a_i \mid 1 \leq i \leq k\} = [\rho a_1 a_2 \ldots a_k]$.

<u>Proof</u>:

Follows easily by repeated applications of the previous lemma and Proposition 3.1.

□

<u>Lemma 3.8</u>

i) If $[\sigma_1] \uparrow [\sigma_2]$ then $[\sigma_1] \sqcup [\sigma_2]$ exists.

ii) $[\sigma_1] \sqcap [\sigma_2]$ exists.

Proof:

To establish the first part of the result, let ρ be a firing sequence of maximum length such that $[\rho] \sqsubseteq [\sigma_1]$ and $[\rho] \sqsubseteq [\sigma_2]$. Since $[\lambda] \sqsubseteq [\sigma_1]$ and $[\lambda] \sqsubseteq [\sigma_2]$ and both σ_1 and σ_2 are of finite length, the existence of ρ is assured, though we have yet to show it is unique. By Proposition 3.5, there exist x and y such that $\rho x \sim \sigma_1$ and $\rho y \sim \sigma_2$.

If $|x| = 0$ ($|y| = 0$) then $[\sigma_1] \sqsubseteq [\sigma_2]$ ($[\sigma_2] \sqsubseteq [\sigma_1]$) so that $[\sigma_1] \sqcup [\sigma_2] = [\sigma_2]$ ($[\sigma_1]$). Hence assume that $|x| > 0$ and $|y| > 0$. We now proceed by induction on $k = |x| + |y|$.

k = 2: The result follows at once from Lemma 3.6.

k > 2

To save space, we will merely sketch the proof idea by considering the concrete case $|x| = 2$ and $|y| = 2$, while assuming the result to be true for k = 3.

Let $x = a_1a_2$ and $y = b_1b_2$. From the maximality of ρ it follows that $[\rho a_1]$ and $[\rho b_1]$ are incomparable and also $[\rho b_1]$ and $[\sigma_1]$ are incomparable (under $\sqsubseteq$). We now claim the situation in Figure 3.2 must prevail.

To see this, fix an upper bound $[\sigma]$ of $[\sigma_1]$ and $[\sigma_2]$. Then, $[\sigma]$ is also an upper bound of $[\rho a_1]$ and $[\rho b_1]$.

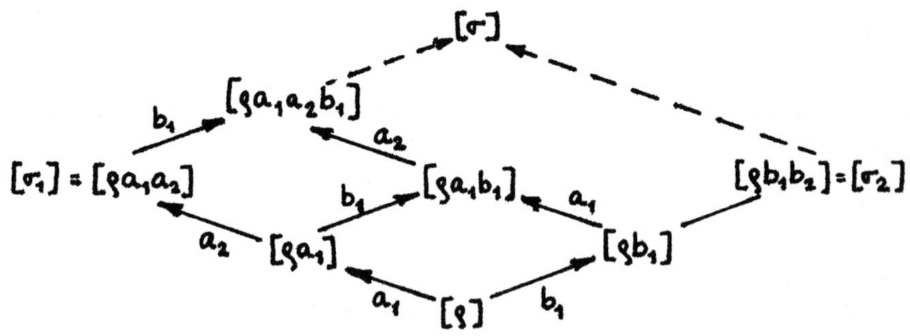

Figure 3.2

Hence, by Lemma 3.6, $\rho a_1 b_1 \in FS$ and moreover $[\rho a_1 b_1] = [\rho a_1] \sqcup [\rho b_1]$. Now $[\rho a_1 b_1] \neq [\rho a_1 a_2]$, because then we would have $[\rho b_1] \sqsubseteq [\sigma_1]$ and $[\rho b_1] \sqsubseteq [\sigma_2]$, which would violate the maximality of ρ.

Since $|\rho a_1 b_1| = |\sigma_1|$, we can now conclude by Proposition 3.3 and Proposition 3.5 that $[\rho a_1 b_1]$ and $[\sigma_1]$ are incomparable. Now $[\rho a_1] \sqsubseteq [\sigma]$ and $[\rho b_1] \sqsubseteq [\sigma]$. Hence $[\rho a_1 b_1] = [\rho a_1] \sqcup [\rho b_1] \sqsubseteq [\sigma]$. We already have $[\sigma_1] \sqsubseteq [\sigma]$. Thus $[\sigma_1] \uparrow [\rho a_1 b_1]$. Hence by Lemma 3.6, we have $\rho a_1 a_2 b_1 \in FS$ and moreover $[\rho a_1 a_2 b_1] = [\sigma_1] \sqcup [\rho a_1 b_1]$. We already know that $[\sigma_1] \sqsubseteq [\sigma]$ and $[\rho a_1 b_1] \sqsubseteq [\sigma]$. We now have that $[\rho a_1 a_2 b_1] \uparrow [\sigma_2]$. The induction hypothesis now applies by using ρb_1 to play the role previously played by ρ. Hence $[\rho a_1 a_2 b_1] \sqcup [\sigma_2]$ exists. It is routine to verify that $[\rho a_1 a_2 b_1] \sqcup [\sigma_2]$ is also the least upper bound of $[\sigma_1]$ and $[\sigma_2]$.

The second part of the result now follows easily. $[\sigma_1]$ and $[\sigma_2]$ have at least one lower bound, namely $[\lambda]$. They can have at most a finite number of lower bounds. If $[\rho_1]$ and $[\rho_2]$ are two lower bounds of $[\sigma_1]$ and $[\sigma_2]$ then $[\rho_1] \uparrow [\rho_2]$. Hence $[\rho_1] \sqcup [\rho_2]$ exists, by the first part of the result. These considerations lead to the conclusion that $[\sigma_1] \sqcap [\sigma_2]$ exists. □

The "reverse" versions of Lemmas 3.6 and 3.7 will also be required to prove our main result.

<u>Lemma 3.9</u>

Let $[\rho_0] \neq [\rho_1]$ such that $\rho_0 a \sim \rho_1 b$. Then there exists ρ such that $[\rho] = [\rho_0] \sqcap [\rho_1]$ and $\rho b \sim \rho_0$ and $\rho a \sim \rho_1$.

<u>Proof</u>:

The situation claimed by the result can be pictured as in Figure 3.3.

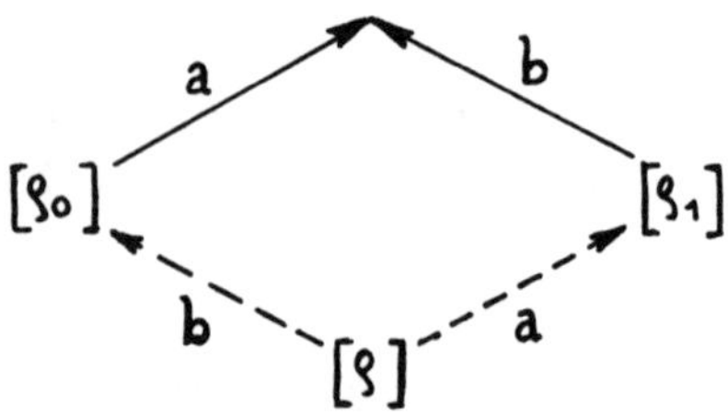

Figure 3.3

Suppose a = b. Then $\rho a \sim \rho b$. But this would imply that $\rho_0 \sim \rho_1$, a contradiction. Hence a ≠ b. Then, a and b must belong to different agents because $\rho_0 a \upharpoonright \{a,b\} \neq \rho_1 b \upharpoonright \{a,b\}$.

<u>Claim</u>

There exists ρ'_0 such that $\rho'_1 b \sim \rho_0$.

<u>Proof of claim</u>:

Since $\rho_0 a \sim \rho_1 b$ and $a \neq b$, we must certainly have $\#_b(\rho_0) > 0$. Hence ρ_0 can be expressed as $\rho_0 = \sigma bx$ with $\#_b(x) = 0$. Let $b \in T_i$. Then $\#_d(x) = 0$ for every $d \in T_i$. This is so because $\sigma bxa \sim \rho_1 b$ and $\#_b(x) = 0$ (and $a \neq b$). We now proceed by induction on $k = |x|$.

<u>k = 0</u>

Set $\rho'_0 = \sigma$ and we are done.

<u>k > 0</u>

Let $x = dy$ with $d \in T_j$. We know that $j \neq i$. Suppose that d is enabled at M_σ. Then by Proposition 3.1, σbdy is also a firing sequence with $\sigma dby \sim \sigma bdy \sim \rho_0$ and the required result follows from the induction hypothesis.

Suppose that d is not enabled at M_σ. Then there exists a buffer place $s \in {}^\cdot d \cap b^\cdot$ such that $M_\sigma(s) = 0$. Clearly $M_{\sigma b}(s) = 1$, but again $M_{\sigma bd}(s) = 0$. Now no transition in T_i appears in $x = dy$ and hence $M_{\rho_0}(s) = 0$. (Recall that $\rho_0 = \sigma bdy$). But a and b belong to different agents and we can therefore conclude that $M_{\rho_0 a}(s) = 0$. This is a contradiction because $M_{\rho_1 b}(s) > 0$ and $M_{\rho_0 a} = M_{\rho_1 b}$ by Proposition 3.3. This completes the proof of the claim.

Returning to the main proof, we can use the above argument to conclude that there exists ρ_1' such that $\rho_1' a \sim \rho_1$. Hence $\rho_0' ba \sim \rho_1' ab$. This at once implies that $\rho_0' \sim \rho_1'$. $[\rho_0']$ is a lower bound for $[\rho_0]$ and $[\rho_1]$ with $\rho_0' b \in [\rho_0]$ and $\rho_0' a \in [\rho_1]$. Suppose $[\rho']$ is another lower bound for $[\rho_0]$ and $[\rho_1]$. Then $[\rho] \uparrow [\rho_0']$ and hence there exists σ such that $[\sigma] = [\rho'] \sqcup [\rho_0']$. Clearly $[\rho_0'] \sqsubseteq [\sigma] \sqsubseteq [\rho_0]$. Now $[\sigma] \neq [\rho_0]$ because $[\sigma] \sqsubseteq [\rho_1]$ also. Hence $[\sigma]$ cannot lie properly between $[\rho_0']$ and $[\rho_0]$, since $|\rho_0| = |\rho_0'| + 1$. Hence $[\rho_0'] = [\sigma]$ and we are done.

□

<u>Lemma 3.10</u>

Let $\rho_1, \rho_2, \ldots \rho_k$ and $a_1, a_2, \ldots a_k$ be such that the following conditions are satisfied.

i) For $1 \leq i,j \leq k$, $(i \neq j \Longrightarrow \rho_i \not\sim \rho_j)$

ii) For $1 \leq i,j \leq k$, $\rho_i a_i \sim \rho_j a_j$

Then there exists ρ such that $\rho a_1 a_2 \ldots a_k \sim \rho_i a_i$ for $1 \leq i \leq k$.

<u>Proof</u>:

Follows easily by repeated applications of the previous lemma.

□

4. THE EVENT STRUCTURE SEMANTICS

We are now in a position to describe the behaviour of the ACSS $\mathscr{A}$ in terms of a finitary $\hat{T}$-labelled event structure. As stated earlier, we shall achieve this by showing that $(FS/\sim, \sqsubseteq)$ — which we shall, for convenience, denote by TR for the rest of this section — is a finitary, prime algebraic, finitely coherent poset. Theorem 2.5 will then at once lead to an event structure representation.

The technique we employ here leans heavily on the characterization of objects called trace monoids in terms of labelled event structures by Rozoy and Thiagarajan [RoT]. To save space, we shall not give detailed proofs in this section. The interested reader is referred to [RoT] for the technical details. However, the proof outline we present will be self-contained so that, in principle, the reader can fill in the details without reference to [RoT].

The notion of a unit interval turns out to be very useful for achieving our goal.

<u>Definition 4.1</u>

The set of <u>unit intervals</u> of TR is the set $UI \subseteq FS/\sim \times \hat{T} \times FS/\sim$ given by:

$$UI \triangleq \{ ([\rho], a, [\rho']) \mid \rho a \sim \rho' \}$$

□

For convenience, we shall denote the unit interval $([\rho], a, [\rho'])$ as $\langle \rho, a \rangle$. Note that according to this convention $\langle \rho, a \rangle = \langle \sigma, b \rangle$ just in case $\rho \sim \sigma$ and $a = b$.

Next, we impose an ordering over UI.

<u>Definition 4.2</u>

Let $\langle \rho, a \rangle, \langle \sigma, b \rangle \in UI$.

Then $\langle \rho, a \rangle \preccurlyeq \langle \sigma, b \rangle$ iff the following conditions are fulfilled.

i) $a = b$.

ii) $[\rho a] \sqcup [\sigma] = [\sigma b]$ and $[\rho a] \sqcap [\sigma] = [\rho]$.

□

It is not difficult to verify that $\preccurlyeq$ is a partial order. Consider the ACSS of Figure 1.2. We then have $\langle ppc,c\rangle \preccurlyeq \langle pcppp,c\rangle$.

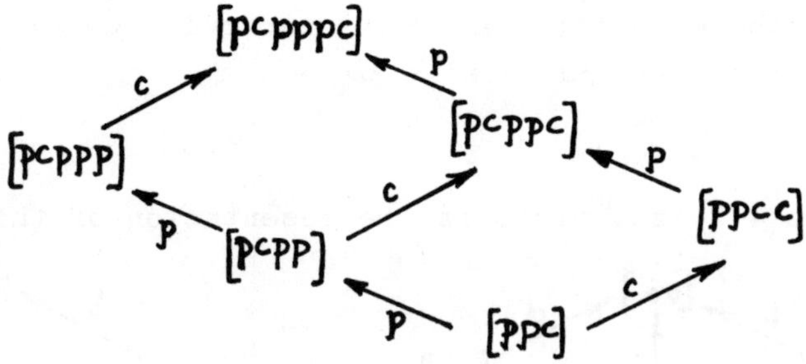

Figure 4.1

<u>Definition 4.3</u>

i) $\succcurlyeq \triangleq (\preccurlyeq)^{-1}$.

ii) $\approx \triangleq (\preccurlyeq \cup \succcurlyeq)^{*}$.

iii) $[\![\langle\rho,a\rangle]\!] = \{\langle\sigma,a\rangle \mid \langle\rho,a\rangle \approx \langle\sigma,a\rangle\}$.

□

Clearly, $\approx$ is an equivalence relation. In general, an equivalence class of $\approx$ may be an infinite set. For instance, in the example of Figure 1.2,

$$[\![\langle p,c\rangle]\!] = \{\langle p,c\rangle,\langle pp,c\rangle,\langle ppp,c\rangle, \; . \; . \; . \; \}$$

It is straightforward to show — using the finitariness of $\sqsubseteq$ — that each equivalence class of $\approx$ has a minimal element. What requires an argument is the assertion that this minimal element is unique; i.e., each equivalence class of $\approx$ has a <u>least</u> element. It turns out that Lemma 3.9 can be used to show the following result. In stating this result, we have used $\prec$ to denote the following relation over unit intervals.

$\langle\rho,a\rangle \prec \langle\sigma,a\rangle$ iff $\rho \nsim \sigma$, $\langle\rho,a\rangle \preccurlyeq \langle\sigma,a\rangle$ and
$\langle\rho,a\rangle \preccurlyeq \langle\rho',a\rangle \preccurlyeq \langle\sigma,a\rangle$ implies that
$\rho \sim \rho'$ or $\rho' \sim \sigma$.

<u>Lemma 4.4</u>

Let $\langle\rho_1, a\rangle$, $\langle\rho_2, a\rangle$ and $\langle\sigma, a\rangle$ be three distinct unit intervals such that $\langle\rho_1, a\rangle \prec \langle\sigma, a\rangle$ and $\langle\rho_2, a\rangle \prec \langle\sigma, a\rangle$. Then there exists a unit interval $\langle\rho, a\rangle$ such that $\langle\rho, a\rangle \prec \langle\rho_1, a\rangle$ and $\langle\rho, a\rangle \prec \langle\rho_2, a\rangle$.

□

Figure 4.2 is a pictorial representation of this result.

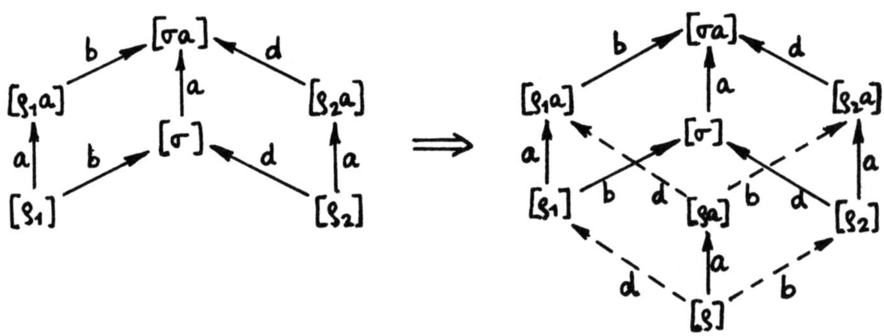

Figure 4.2

Using this lemma, it is straightforward to establish the following result.

<u>Theorem 4.5</u>

Let $\langle\rho, a\rangle$ be a unit interval. Then $\llbracket\langle\rho, a\rangle\rrbracket$ contains a least element (under $\prec$). □

This theorem leads us to the notion of a prime interval, which in turn permits us to identify the set of prime elements of TR.

<u>Definition 4.6</u>

i) PI, the set of <u>prime intervals</u> of TR is the subset of UI given by:

$$PI = \{\langle\rho, a\rangle \mid \langle\rho, a\rangle \text{ is the least element of } \llbracket\langle\rho, a\rangle\rrbracket\}.$$

ii) $PR \subseteq FS/\sim$ (which will soon be called the set of <u>prime elements</u> of TR) is given by:

$$PR \triangleq \{[\rho'] \mid \exists [\rho].\exists a.([\rho],a,[\rho']) \in PI\}.$$

□

For the ACSS of Figure 1.2, <p,c>, <ppc,c> and <pp,q> are examples of prime intervals. The corresponding members of PR are [pc],[ppcc] and [ppq].

PR turns out to be the set of prime elements of TR. In fact, using Theorem 4.5, we can say much more.

<u>Theorem 4.7</u>

i) $[\rho] \in PR$ iff $|{}^{\cdot}[\rho]| = 1$ where
$${}^{\cdot}[\rho] = \{[\rho'] \mid ([\rho'],a,[\rho]) \in UI \text{ for some } a \in \hat{T}\}.$$

ii) PR is the set of prime elements of TR.

iii) TR is prime algebraic.

□

The characterization of the prime elements given in part i) of the theorem has been independently observed — in a different context — by Shields [S]. The subsequent parts of the theorem follow easily from this characterization, whose proof depends crucially on Theorem 4.5.

To show that TR is finitely coherent, we have to do a little more work.

<u>Lemma 4.8</u>

Let $P \subseteq PR$ be a finite set of prime elements such that

i) P is pair-wise consistent.

ii) $P = (\downarrow P) \cap PR$.

Then $\sqcup P$ exists in TR.

<u>Proof sketch</u>:

The proof is by induction on $k = |P|$. If $k = 0$ then $P = \emptyset$ and clearly $\sqcup P = [\lambda]$, so assume $k > 0$. Since P is finite, we know that P has at least one maximal element. If P has exactly one maximal element then obviously this maximal element is the l.u.b. of P. If P has exactly two maximal elements then by Lemma 3.8, P has a l.u.b. So assume that P has at least three maximal elements.

Denote the maximal elements of P by $P_{max} = \{[\rho_1],[\rho_2],\ldots,[\rho_l]\}$, $l \geq 3$. Let $D = P - P_{max}$. Then we can apply the induction hypothesis to D to obtain $[\sigma] = \sqcup D$. For $i \in \{1,2,\ldots,l\}$, we can again apply the induction hypothesis to $D \cup \{[\rho_i]\}$ to obtain $[\sigma_i] = \sqcup(D \cup \{[\rho_i]\})$, with $[\sigma] \sqsubseteq [\sigma_i]$. In fact, we can show that the situation of Figure 4.3 holds, where $([\rho_i'],a_i,[\rho_i])$ is the prime interval corresponding to the prime element $[\rho_i]$.

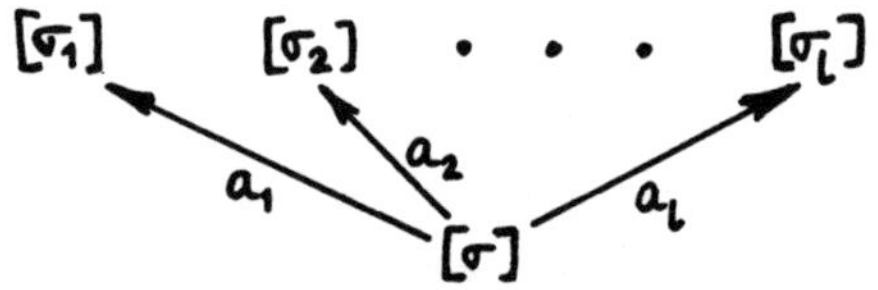

Figure 4.3

For $i,j \in \{1,2,\ldots,l\}$, we apply the induction hypothesis again to $D \cup \{[\rho_i],[\rho_j]\}$ to show that $\{[\sigma_1],[\sigma_2],\ldots,[\sigma_l]\}$ is pair-wise consistent. Then from Lemma 3.10, we know that $\{[\sigma_1],[\sigma_2],\ldots,[\sigma_l]\}\uparrow$, from which it follows that $[\sigma'] = \sqcup\{[\sigma_1],[\sigma_2],\ldots,[\sigma_l]\}$ exists. It is then easy to show that $[\sigma'] = \sqcup P$ as well.

□

<u>Theorem 4.9</u>

TR is finitely coherent.

<u>Proof sketch</u>:

Let $X \subseteq FS/\sim$ be a finite pair-wise consistent set. Define $P = PR \cap (\downarrow X)$. Then it is easy to check that P fulfills the hypotheses of the previous lemma. Hence $\sqcup P$ exists. Using the fact that TR is prime algebraic, it is then straightforward to show that $\sqcup P = \sqcup X$. □

Since TR is obviously finitary we have finally reached our main goal.

Theorem 4.10

TR is a finitary, prime algebraic, finitely coherent poset. □

TR can now be represented as a $\hat{T}$-labelled event structure.

Definition 4.11

$ES_{\mathcal{A}} \triangleq (E, <, \#, \varphi)$ is given by

i) $E = PR$, the set of prime elements of TR.

ii) $\leq$ is $\sqsubseteq$ restricted to PR x PR.

iii) $\# = \{(e_1, e_2) \mid e_1, e_2 \in E$ and $e_1 \not\uparrow e_2$ (in TR)$\}$

iv) φ: $E \rightarrow T$ is defined as:

$\forall e \in E.\ \ \varphi(e) = a$ iff $([\rho], a, e) \in PI$, where $^{\cdot}e = \{[\rho]\}$ (see Theorem 4.7) and PI is the set of prime intervals of TR.

□

By the first part of Theorem 4.7, the labelling function φ is well defined. Clearly $ES_{\mathcal{A}}$ is a $\hat{T}$-labelled event structure. The poset of finite configurations of this event structure ordered under inclusion will be isomorphic to (FS/~) by Corollary 2.6. Thus, we are justified in claiming that $ES_{\mathcal{A}}$ is the event structure representation of the behaviour of $\mathcal{A}$.

5. DISCUSSION

In this paper we have formulated a model of asynchronous communication based on Petri nets. Our model is a restricted one in that we cater only for point-to-point unidirectional message passing, and that too only among a finite number of sequential agents. Nevertheless, this class is an interesting one and is sufficiently expressive to capture the essential features of asynchronous communication, as shown in the related literature we have cited so far.

Our main achievement has been to demonstrate that in this setting, standard notions can be easily applied — in a modified form — to obtain an event structure representation of the behaviour. Our results seem to suggest that the relationship between event structures and trace languages worked out in [RoT] might be applicable in a much larger context. We have shown that their theorem goes through in at least one interesting case where the independence relation used in trace theory is made to be "context dependent". We have also shown that the ideas of trace theory can be applied to a larger class of Petri nets than just the class of safe Petri nets, as has been the case till now [AR]. (A safe Petri net is a marked net in which at each reachable marking, starting with the initial marking, each place carries at most one token.)

At present we do not know much about the properties of the ACSS model, apart from the results contained in [R] concerning a restricted subclass of ACSSs. It will be an interesting task to obtain a characterization of the global behaviour of an ACSS in terms of the autonomous behaviour of its agents (which is easy to compute) and the communication structure.

The event structures that result from ACSSs by our construction fall within a subclass of event structures called n-agent event structures. It has been shown in [LT] that this class of event structures can be characterized with the help of a temporal logic with indexed modalities. (Actually, the proof of the completeness result presented in [LT] contains a flaw. It can however be easily repaired [T2].)

References

[LNCS stands for Springer Lecture Notes in Computer Science]

[AR] Aalbersberg, I. J. and Rozenberg, G.: "Theory of Traces", Theoretical Computer Science 60, 1, pp. 1-82 (1982).

[CL] Chandy, K. M. and Lamport,L.: "Distributed Snapshots: Determining Global States of Distributed Systems", ACM Transactions on Computer Systems 3, 1, pp. 63-75 (1985).

[CM1] Chandy, K. M. and Misra, J.: "A Distributed Algorithm for Detecting Resource Deadlocks in Distributed Systems", Proc. First ACM Symposium on Principles of Distributed Computing, pp. 157-164 (1982).

[CM2] Chandy, K. M. and Misra, J.: "How Processes Learn", Distributed Computing, 1, 1, pp. 40-52 (1986).

[DS] Dijkstra, E. W. and Scholten, C. S.: "Termination Detection for Diffusing Computations", Information Processing Letters 11, 1, pp. 1-4 (1980).

[FM] Finkel, A. and Memmi, G.: "Fifo Nets: A New Model of Parallel Computation", Proceedings of the 6th GI Conference on Theoretical Computer Science, LNCS 145 pp. 111-121 (1982).

[LT] Lodaya, K. and Thiagarajan, P. S.: "A Modal Logic for a Subclass of Event Structures", DAIMI Report PB-220, Computer Science Department, Aarhus University, Denmark (1987).

[M] Mazurkiewicz, A.: "Concurrent Program Schemes and their Interpretations", DAIMI Report PB-78, Computer Science Department, Aarhus University, Denmark (1977).

[NPW] Nielsen, M., Plotkin, G. and Winskel, G.: "Petri Nets, Event Structures and Domains, Part I", Theoretical Computer Science 13,1, pp. 85-108 (1980).

[P] Peterson, J. L.: Petri Net Theory and the Modelling of Systems, Prentice Hall, Inc., Englewood Cliffs, New Jersey (1981).

[R1] Reisig, W.: "Deterministic Buffer Synchronization of Sequential Processes", Acta Informatica 18, pp. 117-134 (1982).

[R2] Reisig, W.: Petri Nets, EATCS Monographs on Theoretical Computer Science, Vol.4, Springer (1985).

[RT] Rozenberg, G. and Thiagarajan, P. S.: "Petri Nets, Basic Notions, Structure, Behaviour", Current Trends in Concurrency, LNCS 224, pp. 585-668 (1986).

[RoT] Rozoy, B. and Thiagarajan, P. S.: "Event Structures and Trace Monoids", Report 87-47, LITP, University of Paris 7, France (1987).

[S] Shields, M. W.: "Behavioural Presentations", to appear in the Proceedings of REX School/Workshop on Linear Time, Branching Time and Partial Order in Logics and Models for Concurrency, Springer.

[T1] Thiagarajan, P. S.: "Some Behavioural Aspects of Net Theory", Proceedings ICALP '88, LNCS 317, pp. 630-653 (1988).

[T2] Thiagarajan, P. S.: "A Correction to a Modal Logic for a Subclass of Event Structures", Manuscript (to appear as an internal report of the Computer Science Department, Aarhus University, Denmark).

[W1] Winskel, G.: "Event Structure Semantics of CCS and Related Languages", Proceedings ICALP '82, LNCS 140, pp. 561-576 (1982).

[W2] Winskel, G.: "Event Structures", Advances in Petri Nets, 1986, Part II, LNCS 255, pp. 325-392 (1987).

Decidability and Undecidability in Distributed Transition Systems

Rohit Parikh[1]

Abstract: We investigate a Propositional Logic for Distributed Computing recently introduced by Lodaya, Ramanujam and Thiagarajan [4], and prove the following two results. (1) The *nondeterministic* version of this logic is decidable in NEXPTIME. (2) The *deterministic* version is highly undecidable. The proof of (1) uses the filtration technique used by Fischer and Ladner for Propositional Dynamic Logic (PDL). The proof of (2) uses the undecidability of one version of the recurring domino problem.

Introduction

In [4] , Lodaya, Ramanujam and Thiagarajan define *Distributed Transition Systems* which generalise the notion of sequential execution of a program to allow for concurrency. They then define a logic by giving a formal language L and a semantics for it. An axiomatic system is given and proved to be sound and complete. Since the system has the finite model property, it follows that the logic is decidable.

In this paper we shall give a direct proof that the system is decidable in non-deterministic exponential time (NEXPTIME). We shall also prove that the *deterministic* version of the system is highly undecidable, and in fact, Π^1_1 complete. For the sake of having this paper self contained, we give a brief account of the system and its semantics.

[1]Brooklyn College of CUNY, CUNY Graduate Center and IBM Watson Research Center. Research supported by NSF grant DCR-8504825-01 and a grant from the CUNY-FRAP program. A preliminary version of this paper appeared as IBM research report RC13930, Aug. 88

Syntax and Semantics

Definition 1: A Distributed Transition System (DTS) is a triple $DTS = (S, \mathcal{A}, \rightarrow)$ where
(a) S is a nonempty set of *states*
(b) $\mathcal{A}$ is a finite set of *actions.* and
(c) $\rightarrow$ is a binary transition relation $\rightarrow \subseteq S \times 2^{\mathcal{A}} \times S$ satisfying:
(i) $s \xrightarrow{\emptyset} s'$ iff $s = s'$
(ii) $s \xrightarrow{u} s'$ iff $\exists f : 2^u \mapsto S$ such that $f(\emptyset) = s,\ f(u) = s'$ and $\forall v_1 \subseteq v_2 \subseteq u, f(v_1) \xrightarrow{v_2 - v_1} f(v_2)$.

Letters s, t etc. will denote states. $a, b, ..$ will denote actions. We shall sometimes refer to a dts as a *frame*. It will be called *deterministic* if $s \xrightarrow{u} s'$ and $s \xrightarrow{u} s''$ imply that $s' = s''$.

The clause c(ii) captures the idea that there is a *concurrent* u-step from s to s'; it is possible to perform the steps in u concurrently and hence in any order and reach the state s'. Moreover, we can do some of the actions concurrently or in any order, and do the rest concurrently too. The set of states reachable in this way forms a hypercube with 2^m states where u has m elements.

Thus for example, if we have $s \xrightarrow{\{a,b\}} s'$ then there exists a square as in figure 1.

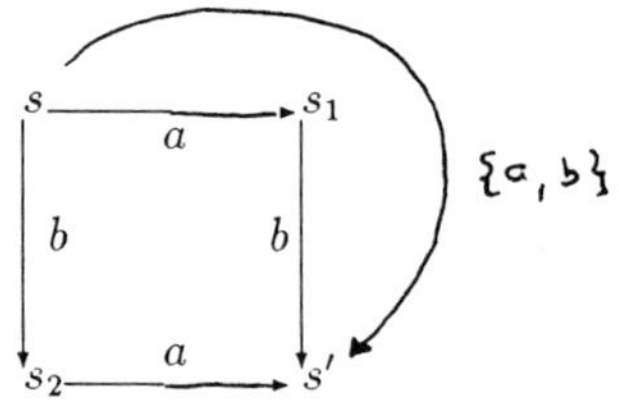

Figure 1

Here $f(\emptyset) = s,\ f(\{a\}) = s_1,\ f(\{b\}) = s_2$ and $f(\{a, b\}) = s'$.

On the other hand, if we do have $s \xrightarrow{a} s_1,\ s_1 \xrightarrow{b} s',\ s \xrightarrow{b} s_2$ and $s_2 \xrightarrow{a} s'$, we might still not have $s \xrightarrow{\{a,b\}} s'$, since it might happen that the actions a and b are performable in either order, but not concurrently. E.g. a and b might be the actions of two processes using the same resource, in which case the actions can be performed in either order, but not simultaneously.

Definition 2: Let $\longrightarrow^*$ be the reflexive transitive closure of $\longrightarrow$, where $s \longrightarrow t$ means $\exists u, s \stackrel{u}{\longrightarrow} t$. Then for $s \in S$, the *reachability class* $RC(s)$ of s is the set $\{s' | s \longrightarrow^* s'\}$.

Remark: In definition 2, above, $\exists u, s \stackrel{u}{\longrightarrow} s'$ could be replaced by $\exists a, s \stackrel{a}{\longrightarrow} s'$. The two relations are distinct, but they have the same reflexive transitive closure. Hence $s' \in RC(s)$ iff there is a chain $s = s_1, ..., s_m = s'$ such that $\forall i < m, \exists a, s_i \stackrel{a}{\longrightarrow} s_{i+1}$. Intuitively, $RC(s)$ is just the set of states that lie in the *future* of s.

The Language: We assume given a finite set *Prop* of atomic *propositional* symbols P_i and a finite set *Act* of *action* symbols a_j. Letters u and v (with subscripts) will denote finite sets of actions. We shall use a_i as an abbreviation for $\{a_i\}$.

Then the language of PDTL (Propositional Distributed Transition Logic) will be formed from the basic P_i by the following rules:

Definition 3:
(i) Each P_i is a formula
(ii) If A and B are formulas, then so are $A \vee B$ and $\neg A$.
(iii) If A is a formula and u is a set of actions, then $< u > A$ is a formula
(iv) If A is a formula, then so is $\Diamond A$.

We will use the usual abbreviations like $A \rightarrow B$ for $(\neg A \vee B)$, $A \wedge B$ for $\neg(\neg A \vee \neg B)$, etc. $\Box$ will stand for $\neg\Diamond\neg$ and $[u]$ for $\neg < u > \neg$.

A *model* for the language will consist of a pair $< Fr, V >$ where Fr is a *frame* or DTS $(S, \mathcal{A}, \longrightarrow)$ and V is the *valuation function* $V : S \mapsto 2^{Prop}$.

Given a formula A, a model $M =< Fr, V >$, and $s \in S$, we define the relation $M, s \models A$, (A is *true* at state s) by induction on the complexity of A as follows:

Definition 4:
(i) $M, s \models P$ iff $P \in V(s)$
(ii) $M, s \models A \vee B$ iff $M, s \models A$ or $M, s \models B$
(iii) $M, s \models \neg A$ iff $M, s \not\models A$
(iv) $M, s \models < u > A$ iff for some $s', s \stackrel{u}{\longrightarrow} s'$ and $M, s' \models A$
(v) $M, s \models \Diamond A$ iff for some $s' \in RC(s), M, s' \models A$.

Note that the $\Diamond$ construct could be expressed in terms of the other symbols if we had the $*$-operator as in PDL. $\Diamond$ is in fact just $< \{a_1, ..., a_k\}^* >$ where $Act = \{a_1, ..., a_k\}$.

Example 1: This is a deterministic example. Let S be $N \times N$, let $\mathcal{A} = \{a, b\}$ and let $(i, j) \stackrel{\{a,b\}}{\longrightarrow} (k, l)$ iff $k = i + 1$ and $l = j + 1$. Moreover $(i, j) \stackrel{a}{\longrightarrow} (k, l)$ iff

$k = i + 1$ and $l = j$. Similarly $(i, j) \xrightarrow{b} (k, l)$ iff $k = i$ and $l = j + 1$. Thus a causes a horizontal movement by one step, b causes a vertical movement by one step, and $\{a, b\}$ causes a diagonal movement by one step. Let (i, j) satisfy Odd iff $i + j$ is odd, and satisfy $Even$ iff $i + j$ is even.

Then at (0,0), $\Box(Odd \lor Even)$, $\Box\neg(Odd \land Even)$, $\Box(Odd \to [a]Even)$ and $\Box(Odd \to [a, b]Odd)$ are all true.

Example 2: Let again, $S = \{a, b, c\}^*$, $\mathcal{A} = \{a, b\}$ and $x \xrightarrow{a} xac^*$, $x \xrightarrow{b} xbc^*$. Note now that $x \xrightarrow{\{a,b\}} y$ can never happen for any x, y, since the "ranges" of a and b are disjoint. Both a, b act nondeterministically.

Example 3: Let again, $S = \{a, b, c, d\}^*/\equiv$, and $\mathcal{A} = \{a, b, c, d\}$, where $\equiv$ is generated by the equations $ab = ba$ and $cd = dc$. E.g. $abacdc \equiv aabdcc$. Now we *can* have $x \xrightarrow{\{a,b\}} xab = xba$ and similarly for $\{c, d\}$, but $x \xrightarrow{\{a,c\}} y$ will never happen.

Decidability

A formula A is said to be *satisfiable* if there is an M, s such that $M, s \models A$. It is *valid* if for all M, s, $M, s \models A$. We will show that if a formula A is satisfiable, then A has a model at most exponential in the length of A. It follows that satisfiability is in non-deterministic exponential time (NEXPTIME).

Definition 5: Given a formula A, we define $FL(A)$, the Fischer-Ladner closure of A, to be the smallest set X satisfying the following properties.
(i) $A \in X$
(ii) If $B \lor C \in X$, then B and C are in X.
(iii) If $\neg B \in X$, then $B \in X$.
(iv) If $< u > B \in X$, then for each $a_i \in u, < a_i > B \in X$ and $B \in X$.
(v) If $\Diamond B \in X$, then $B \in X$, and for every $a_i \in Act$, $< a_i > \Diamond B \in X$.

Definition 6: Given a model M of A, we define a factor model $\overline{M}$ as follows:

If x, y are states of M, then $x \equiv y$, iff for all $B \in FL(A)$, $M, x \models B$ iff $M, y \models B$.
Note that $\equiv$ is an equivalence relation and if $\overline{x}$ is the equivalence class of x under $\equiv$, then $\overline{x} = \overline{y}$ iff $x \equiv y$. We let $\overline{M} = < \overline{S}, \longrightarrow, \overline{V} >$ where $\overline{S} = \{\overline{x} \mid x \in S\}$ and $\longrightarrow$ and $\overline{V}$ are as follows:

$\overline{x} \xrightarrow{u} \overline{y}$ iff $\exists x' \in \overline{x}$ and $\exists y' \in \overline{y}$ such that $x' \xrightarrow{u} y'$.

$\overline{V}(\overline{x}) = V(x)$. In other words, for *atomic* P, $x \models P$ iff $\overline{x} \models P$. Note that this definition of $\overline{V}$ is unambiguous since $\overline{x} = \overline{y}$ implies $V(x) = V(y)$. We ignore those atoms P which do not occur in the formula A.

We have to check that $\overline{M}$ is a model. The only thing to check is that if $\overline{x} \xrightarrow{u} \overline{y}$ in $\overline{M}$, then there exists a function $g : 2^u \mapsto \overline{S}$ as required. However this is easy to verify. For there must have been $x' \in \overline{x}$ and $y' \in \overline{y}$ such that $x' \xrightarrow{u} y'$ in M. This yields a function f from $2^u \mapsto S$ with the required properties (since M *was* a model) and we can define g by: $g(v) = \overline{f(v)}$. g is a function from 2^u to $\overline{S}$ and for $v_1 \subseteq v_2 \subseteq u$, we have $f(v_1) \xrightarrow{v_2 - v_1} f(v_2)$ so that we also get, in $\overline{S}$, $g(v_1) \xrightarrow{v_2 - v_1} g(v_2)$

For a formula A, let $c(A)$ be the number of occurrences in A of logical symbols, propositional letters and action letters, and for a set X, let $card(X)$ be the number of elements in X.

Lemma 1: $FL(A)$ is finite.
If k is $card(Act)$, then $card(FL(A)) \leq (k+1)(c(A))$

Proof: By induction on $c(A)$. If A is a propositional symbol, then the claim is clear.

If $A = B \vee C$ then $c(A) = c(B) + c(C) + 1$ and $FL(A) = FL(B) \cup FL(C) \cup \{A\}$, so
$card(FL(A)) \leq card(FL(B)) + card(FL(C)) + 1$
$\leq (k+1)(c(B) + c(C)) + 1 \leq (k+1)(c(A))$

Similarly, if A is $\neg B$, then $card(FL(A)) = card(FL(B)) + 1$.

If $A = \Diamond B$, then $FL(A) = \{A\} \cup \{< a_i > \Diamond B : i = 1, ..., k\} \cup FL(B)$. Hence $card(FL(A)) \leq k + 1 + card(FL(B)) \leq k + 1 + (k+1)(c(B)) \leq (k+1)(c(A))$.

Similarly if $A =< u > B$. $\Box$

Note that the size bound could be reduced a little if we notice that only the construct $\Diamond$ is costly.

Corollary: The factor model $\overline{M}$ of definition 6 is finite, and indeed of size at most exponential in $c(A)$.

Proof: Clearly there can be at most $2^{card(FL(A))}$ equivalence classes for the equivalence relation $\equiv$ of definition 6. $\Box$.

Lemma 2: For all $B \in FL(A)$, for all $s \in S$, $M, s \models B$ iff $\overline{M}, \overline{s} \models B$.

Proof: By induction on $c(B)$.

(1) If B is an atom, then the claim holds by definition of $\overline{V}$.

(2) The cases where $B = \neg C$ and $B = C \vee D$ are easy.

For example, $\overline{M}, \overline{s} \models \neg C$ iff
$\overline{M}, \overline{s} \not\models C$ iff (by induction hypothesis, IH) $M, s \not\models C$ iff $M, s \models \neg C$.

(3) $B =< u > C$ where $u = \{a_1, ..., a_m\}$.

If $M, s \models B$, then $\exists t, s \xrightarrow{u} t$ such that $M, t \models C$. Hence $\overline{s} \xrightarrow{u} \overline{t}$ and (IH) $\overline{M}, \overline{t} \models C$ hence $\overline{M}, \overline{s} \models B$.

If $\overline{M}, \overline{s} \models B$, then $\exists \overline{t}, \overline{s} \xrightarrow{u} \overline{t}$ and $\overline{M}, \overline{t} \models C$.

Now $\exists s' \in \overline{s}, t' \in \overline{t}$ such that $s' \xrightarrow{u} t'$. Since $t' \equiv t$, $\overline{t'} = \overline{t}$ and so, (IH), $M, t' \models C$. Hence $M, s' \models B$. But $s \equiv s'$, so $M, s \models B$.

(4) $B = \Diamond C$.

(a) If $M, s \models B$, then there is a chain $s = s_1, ..., s_n$ such that $M, s_n \models C$ and for all $i < n, \exists j, s_i \xrightarrow{a_j} s_{i+1}$. This, of course, implies $\overline{s_i} \xrightarrow{a_j} \overline{s_{i+1}}$.

By IH, $\overline{M}, \overline{s_n} \models C$ and hence, since C implies B, $\overline{M}, \overline{s_n} \models B$. Now we will do reverse induction on i from n to 1.

Suppose that $\overline{M}, \overline{s_{i+1}} \models B$, then $\overline{M}, \overline{s_i} \models < a_j > B$. Hence, since $< a_j > B$ logically inplies B, $\overline{M}, \overline{s_i} \models B$.

Thus, by reverse induction as above, $\overline{M}, \overline{s_1} \models B$, i.e. $\overline{M}, \overline{s} \models B$.

(b) Conversely, if $\overline{M}, \overline{s} \models B$, then there is a chain $\overline{s} = \overline{s_1}, ..., \overline{s_n}$ such that for all i there is a j such that $\overline{s_i} \xrightarrow{a_j} \overline{s_{i+1}}$ and $\overline{M}, \overline{s_n} \models C$.

By IH, $M, s_n \models C$ and so $M, s_n \models \Diamond C$, i.e. $M, s_n \models B$. Now for all $i < n$, if $M, s_{i+1} \models B$, then there exist states x_i, x_{i+1}, and action a_j such that $x_i \equiv s_i, x_{i+1} \equiv s_{i+1}$, and $x_i \xrightarrow{a_j} x_{i+1}$.

Now $x_{i+1} \equiv s_{i+1}$ so $M, x_{i+1} \models B$. So $M, x_i \models < a_j > B$ so $M, x_i \models B$. But $x_i \equiv s_i$ and so $M, s_i \models B$. Using reverse induction on i from n to 1, we get, $M, s_1 \models B$, i.e. $M, s \models B$. □

Corollary: PDTL is in NEXPTIME.

Note that the techniques used above could be easily modified to prove NEXPTIME decidability of the logic where the $\Diamond$ construct is replaced by the stronger $*$-operator of PDL. If, for example, the action letters were a, b, c, then $\Diamond$ would be equivalent to $< \{a, b, c\}^* >$, but the construct $< \{a, b\}^* >$ would be *new*, and inexpressible in the old language. Thus a direct decidability result gives us a great deal of flexibility in our choice of the exact language.

A remark about the upper and lower bounds. It is easy to see that the Fischer-Ladner [1], lower bound of *deterministic* exponential time for PDL will also hold for PDTL. The same proof goes through except for the fact that the $[\vdash^*]$ of page 207, line 12 must be replaced by the □ of PDTL. As for the upper bound, PDL has been shown by Pratt [5] to be decidable in deterministic exponential time. However, unlike PDL, the models of PDTL are built from hypercubes corresponding to the relation $\xrightarrow{u}$. Such hypercubes can be exponential in the size of the formula and it is not obvious that guessing these hypercubes can be avoided. Thus we seem to be left with a gap here.

Undecidability of the Deterministic Case

We will show that the deterministic version of PDTL is highly undecidable, by reducing to it a version of the domino (or tile) problem.

Definition 7: A DTS or frame is said to be *deterministic* if for each state s and action a, there is at most one s' such that $s \xrightarrow{a} s'$. A model M is deterministic if its frame is. Finally, a formula A is said to be *deterministically valid* if it is valid over all deterministic models. A formula is said to be *deterministically satisfiable* if it is satisfied in some deterministic model.

Clearly if a formula is valid, it is deterministically valid, but, not necessarily vice versa. For example, the formula $A =< a > P \wedge < a > Q \rightarrow < a > (P \wedge Q)$ is valid in all deterministic models, but not in all nondeterministic ones. Suppose that one can access two states s' and s'' from s, both via the action a, but such that s' satisfies P only and s'' satisfies Q only. Then we have a nondeterministic model in which the antecedent of the formula holds but the succedent fails so the formula A fails to hold. The *negation* of A is satisfiable, but not deterministically satisfiable.

We will show that the validity problem for Deterministic Propositional Distributed Transition Logic (DPDTL) is Π_1^1-complete. i.e. it is in the class Π_1^1 and is as hard as any other problem in this class. For the sake of completeness, we give here a brief discussion of this class.

It is known that the undecidability of the halting problem can be relativised, i.e. if X is a set of natural numbers, then one can consider Turing machines which use X as an oracle. Then the halting problem for such machines is not itself Turing computable (or recursive) in X, i.e. it cannot be computed using X as an oracle, but if X' is this halting problem, then X is computable in it.

Suppose we define X_0 to be the empty set, and $X_{n+1} = (X_n)'$. Then as n increases, the sets X_n get more and more non-recursive. The *arithmetical* sets, sets definable in first order arithmetic, are exactly the sets recursive in X_n for some finite n. However, by diagonalisation, we can now define the set X_ω which is just above all these X_n. In fact we can define X_α where α is any recursive ordinal. Sets recursive in these are exactly the *hyperarithmetic* sets.

Then a Π_1^1-complete set lies just above all these hyperarithmetic sets in that it is not recursive in any of them, but they are all recursive in it. Syntactically, a Π_1^1 predicate P is expressible in the form $P(x) \equiv (\forall X)(\exists y)R(X, y, x)$, where $R(X, y, x)$ is recursive in X, y, x and the variable X ranges over *sets* of natural numbers. A predicate is Σ_1^1 iff its negation is Π_1^1 and another characterisation of hyperarithmetic sets is to say that they are just the sets which are both Π_1^1 and Σ_1^1. See [6].

The Tiling Problem: Suppose we are given a finite set $\mathcal{T}$ of (types of) tiles. A *tile* is essentially a unit square, where each side, north, east, south, and west, is assigned a *color*. Two tiles of the same type are of course identically colored, and there are infinitely many tiles of each type. The *problem of tiling* is, given such a finite set of types, to determine if there is a way to tile the upper right quadrant of the plane in such a way that a tile of a specified initial type T_0 is next to the origin and the colors of adjacent tiles all match. E.g. if a tile t is just to the left of another tile t', then the east color $East(t)$ of t and the west color $West(t')$ of t' are equal. The problem of *recurring* tiling is to decide if there is a tiling which has the additional property that some given tile type T_r occurs infinitely often in the leftmost column. This is the problem R2 of [2].

The problem of tiling is r.e.-complete. i.e. it is recursive in the halting problem and vice versa. The problem of deciding if there exists a recurring tiling is Σ_1^1-complete (see [2]). Thus all we need to do is to show how to reduce the recurring tiling problem to the satisfiability problem for DPDTL, and to show that, moreover, the latter problem *is* in the class Σ_1^1. It will then follow that the *satisfiability* problem is Σ_1^1-complete and the *validity* problem is Π_1^1-complete

The Color Problem: We define another problem, the *color problem*, which will serve as a convenient intermediary. We imagine given a finite set $\mathcal{C}$ of colors. Moreover, for each $c \in \mathcal{C}$, there are two subsets $U(c)$ and $R(c)$ of $\mathcal{C}$. Read *Up* for U and *Right* for R. The problem now is to find a coloring of the set $N \times N$ such that for all $i, j \in N$, $c(i,j) \in \mathcal{C}$, $c(0,0) = c_0$, $c(i, j+1) \in U(c(i,j))$ and $c(i+1, j) \in R(c(i,j))$. In other words, a coloring of the lattice points in the plane such that if a point has color c, then the point just above has a color from the set $U(c)$ and the point to the right has a color from the set $R(c)$.

Reduction of the Tiling Problem to the Color Problem: Given a set $\mathcal{T}$ of types of tiles, let $\mathcal{C} \subseteq \mathcal{T}^4$ be such that if $c = (T_1, T_2, T_3, T_4)$, then $c \in \mathcal{C}$ iff $South(T_1) = North(T_3)$, $East(T_1) = West(T_2)$, $North(T_4) = South(T_2)$ and $West(T_4) = East(T_3)$. In other words, the four tile types can be put at a point so that the tiles T_1, T_2, T_3, T_4 accupy the NW, NE, SW, SE corners respectively and the adjoining colors all match. See figure 2.

T_1	T_2
T_3	T_4

Figure 2

To make the reduction complete, we define
$U(c) = \{c'|c' \textit{ is of the form } (T, T', T_1, T_2) \wedge c' \in \mathcal{C}\}$.
Similarly,
$R(c) = \{c'|c' \textit{ is of the form } (T_2, T, T_4, T') \wedge c' \in \mathcal{C}\}$.
It is straightforward now to see that there is a 1-1 correspondence between tilings for the original tiling problem and colorings for the coloring problem. Thus, for instance, if we are given a tiling, we can get a coloring by looking at the four tiles which meet at each lattice point. On the other hand, given a coloring, we can find a tiling by taking the SW tile of the four at each lattice point. Precisely, if ϕ is the tiling and ψ is the cooresponding coloring, then we have

$$\psi(i,j) = (\phi(i,j+1), \phi(i+1,j+1), \phi(i,j), \phi(i+1,j))$$

and

$$\phi(i,j) = (\psi(i,j))_3$$

where the function $(x,y,z,u)_3 = z$ gives the third component of every quadruple.

Now given a recurring tiling problem, we show how to reduce it to the problem of determining the satisfiability of a formula A of DPDTL. The formula A is expressed in the language of the corresponding color problem. We have a language with two action symbols a, b, a proposition symbol C_i for each $c_i \in \mathcal{C}$, and a proposition symbol F to indicate that the given state is in the leftmost column. a means "one step right" and b means "one step up". A is the conjunction of the seven formulas A_i below.

A_1: $\bigvee C_i : c_i$ is of the form $(T, T', T_0, T'') \wedge c_i \in \mathcal{C}$
A_1 says that the tile type T at the origin is the type T_0. Note that the symbols T, c_i are *used* in describing A_1 but do not *occur* in it. Only the C_i do.

A_2: $\Box[(\bigvee C_i : c_i \in \mathcal{C}) \wedge (\bigwedge C_i \rightarrow \neg C_j : i \neq j)]$
A_2 says that each point of $N \times N$ has exactly one color.

A_3: $\Box < \{a, b\} > \textit{true}$
A_3 says that one can always do a, b *concurrently* from any point.

A_4: $\Box(\bigwedge[C_i \rightarrow [a](\bigvee C_j : c_j \in R(c_i)] : c_i \in \mathcal{C})$

A_4 says that the color to the right of any point is always from the *Right* set of that point. A_5, below, is the same with *Up* instead of *Right*.

A_5: $\Box(\bigwedge[C_i \rightarrow [b](\bigvee C_j : c_j \in U(c_i)] : c_i \in \mathcal{C})$

A_6: $F \wedge \Box(F \rightarrow [b]F) \wedge \Box(\neg < a > F)$

A_6 says that F holds exactly in the leftmost column.

A_7: $\Box(F \rightarrow \Diamond(F \wedge (\bigvee C_i$: type T_r occurs in color $c_i)))$

A_7 says that the tile type T_r occurs infinitely often in the leftmost column. Note again that the symbol T_r does not actually occur in A_7.

Then it is clear that the formula A is deterministically satisfiable iff the original recurring tile problem has a solution. From a model of the formula, one can read off the solution to the tiling problem and conversely, a solution to the tiling problem provides a model. (A model may have extra points which do not belong to the reachability class of the base state, but these can just be ignored as they play no role in whether the formula A holds at the base state).

Now, the problem of the existence of solutions to the repeating tile problem is Σ_1^1-complete. Hence the satisfiability problem for DPDTL is Σ_1^1-hard and therefore the validity problem for DPDTL is Π_1^1-hard. To see that it is in fact in the class Π_1^1 we note that the satisfiability problem is in Σ_1^1. This follows from the fact that if a formula has a model, then it has a countable one and the model can in fact be coded in the full k-ary tree where k is the number of action letters. We skip the details.

Why should the deterministic case be so different? The reason is that the combination of determinism and concurrency forces the model to look like a whole bunch of squares glued together; in other words, to look like $N \times N$. Think of the point satisfying the formula A as $(0,0)$. Now given a point p in the model corresponding to (i,j), we have a point q reachable by doing $\{a,b\}$. Now q can also be reached by doing a and then b or by doing b and then a. However, a and b are deterministic. Hence q is unique and can be thought of as $(i+1,j+1)$. The other two points of the square are $(i+1,j)$ and $(i,j+1)$. Thus the set of points accessible from $(0,0)$ is isomorphic to $N \times N$. Once that happens, then coding the domino problems is easy. By contrast, in the non-deterministic case, the model looks more like a tree and the logic is easier to decide.

References

[1] M. Fischer and R. Ladner, "Propositional Dynamic Logic of Regular Programs", *Jour. Comp. Sys. Sci.* **18** (1981) pp. 194-211.

[2] D. Harel, "Recurring Dominoes: Making the Highly Undecidable Highly Understandable", *Annals of Discrete Mathematics* **24** (1985), pp. 51-72.

[3] D. Kozen and R. Parikh, "An Elementary Completeness Proof for PDL", *Theor. Comp. Sci* **14** (1981) pp. 113-118.

[4] K. Lodaya, R. Ramanujam and P. Thiagarajan, "A Logic for Distributed Transition Systems", Technical Report 88-25, department of Computer Science, leiden University. To appear in *Proceedings of the REX Conference*, Springer Lecture Notes in Computer Science.

[5] V. Pratt, "A Near-Optimal Method for Reasoning About Action" , *J. Computer and System Science* **20** (1980) pp. 231-254.

[6] H. Rogers, *Theory of Recursive Functions and Effective Computability*, McGraw-Hill 1967.

INDISCERNIBILITY, PARTITIONS AND ROUGH SETS

Zdzisław Pawlak
Polish Academy of Sciences

ABSTRACT. The concept of a rough set is a new mathematical tool intended to deal with imprecise knowledge. Some issues concerning basic properties of this concept will be discussed in this paper.

1. INTRODUCTION

We would like to discuss in this paper a basic assumption underlying the concept of a rough set (cf.[1]), which was introduced in order to deal with imprecise knowledge. Our primary assumption is that if we do not have precise knowledge about some objects - we are unable to discern them, i.e. our conjecture is that imprecision is manifested throughout indiscernibility. Moreover we assume that indiscernibility relation is an equivalence relation, and each equivalence (indiscernibility) class of the indiscernibility relation contains elements which can not be discerned at the present level of knowledge. Thus knowledge about certain set of objects is identified in our approach with the ability to classify this object into blocks of the partition induced by the indiscernibility relation. Thus the more knowledge we have about some objects the more exactly we can then classify. In order to formulate these ideas more precisely the concept of the rough set will be employed. Let us mention the idea of the rough set is basically different to that of fuzzy set introduced by Zadeh (cf. [4]).

2. APPROXIMATION SPACE

In this section we define the notion of an approximation space, which will be used as a mathematical model of imprecise knowledge. Informally the approximation space is a partition of a certain universe of discourse, such that the elements of the universe contained in the same block of the partition appear to be indistinguishable due to the lack of knowledge.

We begin our considerations with precise definition of the concept of the approximation space. The *approximation space* is a pair $A = (U,R)$, where U is a non-empty, finite set called the *universe* and R is a binary relation over U, called the *indiscernibility relation*. Elements of U will also be called *objects*. Objects can be anything we can think of, for example states, processes, moments of time, physical or abstract entities etc. In other words the universe is going to represent our domain of interest.

We assume that R is an equivalence relation. This assumption is motivated by many practical applications of the introduced concept.

If R is an indiscernibility relation then R^* is to denote the family of all equivalence classes of R (partition generated by R), i.e. $R^*=\{X_1,X_2,\ldots,X_n\}$, where X_i are equivalence (indiscernibility) classes of R (or *blocks* of R^*). The equivalence class containing element $x\in U$ will be denoted by $[x]_R$ or $[x]$ when R is understood. If $R(x,y)$ we say that x and y are *R-indiscernible*.

If $A=(U,R)$ and $A'=(U',R')$ are two approximation spaces and $U'\subseteq U$, $R'\subseteq R$ we say that A' is an *approximation subspace* of A.

If $B = (U,Q)$ is the approximation subspace of $A=(U,R)$ we say that B is *finer* than A and A is *coarser* than B.

Intuitively, finer approximation space means that our knowledge about the universe is larger than in the case of coarser approximation space. The more knowledge we have the finer is the corresponding approximation space, the better is our ability to discern more precisely elements of the universe. Representing of knowledge by an indiscernibility relation seems to be natural and justified at least in some application areas.

It is worthwhile to mention that the inability to discern exactly objects might be not necessarily a drawback of our knowledge. Sometimes it may be a desired advantage. Suppose for example that we consider a concept of a green colour. Because human beings are able to discern many shades of green thus in order to have one concept of green colour we have to ignore small differences between them. In our terms it means a coarser approximation space, which is in fact a generalization of the concept of green colour, i.e. reduction of our ability to discern shades of green. Conversely, finer approximation space means specification of our knowledge. For example, in order to specify the concept of water we have to have more knowledge so that we are able to distinguish between oceans, lakes, rivers, puddles etc. Thus the concept of indiscernibility may have many applications. We shall concentrate in this paper on the investigation of indiscernibility as a model for imprecise knowledge independently of its possible meanings.

3. APPROXIMATION OF SETS

As we have already demonstrated in the previous section the incompleteness of our knowledge leads to practical difficulties in deciding membership of an object in a set. Consequently, in the rough set approach the basic role is played by the concept of the approximation of a set by another set.

To describe the idea, suppose we are given an approximation space $A = (U, R)$. With each subset $X \subseteq U$ we can associate two related subsets

$$\underline{R}X = \bigcup \{Y \in R^{*}: Y \subseteq X\}$$
$$\bar{R}X = \bigcup \{Y \in R^{*}: Y \cap X \neq \emptyset\}$$

called the *R-lower* and *R-upper approximation* of X respectively.

The set

$$BN_R(X) = \bar{R}X - \underline{R}X$$

will be called the *R-boundary* of X, or a *R-boundary region* of X.

We shall also employ the following denotations:

$POS_R(X) = \underline{R}X$, *R-positive region* of X

$NEG_R(X) = U - \bar{R}X$, *R-negative region of* X.

The positive region $POS_R(X)$ or the lower approximation of X is the collection of those objects which can be classified with full certainty as members of the set X. Similarly, the negative region $NEG_R(X)$ is the collection of objects about which it can be determined without any ambiguity that they do not belong to the set X, that is, there are contained in the complement $-X$.

The boundary region is, in a sense, undecidable area of the universe, i.e. none of the objects belonging to the boundary can be classified with certainty into X or complement $-X$.

Now we are able to define our basic concept of a rough set. Set $X \subseteq U$ is *rough with respect to R* if $\bar{R}X \neq \underline{R}X$; otherwise the set X is *exact*. Thus rough sets are sets with unsharp defined boundary, i.e. sets which can not be uniquely defined.

4. PROPERTIES OF APPROXIMATION

Directly from the definition of approxiamtions we can get the following properties of the R-lower and the R-upper approximations:

Proposition 1.

1) $\underline{R}X \subseteq X \subseteq \overline{R}X$
2) $\underline{R}\emptyset=\overline{R}\emptyset=\emptyset$; $\underline{R}U=\overline{R}U=U$
3) $\overline{R}(X\cup Y)=\overline{R}X\cup\overline{R}Y$
4) $\underline{R}(X\cap Y)=\underline{R}X\cap\underline{R}Y$
5) $X\subseteq Y$ implies $\underline{R}X\subseteq\underline{R}Y$ and $\overline{R}X\subseteq\overline{R}Y$
6) $\underline{R}(X\cup Y)\supseteq\underline{R}X\cup\underline{R}Y$
7) $\overline{R}(X\cap Y)\subseteq\overline{R}X\cap\overline{R}Y$
8) $\underline{R}(-X)=-\overline{R}X$
9) $\overline{R}(-X)=-\underline{R}X$
10) $\underline{R}\underline{R}X=\overline{R}\underline{R}X=\underline{R}X$
11) $\overline{R}\overline{R}X=\underline{R}\overline{R}X=\overline{R}X$

Proof.

1a) If $x\in\underline{R}X$, then $[x]\subseteq X$, but $x\in[x]$ hence $x\in X$ and $\underline{R}X\subseteq X$.

1b) If $x\in X$, then $[x]\cap X\neq\emptyset$ (because $x\in[x]\cap X$) hence $x\in\underline{R}X$, and $X\subseteq\underline{R}X$.

2a) From 1) $\underline{R}\emptyset \subsetneq \emptyset$ and $\emptyset\subseteq\underline{R}\emptyset$ (because the empty set is included in every set) thus $\underline{R}\emptyset=\emptyset$.

2b) Suppose $\overline{R}\emptyset\neq\emptyset$. Then there exists x such that $x\in\overline{R}\emptyset$. Hence $[x]\cap\emptyset\neq\emptyset$, but $[x]\cap\emptyset=\emptyset$, what contradicts the assumption, thus $\overline{R}\emptyset=\emptyset$.

2c) From 1) $\underline{R}U\subseteq U$. In order to show that $U\subseteq\underline{R}U$ let us observe that if $x\in U$, then $[x]\subseteq U$, hence $x\in\underline{R}U$, thus $\underline{R}U=U$.

2d) From 1) $\overline{R}U\supseteq U$, and obviously $\overline{R}U\subseteq U$, thus $\overline{R}U=U$.

3) $x\in\overline{R}(X\cup Y)$ iff $[x]\cap(X\cup Y)\neq\emptyset$

iff $[x] \cap X \cup [x] \cap Y \neq \emptyset$

iff $[x] \cap X \neq \emptyset \vee [x] \cap Y \neq \emptyset$ iff $x \in \overline{R}X \vee x \in \overline{R}Y$ iff $x \in \overline{R}X \cup \overline{R}Y$. Thus $\overline{R}(X \cup Y) = \overline{R}X \cup \overline{R}Y$.

4) $x \in \underline{R}(X \cap Y)$ iff $[x] \subseteq X \cap Y$ iff $[x] \subseteq X \wedge [x] \subseteq Y$ iff $x \in \underline{R}X \cap \underline{R}Y$.

5) Because $X \subseteq Y$ iff $X \cap Y = X$ by virtue of 4) we have $\underline{R}(X \cap Y) = \underline{R}X$ iff $\underline{R}X \cap \underline{R}Y = \underline{R}X$ which yields $\underline{R}X \subseteq \underline{R}Y$.

Because $X \subseteq Y$ iff $X \cup Y = Y$, hence $\overline{R}(X \cup Y) = \overline{R}Y$ and by virtue of 3) we have $\overline{R}X \cup \overline{R}Y = \overline{R}Y$ and hence $\overline{R}X \subseteq \overline{R}Y$.

6) Because $X \subseteq X \cup Y$ and $Y \subseteq X \cup Y$, we have $\underline{R}X \subseteq \underline{R}(X \cup Y)$ and $\underline{R}Y \subseteq \underline{R}(X \cup Y)$ which yields $\underline{R}X \cup \underline{R}Y \subseteq \underline{R}(X \cup Y)$.

7) Because $X \cap Y \subseteq X$ and $X \cap Y \subseteq Y$, we have $\overline{R}(X \cap Y) \subseteq \overline{R}X$ and $\overline{R}(X \cap Y) \subseteq \overline{R}Y$ hence $\overline{R}(X \cap Y) \subseteq \overline{R}X \cap \overline{R}Y$.

8) $x \in \underline{R}(x)$ iff $[x] \subseteq X$ iff $[x] \cap -X = \emptyset$ iff $x \notin \overline{R}(-X)$ iff $x \in -\overline{R}(-X)$, hence $\underline{R}(X) = -\overline{R}(-X)$.

9) By substitution $-X$ for X in 9) we get $\overline{R}(X) = -\underline{R}(-X)$.

10a) From 1) $\underline{R}\underline{R}X \subseteq \underline{R}X$, thus we have to show that $\underline{R}X \subseteq \underline{R}\underline{R}X$. If $x \in \underline{R}X$ then $[x] \subseteq X$, hence $\underline{R}[x] \subseteq \underline{R}X$ but $\underline{R}[x] = [x]$, thus $[x] \subseteq \underline{R}X$ and $x \in \underline{R}\underline{R}X$, that is $\underline{R}X \subseteq \underline{R}\underline{R}X$.

10b) From 1) $\underline{R}X \subseteq \overline{R}\underline{R}X$, thus it is enough to show that $\underline{R}X \supseteq \overline{R}\underline{R}X$.

If $x \in \overline{R}\underline{R}X$, then $[x] \cap \underline{R}X \neq \emptyset$, i.e. there exists $y \in [x]$ such that $y \in \underline{R}X$, hence $[y] \subseteq X$ but $[x] = [y]$, thus $[x] \subseteq X$ and $x \in \underline{R}X$ which is to mean that $\underline{R}X \supseteq \overline{R}\underline{R}X$.

11a) From 1) $\overline{R}X \subseteq \overline{R}\overline{R}X$. We have to show, that $\overline{R}X \supseteq \overline{R}\overline{R}X$. If $x \in \overline{R}\overline{R}X$, then $[x] \cap \overline{R}X \neq \emptyset$ and for some $y \in [x]$ $y \in \overline{R}X$, hence $[y] \cap X \neq \emptyset$ but $[x] = [y]$, thus $[x] \cap X \neq \emptyset$, i.e. $x \in \overline{R}X$, which yields $\overline{R}X \supseteq \overline{R}\overline{R}X$.

11b) From 1) $\underline{R}\overline{R}X \subseteq \overline{R}X$. We have to show, that $\underline{R}\overline{R}X \supseteq \overline{R}X$. If $x \in \overline{R}X$ then $[x] \cap X \neq \emptyset$. Hence $[x] \subseteq \overline{R}X$ (because if $y \in [x]$, then $[y] \cap X = [x] \cap X \neq \emptyset$, i.e. $y \in \overline{R}X$) and $x \in \underline{R}\overline{R}X$, which gives $\underline{R}\overline{R}X \supseteq X$.

5. LOWER AND UPPER MEMBERSHIP

The concept of approximations of sets leads to a new conception of membership relation. Because definition of set in our approach is associated with knowledge (i.e. indiscernibility relation) hence also a membership relation must be related to knowledge. Formally this can be defined as follows:

$$x \underline{\in}_R X \text{ if and only if } x \in \underline{R}X$$

$$x \overline{\in}_R X \text{ if and only if } x \in \overline{R}X$$

where $\underline{\in}_R$ reads "*x surely belongs* to X with respect to R " and $\overline{\in}_R$ - "x possibly *belongs* to X with respect to R ".

Both membership relations again are referring to our knowledge, i.e. indiscernibility relation R.

From **Proposition 1** we obtain the following properties of membership relations (for simplicity we drop the subscript R):

1) $x \underline{\in} X$ implies $x \underline{\in} X$ implies $x \in X$ implies $x \overline{\in} X$
2) $x \underline{\in} \emptyset$ if and only if $x \overline{\in} \emptyset$ if and only if $x \in \emptyset$;
   $x \underline{\in} U$ if and only if $x \overline{\in} U$ if and only if $x \in U$;
3) $X \subseteq Y$ implies ($x \underline{\in} X$ implies $x \underline{\in} Y$ and $x \overline{\in} X$ implies $x \overline{\in} Y$)
4) $x \overline{\in} (X \cup Y)$ if and only if $x \overline{\in} X$ or $x \overline{\in} Y$
5) $x \underline{\in} (X \cap Y)$ if and only if $x \underline{\in} X$ and $x \underline{\in} Y$
6) $x \underline{\in} X$ or $x \underline{\in} Y$ implies $x \underline{\in} (X \cup Y)$
7) $x \overline{\in} (X \cap Y)$ implies $x \overline{\in} X$ and $x \overline{\in} Y$
8) $x \underline{\in} (-X)$ if and only if non $x \overline{\in} X$
9) $x \overline{\in} (-X)$ if and only if non $x \underline{\in} X$

6. ROUGH EQUALITY OF SETS

As we have already indicated the concept of rough set differs essentially from the ordinary concept of the set, because for the rough sets we are unable to define uniquely the membership relation and we have two of them instead (cf. section 5).

There is another important difference between those concepts namely that of equality of sets. In set theory two sets are equal if they have exactly the same elements. In our approach we need another concept of equality of sets, namely approximate (rough) equality.

In fact we need not one but three kinds of approximate equality of sets, as defined below:

Let $A = (U, R)$ and $X, Y \subseteq U$. We say that

a) Sets X and Y are *bottom R-equal* ($X \eqsim_R Y$) if $\underline{RX} = \underline{RY}$.

b) Sets X and Y are *top R-equal* ($X \simeq_R Y$) if $\bar{R}X = \bar{R}Y$.

c) Sets X and Y are *R-equal* ($X \approx_R Y$) if $X \eqsim_R Y$ and $X \tilde{\simeq}_R Y$.

It is easy to see that $\eqsim_R$, $\simeq_R$ and $\approx_R$ are equivalence relations for any indiscernibility relation R.

We can associate the following interpretations, with the above notions of rough equality (For simplicity of notation we shall omit the subscripts.):

a) If $X \eqsim Y$, this means that positive examples of the sets X and Y are the same.

b) If $X \simeq Y$, then the negative examples of sets X and Y are the same.

c) If $X \approx Y$, then both positive and negative examples of sets X and Y are the same.

(By positive or negative examples of a set we mean the elements of the universe belonging to either positive or negative region of the set, respectively.)

The following exemplary properties of relations $\eqsim_R$, $\simeq_R$ and $\approx_R$ are immediate consequences of the definitions:

Proposition 2. For any indiscernibility relation we have the following properties:

1) $X \eqsim Y$ if $X \cap Y \eqsim X$ and $X \cap Y \eqsim Y$

2) $X \simeq Y$ if $X \cup Y \simeq X$ and $X \cup Y \simeq Y$

3) If $X \simeq X'$ and $Y \simeq Y'$, then $X \cup Y \simeq X' \cup Y'$

4) If $X \underset{\sim}{-} X'$ and $Y \underset{\sim}{-} Y'$, then $X \cap Y \underset{\sim}{-} X' \cap Y'$

5) If $X \simeq Y$, then $X \cup -Y \simeq U$

6) If $X \underset{\sim}{-} Y$, then $X \cap -Y \underset{\sim}{-} \emptyset$

7) If $X \subseteq Y$ and $Y \simeq \emptyset$, then $X \simeq \emptyset$

8) If $X \subseteq Y$ and $X \simeq U$, then $Y \simeq U$

9) $X \simeq Y$ if and only if $-X \simeq -Y$

10) $X \cap Y \underset{\sim}{-} \emptyset$ if and only if $X \underset{\sim}{-} \emptyset$ or $Y \underset{\sim}{-} \emptyset$

11) $X \cup Y \simeq U$ if and only if $X \simeq U$ or $Y \simeq U$

■

Let us note that if we replace $\underset{\sim}{-}$ by $\simeq$ (or conversely) the above properties are not valid.

7. ROUGH INCLUSION OF SETS

One of the fundamental notions of the set theory is inclusion relation. Analogous notion can be introduced in rough sets framework. The rough inclusion of sets is defined here in much the same way as the rough equality of sets.

The formal definition of rough inclusion is as follows.

Let $A = (U, R)$ be an approximation space and $X, Y \subseteq U$. We shall say that:

a) Set X is *bottom R-included* in Y ($X \underset{\sim}{\subset}_R Y$) if $\underline{R}X \subseteq \underline{R}Y$, ($\underline{R}X \neq \emptyset$)

b) Set X is *top R-included* in Y ($X \tilde{\subset}_R Y$) if $\bar{R}Y \subseteq \bar{R}X$.

c) Set X is *R-included* in Y ($X \underset{\sim}{\tilde{\subset}}_R Y$), if $X \underset{\sim}{\subset}_R Y$ and $X \tilde{\subset}_R Y$.

One can easily see that $\underset{\sim}{\subset}_R$, $\tilde{\subset}_R$ and $\underset{\sim}{\tilde{\subset}}_R$ are ordering relations.

In fact we have, as in the case of rough equality of sets, three rough inclusion relations of sets. The intuitive meaning of these inclusions is the following:

a) $X \underset{\sim}{\subset} Y$ means that the positive examples of the set X

are also positive examples of the set Y.

b) $X \tilde{\subset} Y$ means that negative examples of set Y are also the negative examples of the set X.

c) If $X \underset{\sim}{\tilde{\subset}} Y$, then both a) and b) hold.

It should be quite clear by now that rough inclusion of sets does not imply the inclusion of sets.

Immediately from the definitions we can derive the following simple properties:

Proposition 3.

1) If $X \subseteq Y$, then $X \underset{\sim}{\subset} Y$, $X \tilde{\subset} Y$ and $X \underset{\sim}{\tilde{\subset}} Y$.
2) If $X \underset{\sim}{\subset} Y$ and $Y \underset{\sim}{\subset} X$, then $X \underset{\sim}{=} Y$.
3) If $X \tilde{\subset} Y$ and $Y \tilde{\subset} X$, then $X \simeq Y$.
4) If $X \underset{\sim}{\tilde{\subset}} Y$ and $Y \underset{\sim}{\tilde{\subset}} X$, then $X \approx Y$.
5) $X \tilde{\subset} Y$ if and only if $X \cup Y \simeq Y$.
6) $X \underset{\sim}{\subset} Y$ if and only if $X \cap Y \underset{\sim}{=} Y$.
7) If $X \subseteq Y$, $X \underset{\sim}{=} X'$ and $Y \underset{\sim}{=} Y'$, then $X' \underset{\sim}{\subset} Y'$.
8) If $X \subseteq Y$, $X \simeq X'$ and $Y \simeq Y'$, then $X' \tilde{\subset} Y'$
9) If $X \subseteq Y$, $X \approx X'$ and $Y \approx Y'$ then $X' \underset{\sim}{\tilde{\subset}} Y'$.
10) If $X' \tilde{\subset} X$ and $Y' \tilde{\subset} Y$, then $X' \cup Y' \tilde{\subset} X \cup Y$.
11) If $X' \underset{\sim}{\subset} X$ and $Y' \tilde{\subset} Y$, then $X' \cap Y' \tilde{\subset} X \cap Y$.
12) $X \cap Y \underset{\sim}{\subset} X \tilde{\subset} X \cup Y$.
13) If $X \underset{\sim}{\subset} Y$ and $X \underset{\sim}{=} Z$, then $Z \underset{\sim}{\subset} Y$.
14) If $X \tilde{\subset} Y$ and $X \simeq Z$, then $Z \tilde{\subset} Y$.
15) If $X \underset{\sim}{\tilde{\subset}} Y$ and $X \approx Z$, then $Z \underset{\sim}{\tilde{\subset}} Y$.

■

The above properties are not valid if we replace $\underset{\sim}{=}$ by $\simeq$ (or conversely).

8. CONCLUSION

It is interesting to compare the the concept of the rough sets with that of conventional set. Basic properties of roughs sets, like membership of elements, equality and inclusion of sets are related to our knowledge about the universe of discourse, expressed by the indiscernibility relation. Consequently whether an element belongs to a set or not is not an objective property of the element but depends upon our knowledge about it. Similarly equality and inclusion of sets are not decidable in absolute sense but depend on what we know about the sets in question. In general all properties of rough sets are not absolute but are related to what we know about them. In this sense the rough set approach could be viewed as a subjective counterpart of the "classical" set theory.

9. REFERENCES

1) **Pawlak, Z.**, Rough Sets. *International Journal of Information and Computer Sciences*, **11**, 341-356(1982).

2) **Novotny, M., and Pawlak, Z.** Characterization of rough top equalities and rough bottom equalities. *Bull. Polish Acad. Sci. Math.*, **33**, 91-97(1985a).

3) **Novotny, M., and Pawlak, Z.**, On rough equalities. *Bull. Polish Acad. Sci. Math.*, **33**, 99-104(1985b).

4) **Zadeh, L. (1965).** Fuzzy Sets. *Information and Control*, **8**, 338-353(1965).

A 4-STATE PROBABILISTIC TABLE APPROXIMATING ALL 2-STATE PROBABILISTIC TABLES

Azaria Paz
Computer Science Department
Technion - Israel Institute of Technology
Haifa 32000, Israel

ABSTRACT

Let K_2 be the set of all tables $T = (S,M)$ where S is a set of 2 states and M is a finite set of 2×2 probabilistic matrices $M = \{A(\sigma):\sigma \in \Sigma\}$. For $x = \sigma_{i_1} \ldots \sigma_{i_k} \in \Sigma^*$ define $A(x) = A(\sigma_{i_1}) \ldots A(\sigma_{i_k})$. A 4-state probabilistic table $T_1 = (S_1,M_1)$ over an alphabet Σ' with 8 letters is shown such that if $S_1 = \{1,2,3,4\}$, $S = \{1,2\}$, $\phi(1) = 1$ and $\phi(2) = 3$. Then for any $\delta > 0$ there exists a mapping $\Psi_\delta : \Sigma \longrightarrow \Sigma^*$, such that

$$|A_{ij}(x)-A'_{\phi(i)\phi(j)}(\Psi_\delta(x))| < \delta$$

for all $x = \sigma_{i_1} \ldots \sigma_{i_k} \in \Sigma^*$, where $\Psi_\delta(x) = \Psi_\delta(\sigma_{i_1}) \ldots \Psi_\delta(\sigma_{i_k})$, $M_1 = \{ A'(\sigma): \sigma \in \Sigma'\}$ and the matrices $A'(\sigma)$ are 4×4 probabilistic matrices.

1. INTRODUCTION

A probabilistic table over an alphabet Σ is a system (S,M) where S is a finite set of states and M is a finite set of $|S| \times |S|$ stochastic matrices $\{A(\sigma); \sigma \in \Sigma\}$.

With every word $x = \sigma_1 \ldots \sigma_k \in \Sigma^*$ we associate the stochastic matrix $A(x) = A(\sigma_1) \ldots A(\sigma_k)$. The ij -entry of $A(x)$, denoted $A_{ij}(x)$, represents the probability that the system defined by the given table moves from state i to state j under the input x.

Probabilistic tables are the underlying structure of Finite Probabilistic Automata and may have other applications as well (random number generation, nonhomogeneous Markov Chains, etc.).

The problem considered in this paper is the following:

Is it possible to construct an m-state probabilistic table (abbreviation: p.t.) such that every n-state, $n < m$, p.t. can be approximated (in a certain sense to be defined in the sequel) by it? We answer this question positively and constructively for $m = 4$ and $n = 2$.

2. SOME DEFINITIONS AND NOTATIONS

If A is a matrix then $|A|$ denotes $|A| = \max_{i,j} |a_{ij}|$.

Definition 1:

Given two p.t.'s (S_1,M_1) and (S_2,M_2) over the alphabets Σ_1 and Σ_2 correspondingly we say that (S_1,M_1) is δ-homomorphic to (S_1,M_1) if there is a mapping $\phi : S_1 \longrightarrow S_2$ and for every $\delta > 0$ there is a mapping $\Psi_\delta: \Sigma_1 \longrightarrow \Sigma_2^*$ such that for every word $x \in \Sigma_1^*$ we have that

$$|A^{(1)}_{ij}(x) - A^{(2)}_{\phi(i)\phi(j)}(\Psi_\delta(x))| \leq \delta$$

where $M_i = \{A^{(i)}(\sigma);\sigma \in\Sigma_i\}$ $i = 1,2$ and $\Psi_\delta(x) = \Psi_\delta(\sigma_1)\ldots \Psi_\delta(\sigma_k)$ for $x = \sigma_1\ldots\sigma_k$.

Definition 2:

Let K be a class of probabilistic tables. A given p.t. $\theta = (S,M)$ will be called δ-universal for the class K if every p.t. in K is δ-homomorphic to θ.

3. SOME PRELIMINARY LEMMAS

The following 3 lemmas are well known. The proof is provided for the sake of completeness.

Let $A = [a_{ij}]$ be a 2 x 2 matrix. Define
$|| A || = \max (|a_{11}-a_{21}|, |a_{12}-a_{22}|)$.

Lemma 1: Given 2 probabilistic 2 x 2 matrices A and B, $|| AB || \leq || A || \; || B ||$.
Proof: Let AB = C. Then

$$\begin{aligned} |c_{11}-c_{21}| &= |a_{11}b_{11} + (1-a_{11})b_{21} - (a_{21}b_{11} - (1-a_{21})b_{21})| \\ &= |(a_{11}-a_{21})b_{11} - (a_{11}-a_{21})b_{21}| \\ &= |(a_{11}-a_{21})(b_{11}-b_{21})| \leq || A || \; || B ||. \end{aligned}$$

In a similar way $|c_{21}-c_{22}| \leq || A || \; || B ||$.

Lemma 2: Given two 2 x 2 probabilistic matrices A and B, $|AB - B| \leq || B ||$.
Proof: Let AB = C. Then

$$\begin{aligned} |c_{ij}-b_{ij}| &= |a_{i1}b_{1j}+(1-a_{i1})b_{2j}-b_{ij}| \\ &= |a_{i1}(b_{1j}-b_{2j})+b_{2j}-b_{ij}| \\ &= \begin{cases} |a_{21}(b_{1j}-b_{2j})| \leq |b_{1j}-b_{2j}| \leq || B || & \text{if } i = 2 \\ |(1-a_{11})(b_{1j}-b_{2j})| \leq |b_{1j}-b_{2j}| \leq || B || & \text{if } i = 1 \end{cases} \end{aligned}$$

Lemma 3: Let $A(0) = \begin{bmatrix} 1 & 0 \\ 0.5 & 1 \end{bmatrix}$, $A(1) = \begin{bmatrix} 0.5 & 0.5 \\ 0 & 1 \end{bmatrix}$ and $A(x) = A(\sigma_1)\ldots A(\sigma_k)$ where $x = \sigma_1 \ldots \sigma_k$ and $\sigma_i \in \{0,1\}$. Then $A_{12}(x) = 0.\sigma_k \ldots \sigma_1$ where $0.\sigma_k \ldots \sigma_1$ is an ordinary binary fraction.

The proof is straightforward, by induction on the length of x, and is left to the reader. Notice that the set $\{A_{12}(x): x \in \Sigma^*\}$ is dense in the interval (0,1).

Let $T = (S,M)$ be an arbitrary p.t. with $M = \{A(\sigma_i): \sigma_i \in \Sigma\}$, Σ is a finite alphabet and $A(\sigma_i)$ are 2×2 probabilistic matrices. Some of the matrices $A(\sigma_i)$ may be equal to the matrix $\begin{bmatrix}1 & 0\\ 0 & 1\end{bmatrix}$ or to the matrix $\begin{bmatrix}0 & 1\\ 1 & 0\end{bmatrix}$. Such matrices will be called degenerate. For a given word $x = \sigma_{i_1}\ldots\sigma_{i_k} \in \Sigma^*$ we define the <u>proper length</u> of the product $A(x) = A(\sigma_{i_1})\ldots A(\sigma_{i_k})$ to be the number of matrices $A(\sigma_{i_j})$ in it which are not degenerate. Let $m(T)$ be defined as

$m(T) = \max_i \{\| A(\sigma_i) \| : \sigma_i \in \Sigma, A(\sigma_i)$ is not degenerate$\}$.

It follows from the definitions that for any T as above and such that M contains some nondegenerate matrices, we have that

$$0 \le m(T) < 1. \qquad (1)$$

This implies, by Lemma 1, that

$$\| A(x) \| \le (m(T))^{|x|_p} \longrightarrow 0, \quad \text{if } |x|_p \longrightarrow \infty \qquad (2)$$

where $|x|_p$ denotes the proper length of $A(x)$. Moreover we can prove the following.

Lemma 4: Let $T_1 = (S,M_1)$ and $T_2 = (S,M_2)$ be 2 p.t.'s over the same alphabet and such that both M_1 and M_2 are sets of 2×2 probabilistic matrices. For any δ there is ε such that if $|A(\sigma_i)-B(\sigma_i)| \le \varepsilon$ whenever $A(\sigma_i)$ is not degenerated and $A(\sigma_i) = B(\sigma_i)$ for degenerate $A(\sigma_i)$ then $|A(x)-B(x)| \le \delta$ for all $x \in \Sigma^*$, where $M_1 = \{A(\sigma_i)\}$ and $M_2 = \{B(\sigma_i)\}$.

Proof: If all matrices in M_1 are degenerate, then $M_1 = M_2$ and there is nothing to prove. Otherwise let t be the minimal integer such that $(m(T_1))^t < \delta/3$. Such an integer exists, as follows from (1).

The set $\{A(z): |z|_p \leq t\}$ is finite, as it is easy to see. Therefore, we can choose $\varepsilon > 0$ such that $(m(T_2))^t < \delta/3$ $(\lim_{\varepsilon\to 0} m(T_2) = m(T_1))$, and such that for all $z \in \Sigma^*$ with $|z|_p \leq t$, $|A(z)-B(z)| < \delta/3$.

Let $x \in \Sigma^*$ be any word. If $|x|_p \leq t$ then $|A(x)-B(x)| < \delta/3 < \delta$ and we are done. Otherwise, let $x = yz$ with $|z|_p \leq t$. By Lemma 2 and (2) and the choice of ε we have that

$$\begin{aligned} |A(x)-B(x)| &\leq |A(y)A(z)-A(z)| + |B(y)B(z)-B(z)| \\ &+ |A(z)-B(z)| \leq \| A(z) \| + \| B(z) \| + |A(z)-B(z)| \\ &< \delta/3 + \delta/3 + \delta/3 = \delta. \end{aligned}$$

The Main Problem

We can prove now the following.

Theorem: Let K_2 be the set of all 2-state p.t.'s and let $\delta > 0$ be any real number. A δ-universal p.t. with 4-state for K_2 can be constructed.

Proof: Define the 4-state p.t. $T = (S,M)$ over an 8-letter alphabet $\Sigma = \{\sigma_1 \ldots \sigma_8\}$ as below:

$$M = \{A(\sigma_i): 1 \leq i \leq 8\}$$

i	1	2	3	4
$M(\sigma_i)$:	$\begin{bmatrix}1&0&0&0\\0&0&1&0\\0&0&1&0\\0&0&1&0\end{bmatrix}$	$\begin{bmatrix}0&0&1&0\\0&0&1&0\\1&0&0&0\\0&0&1&0\end{bmatrix}$	$\begin{bmatrix}1&0&0&0\\1/2&1/2&0&0\\0&0&1&0\\0&0&0&1\end{bmatrix}$	$\begin{bmatrix}1/2&1/2&0&0\\0&1&0&0\\0&0&1&0\\0&0&0&1\end{bmatrix}$

$$
\begin{array}{ccccc}
i & 5 & 6 & 7 & 8 \\
M(\sigma_i): &
\begin{bmatrix} 1 & 0 & 0 & 0 \\ 0 & 1 & 0 & 0 \\ 0 & 0 & 1 & 0 \\ 0 & 0 & 1/2 & 1/2 \end{bmatrix} &
\begin{bmatrix} 1 & 0 & 0 & 0 \\ 0 & 1 & 0 & 0 \\ 0 & 0 & 1/2 & 1/2 \\ 0 & 0 & 0 & 1 \end{bmatrix} &
\begin{bmatrix} 0 & 0 & 1 & 0 \\ 1/2 & 0 & 1/2 & 0 \\ 0 & 0 & 1 & 0 \\ 1/2 & 0 & 1/2 & 0 \end{bmatrix} &
\begin{bmatrix} 0 & 0 & 1 & 0 \\ 1/2 & 0 & 1/2 & 0 \\ 1 & 0 & 0 & 0 \\ 1/2 & 0 & 1/2 & 0 \end{bmatrix}
\end{array}
$$

Let x and y be words over the subalphabets $\Sigma_1 = \{\sigma_3, \sigma_4\}$ and $\Sigma_2 = \{\sigma_5, \sigma_6\}$ respectively. It is easy to verify, based on Lemma 3, by straightforward computation that

$$
A(xy) = \begin{bmatrix} \alpha & 1-\alpha & 0 & 0 \\ \beta & 1-\beta & 0 & 0 \\ 0 & 0 & \gamma & 1-\gamma \\ 0 & 0 & \theta & 1-\theta \end{bmatrix}
$$

where α, β, γ and θ are binary fractions and the sets of values $\{\alpha : x \in \Sigma_1^*\}$, $\{\gamma : y \in \Sigma_2^*\}$ are independently dense in the interval $(0,1)$; $\alpha = \alpha(x)$, $\gamma = \gamma(y)$. Furthermore, one verifies by straightforward computation the following equalities:

$$
A(xy\sigma_7) = \begin{bmatrix} \frac{1-\alpha}{2} & 0 & \frac{1+\alpha}{2} & 0 \\ \frac{1-\beta}{2} & 0 & \frac{1+\beta}{2} & 0 \\ \frac{1-\gamma}{2} & 0 & \frac{1+\gamma}{2} & 0 \\ \frac{1-\theta}{2} & 0 & \frac{1+\theta}{2} & 0 \end{bmatrix}, \quad
A(xy\sigma_8) = \begin{bmatrix} \frac{1-\alpha}{2} & 0 & \frac{1+\alpha}{2} & 0 \\ \frac{1-\beta}{2} & 0 & \frac{1+\beta}{2} & 0 \\ \frac{1+\gamma}{2} & 0 & \frac{1-\gamma}{2} & 0 \\ \frac{1+\theta}{2} & 0 & \frac{1-\theta}{2} & 0 \end{bmatrix}
$$

$$A(xy\sigma_7\sigma_2) = \begin{bmatrix} \frac{1+\alpha}{2} & 0 & \frac{1-\alpha}{2} & 0 \\ \frac{1+\beta}{2} & 0 & \frac{1-\beta}{2} & 0 \\ \frac{1+\gamma}{2} & 0 & \frac{1-\gamma}{2} & 0 \\ \frac{1+\theta}{2} & 0 & \frac{1-\theta}{2} & 0 \end{bmatrix}, \quad A(xy\sigma_8\sigma_2) = \begin{bmatrix} \frac{1+\alpha}{2} & 0 & \frac{1-\alpha}{2} & 0 \\ \frac{1+\beta}{2} & 0 & \frac{1-\beta}{2} & 0 \\ \frac{1-\gamma}{2} & 0 & \frac{1+\gamma}{2} & 0 \\ \frac{1-\theta}{2} & 0 & \frac{1+\theta}{2} & 0 \end{bmatrix}$$

$\alpha = \alpha(x)$, $\beta = \beta(x)$, $\gamma = \gamma(y)$, $\theta = \theta(y)$.

Notice that the subset of states $S' = \{s_1, s_3\} \subset S$ is a closed subset of states in all the above four matrices (i.e. once in S' the system remains in S' for ever).

Let $T_1 = (S_1, M_1)$ be any p.t. in K_2 over the alphabet $\Sigma' = \{a_1 \ldots a_k\}$ and assume that not all the matrices in M_1 are degenerate (the other case is trivial).

Let $S_1 = \{1,2\}$ and let $S = \{1,2,3,4\}$. Define $\phi : S_1 \longrightarrow S$ by:

$$\phi(1) = 1, \quad \phi(2) = 3.$$

Given $\delta > 0$ let ε be as in Lemma 4 for the given p.t. T_1. It is easy to see that for any l such that $A'(a_l)$ is not degenerate, we can find x_l, y_l and z_l such that $x_l \in \Sigma_1^*$, $y_l \in \Sigma_2^*$ and $z_l \in \{\sigma_7, \sigma_8, \sigma_7\sigma_2, \sigma_8\sigma_2\}$ such that

$$|A'_{ij}(a_l) - A_{\phi(i)\phi(j)}(x_l y_l z_l)| < \varepsilon$$

where $M_1 = \{A'(a_l) : 1 \le l \le k\}$. This follows from the structure of the matrices $A(xyz)$ shown above.

Set $\Psi(a_l) = \sigma_1$ if $A'(a_l) = \begin{bmatrix} 1 & 0 \\ 0 & 1 \end{bmatrix}$, $\Psi(a_l) = \sigma_2$ if $A'(a_l) = \begin{bmatrix} 0 & 1 \\ 1 & 0 \end{bmatrix}$ and $\Psi(a_l) = x_l y_l z_l$ as defined above.

Our main theorem now follows from Lemma 4.

Remark 1: It is natural to ask whether it would be possible to generalize the result of the main theorem to the class K_n of the n-state p.t.'s for n = 3,4... etc. It appears to this author that such a generalization is impossible. Moreover, it seems reasonable to assume that the proof of any restricted generalization of the theorem would be very cumbersome.

Remark 2: A full coverage of probabilistic automata as well as an extensive bibliography can be found in A. Paz, Introduction to Probabilistic Automata, Academic Press, 1971.

APPLICATION OF L-SYSTEMS TO ALGORITHMIC GENERATION OF SOUTH INDIAN FOLK ART PATTERNS AND KARNATIC MUSIC*

PRZEMYSLAW PRUSINKIEWICZ
Department of Computer Science
University of Regina
Regina, Saskatchewan,Canada S4S 0A2

and

KAMALA KRITHIVASAN
M. G. VIJAYANARAYANA
Department of Computer Science
Indian Institute of Technology
Madras, India 600 036.

Abstract

Kolams are a form of graphical folk art practised in South India. Many kolams form families with a sophisticated recursive structure. This presents a challenging problem of describing kolam patterns formally, and creating them using computer graphics techniques. The method introduced in this paper applies L-systems to generate sequences of commands which control a turtle drawing the pattern. A variant uses turtle positions as the control points for B-spline approximation. Application of L-systems to generation of Karnatic music is shown by generating some tunes.

1. INTRODUCTION

Rewriting systems can be used to generate images in two different ways. In the first case, the rewriting system operates directly on two-dimensional objects, such as arrays[6,8] and graphs[10]. In the second case, grammars (in the broad sense of the word, including parallel rewriting systems) are used to define strings of symbols. A graphic interpretation function subsequently translates these strings into images. The method discussed in this paper belongs to this second category. The strings are generated using L-systems[7] and interpreted graphically as sequences

---

*An earlier version of this paper was presented at the International Conference on Computer Graphics held at Singapore, September 1988.

of commands controlling a LOGO-style turtle. This approach to image generation was first mentioned by Szilard and Quinton[17], and further developed to generate fractal Koch curves and realistic images of plants by Prusinkiewicz[11,12]. This paper applies L-systems with the turtle interpretation to a new domain : a form of folk art from South India called kolam.This provides an alternative to the previous formal description of kolam designs using a variant of array grammars[15]. The L-systems provide a particularly concise description of many kolam patterns and lend themselves to software implementations which properly render all details of kolams using computer graphics techniques. This paper also considers application of L-systems to automatic generation of Karnatic music tunes.

2. L-SYSTEMS

This section summarises fundamental definitions and notations related to L-systems. For their tutorial introduction, see (5,13,14).

Let V denote an alphabet, V^* the set of all words over V, and V^+ the set of all nonempty words over V.

Definition 2.1. A **0L-system** is an ordered triplet $G = \langle V, \omega, P \rangle$ where V is the **alphabet** of the system, $\omega \in V^+$ is a nonempty word called the **axiom,** and $P \in V \times V^*$ is a finite **set of productions.** If a pair (a, α) is a production, we write $a \rightarrow \alpha$. The letter a and the word α are called the **predecessor** and the **successor** of this production, respectively. It is assumed that for any letter $a \in V$, there is at least one word $\alpha \in V^*$ such that $a \rightarrow \alpha$. A 0L-system is **deterministic** iff for each $a \in V$ there is exactly one $\alpha \in V^*$ such that $a \rightarrow \alpha$.

Definition 2.2. Let $G = \langle V, \omega, P \rangle$ be a 0L-system, and suppose that $x = x_1 \ldots x_m$ is an arbitrary word over V. We will say that the word $y = y_1 \ldots y_m \in V^*$ is **directly derived** from (or **generated** by) x and write $x \Rightarrow y$ iff $x_i \rightarrow y_i$ for all i = 1,...,m. A word x is generated by G in a derivation of **length** n if there exists a sequence of words $x_0, x_1, \ldots, x_n$ such that $x_0 = \omega$, $x_n = x$ and $x_0 \Rightarrow x_1 \Rightarrow \ldots \Rightarrow x_n$.

Definition 2.3. A **T0L-system** is an ordered quadruplet $G_T = \langle V, \omega, P, T \rangle$

where V, ω and P are as in the definition of a 0L-system and T is a finite nonempty collection of subsets of P, called **tables.** It is assumed that for each table $t \in T$ and each letter $a \in V$ there is at least one production $p \in t$ with the predecessor a.

Definition 2.4. A word x is **directly derived** from the word y in a T0L-system $G_T = \langle V, \omega, P, T \rangle$ if x is directly derived from y in 0L-system $G = \langle V, \omega, P \rangle$ and all productions used in this derivation belong to the same table $t \in T$.

The notion of the direct derivation in a T0L-system generalizes to the derivation of length n, as in definition 2.2. All productions used in a given derivation step must belong to the same table but different tables may be used in different derivation steps.

Convention: If no production is explicitly specified for a given predecessor $a \in V$, we assume that the **identity production** $a \rightarrow a$ belongs to the set of productions P or to the table t under consideration.

3. THREE-DIMENSIONAL TURTLE INTERPRETATION OF STRINGS

This section presents a method for mapping strings of symbols into graphical objects. This method is based on manoeuvring a LOGO-like turtle in three dimensions[1]. The key concept is to represent current **orientation** of the turtle in space by three vectors $\vec{H}$, $\vec{L}$, $\vec{U}$, representing the turtle's **heading,** the direction to the **left,** and the **up** direction respectively. Obviously, these three vectors are perpendicular to each other. Additionally, they are assumed to have the unit length and to satisfy the equation $\vec{H} \times \vec{L} = \vec{U}$. Rotations of the turtle can be then expressed by the equation:

$$[\ \vec{H'}\ \vec{L'}\ \vec{U}\ ] = [\ \vec{H}\ \vec{L}\ \vec{U}\ ]\ \mathbf{R} \qquad (3.1)$$

where **R** is a 3x3 **rotation** matrix. Specifically, rotations by angle α about vectors $\vec{U}$, $\vec{L}$ and $\vec{H}$ are represented by matrices:

$$R_U(\alpha) = \begin{bmatrix} \cos\alpha & \sin\alpha & 0 \\ -\sin\alpha & \cos\alpha & 0 \\ 0 & 0 & 1 \end{bmatrix} \quad (3.2)$$

$$R_L(\alpha) = \begin{bmatrix} \cos\alpha & 0 & -\sin\alpha \\ 0 & 1 & 0 \\ \sin\alpha & 0 & \cos\alpha \end{bmatrix} \quad (3.3)$$

$$R_H(\alpha) = \begin{bmatrix} 1 & 0 & 0 \\ 0 & \cos\alpha & -\sin\alpha \\ 0 & \sin\alpha & \cos\alpha \end{bmatrix} \quad (3.4)$$

Definition 3.1. A three-dimensional **turtle** is a triplet T = < V, S, N > where V is called the turtle's **alphabet,** S is a **set of states** and N: $V \times S \rightarrow S$ is a **state transition function.** The alphabet V consists of symbols:

F f @ + - & ^ \ / | # ! ' ` { } [ ] (3.5)

The **state** of the turtle is a six-tuple s = < $\vec{P}$, $\vec{H}$, $\vec{L}$, $\vec{U}$, w, c>. The position vector $\vec{P}$ represents the turtle's **position** in Cartesian coordinates. Vectors $\vec{H}$, $\vec{L}$, $\vec{U}$ represent the turtle's **orientation,** as described above. Number w represents the **width** of the line drawn by the turtle. Number c corresponds to the **colour** of the lines and polygons drawn**.

The state transition function has four parameters: the **step size** d, the **angle increment** δ, the **width increment** w_inc and the **colour increment** c_inc. Given these parameters, the turtle responds to the symbols of V as follows:

f Move forward a step of length d. The position of the turtle changes to $\vec{P}' = \vec{P} + dH$. A line segment of width w and colour c between points P and P′ is drawn.

F Move forward a step of length d without drawing a line.

@ Draw a dot of diameter w and colour c at the current position P.

**In the actual software implementation of the described concepts on a SUN 2/160 workstation, w is a parameter to the SunCore function set_linewidth, and c is the index to the colour table. (SunCore is a trademark of Sun Microsystems, Inc..)

+ Turn left by angle δ . The orientation of the turtle changes according to formula (3.1), with the rotation matrix equal to $\mathbf{R}_U(\delta)$.

- Turn right by angle δ. The rotation matrix is equal to $\mathbf{R}_U(-\delta)$.

& Pitch down by angle δ. The rotation matrix is equal to $\mathbf{R}_L(\delta)$.

^ Pitch up by angle δ. The rotation matrix is equal to $\mathbf{R}_L(-\delta)$.

\ Roll left by angle δ. The rotation matrix is equal to $\mathbf{R}_H(\delta)$.

/ Roll right by angle δ. The rotation matrix is equal to $\mathbf{R}_H(-\delta)$.

| Turn away. The rotation matrix is equal to $\mathbf{R}_U(180°)$.

Increment current line width according to the formula: w′ = w + w_inc.

! Decrement current line width according to the formula: w′ = w - w_inc.

' Increment current colour according to the formula: c′ = c + c_inc.

` Decrement current colour according to the formula: c′ = c - c_inc.

{ Start saving the subsequent positions of the turtle as vertices of a polygon to be filled.

} Fill the saved polygon using the current colour c.

[Push current state of the turtle into a pushdown stack.

] Pop a state from the stack, and make it the current state of the turtle. No line is drawn, although the position of the turtle may change.

All other symbols are ignored by the turtle (the turtle preserves its state).

Remark 3.1. The above definition specifies only the essential aspects of the turtle's behaviour. Specifically, exception handling is left undefined and may depend on the particular implementation of the turtle. An exception occurs, for example, if the width decreases to a negative value or if an attempt is made to pop a state from the empty stack.

Definition 3.2. Let $s_0 = \langle \vec{P}_0, \vec{H}_0, \vec{L}_0, \vec{U}_0, w_0, c_0 \rangle$ be the initial state of the turtle and suppose that d, δ, w_inc and c_inc are fixed parameters. The object (set of lines and polygons) created by the turtle corresponding to a word x is called the **turtle interpretation** of x.

4. KOLAM PATTERNS

4.1 What Is A Kolam?

In villages in the South of India, women decorate the courtyards in front of their homes with traditional designs called kolam. The art of kolam is of ancient origin; it is estimated to have developed as early as 5,000 years ago. Vivid descriptions of the beauty of kolams and the techniques for working them out can be found in Sanskrit works.

Many kolam designs are geometric patterns formed by means of interleaving straight or curved lines. They can be of different sizes and complexities. Designs as big as 3m × 3m, with total line length of hundreds of metres, can be encountered. One method of covering a large area with drawings is to repeat a small design many times. This is seldom done. A more elegant approach is to connect small elements into sophisticated structures. In mathematical terms, this amounts to exploring the recursive structure of a family of increasingly complex patterns.

4.2 Kolams And L-systems

The first formal model for describing kolam patterns was proposed in (11). According to this model, kolam patterns can be generated by a variant of array grammars. Recently, we have noticed that L-systems with turtle interpretation offer a simpler and more intuitive method for generating kolam patterns and describing their families.

Generally, kolam patterns can be divided into three classes: non-recursive designs, recursive designs with an exponential growth, and recursive designs with a polynomial growth. The term "growth" refers to the increase in the number of primitive elements (such as vectors or spline control points) present in subsequent patterns belonging to the same family. A kolam family is understood as the sequence of patterns produced by a given L-system in derivations of length 0,1,2,3,... .

Non-recursive kolams are the only members of one-element families. They can be generated by trivial L-systems in which the axiom describes the entire pattern. From the viewpoint of image generation techniques, non-recursive kolams are of little interest.

4.3 Kolams With Exponential Growth

The L-systems which generate kolam patterns with an exponential growth are remarkably simple. For example, consider the variant of the snake kolam shown in Figure 1. It can be divided into two congruent parts by a diagonal line passing through opposite corners of the pattern. The recursive structure of the bottom right corner is analysed in Figure 2. The main component of the design is the open polygon **a**. The design starts with two line segments meeting at the right angle **b**. These lines are disconnected at the vertex marked with a dot to accomodate the insertion of the polygon **a**. The polygon **c** results. The subsequent shape **d** is obtained by properly inserting polygon **a** in all marked vertices of **c**. Thus, the recursion consists of concurrently inserting the predefined shape **a** in all marked vertices of the polygon from the previous level. It is obvious that the number of polygon edges grows exponentially with the recursion depth.

The L-system generating the family of snake kolams can be obtained in a straightforward way by coding the inserted polygon **a** and the initial angular shape **b** using the following L-system:

$$\omega : f + Xf + f + Xf \tag{4.1}$$

$$p : X \rightarrow Xf - f - f + Xf + f + Xf - f - f + X \tag{4.2}$$

The angle increment δ is equal to 90°. In order to render the curvature of the original design, the consecutive positions of the turtle are used as the control points for a B-spline approximation. The snake shown in Figure 1 was obtained using a derivation of length 4. Note the similarity between the snake kolam and the Sierpinski space-filling curve. It is fascinating to discover a fractal curve in folk art!

Another kolam pattern with exponential growth, called the Anklets of Krishna, is shown in Figure 3. Its structure is close to that of the snake and can be analysed in a similar way. Figure 3 was generated using the following L-system:

$$\omega : - X - - X \tag{4.3}$$

$$p : X \rightarrow XfX - - XfX \tag{4.4}$$

The derivation length n was equal to 5 and the angle increment δ was equal to 45°.

In a modification of the Anklets of Krishna shown in Figure 4a, the basic structural elements (bold squares) are seperated from each other and ornamented using decorative elements **b** and **c**. The pattern is described by the following table L-system:

$$\omega : - X - - X \tag{4.5}$$

Table 1

$$p_1 : X \rightarrow XfX - - XfX \tag{4.6}$$

Table 2

$$p_2 : X \rightarrow BfA - - BfA \tag{4.7}$$

$$p_3 : A \rightarrow f + + ffff - - f - - ffff + + f + + ffff - - f \tag{4.8}$$

$$p_4 : B \rightarrow f - - ffff + + f + + ffff - - f - - ffff + + f \tag{4.9}$$

Table 1 (production p_1) is applied in the first n-2 derivation steps. Table 2 is then used to insert the decorative elements. To make the structure legible, Figure 4a was generated with only 3 derivation steps. The angle increment δ was equal to 45°.

The L-system generating the family of kolams of crosses is obtained using the following L-system:

$$\omega : X+f-f+X+f-f+X+f-f+X+f-f \tag{4.10}$$

$$p_1 : X \rightarrow X+X-X+X-f-X+X-X+X \tag{4.11}$$

$$p_2 : f \rightarrow f \tag{4.12}$$

The angle increment is 90°. The kolam obtained from a derivation of length 4 is shown in figure 5.

4.4 Kolams With Polynomial Growth

The mango leaves kolam shown in Figure 6a was generated by the following L-system:

$$\omega : A - - - A \tag{4.10}$$

$$p_1 : A \rightarrow F - f + Z + f - FA \tag{4.11}$$

$$p_2 : Z \rightarrow f - ff - f - -[- -Z]f - ff - f - - f - ff - f - - \tag{4.12}$$

The derivation length n was equal to 7 and the angle increment δ was equal to 60°. The axiom defines the structure as consisting of two parts, originating from the letters A and symmetric with respect to the kolam centre. Production p_1 describes the formation of a sequence of wedges **b** which form the axis of the structure. Attached to each wedge is a branch **c**, generated from the symbol Z by production p_2. The number of branch elements increases in each derivation step. Since the branches near the kolam base are created first, they are longer than those situated in the higher portions of the structure. The structure exhibits polynomial growth, with the number of line segments proportional to the square of the derivation length.

Other examples of kolam patterns with polynomial growth functions are shown in Figures 7 and 8.

It is interesting to note the relationship between kolam patterns, fractal curves and plants. On one hand, kolam patterns with exponential growth are closely related to space-filling curves. On the other hand, the patterns with polynomial growth exhibit phase effects common to many plants. As in the case of plants, it is easier to design an L-system capturing the entire sequence of kolam patterns forming a given family than attempt to characterise a particular "developmental stage" without referring to the growth dynamics. More results on the formal structure of kolam patterns were recently published by G. Siromoney and R. Siromoney[16].

5. GENERATION OF KARNATIC MUSIC

In Indian music, the concept of *raga* is of main importance. There are seven basic notes. Five of them can be further subdivided into two sub notes. Indian music is famous for its improvisation. When any composition is performed, there are three stages.

(1) Before the actual composition is performed, improvisation is done. The *raga* is exposed and elaborated here; *thalam* and lyric are absent in this first stage of improvisation.

(2) *Thanam* : Here also there is no lyric and *thalam* but the piece of music will have tempo (*laya*). This is also a way of improvising *raga*.

(3) During the time of performing the composition also, we can have improvisation, but it is set to a particular *thalam*. It is in the form of *Kalpanaswara*.

The construction of tables and use of L-systems can be used to generate tunes. This is mainly helpful for a beginner who is in the stage of understanding different ways of improvising a *raga*. Proper concatenation of tables or derivation using L-systems can be used. Thus the above mentioned three levels of improvisation can be tested and practised with the help of a computer.

Here, eight tables have been used for any *raga*. Initially the attempts made were towards *purna ragas* which consist of all seven notes; later they were extended to *janya ragas* where some notes may be missing. Wipro PC was used for implementation. The basic frequency has to be chosen by the user, and other frequencies are determined relative to this. One typical table is given below.

S → S R G R

R → R G M G

G → G M P M

M → M P D P

P → P D N D

D → D N S N

N → N S R S

More tables can be added. If the L-system is used, initially not more than 4 derivation steps are used. The *arohanam* and *avarohanam* of a *raga* form the axiom of the L-system. eg. S R G M P D N S S N D P M G R S for a *purna raga*. Concatenation of tables also gives very good effect. The music thus generated is pleasing to the ears and will be of much help to a student of Karnatic music.

6. CONCLUSION

In this paper we have considered the application of L-systems to the generation of kolam patterns and generation of Karnatic music. It would also be interesting to find if an L-system could describe animation by generating a sequence of pictures. Probably a graph L-system or array L-system could be tried.

ACKNOWLEDGEMENT

Prof. Rani Siromoney kindly provided us with some kolam examples. The support and facilities of the Computer Science Department at the University of Regina were essential to carry out this project. The support from the Natural Sciences and Engineering Research Council of Canada (grant number AO324) is also gratefully acknowledged.

References

1. Abelson, H. and Disessa, A. A., "Turtle Geometry", M.I.T. Press, Cambridge and London (1982).

2. Bairi, B. P., "Rangavalli", Parts 1-3, Navayuga Press, Udupi, India (1984).

3. Foley, J. D. and van Dam, "Fundamentals of Interactive Computer Graphics", Addison-Wesley, Reading (1982).

4. Freeman H., "On encoding arbitrary geometric configurations", IRE Trans. Electron. Comput., 10,pp. 260-268 (1961).

5. Herman, G. T., and Rozenberg, G., "Developmental Systems and Languages", North-Holland, Amsterdam and Oxford (1975).

6. Kirsch, R. A., "Computer Interpretation of English text and picture

patterns", IEEE Trans. EE, 13, pp. 363-376 (1964).

7. Lindenmayer, A., "Mathematical models for cellular interaction in development", Parts I & II,Journal of Theoretical Biology, 18, pp. 280-315 (1968).

8. Milgram, D., and Rosenfeld, A. "Array automata and array grammars", IFIP Congress 71, Booklet TA2, North Holland, Amsterdam, pp. 166-173 (1971).

9. Papert, S., "Mindstorms: children, computers and powerful ideas", Basic Books, New York (1980).

10. Pfaltz, J. L., and Rosenfeld, A., "Web grammars", Proc. Int. Joint Conf. Artificial Intelligence, Washington, pp. 609-619 (1969).

11. Prusinkiewicz, P., "Graphical Applications of L-systems", Proceedings of Graphics Interface '86 - Vision Interface '86, pp. 247-253 (1986).

12. Prusinkiewicz, P., "Applications of L-systems to computer imagery", Proceedings of 3rd International Workshop on Graph Grammars and their Application to Computer Science, LNCS 291, pp. 534-548 (1987).

13. Rozenberg, G., and Salomaa, A., "The Mathematical Theory of L-systems", Academic Press, New York and London (1980).

14. Salomaa, A., "Formal Languages", Academic Press, New York and London (1973).

15. Siromoney, G., Siromoney, R., and Krithivasan, K. "Array grammars and kolam", Computer Graphics and Image Processing, 3, pp. 63-82 (1974).

16. Siromoney, G., and Siromoney, R., "Rosenfeld's cycle grammars and kolam", Proceedings of 3rd International Workshop on Graph Grammars and

their Application to Computer Science, LNCS 291, pp. 564-579 (1987).

17. Szilard, A. L., and Quinton, R. E., "An interpretation for D0L systems by computer graphics", The Science Terrapin, 4, pp. 8-13 (1979).

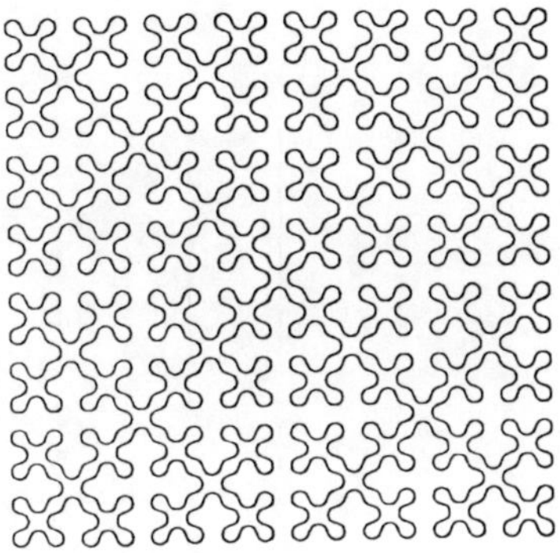

Figure 1 : The snake kolam

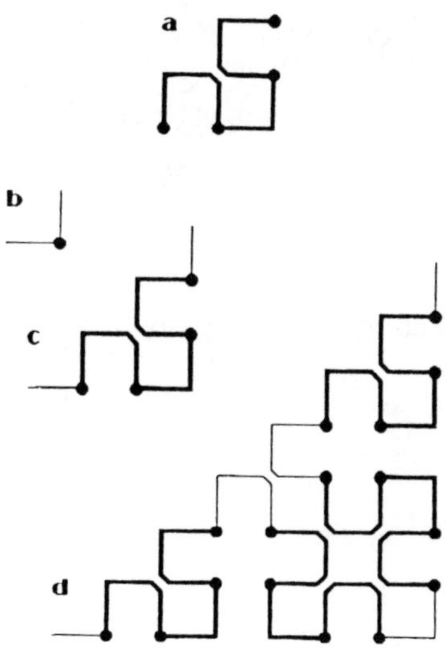

Figure 2 : The recursive structure of the snake kolam

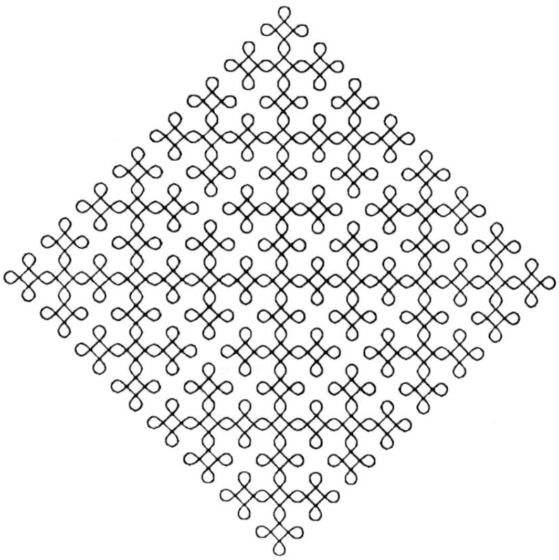

Figure 3 : Anklets of Krishna

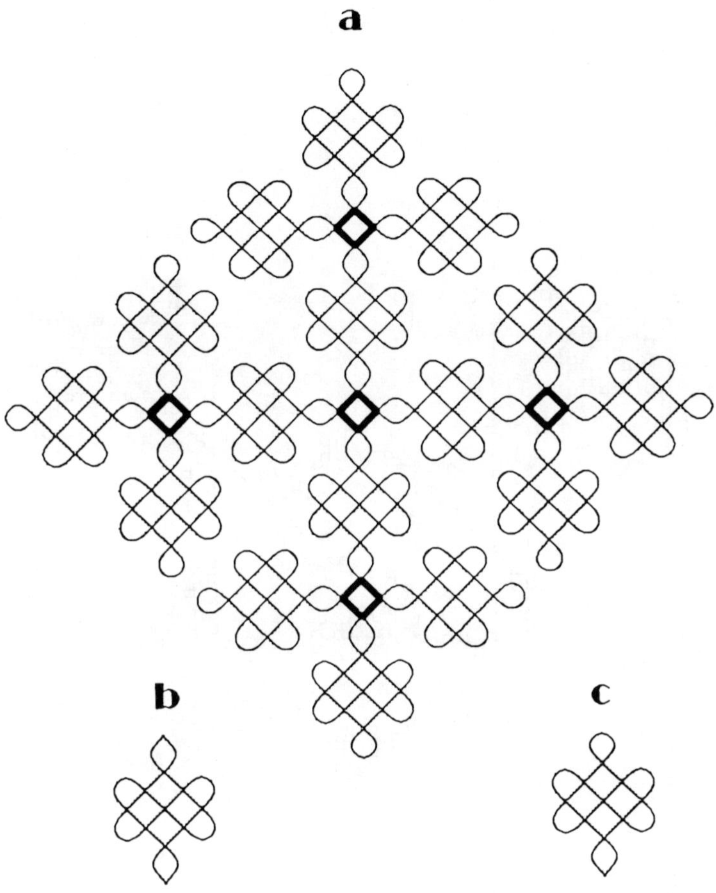

Figure 4 : (a) The bag of candies kolam, and (b,c) its decorative elements

Figure 5 : Kolam of crosses

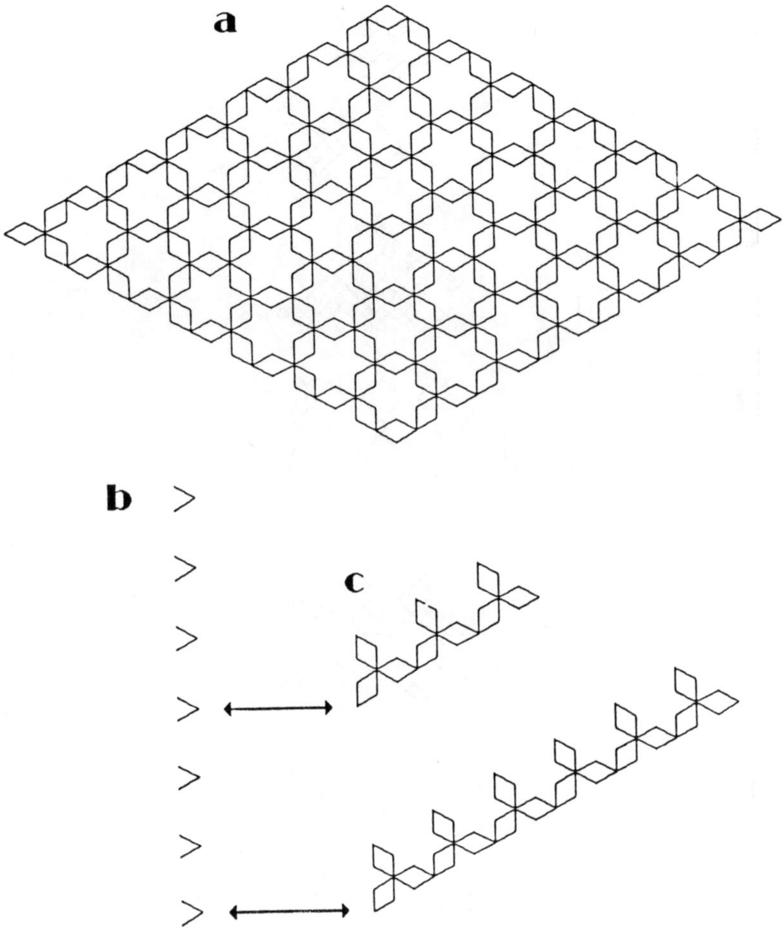

Figure 6 : (a) The mango leaves kolam, and (b,c) its structural components

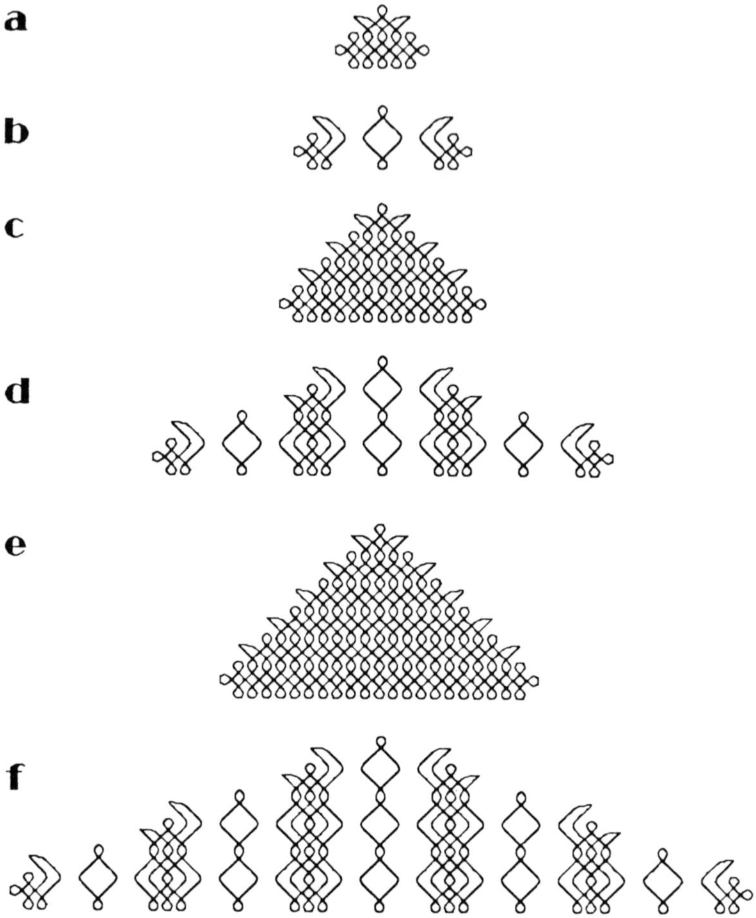

Figure 7 : The <u>mountain</u> kolams
(a,c,e) The kolams obtained in 0,2, and 4 derivation steps
(b,d,f) Exploded views revealing the structure of the <u>mountain</u> family

Figure 8 : Further examples of kolam patterns with polynomial growth function : (a) Kooja and (b) Scissors

AN ARCHITECTURE FOR PICTURE PARSING

Azriel Rosenfeld

Center for Automation Research
University of Maryland
College Park, Maryland 20742-3411 USA

Abstract

This paper suggests that pyramid cellular computers are a natural architecture for implementing a general method of syntactic pattern recognition. It outlines how such computers can be used to extract syntactic primitives (local features, edges/curves, or regions of simple shapes) from an image and to compute their properties. It also sketches how they can be used to identify hierarchical arrangements of primitives, thereby parsing the image (in parallel) in accordance with the rewriting rules of a "coordinate grammar".

1. INTRODUCTION

Objects are usually described as consisting of parts that have given properties (or whose properties satisfy given constraints) and that satisfy given relations (or constraints on relations). The description is often hierarchical, i.e. the parts are themselves composed of subparts, and so on (although in practice the hierarchy is at most a few levels deep). This method of object description can be regarded as "syntactic"; a given class of objects is defined by a "grammar" in which the start symbol represents the class; the nonterminal symbols represent (classes of) (sub...)parts; and the terminal symbols represent (classes of) "primitive" or "atomic" parts that are not themselves composed of subparts.

An analogous approach can be used to describe how the objects of a given class appear in an image (or "picture") taken from a given viewpoint. Here the start symbol represents the set of such images, and the other symbols represent image (sub...)parts; the rules of the grammar specify how parts are made up of subparts. Such a grammar can be used to recognize the presence of an object of the given class in the image, by "parsing" the image using the rules. We first find instances of the primitive parts in the image, and then successively combine parts into

The support of the National Science Foundation and the U.S. Air Force Office of Scientific Research under NSF Grant IRI-86-03723 is gratefully acknowledged, as is the help of Sandy German in preparing this paper.

larger parts as specified by the rules. *Syntactic pattern recognition* is concerned with defining grammars for classes of objects as they appear in images, and using these grammars to recognize the objects by parsing the images. For a general introduction to syntactic pattern recognition see [1].

The grammars used in syntactic pattern recognition can be formalized in various ways. At one extreme, we can define "array grammars" whose languages are digital images; in effect, this approach uses single pixels as the primitives. More generally, we can use arbitrary regions as primitives, and define "graph grammars" whose languages are (hierarchical) region adjacency graphs. We will not review these approaches here. Instead, we will propose an approach in which the primitives are all of simple types: local features (at various scales), such as spots, corners, line ends, or line crossings; smooth pieces of edge or curve; or regions that are "bloblike" or "ribbonlike". To parse the image, we will use a "coordinate grammar" [2,3] in which the rules specify spatial arrangements of parts in given relative positions. We will show that a pyramid cellular computer is a natural architecture for parsing with respect to such a grammar, and that such a computer can also be used to extract the primitives from a given image [4].

Section 2 of this paper discusses image primitives, and Section 3 defines coordinate grammars. Section 4 describes pyramid cellular computers. Section 5 shows how such computers can be used to extract primitives, and Section 6 discusses their use for parsing the spatial arrangements of parts defined by a coordinate grammar.

2. PRIMITIVES

We suggest that a region of an image is appropriately regarded as a "primitive" if it has the following properties:

a) It is "homogeneous"—i.e., it has approximately constant gray level. (More generally, we could allow primitives that are homogeneously textured; but we will not consider this generalization here.)

b) It has a simple shape. (We will define this requirement more precisely below.)

c) It is maximal with respect to properties (a–b)—i.e., it is not a proper subset of a homogeneous connected region of simple shape.

It is straightforward to extract maximal connected homogeneous regions from an image (e.g., using split-and-merge techniques); but these regions will not necessarily have simple shapes. However, such a region can be decomposed into maximal connected subregions of simple shapes by using its medial axis transformation (MAT) [5]. Any region R can be represented as a union of maximal disks; the centers of these disks lie along the "skeleton" of R. If we ignore maximal disks that have small radii, we obtain approximations to R. The skeleton of R can be (approximately) decomposed into a set of simple arcs and curves, which we call its "branches". The union of the maximal disks whose centers lie along a given branch constitute a primitive part of R. Such primitive parts are (approximately) bloblike (i.e., compact) or ribbonlike (i.e., elongated). These remarks suggest that a natural class of image primitives are the (maximal) bloblike or ribbonlike homogeneous regions.

In addition to region-like primitives, we will also allow primitives of two other types: isolated features (e.g., spots, corners, line ends, or line crossings), defined by local patterns of gray levels (at some scale); and maximal pieces of smooth edges or curves.

Any primitive has a uniquely defined centroid and (in general) a uniquely defined principal axis of inertia. The position and orientation of a primitive in the image are determined by specifying the position of its centroid and the orientation of its principal axis.

3. COORDINATE GRAMMARS

"Coordinate grammars" were introduced independently by several authors in the 1960's to provide formal models for sets of (image) parts that satisfy constraints on their spatial arrangement—e.g., mathematical expressions. (For references to this early work, see [2].) In such a grammar each symbol has coordinates associated with it, and each rewriting rule has partial functions associated with it that compute the coordinates of the symbols on the right hand side of the rule in terms of those on the left hand side. Formally, such a rule is of the form $(A_1, \ldots, A_m) \rightarrow (B_1, \ldots, B_n);\ f_1, \ldots, f_n$, where the f's are (in general) vector-valued partial functions of m vector-valued variables, and f_i computes the coordinates of B_i in terms of those of $(A_1, \ldots, A_m)$. For a more detailed definition, see [2].

We shall assume from now on that coordinate grammars are diameter-limited, in the sense that in any rule, the A's and B's all lie within a bounded distance of each other. (If we do not make this assumption, even the simplest types of coordinate grammars can generate arbitrary languages; indeed, the positions of the symbols can be used to simulate counters, which immediately makes such grammars as powerful as Turing machines [2].) In particular, a "context-free" rule in a diameter-limited coordinate grammar rewrites a single symbol A into a tuple of symbols that lie withing a bounded distance of A. If we assume that the terminal symbols of a coordinate grammar are single pixels, that the rules are shift-invariant, and that the coordinates are discrete-valued (e.g., integer-valued), then it can be shown [3] that diameter-limited coordinate grammers are essentially equivalent to isometric array grammars, so that they have a natural hierarchy.

It is convenient to generalize the concept of a coordinate grammar to allow orientations, as well as positions, to be associated with the symbols; each rule now specifies the orientations (as well as positions) of the new symbols related to the old ones. (Note that if we allow orientations that are not multiples of 90°, this can give rise to positions that are not discrete-valued; if we want only discrete-valued positions, we must re quantize the coordinate values after we apply a rule.) This allows us to compactly represent sets of rules that define objects having various orientations, or whose parts have various relative orientations.

We will assume from now on that our coordinate grammars are shift-invariant and diameter-limited, but we will not require the coordinates to be integer-valued. Thus a symbol can, for example, represent an image primitive; in this case, it is convenient to assume that the coordinates associated with the symbol are the coordinates of the primitive's centroid, and the orientation associated with the symbol is the orientation of the primitive's principal axis.

In our approach to syntactic pattern recognition we will make use of two types of coordinate grammars. The first type defines primitives as hierarchical arrangements of pixels, and the second type defines objects as hierarchical arrangements of primitives. This breakdown into two types is simply a convenience; they could be combined into a single grammar, with the start symbols of the first type of grammar becoming the terminal symbols of the second type. Note that in the first type of grammar the terminal symbols are single pixels. For simplicity, we will assume that the rules of these grammars are all context-free; thus a symbol represents a group of... groups of pixels. We will also assume that the coordinates and orientation associated with each symbol are the centroid coordinates and principal axis orientation of the corresponding group (...) of pixels.

4. PYRAMID CELLULAR COMPUTERS

A pyramid cellular computer (for short: a pyramid) is an exponentially tapering stack of arrays of processors ("cells"); for example, if the base of the pyramid ("level 0") is a $2^n \times 2^n$ array, the succeeding levels $(1, 2, \ldots, n)$ might be arrays of sizes $2^{n-1} \times 2^{n-1}$, $2^{n-2} \times 2^{n-2}, \ldots, 1 \times 1$. Each cell is connected to a set of neighbors on its own level; e.g., cell (i,j) is connected to the eight cells $(i \pm 1,j)$, $(i,j \pm 1)$, and $(i \pm 1,j \pm 1)$ (if they exist). Furthermore, each cell is connected to a "parent" on the level above and to a block of "children" on the level below; e.g., cell (i,j) on level k is connected to cell $([i/2],[j/2])$ on level $k+1$ and to the four cells $(2i,2j)$, $(2i+1,2j)$, $(2i,2j+1)$ and $(2i+1,2j+1)$ on level $k-1$ (if they exist). To process a $2^n \times 2^n$ image on such a computer, the image is input to the base of the pyramid, one pixel per cell.

Many parallel algorithms have been developed for processing or analyzing images on pyramids; see, e.g., [6–7]. In the next section of this paper we indicate how pyramids can be used to extract primitives from an image and to compute their positions and orientations. As we shall see, the process of extraction can be regarded as a form of parallel parsing with respect to a coordinate grammar; the pixels belonging to the primitive are hierarchically grouped, with the groups being represented by cells at successively higher levels of the pyramid, until we reach a level at which a single cell represents the entire primitive.

5. PRIMITIVE EXTRACTION[1]

a) Blocks

We first show how a pyramid can detect maximal homogeneous blocks whose sizes and positions are powers of 2. When the image is input to the base of the pyramid (level 0), the cells at levels 1, 2, ..., can successively compute information about 2×2, $4 \times 4, \ldots$ blocks of pixels in the image by combining information obtained from their children. (For example, if

[1]For further details on the algorithms described in this section, see [4].

each cell simply adds its children's values, the cells at levels 1, 2, ... compute the sums of the gray levels in these image blocks.) It is not hard to show that in this way, each cell can compute the mean and standard deviation of the gray levels of its image block, using the corresponding information about its children's blocks (which are the quadrants of its block). This allows us to detect maximal homogeneous blocks, i.e., blocks that have low standard deviations but whose parents do not. Note that in this process, each cell performs only a bounded amount of computation.

b) **Blobs**

Let us call a region R "bloblike" if there exists a block B such that B is contained in R and R is contained in the union of B and its eight neighbors. If we assume that B is as large as possible, then it is not hard to see that if R is a maximal homogeneous region, B must be a maximal homogeneous block. Given B (which can be found as described in (a) above), we can extract R by "growing" a subtree of the pyramid, starting from B as the root. This is done as follows: Let C be (the image block of) a cell on (say) level h ($<$ B's level). C compares its mean gray level to the mean gray levels of its parent and its parent's neighbors. If the closest of these means is that of a cell belonging to the tree, C joins the tree; if not, it does not. The leaves of the tree constructed in this way, which correspond to single pixels of the image, turn out to be (essentially) the pixels that belong to R.

The tree-growing process just described can be regarded as a top-down (parallel) "parse"; it constructs R by successively "rewriting" blocks as unions of blocks of half their size. It also constructs a tree representation of R (a sort of "parse tree") in which the nodes represent subblocks of R of various sizes. (This representation is related to, but less compact than, a quadtree representation [5]; in particular, even if node (= cell) C and all its children belong to R, the tree contains both C and its children, whereas a quadtree would not contain the children in such a case.) Note that in the process of growing the tree, each cell does only a bounded amount of computation.

c) **Ribbons**

Let us call a region "ribbonlike" if there exists a set of distinct blocks $B_1, \ldots, B_m$ of the same size (or of two sizes that differ by a factor of 2)[2] such that

(1) Each B_i is contained in R.

(2) R is contained in the union of the B_i's and their neighbors.

(3) The neighborhoods of B_i and $B_{i\pm 1}$ (modulo m) overlap (so that the B_i's and their neighbors constitute a connected region).

(4) If $j \neq i \pm 1$ (modulo m), the neighborhoods of B_i and B_j are disjoint. (This criterion insures that the ribbon does not double back on itself and cover a region of width greater

[2]This condition restricts us to ribbons of approximately constant width. The generalization to ribbons whose widths can vary by more than a factor of 2 will not be treated here.

than its own.)

If we assume that the B's are as large as possible, they constitute a "blocky" approximation to R, and their centers lie near R's medial axis. Moreover, if R is a maximal homogeneous ribbon, the B's are maximal homogeneous blocks, and they all have similar mean gray levels.

To detect maximal homogeneous ribbons in an image, we first detect maximal homogeneous blocks as described in (a). Consider the set of such blocks on two consecutive levels, say h and $h+1$. Each cell at level $h+2$ looks for sequences of such blocks among its children and grandchildren that have similar means and that satisfy condition (3); the level $(h+2)$ cells also verify that the blocks do not violate condition (4). Each cell at levels $h+3$, $h+4, \ldots$ now tries to combine the sequences detected by its children by joining their ends; it does not keep a list of all the blocks, but only of the endpoints of the sequences. [We assume that the number of sequences that a cell has to handle remains bounded to insure that each cell has to do only a bounded amount of computation. The algorithms in this paragraph can be implemented more effectively on a pyramid in which cells have overlapping blocks of children (e.g., 3×3 rather than 2×2); for simplicity, we omit the details.] A sequence constructed by cell C is called "maximal" if it cannot be combined with sequences in any of C's neighbors.

When a cell C has constructed a maximal sequence σ, we can extract the ribbon corresponding to σ by proceeding as follows: C transmits a signal to those of its children that contain subsequences of σ, identifying these subsequences by specifying their endpoints. These cells in turn pass the signal on to their appropriate children, until we reach level $h+2$. The cells at level $h+2$ that receive the signal transmit it to the maximal blocks at levels $h+1$ and h that comprised their sequences. The blocks that receive the signal initiate tree growing processes like that described in (b) above. Note that this is actually a "forest growing" process, since trees are grown from many blocks simultaneously; but note that the trees may intersect. As in (b), the leaves of the trees should be the pixels belonging to the ribbon that gave rise to the maximal blocks.

The process just described can be regarded as a two-stage top-down parallel "parse"; the first stage constructs the maximal sequence of blocks (starting from a node that "sees" the entire sequence), and the second stage constructs the ribbon starting from this set of blocks. The first stage involves a hierarchical representation of the medial axis of the ribbon (based on subarcs of increasing size, represented by their endpoints), while the second stage involves a forest-like representation of the ribbon, with a set of roots that lie along the medial axis. Once again, the total amount of computation performed by each cell in carrying out this process is bounded.

d) **Edges and curves**

A method similar to that in (c) can be used to extract maximal pieces of smooth edge or curve from an image. A curve is a special case of a ribbon (if it is thin, the blocks are single pixels), and we have already described how to extract it. As regards edges, we first apply a local "edge detection" operator at each pixel of the image. (This can be done in parallel by the cells at the base of the pyramid, using information obtained from their neighbors.) If the original image contains a piece of smooth edge, it should give rise to high "edge values" that lie along a smooth curve, and we can now extract this curve as before. As in (c), in extracting a curve or edge we also create a hierarchical representation of it, so that the process once again resembles parallel parsing; and it requires each cell to perform only a bounded amount of computation.

e) **Local features**

Detection of features such as spots, corners, line ends or line crossings in an image is very easily done on a pyramid. Suppose first that the features are local, i.e. detectable in the neighborhood of a pixel—e.g., a spot is an isolated pixel that contrasts with all its neighbors. Such features are obviously detectable by the cells at the base of the pyramid, which can apply local "feature detection" operators to the image in parallel. Suppose now that the features are larger—e.g., suppose that a spot is approximately k pixels in diameter. We use the pyramid to compute local averages of image blocks of sizes 2×2, $4 \times 4, \ldots,$ $2^h \times 2^h$ at levels 1, 2, . . . , h of the pyramid, where 2^h is the power of 2 closest to k. This produces reduced-resolution versions of the image at successive pyramid levels. At level h the size-k spot appears as a local spot, and can be detected by a local spot detection operator. (It may also be detectable at levels above and below h, but the strongest response of the operator should be at level h.) Similar remarks apply to local features of other types. Thus local features of all sizes can be detected by using the pyramid to produce a set of reduced-resolution versions of the image and then applying local operators at each level. The features can then be extracted by essentially the same tree-growing process as we described in (a). This process creates tree representations of the features, and once again is akin to parallel parsing; and the amount of computation performed by each cell is bounded.

f) **Computing properties of primitives**

All of our primitive extraction processes represent the primitives by (sets of) trees whose leaves are the pixels belonging to the primitive, and which culminate in a single root node (the root of the tree, or the cell that detects the maximal curve or ribbon sequence). Using this tree structure, it is straightforward to compute various moments of the primitive, by recursively computing weighted sums of the gray levels of the primitive's pixels at successive pyramid levels, until the moments of the entire primitive are obtained at its root node. In particular, the coordinates of the primitive's centroid, and the slope of its principal axis, can be computed as simple combinations of moments. Note that these are precisely the computations used in the coordinate-grammar rules; and that each cell only needs to do a bounded amount of computation.

6. PARSING ARRANGEMENTS OF PRIMITIVES

In Section 5 we outlined how a pyramid can extract various types of primitives from an image by a parallel parsing process. We further showed how the pyramid can compute moments of these primitives, and in particular can compute their centroids and principal axes. Thus the pyramid provides us with position and orientation information about a set of image primitives. In addition, it can provide us with various shape properties of the primitives, defined by combinations of moments; this allows us to identify the primitives as being of various types.

We can now regard these primitives as terminal symbols of a coordinate grammar; each symbol represents a primitive of a given type, and we also know its position and orientation. If we have a coordinate grammar for objects of a given class that has these primitives in its terminal vocabulary, we can now recognize such objects in the image by using the grammar to parse subsets of the primitives.

Since our coordinate grammars are diameter-bounded, it is straightforward to carry out the parsing in parallel using a pyramid. We input the terminal symbols into the base of the pyramid, and pass them up to successively higher levels until a cell sees a set of symbols that correspond to the right-hand side of a rule. (This is best done using a pyramid in which the cells' image blocks overlap; if not, the cells must obtain information from their neighbors as well as their children.) The cell can then replace these symbols by the symbol on the left-hand side, and pass this symbol up. In worst cases, this may require a cell to keep track of many symbols; but if the grammar is expansive (i.e., each rule application reduces the number of symbols), and the set of primitives in the image does not have many ambiguous parses, the number of symbols that a given cell needs to handle should not become very large. Thus in such cases it should be possible for the pyramid to construct all the parses of sets of the primitives that represent occurrences of objects, with each cell doing only a bounded amount of computation.

7. CONCLUDING REMARKS

This paper has outlined a general method of defining objects as hierarchical arrangements of image primitives, using coordinate grammars. It has indicated how a pyramid cellular computer can be used to parse expressions in a diameter-bounded coordinate grammar; if the grammar is (sufficiently) expansive (i.e., the number of symbols shrinks rapidly as the parse proceeds), doing this should require each cell in the pyramid to perform only a bounded amount of computation.

We have also shown how a pyramid can be used to extract various basic types of primitives from an image and compute their positions, orientations, and other moment-based properties. These types include local features (at various scales), edges or curves, and ribbon-like or blob-like regions. Such primitives can be extracted using pyramid algorithms in which each cell does only a bounded amount of computation, provided the curves or ribbons are not too complex in shape and the image does not contain too many of them. The process of extracting such a primitive also creates a tree representation in which the features are the pixels belonging to the primitive and the root represents the primitive as a whole; this process too can be regarded as parallel parsing with respect to a coordinate grammar.

The methods described in this paper have not been specified in detail; more information can be found in the cited references. Our discussion of these methods has been informal and sketchy. Nevertheless, it is hoped that this paper has served to convey the flavor of the approach, and to suggest why pyramid cellular computers seem to be a very appropriate architecture for syntactic object recognition.

REFERENCES

1. Fu, K.S., *Syntactic Pattern Recognition and Applications*, Prentice-Hall, Englewood Cliffs, NJ (1982).
2. Milgram, D.L. and Rosenfeld, A., A note on "grammar with coordinates", in F. Nake and A. Rosenfeld, eds., *Graphic Languages*, North-Holland, Amsterdam, 187–194 (1972).
3. Rosenfeld, A., Coordinate grammars revisited: generalized isometric grammars, CS-TR-1918, Center for Automation Research, University of Maryland, College Park (September 1987).
4. Rosenfeld, A., Pyramid algorithms for finding global structures in images, *Information Sciences*, in press.
5. Rosenfeld, A. and Kak, A.C., *Digital Picture Processing*, Academic Press, New York, Ch. 11 (1982).
6. Rosenfeld, A., ed., *Multiresolution Image Processing and Analysis*, Springer, Berlin (1984).
7. Cantoni, V. and Levialdi, S., eds., *Pyramidal Systems for Computer Vision*, Springer, Berlin (1986).

PUBLIC-KEY CRYPTOSYSTEMS AND LANGUAGE THEORY

Arto Salomaa
Mathematics Department
University of Turku
Finland

ABSTRACT. Public-key cryptosystems based on language theory are discussed. Two types of such systems - functional and rewriting-based - are distinguished.

1. INTRODUCTION

During recent years the increase in the amount of studies concerning cryptography has been really explosive, and there are two main reasons for this. In the first place, the seminal idea of public-key cryptography, apart from being of extraordinary interest on its own right, has created entirely new types of applications, some of which are rather contraintuitive with respect to the common sense notions concerning communication between different parties. In the second place, the need for cryptography has increased tremendously due to various aspects of data security. This can be expressed briefly by saying that there are now really many "positive" applications of cryptography, whereas the earlier applications were mainly "negative", i.e., secret communication during wars, criminal activities, etc. Besides, it seems that the range of applications will become larger and larger with the expansion of electronic mail and similar systems. The positive applications which we refer to are all somehow connected with the very important task of assuring that the information stored in an information system can be accessed by proper, or authorized, persons only.

Public-key cryptosystems are constructed along the following guidelines.

(i) Start with a difficult (intractable) problem P.

(ii) Pick up an easy subproblem P_1 of P.

(iii) "Shuffle" P_1 in such a way that the resulting problem P_2 "looks like" the original problem P. Use P_2 as the public encryption key.

(iv) Keep secret the information concerning how P_1 can be recovered from P_2. This information is referred to as the "trapdoor".

(v) A legal user of the system is able to decrypt by solving the easy problem P_1. Others have to solve P_2 that at least looks like the intractable P.

The guidelines (i)-(v) are still on a very abstract level. How the details can be filled in decides the quality of the resulting cryptosystem.

In some of the most common public-key cryptosystems, such as RSA or knapsack systems, the underlying problem P belongs to number theory. However, in principle there are no restrictions as regards the area of the problem P. In the systems considered in this paper P belongs to language theory. The purpose of the paper is to discuss some pros and cons of language-theory based public-key cryptosystems. A brief outline about the contents of the paper follows.

Sections 2-4 discuss "functional" cryptosystems. There are, say, two functions f_0 and f_1 operating on words, as well as an initial word w. A sequence of bits (plaintext word) is encrypted by applying the functions to the initial word in the corresponding order. For instance, 0100 is encrypted as $wf_0f_1f_0f_0$. Section 2 discusses the oldest among such systems - see, for instance, [4]. A common cryptanalytic attack, [2], is presented in Section 3. Further such cryptosystems, [6], are considered in Section 4. The final Section 5 deals with language-based public-key cryptosystems of a different type, [3], [5] and [7]. Two rewriting systems R_0 and R_1 are given. A bit i is encrypted by randomly creating a word according to R_i. It is taken care of that decryption is unique.

2. A DT0L-T0L-BASED CRYPTOSYSTEM

More details of the system are contained, for instance, in [4]. The cryptosystem designer starts with a DT0L system, where parsing is easy, and shuffles it by adding new letters to get a T0L system. The secret trapdoor is the information concerning how to get back from the T0L system to the DT0L system. Thus, the cryptanalyst has to deal with the T0L system, whereas the legal receiver may deal with the DT0L system that should be chosen in such a way that parsing is easy. Some details will now be given.

Let Σ be an alphabet and consider two morphisms $h_0, h_1 : \Sigma^* \to \Sigma^*$, as well as a nonempty word w in Σ^*. We say the quadruple $G = (\Sigma, h_0, h_1, w)$ is <u>backward deterministic</u> if the condition

(1) $(w)i_0i_1 \ldots i_n = (w)j_0j_1 \ldots j_m$, each i and j in $\{h_0, h_1\}$,

always implies the condition

(2) $i_0i_1 \ldots i_n = j_0j_1 \ldots j_m$.

More specifically, (1) indicates that the two words over Σ appearing on the two sides of the equation are equal, whereas (2) indicates that m = n and the two words over the alphabet $\{h_0, h_1\}$ appearing on the two sides of the equation are equal. Here we have written $(w)i_0$ instead of $(w)h_{i_0}$.

By the terminology of L systems, the quadruple $G = (\Sigma, h_0, h_1, w)$ is a <u>DT0L system</u>. The condition of backward determinism means that the final outcome always determines uniquely the sequence of tables used. An obvious way to obtain backward determinism is to include a special letter t in Σ ("table indicator") with productions

$$t \to t0 \ , \ 0 \to 0 \ , \ 1 \to 1 \ , \text{ in } h_0 \ ,$$

$$t \to t1 \ , \ 0 \to 0 \ , \ 1 \to 1 \ , \text{ in } h_1 \ .$$

Further details are omitted.

Backward deterministic DT0L systems G can be used as <u>classical cryptosystems</u>: a sequence of bits $i_0 i_1 \dots i_n$ is encrypted as the word over Σ

$$(w)h_{i_0} h_{i_1} \dots h_{i_n} \ .$$

Then G has to be kept secret. Otherwise, there is no difference between the (legal) decryption and the (illegal) cryptanalysis.

We will see how the classical cryptosystem can be changed into a public-key one. Before that we want to point out that backward determinism guarantees only that unique parsing is possible, i.e., to every cryptotext corresponds a unique plaintext. It does not guarantee that parsing is easy. This is guaranteed by <u>strong backward determinism</u>. By definition, a DT0L system $G = (\Sigma, h_0, h_1, w)$ is strongly backward deterministic iff the condition

$$z = (w)i_1 \dots i_t = (y)i_k \ , \ i,j \in \{0,1\} \ , \ x,y \in \Sigma^* \ ,$$

always imply the conditions

$$i_k = i_t \quad \text{and} \quad y = (w)i_1 \dots i_{t-1} \ .$$

For instance, the DT0L system determined by the initial word ab and morphisms

$$h_0 : a \to ab \ , \ b \to bb \ ; \ h_1 : a \to bb \ , \ b \to ab$$

is backward deterministic but not strongly. A drastic difference between the two notions is that backward determinism is undecidable, [1], whereas strong backward determinism is decidable, [4].

Thus, every word generated by a strongly backward deterministic DT0L system has a unique predecessor in Σ^*, and is derived from this predecessor by a unique morphism. A word generated by a backward deterministic DT0L system may have several predecessors. This means that the parsing sequence of a word in a backward deterministic DT0L system depends on both the word and the axiom. The parsing sequence of a word in a strongly backward deterministic DT0L system depends on the word itself only. The axiom only decides where the parsing should end. Let us now define the public-key cryptosystem that will be a T0L system.

Let Δ be an alphabet of a much greater cardinality than Σ. Typically, Σ consists of five letters, whereas Δ consists of 200 letters. Let $g : \Delta^* \to \Sigma^*$ be a morphism mapping every letter to a letter or to the empty word in such a way that $g^{-1}(a)$ is nonempty for all letters a of Σ. Define two finite substitutions σ_0 and σ_1 on Δ^* by letting $\sigma_i(d)$ to be a finite nonempty subset of

$$g^{-1}(h_i(g(d))) \text{ for all } d \text{ in } \Delta,\ i = 0, 1 .$$

Intuitively, the morphism g divides the letters of Δ into descendants of letters of Σ and into dummy symbols that are mapped into the empty word λ.

Finally, choose a word u from $g^{-1}(w)$.

The quadruple $H = (\Delta, \sigma_0, \sigma_1, u)$ now constitutes the public encryption key. The encryption of a sequence $i_0 i_1 \ldots i_n$ of bits happens by choosing an arbitrary word from the (finite) set

$$(3) \qquad (u)\, \sigma_{i_0} \sigma_{i_1} \cdots \sigma_{i_n} .$$

The <u>secret trapdoor</u> consists of the items Σ, h_0, h_1, w and g. In fact, g is the essential item because the other items can be determined from g and the public encryption key.

It follows by the definitions that whenever y is a word in the set (3), then

$$g(y) = (w)\, h_{i_0}\, h_{i_1} \cdots h_{i_n} .$$

Thus, the knowledge of the secret trapdoor reduces decryption to the parsing problem of the DT0L system G.

In the terminology of L systems, H is a <u>T0L system</u>.

Plaintext can and should be divided into blocks before encryption is begun. The blocks may be of variable size. The size should not be too large. Otherwise, the cryptotext will be too long in comparison with the plaintext. In the normal case the cryptotext blocks are separated by a boundary marker #.

Instead of two morphisms and substitutions, the systems G and H might have more of them. For instance, if we want to encrypt directly a plaintext given in decimal notation, we should use ten morphisms and substitutions.

Let us still consider an example. The DT0L system G is determined by w = ab and by the two morphisms

$$h_0 : a \to ab \ , \ b \to b \ ;$$

$$h_1 : a \to a \ , \ b \to ba \ .$$

Strong backward determinism follows because the last morphism applied is h_0 exactly in case the word under scan ends with b. (It is also true that the last morphism is h_0 exactly in case the word under scan has the subword b^2.)

Define now $\Delta = \{c_1, c_2, c_3, c_4, c_5\}$ and g by

$$g(c_2) = g(c_4) = a, \ g(c_1) = b, \ g(c_3) = g(c_5) = \lambda .$$

Choose $u = c_2c_3c_1$ and define two substitutions σ_0 and σ_1 by

$$\sigma_0 : c_1 \to c_5c_1 \ , \ c_2 \to c_2c_3c_1 \ , \ c_2 \to c_4c_5c_1 \ , \ c_3 \to c_3c_5,$$
$$c_3 \to c_5c_3 \ , \ c_4 \to c_2c_1c_3c_5 \ , \ c_5 \to c_5c_5 \ ;$$
$$\sigma_1 : c_1 \to c_1c_2 \ , \ c_1 \to c_1c_4 \ , \ c_2 \to c_4 \ , \ c_3 \to c_3c_5c_3 \ ,$$
$$c_3 \to c_5c_5 \ , \ c_4 \to c_2 \ , \ c_4 \to c_4 \ , \ c_5 \to c_5 \ .$$

3. A CRYPTANALYTIC METHOD APPLICABLE FOR MANY FUNCTIONAL CRYPTOSYSTEMS

The cryptosystem discussed in the previous section has many desirable features. The encryption and legal decryption are easy and possess fast algorithms. The size of the plaintext blocks is very flexible. It can be taken care of that the cryptotext will not be too long, as is often the case with similar systems. The problem of finding the letters mapped into the empty word by g is NP-complete, [4].

However, the system, as well as many similar systems, is vulnerable with respect to the following cryptanalytic attack due to Jarkko Kari, [2]. For the sake of completeness we outline the attack.

The basic idea is the following. Let A be a nondeterministic finite automaton accepting the language L, and let σ be a finite substitution. Then a nondeterministic finite automaton A′ with the following properties may be constructed: A′ accepts the language $\sigma^{-1}(L)$ and <u>has the same state set</u>, as well as initial and final states, as A. Indeed, for a letter a, word x in $\sigma(a)$ and state q of A, compute the set S_x of states that can be reached in A from q with the input word x. In A′ a transition from q caused by a goes to exactly the states in S′, where S′ is the union of the sets S_x when x ranges over $\sigma(a)$.

Given now the public encryption key $H = (\Delta, \sigma_0, \sigma_1, u)$ and a cryptotext $c = c_1c_2 \ldots c_n$, we let first A be a nondeterministic finite automaton accepting only the word c. Let then A_i' be an automaton accepting the language $\sigma_i^{-1}(L(A))$, for i = 0, 1. By strong backward determinism, exactly one of the languages $L(A_i')$, say $L(A_0')$ is nonempty. Then the last bit of the plaintext is 0, and the new A is A_0'. The procedure is repeated. The iteration is finished when u is reached. The procedure runs in cubic time, [2], but probably not in quadratic time. Strong backward determinism is essential. This is not required in general for the system discussed in Section 2. However, at least a similar requirement is quite essential for efficient legal decryption.

4. OTHER FUNCTIONAL CRYPTOSYSTEMS

Cryptosystems can be modified by the use of nonterminals. This approach transforms the system discussed in Section 2 into an EDT0L-ET0L-based system. We now have to require that derivations begin and end with a terminal word. Otherwise, there is no essential difference with the earlier case. The requirement excludes some end words, namely, those containing nonterminals. In the general case this means the exclusion of some plaintext words as well. However, this can be taken care of. The cryptanalysis is of essentially the same complexity as for systems without nonterminals. Thus, nonterminals seem not to buy you anything.

Similar ideas can be applied for grammars, matrix grammars, etc. We hope to return to these matters in another paper.

The system presented in [6] is not backward deterministic and, thus, Kari's cryptanalytic method is not as such applicable. However, the same cryptotext may lead to very many plaintexts and, thus, legal decryption is very ambiguous. (It is possible that this can be taken care of.) Let us use the notation of [6]. Set T = {a}, g(a) = a, g(e) = λ for $e \neq a$ (big V!), $u_1 = x_1 = a$, $\sigma_0 : a \to a^2$, $\sigma_1 : a \to a^4$. Other letters are mapped arbitrarily by σ_i. Then the plaintext corresponding to a^{2^i} is very ambiguous because (i) the starting point of the encryption is not known, (ii) the last substitution used cannot be found out. More sophisticated examples can be constructed.

It is customary to require that in a given cryptosystem only one plaintext corresponds to any given cryptotext, although a plaintext may give rise to several cryptotexts.

5. REWRITING-BASED CRYPTOSYSTEMS

Consider two rewriting systems (in a very general sense) R_0 and R_1 such that the generated languages $L(R_0)$ and $L(R_1)$ are disjoint. The bit i is encrypted by generating an arbitrary word in $L(R_i)$. It should be hard to decide of an arbitrary word to which of the languages it belongs. The same decision should be easy for modified rewriting systems R_i'. The systems R_i are public, whereas the information concerning how to obtain the systems R_i' constitutes the secret trapdoor.

A common remark concerning all systems of this type is in order. The original decision problem concerning the systems R_i may be undecidable. However, it cannot be undecidable for the special systems obtained by shuffling R_i'. This follows because, for any public-key cryptosystem, cryptanalysis is in NP provided the encryption method is in P. Given a cryptotext, one just guesses the plaintext and the encryptionsequence. (The latter is needed only if the encryption is not unique.) The verification of the guess is in P, by our assumption.

The oldest cryptosystem of this type is due to [7]. Let w_0 and w_1 be two non-equivalent words in a group G with an unsolvable word problem. The bit i is encrypted by using the defining relations of G to generate an arbitrary word equivalent to w_i. The legal recipient decrypts by considering another group G′ with an easy word problem. The words w_0 and w_1 are still non-equivalent in G′.

In this system the cryptotext tends to be long. The cryptanalyst may find a trapdoor that is not actually used by the system designer.

The system considered in [5] is based similarly on Thue systems and contains many promising ideas.

The system discussed in [3] uses similarly two grammars G_0 and G_1 with disjoint languages $L(G_i)$. Two disjoint regular languages $R_i \supseteq L(G_i)$ constitute the secret trapdoor. It can be shown that the problem of finding two such R_i (not necessarily the ones used by the system designer) is NP-complete.

REFERENCES

[1] Dassow, J., A note on DT0L systems. EATCS Bulletin 22 (1984) 11-14.

[2] Kari, J., A cryptanalytic observation concerning systems based on language theory. Discr. Appl. Math. 21 (1988) 265-268.

[3] Niemi, V., Hiding regular languages. In preparation.

[4] Salomaa, A. and Yu, S., On a public-key cryptosystem based on iterated morphisms and substitutions. Theor. Comp. Sci. 48 (1986) 283-296.

[5] Siromoney, R. and Siromoney, G., A public key cryptosystem, that defies cryptanalysis. EATCS Bulletin 28 (1986) 37-43.

[6] Subramanian, K.G., Siromoney, R. and Abisha, P.J., A D0L-T0L public-key cryptosystem. Inf. Proc. Letters 26 (1987/88) 95-97.

[7] Wagner, N.R. and Magyarik, M.R., A public key cryptosystem based on the word problem. Springer Lecture Notes in Computer Science 196 (1985) 19-36

KAMBI KOLAM AND CYCLE GRAMMARS*

Gift Siromoney
Rani Siromoney
and
T. Robinson

Madras Christian College
Tambaram
Madras 600 059, INDIA

ABSTRACT

Cycle grammar for the generation and description of pictures having a rotational symmetry was advocated by Rosenfeld, as early as 1974. Kambi kolam patterns, fractals, and several other natural families provide us with interesting examples of cycle languages. Methods of describing these, using turtle moves, chain-code interpretation and kolam moves are examined. Cycle rewriting rules are introduced and appplied to the generation of kambi kolam patterns. Conditions for the pictures to represent cycles are examined.

1. INTRODUCTION

Graph grammars and array grammars for the description and analysis of two-dimensional structures have been studied extensively [2,4,9,18]. More than a decade ago, Rosenfeld [8] argued the case for cycle grammars for generating patterns having various types of rotational symmetry [12,13]. Languages generated by cycle

---

* Revised version of Gift Siromoney and Rani Siromoney, Rosenfeld's Cycle Grammars and Kolam, Proc. 3rd International Workshop on Graph Grammars and their applications to Computer Science, Lecture Notes in Computer Science, 291, Springer-Verlag, Berlin, 1987.

grammars consist of cycles ("necklaces") of symbols i.e. cyclically ordered sequences of symbols. There are several interesting families of pictures - both natural as well as artificial - which are cycle languages. Outlines of chromosome shapes regarded as sequences of basic shape elements form a natural family of cycles. These were among the earliest examples for which grammars were given. Several of the fractals, including some classical space filling curves provide us with interesting examples of picture cycles. Edge label controlled map systems have been used extensively in the generation of observed cell division patterns in plant tissues [3]. Those based on control by 'circular words' provide us with natural examples of picture cycles. Certain families of kolam patterns viz. the kambi kolam - literally meaning wire decoration - which can be represented as a single strand, provide us with illustrative examples of picture cycle languages. Each kambi begins and ends at the same point. i.e. each kambi is an unending line or a closed curve with or without loops.

Kolam is a traditional art practised extensively in the southern part of India, for decorating courtyards of dwellings. Motivated by these designs, we have introduced earlier, different types of array grammars generating array languages [14] and we have given specific instructions for drawing certain kinds of kolam patterns graphically [15]. There, the approach was syntactic and the emphasis was on considering each pattern as made up of subpatterns which in turn could be reduced ultimately to certain primitive patterns. Siromoney kolam array grammar [1] can generate digital rectangular arrays of different sizes, but with same proportion between the length and breadth. This property is a requirement when a camera on a robot does not maintain a fixed distance from the object of interest and the grammar has proved to be useful in an inference scheme.

We conducted an experiment to find out how simple village women (very often not literate) store such complicated patterns in their memory and retrieve them with ease while drawing the kolam. In the course of the study, it was found that kolam practitioners remember, describe and draw the designs in terms of "moves" such as 'going forward', 'taking a right turn', 'taking a U-turn to the right' and so on, reminiscent of the "interpretations" which are used in computer graphics as sequences of commands which control a "turtle" [7]. Treating each kind of a move as a terminal sign, each single kambi kolam represents a "necklace" or picture cycle. Thus kolam designs provide us with illustrative examples of a variety of patterns including several picture cycle languages.

These picture cycle languages can be viewed and generated in several ways - (i) some of them may be regarded as cycles in the graph-theoretic sense - as a sequence of nodes and arcs, or (ii) they may be converted into strings and generated by string grammars either Chomskian or L-type, or (iii) as necklaces of terminal symbols. The terminal symbols may be of different types - each symbol may have a graphic interpretation as in [19] or represent simpler turtle moves as in [7] or chaincode alphabet as in [6] with coordinates specified or not or "kolam moves" as in [16]. Each of these representations has its own advantage and is applicable to specific problems. Picture necklaces described using any one of these terminal symbols in turn may be generated by Chomskian grammars or L-systems or cycle-rewriting rules.

In this paper, after introducing the graphic representation, turtle moves and chain code pictures, and giving examples of generations of picture necklaces by Chomskian, L-type grammars we examine conditions for cycleness in terms of the grammar. Then we introduce cycle catenation and other operations mainly motivated by the manner in which the kolam practitioners draw the kolam designs.

2. PRELIMINARIES

Cycles or necklaces are formed either (i) by allowing a grammar to generate a string and then bending the string until it closes itself or (ii) starting from sentential forms that are "cycles" and using production rules for the generation of cycles.

If G is a grammar (context-free or 0L) and L(G) the string language generated by G, $\widehat{L(G)}$ the set of cycles resulting from bending the strings of L, and $\tilde{L}(G)$ the language generated when sentential forms are regarded as cycles, it is clear that $\widehat{L(G)} = \tilde{L}(G)$ [8]. When a picture in the form of a cycle is considered as a necklace of terminal symbols , we further require that starting from anywhere in the string, we should obtain the same picture. This additional requirement is needed in view of the fact that necklaces with graphic interpretations for drawing certain fractal curves need not necessarily yield unending lines with arbitrary starting points (examples 3 and 4).

Formally, this requirement may be given as follows: Let $x = x_1x_2 \ldots x_n$ be a string of terminal symbols. Then $\hat{x} = \widehat{x_1x_2 \ldots x_n}$ is obtained by bending x and forming a Rosenfeld cycle denoted $\not{c}$ x.

If $x' = x_2x_3 \ldots x_nx_1$, $x'' = x_3x_4 \ldots x_nx_1x_2, \ldots$ then $\hat{x} = \hat{x}' = \hat{x}'' = \ldots$ showing that $\hat{x}$ is a cyclically ordered sequence of symbols over a terminal alphabet.

Let I(x) be an interpretation of the string x (I may be a graphical interpretation and may represent the pen-command of turtle or a chain code representation). Then $I(x) = I(x_1)\ I(x_2) \ldots I(x_n)$.

Let P(I(x)) be the picture represented by I(x). It is a pictorial necklace with or without loops if $I(\hat{x}) = I(x') = I(x'') = \ldots$. Note that Rosenfeld's cycle need not represent a picture necklace.

We illustrate with a few examples.

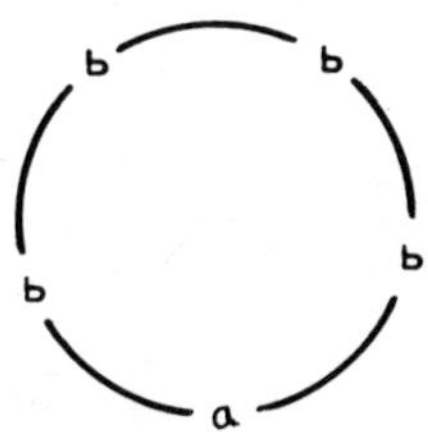

(a)

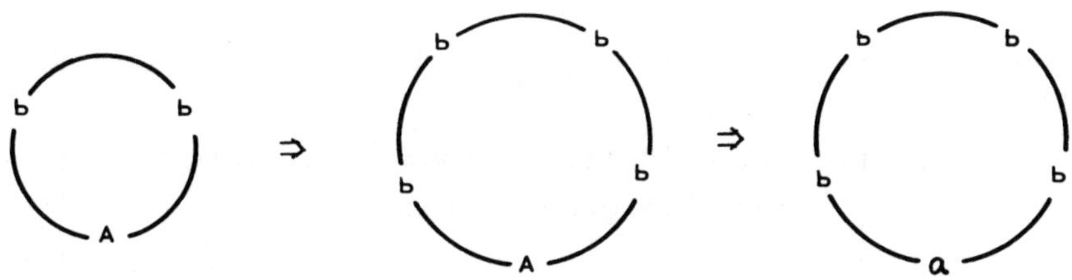

(b)

Figure 1(a). The string bbabb bent in the form of a cycle.

(b). Cycle derived from a sentential form in the form of a necklace.

Example 1: Let G consist of the context-free productions $A \longrightarrow a$, $B \longrightarrow b$, $A \longrightarrow bAb$, were A is the start symbol and a,b are terminal symbols. Then, the derivation $A \Rightarrow bAb \Rightarrow b^2Ab^2$ yields b^2ab^2 which can be represented as the cycle in Fig. 1a. If we treat the sentential form bAb as a cycle we can derive the cycle in Fig. 1b. which is the same as the one in Fig. 1a.

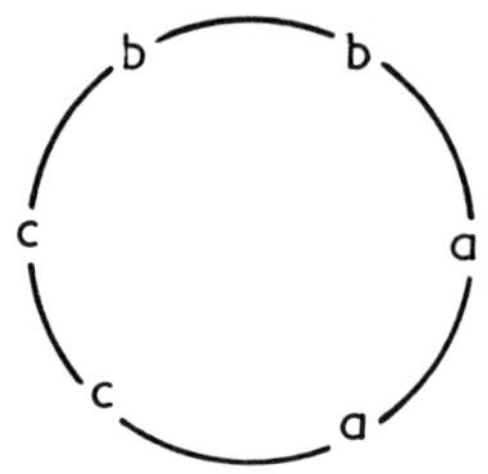

(a)

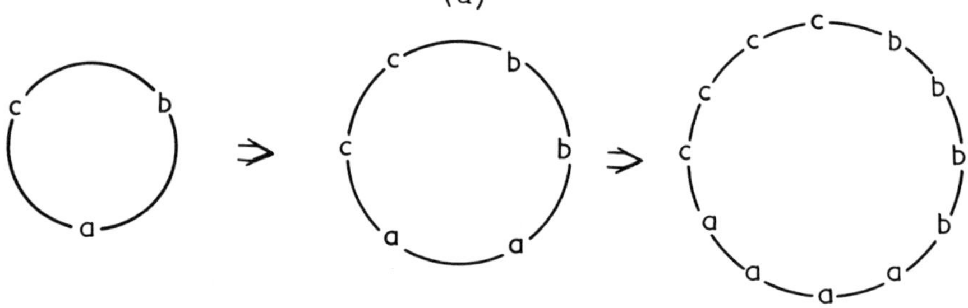

(b)

Figure 2(a). The string aabbcc bent in the form of a cycle.

(b). Cycles derived from a circular sentential form using D0L rules.

Example 2: Let H be the D0L system $< \Sigma, h, w >$ where $\Sigma = \{ a,b,c \}$, w = abc, h(a) = aa, h(b) = bb, h(c) = cc. Then the derivation $abc \Rightarrow a^2b^2c^2 \Rightarrow a^4b^4c^4$ yields the cycle in Fig. 2a. We also have the cycle derivation (Fig. 2b). Both the derivations yield same set of cycles (Fig. 2)

Example 3: Von Koch curve

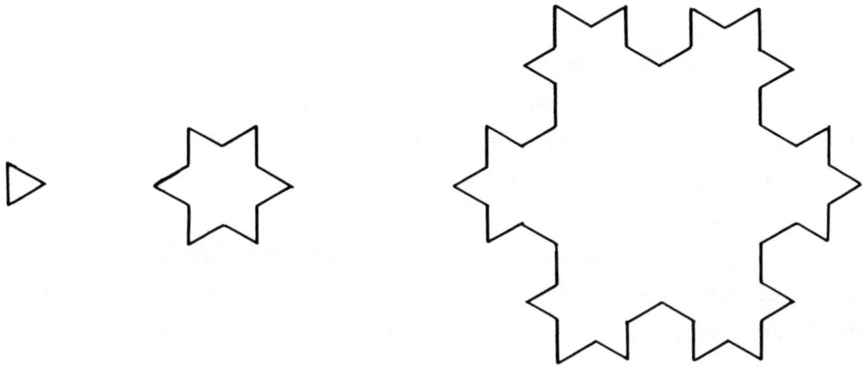

Figure 3. A sequence of patterns in Example 3 (Von Koch curve).

It is clear that the sequence of patterns in Fig. 3 are cycles in the graph-theoretic sense. The sequence of pen commands with graphic interpretation function I is given by

$I(a)$ = Forward, $I(r)$ = right 60°, $I(\ell)$ = left 60° [19]. Consider the DOL system $G = < \Sigma, h, w >$, $\Sigma = \{ a, r, \ell \}$, $w = a\ell a\ell a$, and $h(a) = ara\ell ara$, $h(r) = r$, $h(\ell) = \ell$. It is clear that $\widehat{L(G)} = \tilde{L}(G)$ and $I(L(G))$ represents the sequence of patterns. But it is not a picture necklace since in $I(\tilde{L}(G))$, if we start at an arbitrary point and execute the commands, the pen does not produce the same sequence of patterns - $ara\ell ara$ considered as a necklace has 2 consecutive a's. For pictoral necklaces, $I(\hat{x})$ must be a necklace and unique.

One way of overcoming this is to make the requirement that the turtle returns to the original position and direction. In such a case it is clear that we get a pictorial necklace. We can also consider the sequence of patterns represented by chaincode on a hexagonal grid. Let a,b,c stand for unit length in the direction ↗, ↖, ↓ of the hexagonal grid  and a, b, c in the reverse directions. Consider the DOL system $G = \langle \Sigma, h, w \rangle$ where $\Sigma = \{ a,b,c,\bar{a},\bar{b},\bar{c} \}$, $w = abc$ and $h(a) = a\bar{b}\bar{c}a$, $h(b) = b\bar{c}\bar{a}b$, $h(c) = c\bar{a}\bar{b}c$, $h(\bar{a}) = \bar{a}$, $h(\bar{b}) = \bar{b}$, $h(\bar{c}) = \bar{c}$. Derivations proceed as follows.

$$abc \Rightarrow a\bar{b}\bar{c}ab\bar{c}\bar{a}bc\bar{a}\bar{b}c$$

$$\Rightarrow a\bar{b}\bar{c}a\bar{b}\bar{c}a\bar{b}\bar{c}ab\bar{c}\bar{a}b\bar{c}\bar{a}b\bar{c}\bar{a}bc\bar{a}\bar{b}c\bar{a}\bar{b}c\bar{a}\bar{b}c$$

It is clear that $\widehat{L(G)} = \tilde{L}(G)$ and $I(L(G))$ is a pictorial necklace and $P(L(G))$ represents the picture necklaces depicted in Fig. 3. Perhaps we can call this a DOL necklace system.

Here we describe a graphical interpretation of strings based on the notion of a LOGO - style turtle which is made use of in [7].

A state of the turtle is defined as a triplet (x,y,α), where the cartesian coordinates (x,y) represent the turtle's position and the angle α, called the turtle's heading, is interpreted as the direction in which the turtle is facing. Given the step size d and the angle increment δ, the turtle can respond to commands represented by the following symbols:

F - Move forward a step of length d. The state of the turtle changes to (x',y',α), where $x' = x + d\cos\alpha$ and $y' = y + d\sin\alpha$. A line segment between points (x,y) and (x',y') is drawn.

f - Move forward a step of length d without drawing a line.

\+ - Turn right by angle δ. The next state of the turtle is $(x,y,\alpha+\delta)$. It is assumed here that the positive orientation of angles is clockwise.

\- - Turn left by angle δ. The next state of the turtle is $(x,y,\alpha-\delta)$.

All other symbols are ignored by the turtle (the turtle preserves its current state).

Let γ be a string, (x_0, y_0, α_0) the initial state of the turtle, and d, δ fixed parameters. The picture (set of lines) drawn by the turtle responding to the string γ is called the turtle interpretation of γ.

For the DOL necklace system in example 3, the representation and generation by turtle moves is simple, and is given by ({ F,+,- }, { F $\longrightarrow$ F+F--F+F }, F--F--F) with $\delta = 60^{\circ}$. It is of interest to note that the antisnow flakes (Fig.4) can also be generated in a very simple way by the following DOL system with turtle commands.

({ F,+,- }, { F $\longrightarrow$ F-F++F-F }, F--F--F--) with $\delta = 60^{\circ}$.

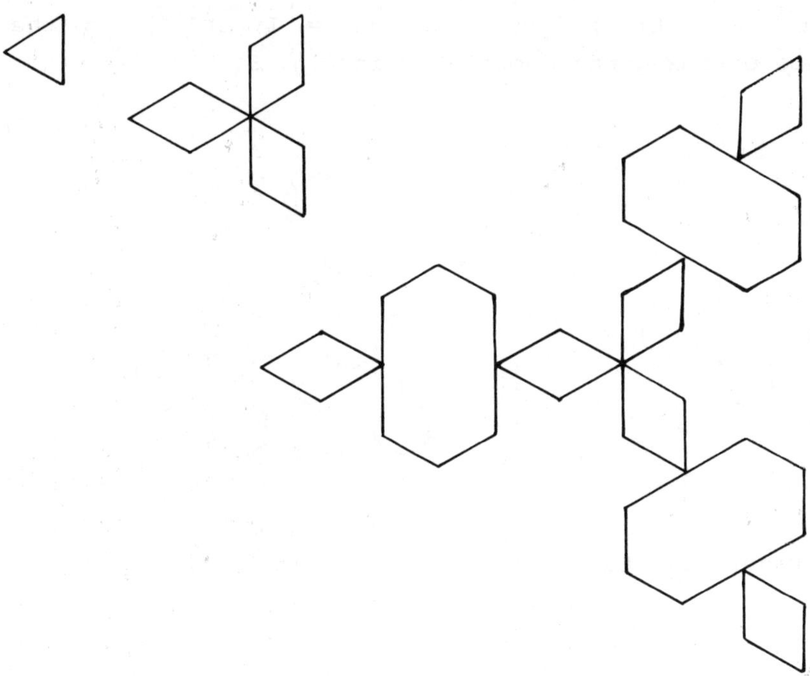

Figure 4. A sequence of antisnowflake patterns

Example 4: (Hexagonal snowflake)

The sequence of patterns in Fig.5 represents cycles in the graph-theoretic sense. Consider the DOL system $H = \langle \Sigma, h, w \rangle$, where $\Sigma = \{ a, r, \ell \}$, $h(a) = ara\ell aa$, $h(r) = r$, $h(\ell) = \ell$ and $w = a\ell a\ell a\ell$. The graphic interpretation function I is defined as I(a) = Forward, I(r) = Right 60°.Forward.Right 60°, I(ℓ) = left 60°.Forward. Left 60° [19]. It is clear that $\widehat{L(H)} = \tilde{L}(H)$ and $I(\widehat{L(H)})$ yields the sequence of patterns in Fig. 5 but is not a picture necklace. However, we can choose the pen commands as follows:

I′(R) = Forward. Right 60°. Forward. Right 60°

I′(L) = Forward. Left 60° . Forward. Left 60°

Consider the DOL system $H' = \langle \Sigma', h', w' \rangle$ where $\Sigma' = \{ R, L \}$, $h'(L) = RL^2$, $h'(R) = RLR$, and $w' = L^3$. Then $\widehat{L(H')} = \tilde{L}(H')$ and $I'(\widehat{L(H')}) = I'(\tilde{L}(H'))$ is the sequence of hexagonal snowflakes in Fig. 5.

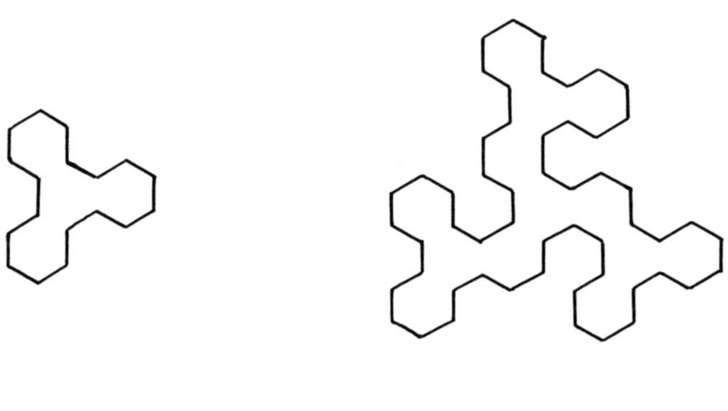

Figure 5. Hexagonal snowflakes in Example 4.

When a DOL-system is given in terms of the turtle commands, we note that a simple criterion enables us to check whether it generates a family of necklaces.

Let a D0L-system over turtle interpretation be given by $H = < T, P, w_o >$ where $T = \{ F,+,- \}$ with some δ. Let t^+, t^- denote the number of +'s and -'s present in a word $w \in T^*$.

The condition is given as follows:

(i) If w_o represents a cycle and

(ii) if $t^+ = t^-$ in the right-hand side of all $p_i \in P$,

then all w_i, such that $w_o \overset{*}{\Rightarrow} w_i$ are cycles.

In the following examples, by verifying the condition we establish the effectiveness of checking whether a D0L-system over the T generates a necklace family.

The turtle interpretation based D0L-system to generate the hexagonal snowflakes (Fig 5.) is

$$\left(\{ F, F', +, - \}, \quad \begin{Bmatrix} F \longrightarrow F{+}F'{+}F{-}F'{-}F \\ F' \longrightarrow F' \end{Bmatrix}, \quad F{-}F'{-}F{-}F'{-}F{-}F' \right)$$

with $\delta = 60^o$. Here F and F' have the same interpretation of 'move forward'. We see that $t^+ = t^- = 2$ in the first production and $t^+ = t^- = 0$ in the second production. w_o represents a picture which is a closed cycle.

Example 5: (Quadratic Koch Island)

The D0L-system based on the turtle interpretation to generate the Quadratic Koch island (Fig. 6) is

$$(\{ F,+,- \}, \{ F \longrightarrow F{+}F{-}F{-}FF{+}F{+}F{-}F \}, F{+}F{+}F{+}F)$$

with $\delta = 90^o$. Here $t^+ = t^- = 3$ and the axiom represents a cycle. Hence, this system generates a family of cycles.

Figure 6: Quadratic Koch Island

Example 6:

The octagonal dragon curve generated by the DOL-system

$$\left(\{ F, F', +, - \}, \begin{Bmatrix} F \longrightarrow F+F+F' \\ F' \longrightarrow F-F-F' \end{Bmatrix}, F \right)$$

with $\delta = 45^o$ does not satisfy the necessary condition and hence it is not a cycle.

3. CYCLE - REWRITING RULES

In this section we introduce picture necklace rewriting rules. We consider the class of picture necklace rules that are applicable to angular versions of kambi kolam with chain code interpretation. The picture necklace catenation operator is introduced with rules as to when it is applicable. After defining picture necklace grammar, we give illustrative examples. We note that there can be several types of productions within the grammar i.e., either Chomskian with or without parallel rewriting [11] or L-type [10].

A kambi is a closed curve with or without loops represented in the form of Rosenfeld cycle which is a string joined at two ends. Each element of the string (or Rosenfeld cycle) belongs to the set

$$K = \{ F, R(1), R(2), R(3), L(1), L(2), L(3) \}$$

where F stands for "move forward one unit", R(1) represents a "half turn to the right", R(2) a "U-turn to the right", R(3) a "complete loop to the right" and similarly for L(1), L(2) and L(3) (Fig. 7a,b).

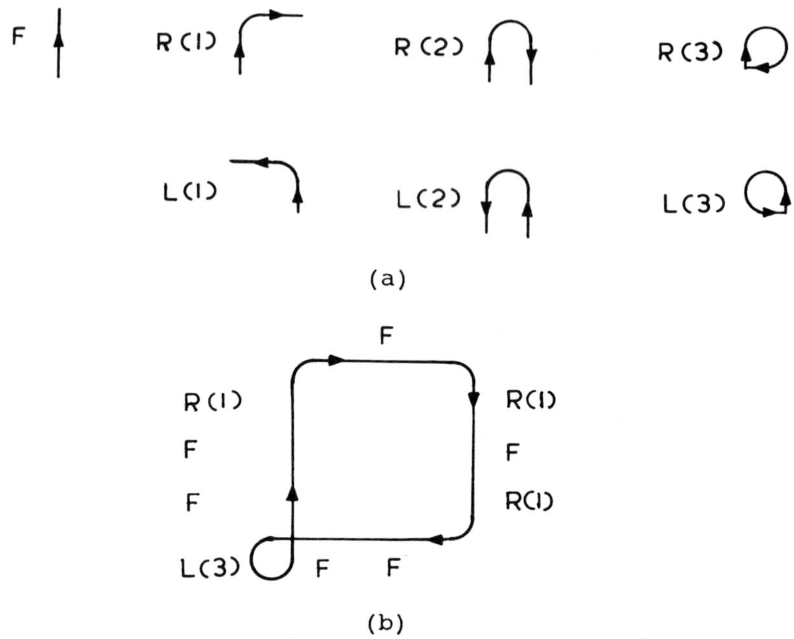

Figure 7. a) Interpretations of moves in a pictorial necklace.
b) A pictorial necklace.

A kambi in general can turn in many otherways but we have restricted ourselves to this limited number of turning moves.

A kolam design contains one or more kambi's and each kambi can be represented by a string of F's, R's and L's which form a necklace. If x is a string of F's, R's and L's, we can write ø w to represent the necklace. For curvilinear kolam cycle if I is the interpretation function on K^*, where

$$K = \{ F, R(1), R(2), R(3), L(1), L(2), L(3) \}$$

then $I(x) = I(\hat{x})$ where $x \in K^*$ and represents a pictorial necklace. $P(I(\hat{x}))$ is unique. For angular kolam cycle $\Sigma = \{ e,w,n,s \}$ and $I(x)$ the interpretation function. $I(x)$ is a pictorial necklace since $P(I(x)) = P(I(\hat{x}))$ and represents a unique picture. In general it is possible that $P(I(x))$ is a pictorial cycle. However $P(I(\hat{x}))$ need not be unique but we note for curvilinear and angular kolam cycles this is unique and hence we have selected this case for our study - for introducing cycle rewriting rules.

We now illustrate with examples.

Example 7:

Fig. 8 represents an aesthetically pleasing family of kambi kolam patterns which can be described by a language consisting of strings over K,

$$L = \{(F^{2n}R(2)F^{2n}L(2))^n F^{2n}R(3)(F^{2n}L(2)F^{2n}R(2))^n L(3)/n \geq 1\}$$

Then L is generated by an ETOL grammer G with control, where $G = (V,T,P,S)$, $V = K \cup \{A_i, B_i, C_i, D_i \ / \ i = 1,2,3 \}$.

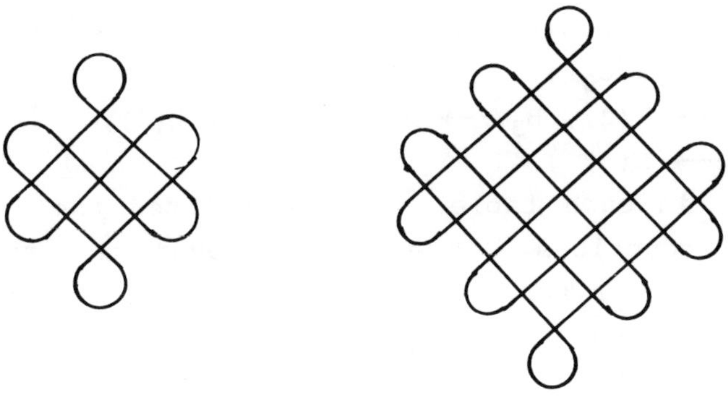

Figure 8. A sequence of Kambi Kolam patterns with a single unending line.

$P = \{ T_1, T_2, T_3, T_4, T_5 \}$, $T_0 : S \longrightarrow A_1B_1C_1D_1$

$T_1 = \{ A_1 \longrightarrow A_2A_1,\ B_1 \longrightarrow B_1,\ C_1 \longrightarrow C_2C_1,\ D_1 \longrightarrow D_1 \}$

$T_2 = \{ A_1 \longrightarrow \lambda,\ B_1 \longrightarrow B_2,\ C_1 \longrightarrow \lambda,\ D_1 \longrightarrow D_2 \}$

$T_3 = \{ A_2 \longrightarrow A_3L(2),\ B_2 \longrightarrow B_3,\ C_2 \longrightarrow C_3R(2),$
$D_2 \longrightarrow D_3 \}$

$T_4 = \{ A_3 \longrightarrow F^2A_3F^2,\ B_3 \longrightarrow F^2B_3,\ C_3 \longrightarrow F^2C_3F^2,$
$D_3 \longrightarrow F^2C_3 \}$

$T_5 = \{ A_3 \longrightarrow R(2),\ B_3 \longrightarrow R(3),\ C_3 \longrightarrow L(2),$
$D_3 \longrightarrow L(3) \}$

Note that in each table, we have omitted the remaining identity productions. The control over the table is given by $T_0T_1^nT_2T_3T_4^nT_5$, $n \geq 1$. We note the context-sensitive nature of the language.

Example 8: (Anklets of Krishna)

The following D0L-system with the "kolam moves" as terminals generates the sequence of single kambi kolam generally known as anklets of Krishna (Fig. 9).

H = < K,P,w > where w = R(1) FR(3) FR(3) FR(3) FR(1)

K = { F, R(1), R(3) } and productions .

F ⟶ F, R(1) ⟶ R(1) FR(3) FR(1)

R(3) ⟶ R(1) FR(3) FR(3) FR(3) FR(1)

Figure 9. Anklets of Krishna.

Example 9: We give one example (Fig. 10) to show the complex nature of the sequence of kolam patterns with a single unending line. It is amazing how kolam practitioners memorize it and recall it in terms of a string over the alphabet K while drawing it.

$$\begin{aligned} \text{Let } w &= R(1)\ F(FL(1))^3\ FR(1) \\ x &= FR(2)\ L(1)\ FF \\ y &= R(1)\ FF\ L(1)\ FF \\ z &= FR(2)\ L(1)\ FL(3)\ FF \end{aligned}$$

We note that $(y_1y_2)^R = y_1^R y_2^R$ where R stands for the reversal of a string. But $(yy)^R = y^R y^R$ and $(y^n)^R = (y^R)^n$
$L(G) = \{\ (y^n w (y^R)_n x y^{n-1} w (y^R)^{n-1} \ldots x y w y^R x w z)\ /\ n \geq 1\ \}$ is context-sensitive and I(L(G)) represents the sequence of kambi kolam patterns. P(I(L(G))) is unique and represents a sequence of picture necklaces.

Let K = { F, R(1), R(2), R(3), L(1), L(2), L(3) }. We define an angular measure μ on K as follows:

$\mu(F) = 0,\ \mu(R(1)) = \pi/2,\ \mu(R(2)) = \pi,\ \mu(R(3)) = 3\pi/2$
$\mu(L(1)) = -\pi/2,\ \mu(L(2)) = -\pi,\ \mu(L(3)) = -3\pi/2$

Let $x = x_1x_2 \ldots x_n$, $n \geq 1$, where each x_i is in K for $i = 1,2,\ldots,n$. Then $\mu(x) = \mu(x_1)+\ldots+\mu(x_n)$ and it is easy to see that if the necklace x represents a kambi, then $\mu(x) = 0 \bmod 2\pi$. Thus μ deals with the amount of turning or angular measure of kambi. The R's and L's contribute to the amount of change in direction and the F's in the context of R's and L's represent translation. The symbol F is translated as "move forward by one unit" but the direction depends upon the context. We shall apply some rules of transformation to transform $\not{c}$ x into $\not{c}$ y where y is a string over the alphabet { n,s,e,w }. This will enable us to consider the angular version of the kambi kolam and this amounts to representing the picture in terms of chain-code interpretation.

Figure 10(a)

Figure 10(b)

Figure 10. Kambi kolam patterns with a single unending line (Example 9)

Let the rules of transformation be as follows:

¢F ⟶ n

¢R(1) ⟶ ne	¢R(2) ⟶ nes	¢R(3) ⟶ nesw
nR(1) ⟶ nne	nR(2) ⟶ nnes	nR(3) ⟶ nnesw
sR(1) ⟶ ssw	sR(2) ⟶ sswn	sR(3) ⟶ sswne
eR(1) ⟶ ees	eR(2) ⟶ eesw	eR(3) ⟶ eeswn
wR(1) ⟶ wwn	wR(2) ⟶ wwne	wR(3) ⟶ wwnes
nL(1) ⟶ nnw	nL(2) ⟶ nnws	nL(3) ⟶ nnwse
sL(1) ⟶ sse	sL(2) ⟶ ssen	sL(3) ⟶ ssenw
eL(1) ⟶ een	eL(2) ⟶ eenw	eL(3) ⟶ eenws
wL(1) ⟶ wws	wL(2) ⟶ wwse	wL(3) ⟶ wwsen

nF ⟶ nn, sF ⟶ ss, eF ⟶ ee, wF ⟶ ww

¢x $\overset{*}{\Rightarrow}$ ¢y by leftmost derivation, using these rules. We are now ready to define a picture necklace:

A picture necklace is a cyclically ordered sequence of letters over the alphabet { n,e,s,w } i.e. a chain code necklace over a square grid. Alternately, it can be a hexagonal grid with a suitable six letter alphabet or an octagonal grid over an eight letter alphabet. We note here that transformation of kolam moves into the corresponding angular version is the reverse of a B-spline approximation described in [7]. The following necessary conditions are to be satisfied:

(i) ns, ew, sn, we cannot be subwords of a necklace.

(ii) Let $\not{c}x$ be a necklace where $x \in \{ n,e,s,w \}^+$

$\Psi(x) = \{ \#_n(x), \#_e(x), \#_s(x), \#_w(x) \}$

is the Parikh vector.

If $\not{c}x$ is a necklace then $\#_n(x) = \#_s(x)$ and $\#_e(x) = \#_w(x)$ and we say that the Parikh vector satisfies the biequality condition.

While studying single kambi kolam patterns, it is of interest to know when a given string represents a cycle, whether a particular path is traversed again (either in the same direction or in the opposite direction) or whether certain substrings represent loops. Similar problems have been dealt with for chain-code picture languages. For certain questions it is easier to consider the picture drawn over the coordinate system of the set of lattice points $\mathbb{Z} \times \mathbb{Z}$. There are several well-known algorithms to detect repetitions, retraces etc. and we could make use of them here to enable us to check whether a single kambi kolam pattern is represented the way in which kolam-practitioners draw it. (i.e. without retreats and without retraces).

Now we give a simple procedure which checks whether the given pattern over the alphabet $\{ n,e,s,w \}$ represents a kambi kolam or not.

Let $w{:}a_1a_2 \ldots a_n$ be the given word over $\{n,e,s,w\}$. Form a word $w'{:}(i,j)_0(i,j)_1 \ldots (i,j)_n$ in the coordinate system for w as follows.

set $(i,j)_0 = (0,0)$

$$(i,j)_k = \begin{cases} (i,j)_{k-1} + (1,0) & \text{if } a_k = e \\ (i,j)_{k-1} - (1,0) & \text{if } a_k = w \\ (i,j)_{k-1} + (0,1) & \text{if } a_k = n \\ (i,j)_{k-1} - (0,1) & \text{if } a_k = s \end{cases}$$

for $k = 1,2,\ldots,n$.

if there exists r,s such that $(i,j)_r = (i,j)_{r+2}$
or $((i,j)_r = (i,j)_{r+s}$ and $(i,j)_{r+1} = (i,j)_{r+s+1})$
or $((i,j)_r = (i,j)_{r+s+1}$ and $(i,j)_{r+1} = (i,j)_{r+s})$
then "not a kambi kolam"
else if $(i,j)_0 = (i,j)_n$ then "kambi kolam"
else "not a kambi kolam"

Next we use the graph theoretic concept to find the number of loops of a particular length.

For a directed graph D, its adjancency matrix, A(D) is the $p \times p$ matrix $[a_{ij}]$ with $a_{ij} = 1$ if $v_i v_j$ is an arc of D

$= 0$ otherwise.

Also we make use of the following theorem which is related to A(D) of a digraph D.

"The i,j entry $a_{ij}^{(n)}$ of A^n is the number of directed walks of length n from v_i to v_j".

Thus if we consider the word w′ of the coordinate system as a digraph, then number of loops of different length can be obtained. The digraph D is constructed from w′ as follows.

- Each distinct $(i,j)_k$ represents a node.
- an arc from $(i,j)_{k-1}$ to $(i,j)_k$ if $(i,j)_{k-1}\,(i,j)_k$ is a subword of w′.
- an arc is drawn between $(i,j)_0$ and $(i,j)_n$ only if $(i,j)_0 \sim (i,j)_n$ is either (1,0) or (0,1). Then in the matrix $A^m(D)$, (i,i) entry gives the number of loops of length m, $4 \leq m \leq n$.

  Notation: We write a cycle in the form of a string but with a special symbol ¢ to indicate that it is a cycle.

  For example C = ¢ wnes

  C^R = ¢ senw

It is clear that the reverse of a cycle is also a cycle. Sometimes we need to specify the particular string representation of the cycle. For this purpose, a cycle "starting" with w and ending with s is denoted by $C = c(w,s)$ then $C^R = c(s,w)$.

We can also use the notation

$C = .wnes.$ then $C^R = .senw.$

Definition of Cycle Grammar:

A cycle grammar $G = (V,T,P,C)$ where V is a finite set of non-terminal and terminal symbols including cycle symbols.

$T = \{n,e,s,w\}$

P is a set of cycle rewriting rules.

C is the start cycle symbol (or axiom)

Note that in P we can incorporate Chomskian type productions [11] or parallel rewriting without distinction between terminals and non-terminals as in L-systems [10].

A cycle language is the set of picture necklaces generated by a cycle grammar i.e., the corresponding set of pictures.

We introduce now the catenation operator denoted by $\odot$ and state the conditions under which it is defined - these are also motivated by the manner in which the kolam practitioner draws the kolam.

1. The first rule shows how to catenate strings in order to get cycles. Let $x,y \in \Sigma^+$, $\Sigma = \{n,e,s,w\}$, and $x = ax'b$, $y = cy'd$, $x',y' \in \Sigma^*$, $a,b,c,d \in \Sigma$.
Then $x \odot y$ is defined if $a = d$, $b = c$ and if $x \odot y$ represents a cycle.

2. The second rule shows how to insert a cycle. If C represents a cycle and $C = fzg$, $f,g \in \Sigma$, $z \in \Sigma^+$ then $x \odot C \odot y$ is defined if

(i) $x \odot y$ is a cycle

(ii) $a = d$, $b = f$, $c = g$.

(iii) $x \odot C \odot y$ is a cycle.

3. Third rule shows how to catenate two cycles (which can be extended to a finite number of cycles)

If C_1 and C_2 are cycles with $C_1 = f_1 z_1 g_1$ and $C_2 = f_2 z_2 g_2$, $f_1, g_1, f_2, g_2 \in \Sigma$, $z_1 z_2 \in \Sigma^+$, $C_1 \odot C_2$ is defined if $f_1 = g_2$ and $g_1 = f_2$. It is useful to introduce a null sign * such that $|*| = 0$. This a kind of marker which can be used when necessary.

* Catenation rules are defined as follows:

$C_1 \odot C_2$ is defined if $C_1 = .* f_1 z_1 g_1 *.$; $C_2 = .* f_2 z_2 g_2 *.$; and $f_1 = g_2$, $g_1 = f_2$.

Having introduced the catenation operator *, we note that the cycle rewriting rules may be of any of the following types:

1. $C \longrightarrow .x_1 \odot x_2 \cdots \odot x_n.$
2. $C \longrightarrow .x_1 \odot C_1 \odot x_2 \cdots x_n C_n \odot x_{n+1}.$
3. $C \longrightarrow .x_1 \odot C_1 \odot C_1' \odot x_2 \cdots C_n \odot C_n' \odot x_{n+1}.$

   $x_i \in \Sigma^*$, $i = 1, \ldots n+1$ and $n \geq 1$.
4. $C \longrightarrow .NESW.$

$$\begin{bmatrix} N \longrightarrow nN \\ E \longrightarrow eE \\ S \longrightarrow sS \\ W \longrightarrow wW \end{bmatrix} \quad \begin{bmatrix} N \longrightarrow N \\ E \longrightarrow \lambda \\ S \longrightarrow sS \\ W \longrightarrow \lambda \end{bmatrix} \quad \begin{bmatrix} N \longrightarrow \lambda \\ E \longrightarrow eE \\ S \longrightarrow \lambda \\ W \longrightarrow wW \end{bmatrix} \quad \begin{bmatrix} N \longrightarrow n \\ E \longrightarrow e \\ S \longrightarrow s \\ W \longrightarrow w \end{bmatrix}$$

5. $C \longrightarrow \lambda$
6. $x \odot C \odot y \longrightarrow x \odot C_1 \odot y$

We illustrate with examples:

Example 10: Let $G = (V,T,P,C)$ be the cycle grammar where $V = \{C,n,e,w,s\}$, $T = \{n,e,w,s\}$, C is the start cycle and P consists of following productions.

$1 : C \longrightarrow e^2 Cnws^2 wn$

$2 : C \longrightarrow e^2 nws^2 wn$

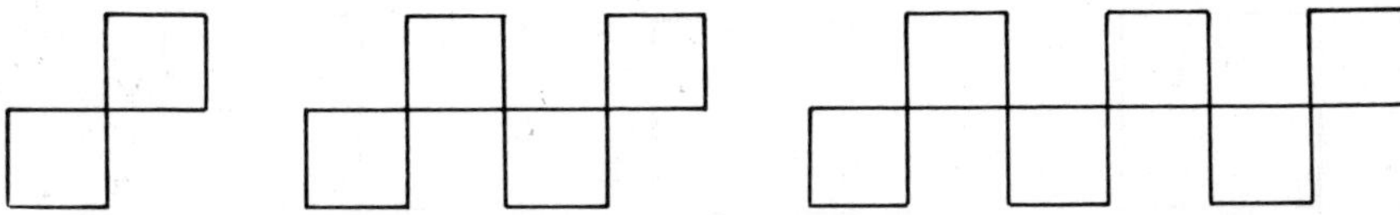

Figure 11. A sequence of even number of chains (Example 10)

Derivations proceed as follows:

$$C \overset{\pi_2}{\Longrightarrow} e^2nws^2wn \qquad \text{(i)}$$

$$C \overset{\pi_1}{\Longrightarrow} e^2Cnws^2wn$$
$$\overset{\pi_2}{\Longrightarrow} e^2e^2nws^2wnnws^2wn \qquad \text{(ii)}$$

$$C \overset{\pi_1}{\Longrightarrow} e^2Cnws^2wn$$
$$\overset{\pi_1}{\Longrightarrow} e^2e^2Cnws^2wnnws^2wn$$
$$\overset{\pi_2}{\Longrightarrow} e^2e^2e^2nws^2wnnws^2wnnws^2wn \qquad \text{(iii)}$$

and so on, yielding a sequence of even number of chains as depicted in Fig. 11. We note that the cycle productions are context-free.

Example 11: Let $G = (V,T,P,C)$ be the cycle grammar, where $V = \{C,n,e,w,s\}$, $T = \{n,e,w,s\}$, C is the start cycle and P consists of the productions

$$\pi_1 : C \longrightarrow n^2e^2s^2w^2$$
$$\pi_2 : C \longrightarrow e^2n^2w^2s^2$$
$$\pi_3 : C \longrightarrow en \odot C \odot ws$$
$$\pi_4 : C \longrightarrow ne \odot C \odot sw$$

It is clear that G is context-free and L(G) is the sequence of kites with a fixed head (Fig. 12).

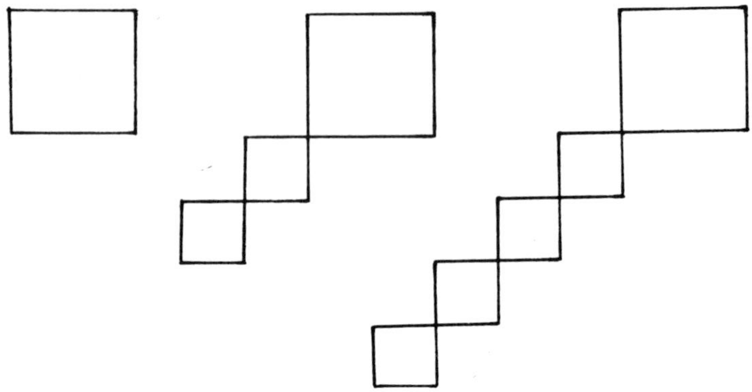

Figure 12. A sequence of patterns in example 11.

In [7], the recursive kolam patterns are classified into two types: those with polynomial growth and those with exponential growth. These can be thought of as the rate at which the ratio between one stage of development depicted by the pattern and the next stage of pattern grows - this can be measured either in terms of primitives or in terms of lengths as for DOL growth functions. The interesting fact is that we note that kolam pattern with polynomial growth can be generated by simple context-free cycle-rewriting rules whereas the kolam patterns with exponential growth require parallel rewriting with tables. In other words, the complexity of the patterns with respect to growth is reflected by the complexity of the grammar in the cycle-rewriting rules.

To illustrate the compactness of the cycle-rewriting rules we give examples of kolam patterns with polynomial growth (border kolam) and with exponential growth (the bag of candies and anklets of krishna).

Example 12. (Border kolam)

The kolam patterns (Fig. 13) which have

Figure 13.

polynomial growth can be generated by the cycle grammar $G = (V,T,P,C_1)$, where $V = \{C_1, C_2, C_3, n, e, s, w\}$ $T = \{n, e, s, w\}$, and P consists of the productions

$C_1 \longrightarrow .s^3wne^3n^2w^2C_2.$ $\qquad C_1 \longrightarrow .s^3wne^3n^2w^2.$

$C_2 \longrightarrow .w^3sen^3C_3e^2s^2.$ $\qquad C_2 \longrightarrow .w^3sen^3e^2s^2.$

$C_3 \longrightarrow .n^2w^2C_2s^3enw^3.$ $\qquad C_3 \longrightarrow .n^2w^2s^3enw^3.$

C_1 is the start cycle. The angular version of this border kolam patterns are

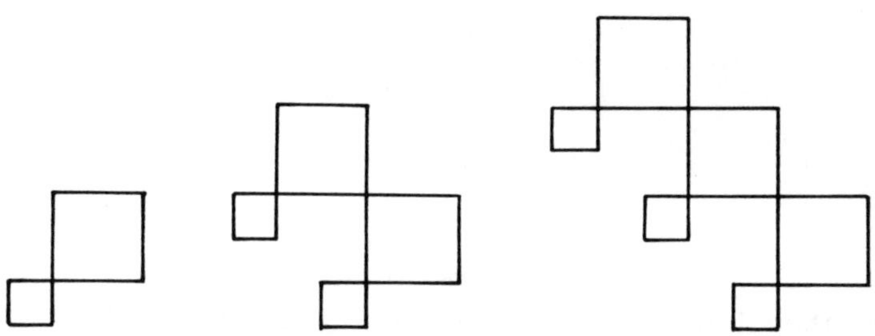

Figure 14.

Example 13: Another sequence of border kolam patterns (Fig. 15) with polynomial growth

Figure 15.

whose angular versions are

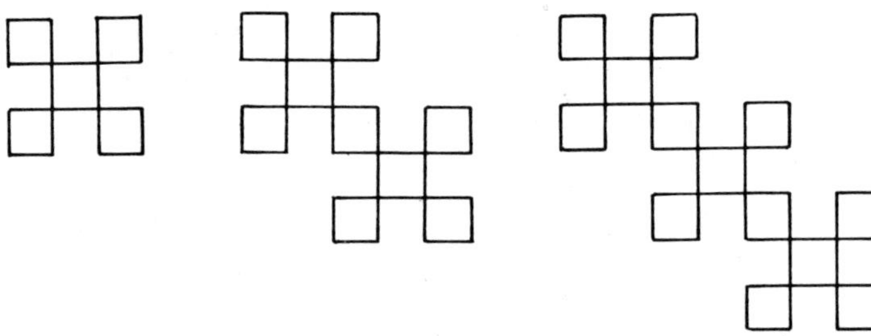

Figure 16.

is generated by the cycle grammar $G = (V,T,P,C_1)$ where

$V = \{C_1,C_2,n,e,s,w\}$ $T = \{n,e,s,w\}$

P consists of the following productions

$C_1 \longrightarrow .wn^3esw^3nes^3wne^3sC_2.$ $C_1 \longrightarrow .wn^3esw^3nes^3wne^3s.$

$C_2 \longrightarrow .s^2wne^3sC\ wn^3esw^2.$ $C_2 \longrightarrow .s^2wne^3swn^3esw^2.$

C_1 is the start cycle

Example 14: The cycle grammar $G = (V,T,P,C_1)$ where

$V = \{C_1,C_2,C_3,n,e,w,s\}$, $T = \{n,e,s,w\}$,

with production rules

$C_1 \longrightarrow .wn^4ws^4wn^4wse^4sw^4se^4sC_2.$
$C_1 \longrightarrow .wn^4ws^4wn^4wse^4sw^4se^4s.$
$C_2 \longrightarrow .s^3en^4es^4eC_3nw^4ne^4nw_3.$
$C_2 \longrightarrow .s^3en^4es^4enw^4ne^4nw^3.$
$C_3 \longrightarrow .e^3sw^4se^4sC_2wn^4ws^4wn^3.$
$C_3 \longrightarrow .e^3sw^4se^4swn^4ws^4wn^3.$ and C_1 being the start cycle, generates the following kolam patterns. (Fig. 17)

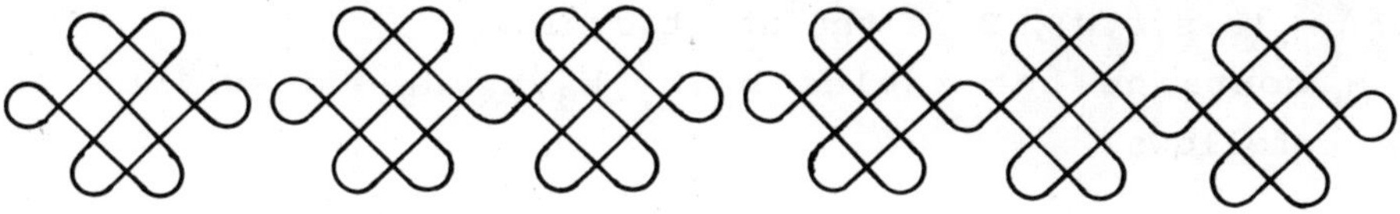

Figure 17.

Now we give two examples of kolam patterns of exponential growth.

Example 15: (Anklets of Krishna)

The kolam pattern given in Figure 9 is generated by the following ETOL cycle grammar. $G = (V,H,\Delta,S)$ where

$V = \{S,A,B,C,D,E,F,G,H,n,e,s,w\}$ $\quad \Delta = \{n,e,s,w\}$

H contains the tables h_1, h_2, h_3, h_4

$$h_1 = \begin{bmatrix} S \longrightarrow AwBsCeDn \\ S \longrightarrow EwFsGeHn \end{bmatrix} \qquad h_2 = \begin{bmatrix} A \longrightarrow .nesw. \\ B \longrightarrow .wnes. \\ C \longrightarrow .swne. \\ D \longrightarrow .eswn. \end{bmatrix}$$

$$h_3 = \begin{bmatrix} E \longrightarrow .ne^3swn^3esw^3nes^3w. \\ F \longrightarrow .wn^3esw^3nes^3wne^3s. \\ G \longrightarrow .sw^3nes^3wne^3swn^3e. \\ H \longrightarrow .es^3wne^3swn^3esw^3n. \end{bmatrix}$$

$$h_4 = \begin{bmatrix} E \longrightarrow .ne^2Dn^2e^2HnEwFs^2w^2Bs^2w. \\ F \longrightarrow .wn^2Aw^2n^2EwFsGe^2s^2Ce^2s. \\ G \longrightarrow .sw^2Bs^2w^2FsGeHn^2e^2Dn^2e. \\ H \longrightarrow .es^2Ce^2s^2GeHnEw^2n^2Aw^2n. \end{bmatrix}$$

Example 16: (Bag of candies) The following ETOL cycle grammar generates these kolam patterns. (Fig. 18)

G = (V,H,Δ,S) where V = {S,A,B,C,D,E,F,G,H,n,e,s,w}
Δ = {n,e,s,w}, S is the start cycle.
H contains the tables h_1, h_2, h_3, h_4, h_5 described as follows.

Let $x = ne^4nw^4ne^4n$ $\quad y = ws^4wn^4ws^4w$
$w = wn^4ws^4wn^4w$ $\quad v = se^4sw^4se^4s$

$$h_1 = \begin{bmatrix} S \longrightarrow .nAwBsCeD. \end{bmatrix}$$

$$h_2 = \begin{bmatrix} A \longrightarrow .xy. \\ B \longrightarrow .wv. \\ C \longrightarrow .x^{-1}y^{-1}. \\ D \longrightarrow .w^{-1}v^{-1}. \end{bmatrix} \qquad h_4 = \begin{bmatrix} E \longrightarrow .y^{-1}x^{-1}. \\ F \longrightarrow .v^{-1}w_{-1}. \\ G \longrightarrow .yx. \\ H \longrightarrow .vu. \end{bmatrix}$$

$$h_3 = \begin{bmatrix} A \longrightarrow .xnFeEsFwy. \\ B \longrightarrow .wwGnFeEsv. \\ C \longrightarrow .x^{-1}sHwGnFey^{-1}. \\ D \longrightarrow .w^{-1}eEsHwGnv^{-1}. \end{bmatrix} \qquad h_5 = \begin{bmatrix} E \longrightarrow .y^{-1}eDnAwbsx^{-1}. \\ F \longrightarrow .v^{-1}nAwBsCew^{-1}. \\ G \longrightarrow .ywBsCeDnx. \\ H \longrightarrow .vsCeDnAww. \end{bmatrix}$$

Figure 18. Kolam pattern of bag of candies.

4. CONCLUSION

In this paper, we have considered picture necklaces generated by cycle rewriting rules. The study is motivated by the manner in which kolam designs are drawn, making use of several kinds of "moves" which resemble pen-commands used in computer graphics. These moves may be considered as pen-commands for computer graphics for generating new sets of pattern classes. Also there is need for extending the class of necklace languages to wider classes of pictures.

ACKNOWLEDGEMENT

Dr. R.Chandrasekaran and Ms L.Revathi generated these patterns in our Kibble Computer Centre. We acknowledge the help of Mr. C.R.Boyd, Ms L.Revathi, Ms Lisa Mathew in the preparation of the paper and Mr.R.Rajagopalan for the drawings.

REFERENCES

[1] Biswas, G. and Dubes, R.C., Some experiments in two-dimensional grammatical inference, Pattern Recognition Letters, **2**, 173-177 (1984).

[2] Claus, V., Ehrig, H. and Rozenberg, G., Eds., Graph grammars and their application to computer science and biology, Lecture Notes in Computer Science, **73**, Springer-Verlag, Berlin (1979).

[3] de Boer, M.J.M., Lindenmayer, A., Map OL-system with edge label control: Comparison of marker and cyclic system, Lecture Notes in Computer Science, **291**, Springer-Verlag, 378-392 (1987).

[4] Ehrig, H., Nagl, M. and Rozenberg, G., Eds., Graph grammars and their application to computer science, Lecture Notes in Computer Science, **153**, Springer-Verlag, Berlin (1983).

[5] Lindenmayer, A. and Rozenberg, G., Parallel generations of maps: Developmental systems for cell layers, Lecture Notes in Computer Science, **73**, Springer-Verlag, 301-316 (1979).

[6] Maurer, H.A., Rozenberg, G. and Welzl, E., Using string languages to describe picture languages, Inform. Contr. **54**, 155-185 (1982).

[7] Prusinkiewicz, P., Graphical applications of L-systems, Proceedings of Graphics Interface '86, Vision Interface '86, Vancouver, B.C., 247-253 (1986).

[8] Rosenfeld, A., A note on cycle grammars, Inform. Contr. **27**, 374-377 (1975).

[9] Rosenfeld, A., "Picture Languages", Academic Press, London - New York (1979).

[10] Rozenberg, G. and Salomaa, A., "The Mathematical Theory of L-systems", Academic Press, New York - London (1980).

[11] Salomaa, A., "Formal Languages", Academic Press, London (1973).

[12] Siromoney, G. and Siromoney, R., Radial grammars and biological systems, Proceedings of the conference on Biologically Motivated Automata Theory, Mclean, Virginia, IEEE Publication 74 C40 - 889 - C, 92-96 (1974).

[13] Siromoney, G. and Siromoney, R., Radial grammars and radial L-systems, Comp. Graphics and Image Proc. **4**, 361-374 (1975).

[14] Siromoney, G., Siromoney, R. and Krithivasan, K., Picture languages with array rewriting rules, Inform. Contr. **22**, 447-470 (1972).

[15] Siromoney, G., Siromoney, R. and Krithivasan, K., Array grammars and kolam, Computer Graphics and Image Processing, **3**, 63-82 (1974).

[16] Siromoney, G. and Siromoney, R., Rosenfeld's cycle grammars and kolam in Graph-grammars and application to computer science, Lecture Notes in Computer Science, **291**, Springer-Verlag, 19 (1987).

[17] Siromoney, G., Subramanian, K.G. and Siromoney, R., A map generating system, Proc. Conf. Foundations of Software Technology and Theoretical Computer Science 3, Bangalore, India, 145-170 (1983).

[18] Siromoney, R., Array languages and Lindenmayer systems - a survey, in "The Book of L" eds. Rozenberg, G. and Salomaa, A., Springer-Verlag, Berlin (1985).

[19] Szilard, A.L. and Quinton, R.E., An interpretation for DOL system by computer graphics, The Science Terrapin (Faculty of Science, University of Western Ontario, London), **4**, 8-13 (1979).

GENERALIZED PARIKH VECTOR AND PUBLIC KEY CRYPTOSYSTEMS

Gift Siromoney
Rani Siromoney
K.G. Subramanian
V. Rajkumar Dare
and
P.J. Abisha

Madras Christian College
Tambaram
Madras 600 059, INDIA

ABSTRACT

The parikh mapping enumerates the number of occurrences of each letter of the alphabet in a given word. The notion of position vector introduced in [15] is a generalization of the parikh vector. It indicates the position of each letter of the alphabet in a word. We provide characterization of regular languages and morphisms using generalized parikh vector (GPV). We also relate this concept with series expansion of the real numbers between 0 and 1. Recently public key cryptosystems (PKC) based on formal language theory have been of interest. The use of GPV is examined here for purposes of decryption of PKC based on DOL/TOL systems [18]. We also discuss a PKC based on the word problem for Thue systems and in particular for finitely presented groups. Here again GPV is found useful for decryption.

1. INTRODUCTION

The classical parikh mapping [11] (referred to as parikh vector in later usage) has played a very important and significant role in formal language theory. The parikh vector counts the number of occurrences of each letter of the alphabet in a word but it does not reflect the positions of letters. A position vector is introduced in [15] which can be obtained either directly, or indirectly from a metric defined on the set of all finite and infinite words over an alphabet. This new measure is a generalization of the parikh vector and indicates the positions of each letter in a word. We first review some of the results from [15], concerning the generalized parikh vector. We then provide characterizations of regular languages and morphisms using the notion of generalized parikh vector. We also relate generalized parikh vector with series expansion of real numbers between 0 and 1.

There has been a lot of interest in the construction of safe and effective public key cryptosystems [5] which ensure secrecy of data. In a public key cryptosystem, the encryption key is made public but the decryption key with a trapdoor is kept secret. Both encryption and decryption are made easy but cryptanalysis, namely breaking the system without the knowledge of the trapdoor is made hard. Several public key cryptosystems based on different principles are known. Recently public key cryptosysytems based on formal language theory have been investigated [13].

We briefly review here the public key cryptosystem based on D0L/T0L systems introduced in [18]. Sufficient conditions which ensure correct decryption are given. These conditions did not get incorporated in [18] as they were sent to the publishers in the proof correction stage. Futhermore, the characterization of morphisms examined here are utilized to provide a decryption technique using generalized parikh vector.

We also discuss a public key cryptosystem based on the word problem for Thue systems and in particular, for finitely presented groups. The latter has some definite advantages over the other. These systems are different from the public key cryptosystems based on the word problem first introduced and studied in [19]. We have pointed out the differences in the last section. Furthermore, the notion of generalized parikh vector can be utilized for decryption purposes in this public key cryptosystem, as indicated for the DOL/TOL system.

2. GENERALIZED PARIKH VECTOR

Let V be a finite alphabet and V^* the free monoid generated by V. Let V^ω be the set of all mappings $u:N \longrightarrow V$ where N is the set of all natural numbers. Elements of V^ω are called infinite words over V. $u \in V^\omega$ is denoted by $u_1u_2\ldots$ or $u(1)u(2)\ldots.$ The set of all finite and infinite words is denoted by V^∞. If $u \in V^*$, then $|u|$ denotes the length of u and #V denotes the number of elements in V.

A mapping $\Psi : V^* \longrightarrow N^n$ where $V = \{ a_1, a_2, \ldots, a_n \}$ is called the parikh mapping if $\Psi(x) = (q_1, q_2, \ldots, q_n)$ where q_i gives the number of a_i's in x.

Definition 2.1

For each $u \in V^\infty$, let $p(u) = (p_1, p_2, \ldots, p_n)$ where $p_i = \sum_{j \in A_i} 1/2^j$ with $A_i \subset N$, is the set of all positions in u of the letter $a_i \in V$. p(u) is called the generalized parikh vector or p-vector or position vector of u.

We note that we can define $p_i = \sum_{j \in A_i} r^j$ for any positive real number r in the case of a finite word u. When u is an infinite word, to ensure convergence of $\sum_{j \in A_i} r^j$, we assume $0 < r < 1$. In the case of a finite word we note that if $r = 1$, then the position vector gives the number of occurrences of each letter of the alphabet and hence coincides with the parikh mapping. The significance of the map p is that it gives the position of each letter of the word.

We now examine the properties of p.

Theorem 2.1

The restriction of p to V^* is one to one.

Proof

For $u, v \in V^*$, let $p(u) = p(v) = (p_1, p_2, \ldots, p_n)$. Then $p_i = r_i / 2^{n_i} = \sum_{j \in A_i} 1/2^j$ where A_i is a finite subset of the set of all natural numbers. Thus $(p_1, p_2, \ldots, p_n)$ uniquely fixes the positions of the letters of the alphabet in the words u and v.

Hence $u = v$.

We now define a topology in V^∞.

Definition 2.2

Let the function $d: V^\infty \times V^\infty \longrightarrow R$ be given by

$$d(u, v) = \sum_{n=1}^{\min\{|u|,|v|\}} r_n + \sum_{n=\min\{|u|,|v|\}+1}^{\max\{|u|,|v|\}} (1/2)^n$$

where $r_n = 0$ if $u_n = v_n$
$= 1/2^n$ if $u_n \neq v_n$.

Then d is a metric on V^∞.

The topology induced by d coincides with the topology defined by Nivat [9].

Theorem 2.2

The mapping $p: V^\infty \longrightarrow R^n$ is continuous in the usual topology in R^n.

We now examine the relation between the coordinates of $p(u)$.

Theorem 2.3

Let $u \in V^\infty$ and $p(u) = (p_1, p_2, \ldots, p_n)$. Then

a) $\sum_{i=1}^{n} p_i = 1$ if $u \in V^\omega$,

b) $\sum_{i=1}^{n} p_i = 1 - 1/2^{|u|}$ if $u \in V^*$, where $n = \#V$.

It is interesting to note that there is a well-formed linear pattern among words of the same length. The position vectors of words of the same length lie on a hyper-plane. For example, in the case of a binary alphabet, we note that the p-vector of words of the same length lie on a stright line. If we take a line through a point p(u) parallel to the i th coordinate axis, then the point $p(ua_i)$ lies on it.

Theorem 2.4

Let $x, y \in V^*$. Then

a) $p(xy) = p(x) + p(y)/2^{|x|}$,

b) $p(x^n) = p(x)\ (1 - 1/2^{n|x|})/(1 - 1/2^{|x|})$,

c) $p(x^\omega) = p(x)\ /\ (1 - 1/2^{|x|})$.

The proofs are straight forward.

3. CHARACTERIZATION OF REGULAR LANGUAGES, AND MORPHISMS

We now examine the structure of $p(V^*)$.

Definition 3.1

Let $M = \{(m_1, m_2, \ldots, m_n) \in R^n\} \cup (0, 0, \ldots, 0)$ satisfying the following conditions:

i) Each m_i is a finite sum of powers of (1/2).

ii) $\sum_{i=1}^{n} m_i = \sum_{j=1}^{k} (1/2)^j$ where k is the maximum power of (1/2) in $\{m_i\ /\ i = 1,\ldots,n\}$.

k is called the order of $m = (m_1, m_2, \ldots, m_n)$ and it is denoted by $|m|$. We set $|(0, 0, \ldots, 0)| = 0$. We note that if $u \in V^*$ and $p(u) = m$, then $|m| = k = |u|$.

We now define an operation called p-addition on M which makes M a monoid. This monoid will reflect the structure of words in V^*.

Definition 3.2

Let $p, q \in M$, define

$p \oplus q = (p_1 + (1/2)^{|p|}q_1,\ p_2 + (1/2)^{|p|}q_2,\ \ldots\ )$.

Remark

We note that instead of the usual vector addition, this p-addition takes care of the translation of positions needed while catenating two words.

Theorem 3.1

a) $(M, \oplus)$ is a monoid with $(0, 0, \ldots, 0)$ as identity.

b) p is a monoid morphism of V^* onto M.

These results follow from the definition of the operation $\oplus$ on M and from the fact that $p(xy) = p(x) \oplus p(y)$.

Remark

If $L_1, L_2 \subseteq V^*$, then

$p(L_1L_2) = p(L_1) \oplus p(L_2)$.

We now characterize the position vectors of regular languages.

Theorem 3.2

Let $L_1, L_2 \subseteq V^*$. Then

i) $p(L_1 \cup L_2) = p(L_1) \cup p(L_2)$

ii) $p(L_1L_2) = p(L_1) \oplus p(L_2)$

iii) $p(L^*) = \langle p(L) \rangle$ where $\langle A \rangle$ is the monoid generated by A.

Proofs follow from the properties of M.

Theorem 3.3

The position vectors of regular languages are the finite sum and union of finitely generated submonoids of M.

Proof follows from the regular expression characterization of regular sets and theorem 3.2.

In order to characterize morphisms in V^*, we first define a monoid.

Let $POS_n = \{A = (A_1, A_2, \ldots, A_n) / A_i \subset N, A_i \cap A_j = \phi$ and $\bigcup_{i=1}^{n} A_i = \{1, 2, \ldots, m\}$ for some $m\}$.

If for $A = (A_1, A_2, \ldots, A_n)$, $\bigcup_{i=1}^{n} A_i = \{1, 2, \ldots, m\}$, then $|A| = m$.

If $A = (\phi, \phi, \ldots, \phi)$, then $|A| = 0$.

Let $A, B \in POS_n$,

$A \circ B = (A_1 \cup \{m+B_1\}, \ldots, A_n \cup \{m+B_n\})$, where $m = |A|$.

Then we have a morphism $\theta: V^* \longrightarrow POS_n$ where

$V = \{a_1, a_2, \ldots, a_n\}$ given by $\Theta(x) = (A_1, A_2, \ldots, A_n)$ where A_i contains the positions of a_i in the word x and $\Theta(\lambda) = (\phi, \phi, \ldots, \phi)$. If $p(x)$ is the generalized parikh vector of x, then $p_i = \sum_{j \varepsilon A_i} 1/2^j$ where $\Theta(x) = (A_1, A_2, \ldots, A_n)$.

Theorem 3.4

Let $L \subset V^*$ where $\# V = n$. Then L is generated by a DOL-system iff $\Theta(L) = M$ satisfies the following conditions:

a) there exists a finite set $\{A^{(1)}, A^{(2)}, \ldots, A^{(n)}\}$ of elements of POS_n where $|A^{(i)}| = r_i$.

b) there exists an element $B = (B_1, B_2, \ldots, B_n) \varepsilon M$ called basic element.

c) if $C = (C_1, C_2, \ldots, C_n) \varepsilon M$, then
$C' = (C_1', C_2', \ldots, C_n') \varepsilon M$ where
$C_k' = \bigcup_{i=1}^{n} (\sum_{\ell < j} k_\ell + A_k^{(i)} : j \varepsilon C_i)$ and
$k_\ell = r_s$ if $\ell \varepsilon C_s$.

Proof

Let L be generated by a DOL-system $G = (V, h, \omega)$. Let $V = \{a_1, a_2, \ldots, a_n\}$ and $h(a_i) = x_i$. Let $\Theta(x_i) = A^{(i)}$ for $i = 1, 2, \ldots, n$. If ω is the axiom, then $\Theta(\omega) = (B_1, B_2, \ldots, B_n)$. If $y \varepsilon L$, then $\Theta(h(y))$ satisfies the conditions (a), (b) and (c) of the theorem. Similarly we can prove that if $M \subset POS_n$ satisfies the conditions (a), (b) and (c) then there exists a $L \subset V^*$ which is generated by a DOL-system such that $\Theta(L) = M$.

Theorem 3.5

Let $L \subset V^*$, then L is generated by a DOL-system iff $p(L)$ satisfies the following properties:

a) there exists a finite set of elements $m^{(1)}, m^{(2)}, \ldots, m^{(n)}$ of M such that $|m^{(i)}| = r_i$.

b) there exists an element $m \varepsilon P(L)$ called basic element,

c) if $p = (p_1, p_2, \ldots, p_n) \varepsilon p(L)$ then

$p' = (p_1', p_2', \ldots, p_n') \in P(L)$ where

$p_k' = \sum_{i=1}^{n} m_k^{(i)} p_i''$ where p_i'' is defined in the following way:

if $p_i = 1/2^{l_1} + 1/2^{l_2} + \ldots + 1/2^{l_s} = \sum_{j \varepsilon C_i} 1/2^j$, then

$p_i'' = 1/2^{m_1} + 1/2^{m_2} + \ldots + 1/2^{m_s}$ where

$m_j = \sum_{p < l_j} k_p$ and $k_p = r_t$ where $p \varepsilon C_t$.

Proof folows from theorem 3.4.

4. GENERALIZED PARIKH VECTOR AND NUMERATION

In this section we relate generalized parikh vector with series expansion of real numbers between 0 and 1.

We know that any real number in [0, 1] has a series expansion in powers of 1/r, for any $r \varepsilon N$.

For $y \varepsilon [0, 1]$, we have a representation $y = \sum_{i=1}^{\infty} x_i/r^i$ where $x_i \varepsilon V = \{0, 1, \ldots, r-1\}$. Then we have the representation for y as $x = x_1 x_2 \ldots \varepsilon V^{\omega}$.

Hence we have a mapping $\mu_r : V^{\infty} \longrightarrow [0, 1]$ such that $\mu_r(x) = y$. If $p(x) = (p_1, p_2, \ldots, p_r)$ is the generalized parikh vector for x with base 1/r instead of 1/2, then

$y = p_2 + 2p_3 + \ldots + (r-1)p_r$.

It is known that μ_r is a continuous function [6].

Here we note that $x_1 \leqslant x_2$ in V^{∞} in lexicographical ordering iff $\mu_r(x_1) \leqslant \mu_r(x_2)$.

Definition 4.1

In a topological space X, a subset A is said to be a G_δ set if it is a countable intersection of open sets.

Theorem 4.1

If I is a G_δ set in [0, 1] in the usual topology then $\mu_r^{-1}[I]$ is deterministic ω - regular in V^{ω}.

Proof

We have that $L \subset V^{\omega}$ is deterministic ω - regular iff L is G_{δ} set in V^{ω}. Since μ_r is continuous, the result follows.

Theorem 4.2

Let C be the cantor set in [0, 1], then $\mu_3^{-1}(c)$ is ω - regular.

Proof

We know that $\mu_3^{-1}(c) = \{0, 2\}^{\omega}$. Hence $\mu_3^{-1}(c)$ is ω-regular.

5. THE DOL/TOL PUBLIC KEY CRYPTOSYSTEM

In the DOL/TOL public key cryptosystem(PKC) [18] the encryption key involves a TOL system which is obtained by shuffling an unambiguous DOL system. The security of the PKC depends on the facts that membership problem for DOL system is decidable in linear time whereas it is NP-complete for the TOL system [13].

The construction of the PKC is as follows:

Let $\Sigma = \{0,1\}$ be the plaintext alphabet and h a homomorphism from Σ to Σ^*. Let x_0 and x_1 be two words in Σ^*. In order to ensure that the decryption yields the correct plain text uniquely, we have to impose the condition that the set $X = \{h(0), h(1), x_0, x_1\}$ is a code, that is, any word in Σ^* has atmost one decomposition over X.

Let Δ be another alphabet of cardinality much greater than that of Σ. Let g be a morphism from Δ to $\Sigma \cup \{\lambda\}$ where λ is the empty word. Define substitutions t_i, $i = 1,2,\ldots,m$ for some $m > 1$ on Δ^* such that $t_i(c)$ is a finite nonempty subset of $g^{-1}(h(g(c)))$, for every $c \in \Delta$. Let u_0 and u_1 be any two words in $g^{-1}(x_0)$ and $g^{-1}(x_1)$ respectively.

The public encryption key is $(t_1, t_2, \ldots, t_m, u_0, u_1)$. Encryption of a plain text $i_1 i_2 \ldots i_n$ in Σ^* is done as follows: A word u is obtained by replacing every occurrence of 0 by u_0 and 1 by u_1. The cryptotext is obtained by choosing any word from

$t_{j_k}(\ldots(t_{j_2}(t_{j_1}(u)))\ldots), \quad k \geqslant 1$

where $j_1, j_2, \ldots, j_k \in \{1,2,\ldots m\}$.

The secret decryption key is (g,h,x_0,x_1). If z is the cryptotext obtained then $g(z) = h^k(w)$ where $w = x_{i_1}\ldots x_{i_n}$ for some $k \geqslant 1$, $i_j \in \{0,1\}$, $j = 1,\ldots,n$ and $i_1 i_2 \ldots i_n$ is the plain text. We can obtain the correct w because $X = \{h(0), h(1), x_0, x_1\}$ forms a code and hence factorization is unique at every step.

The notion of GPV studied in the earlier sections is found suitable for purposes of decryption in the PKC discussed above.

Suppose z is the cryptotext received, we can find the word $x = g(z)$ over $\Sigma = \{0,1\}$ where g is the trapdoor morphism. Then the repeated application of the following algorithm will give the plain text. We use the notations in section 3.

Input: $\Theta_h(0) = (A_0^{(0)}, A_1^{(0)})$, $\Theta_h(1) = (A_0^{(1)}, A_1^{(1)})$ where $A_i^{(j)}$ is the set of positions at which i occurs in $h(j)$, $i,j \in \{0,1\}$. These are stored in lists in the ascending order. Let $k(i,j)$ denote the length of list $A_i^{(j)}$, $i,j \in \{0,1\}$. A word x in Σ^* which has a unique decomposition over $\{h(0),h(1)\}$.

Step 1: Find the positions of 0 and 1 in x and store them in two lists $A_0(x)$ and $A_1(x)$. Let the indices t_0 and t_1 represent any two registers of the lists $A_0(x)$ and $A_1(x)$ respectively.

Step 2: Find the lists $D_i^{(j)}$ which gives the difference between the consecutive positions in lists $A_i^{(j)}$. If $k(i,j) = 1$ then set the difference to be 0.

Step 3: (3.1) Set $t_0 = 0$, $t_1 = 0$, $z = \lambda$

(3.2) $j = 0$, $i = 0$, $i_1 = 1$

(3.3) Consider the $k(i,j)$ entries of $A_i(x)$ starting from the t_ith position $A_i(x)$. Calculate the list of consecutive differences (difference is assumed to be zero when a single entry is considered).

If it is equal to list $D_i^{(j)}$ then $i = i_1$, $i_1 = i$ and execute (3.3)

If satisfied then $t_\ell = t_\ell + k(\ell,j)$, $\ell = 0,1$, $z = zj$

else $j = 1$, $t_\ell = t_\ell + k(\ell,j)$, $\ell = 0,1$, $z = zj$

else $j = 1$, $t_\ell = t_\ell + k(\ell,j)$, $\ell = 0,1$, $z = zj$.

6. PKC BASED ON WORD PROBLEM

In the previous section, a PKC based on the membership problem of DOL/TOL systems was discussed. Constructions of PKCs on word problem have also been investigated in the literature [16,17,19]. In [16, 19] the PKCs depend on the word problem for Thue system namely, the equivalence of two words x_0 and x_1 under a given Thue system.

The system given in [17] depends on Dyck sets and the word problem for special Thue system. But the division of the alphabet chosen might leak out information about the secret trapdoor and hence the system is not very safe.

We describe PKCs based on the word problem for Thue system and finitely presented groups.

6.1 PKC Using Thue Systems.

We give the necessary definitions.

Definition 6.1.1

Let Σ be an alphabet. A Thue system on Σ is a subset T of $\Sigma^* \times \Sigma^*$. Each element (u,v) of the Thue system is called a rule. The Thue congruence $\overset{*}{\underset{T}{\longleftrightarrow}}$ generated by T is the reflexive, transitive closure of the relation $\underset{T}{\longleftrightarrow}$ defined as follows:

For (u,v) ε T and x,y ε Σ^*, xuy $\underset{T}{\longleftrightarrow}$ xvy. When there is no confusion we write $\longleftrightarrow$ and $\overset{*}{\longleftrightarrow}$ for $\underset{T}{\longleftrightarrow}$ and $\overset{*}{\underset{T}{\longleftrightarrow}}$ respectively.

Definition 6.1.2

Two strings x, y ε Σ^* are congruent (mod T)if x $\overset{*}{\underset{T}{\longleftrightarrow}}$ y and the congruence class (mod T) of w ε Σ^* is $[w]_T = \{z \ \varepsilon\ \Sigma^* \ / \ z \overset{*}{\underset{T}{\longleftrightarrow}} w\}$.

Definition 6.1.3

A string x ε Σ^* is minimal with respect to $\overset{*}{\underset{T}{\longleftrightarrow}}$ if there is no y in Σ^* such that x $\overset{*}{\underset{T}{\longleftrightarrow}}$ yand $|x| > |y|$. The minimal element of a congruence class $[u]_T$ is denoted by min[u].

If x, y ε Σ^*, x $\longleftrightarrow$ y and $|x| > |y|$, then we write x $\underset{T}{\longrightarrow}$ y. $\overset{*}{\underset{T}{\longrightarrow}}$ is the reflexive, transitive closure of $\underset{T}{\longrightarrow}$ and it is called a reduction.

Definition 6.1.4

Let T be a Thue system over Σ. T is said to be Church-Rosser if for every x, y ε Σ^* such that x $\overset{*}{\longleftrightarrow}$ y, there exists a z ε Σ^* such that x $\overset{*}{\underset{T}{\longrightarrow}}$ z, y $\overset{*}{\underset{T}{\longrightarrow}}$ z.

Construction of the PKC

Consider a Church-Rosser Thue system T over an alphabet Σ. Choose two words x_0, x_1 $\varepsilon\ \Sigma^+$ satisfying the following conditions:

(i) x_0, x_1 are not congruent mod T
and $x_i = \min[x_i]$, for $i = 0,1$. (6.1.1)

(ii) $\{x_0, x_1\}$ is a code (6.1.2)

(iii) $\min[x_{i_1} x_{i_2} \ldots x_{i_n}] = x_{i_1} x_{i_2} \ldots x_{i_n}$
for $i_j\ \varepsilon\ \{0,1\}$, $j = 1,2,\ldots,n$, $n \geqslant 1$. (6.1.3)

It is well known that the word problem for a Church-Rosser Thue system is solvable in linear time and each congruence class of such a system contains a unique minimal element. The minimal element can be found using the linear time algorithm given in [4]. Also the existence of an algorithm for verifying whether a set is a code or not is guaranteed [2]. Thus conditions (6.1.1) - (6.1.3) can be effectively checked for a Church-Rosser Thue system T.

Let Δ be an alphabet whose cardinality is much greater than that of Σ . Let $g:\Delta^* \longrightarrow \Sigma^*$ be a morphism, mapping every letter of Δ to a letter of $\Sigma \cup \{\lambda\}$ where λ is the empty word.

Consider a Thue system $\overline{T}$ over Δ such that $\overline{T} \subseteq \{(q,r)/g(q) \underset{T}{\longleftrightarrow} g(r)\}$. Choose two words u_0, $u_1 \in \Delta^+$ such that $u_i \in g^{-1}([x_i])$, i = 0,1. The public encryption key is ($\overline{T}$, u_0, u_1). The encryption of a plain text over the alphabet {0,1}, that is, a word $i_1 i_2 \ldots i_n$ in $\{0,1\}^*$, is done by choosing an arbitrary word $w = c_1 c_2 \ldots c_n$ where $c_j \in [u_{i_j}]_{\overline{T}}$, j = 1, 2, ..., n.

This yields the cryptotext w.

The secret decryption key is (T, x_0, x_1, g). If w is a cryptotext, then

$$g(w) \in [x_{i_1}]_T [x_{i_2}]_T \cdots [x_{i_n}]_T$$

We reduce g(w) using T. This yields the word $x_{i_1} \ldots x_{i_n}$. Thus the plaintext $i_1 \ldots i_n$ is recovered.

During encryption, we search for the occurrence of words in the rules of the Thue system $\overline{T}$, in a given word. By using the pattern matching machine [1], this can be done in linear time. This pattern matching machine (PMM) is a finite state automaton which recognizes a set of pattern words. Given a text word w as input, that is, Input (PMM) = w, the PMM gives the output, Output (PMM) = (positions, S), where positions is the set of end positions at which the words in S occur as pattern in w.

We now describe algorithms for decryption.

Encryption:

Input: The Thue system $\bar{T} = \{(q_1, r_1), \ldots, (q_n, r_n)\}$ over the alphabet Δ and the two words $u_0, u_1 \in \Delta^*$ in the public encryption key. A pattern matching machine PMM [1] for $q_1, q_2, \ldots, q_n$ and $r_1, r_2, \ldots, r_n$. Input (PMM) is the text word. Output(PMM) = (positions, S) where "position" is the end positions at which words in S occur as pattern. A plaintext $p = p_1 p_2 \ldots p_m$ where $p_i \in \{0,1\}$.

```
begin
     for i = 1 to m do
         if p_i = 0 then APPLY RULE (u_0)
         else APPLY RULE (u_1)
         replace in p, p_i by u
     return p
end;
```

APPLY RULE (u_j)

Let s be a random number less than or equal to n. Let $r_1, r_2, \ldots, r_s$ be a sequence of random numbers.

```
begin
     for i = 1 to s do
        let Input(PMM) = u_j
        if q_{r_i} ε S where Output(PMM) = (positions, S)
             then replace in u_j, q_{r_i} by r_{r_i}
        else if r_{r_i} ε S then replace in u_j, r_{r_i} by q_{r_i}
        u = u_j
     return u
end;
```

Decryption:

Input: The Thue system T over Σ , which is Church-Rosser and the two words x_0, $x_1 \in \Sigma^*$ satisfying (6.1.1), (6.1.2) and (6.1.3). A cryptotext $c = c_1c_2 \ldots c_n$ is over the alphabet Δ . The map g: $\Delta \longrightarrow \Sigma \cup \{\lambda\}$. Given a word w, $w \xrightarrow[\ell]{*} w_1$ means that w is reduced to w_1 where w_1 is minimal, by applying left-most reductions in T which takes time linear in length of w, by the standard algorithm in [4]. Let $|x_0| \geq |x_1|$, without loss of generality.

```
begin
     for i = 1 to n do
         c_i = g(c_i) in c.
           find w such that c -*->_l w
     return w
end;
```

```
Decode (w)
begin
     Let w(i,r) stand for the subword of w with starting
          position i and length r.
     i = 0, j = 1
     if w(i,|x_0|) = x_0 then
           p_j = 0 and i = i + |x_0|
     else p_j = 1, and i = i + |x_1|
             j = j + 1
                 repeat DECODE (w) until i = |w|
     return p_1p_2 ... p_j
end;
```

Clearly encryption takes polynomial time, decryption takes linear time.

Cryptanalysis:

We now discuss a few possible cryptanalytic attacks on a cryptosystem of this type.

One possible attack is to find a morphism $f: \Delta \longrightarrow \Delta'$, that maps a Thue system $\bar{T}$ over Δ, which has been made public, into a Church-Rosser Thue system $\bar{T}'$, over a smaller alphabet Δ'. From f, one can get a Thue system $\bar{T}' = \{(f(u), f(v))/(u,v) \in \bar{T}\}$. Even if $\bar{T}'$ is Church-Rosser, this will not assert that $f(x_1)$ and $f(x_2)$ are not congruent (mod $\bar{T}'$) whenever x_1 and x_2 are not congruent (mod T). But this property is essential for decryption. Hence a cryptanalyst has to calculate different morphisms for Δ', with different cardinalities. Even if he arrives at the correct Thue system, there is no way of checking it.

A second cryptanalytic approch is to try to remove dummy letters in the rules. In the case of PKCs described in [14,18] if a letter in the leftside of a rule is dummy, then all letters on the right side of the rule are dummy. But this is not the case in our system. Hence reduction of the size of the alphabet by dropping the dummy letters does not help much.

In the brute-force approach, it is evident that even though the cryptanalyst has enough time for preprocessing there is no way of checking whether the system he has arrived at is the one used for decryption.

In fact, finding the trapdoor morphism g is NP-complete.

The role of growth and the block size of the plaintext

It is desirabe to costruct the PKC in such a way that the length of the cryptotext is not much greater than that of plaintext, that is, the encryption function should not have a high growth rate. This problem does not arise in this system mainly because of the fact that a word u replaces a word v when we use a rule (u,v) of T, instead of a single letter as is the case of the PKCs considered in [14,18].

6.2 Public Key Cryptosystems Using Finitely Presented Groups

We now propose a public key cryptosystem based on the word problem for finitely presented groups. This is a special case of the earlier system but has certain advantages over the other, namely encryption is very simple and the number of possible cryptotexts for a given plaintext is much more and so cryptanalysis more difficult.

We first recall some definitions.

Definition 6.2.1

Given an alphabet Σ we write $\Sigma^{-1} = \{a^{-1} / a \in \Sigma\}$ and $\Sigma^{\pm 1} = \Sigma \cup \Sigma^{-1}$. A word x in $(\Sigma^{\pm 1})^*$ is called reduced if it does not contain any subword of the form $a^{\sigma} a^{-\sigma}$, $a \in \Sigma$ $\sigma = \pm 1$.

Definition 6.2.2

A group G, or more precisely a presentation of the group G, denoted $G = < \Sigma , R >$, is given by an alphabet Σ and a set R of words in $(\Sigma^{\pm 1})^*$ called defining relators of G. If Σ and R are finite we say that G is a finitely presented group. If $R = \phi$, G is called the free group generated by Σ and denoted by $F(\Sigma)$.

Given a group $G = < \Sigma ,R >$ we consider the binary relation on $(\Sigma^{\pm 1})^*$, denoted by $\underset{G}{\Longleftrightarrow}$ or simply $\Longleftrightarrow$ and defined as follows. For any $x, y \in (\Sigma^{\pm 1})^*$, $x \underset{G}{\Longleftrightarrow} y$ iff one of the following cases holds:

1) $x = urv$, $y = uv$, with $r \in R$ and $u,v \in (\Sigma^{\pm 1})^*$
2) $x = uv$, $y = urv$ with $r \in R$ and $u,v \in (\Sigma^{\pm 1})^*$
3) $x = ua^{\sigma}a^{-\sigma}v$, $y = uv$ with $a \in \Sigma$, $\sigma = \pm 1$
4) $x = uv$, $y = ua^{\sigma}a^{-\sigma}v$ with $a \in \Sigma$, $\sigma = \pm 1$.

Then we define $\overset{*}{\underset{G}{\Longleftrightarrow}}$ to be the reflexive, transitive closure of $\underset{G}{\Longleftrightarrow}$. It is easy to see that $\overset{*}{\underset{G}{\Longleftrightarrow}}$ is a congruence and the quotient $(\Sigma^{\pm1})^* / \overset{*}{\underset{G}{\Longleftrightarrow}}$ is a group, also denoted by G. The congruence class of a word x is denoted by $[x]_G$ or simply $[x]$. Evidently $x \overset{*}{\underset{G}{\Longleftrightarrow}} y$ iff $[x]_G = [y]_G$. We usually write $x =_G y$ instead of $[x]_G = [y]_G$ and say that the words x and y are equal in G.

Definition 6.2.3

The word problem for the group G consists in deciding, for any given two words x, y in $(\Sigma^{\pm1})^*$, whether $x =_G y$, or equivalently in deciding, for any given word x, whether $x =_G 1$, where 1 is the empty word.

A very well-known result, due to Novikov [10] says that the word problem for finitely presented groups is undecidable. But the algorithm solving the word problem for free groups is quite simple because for any free group $F(\Sigma)$ and for any x,y in $(\Sigma^{\pm1})^*$, $x =_F y$ iff x and y can be led to the same reduced word by reduction, that is, by removing (by any way) subwords of the form $a^{\sigma} a^{-\sigma}$ with $a \in \Sigma$, $\sigma = \pm 1$.

Using these results we now construct a public key cryptosystem as follows.

Construction of PKC:

Consider a free group $F(\Sigma)$ which is non-empty and finite. Fix two different reduced words x_0, x_1 in $(\Sigma^{\pm1})^*$ such that

i) $X = \{x_0, x_1\}$ is a code (6.2.1)

ii) The words x_0x_0, x_0x_1, x_1x_0, x_1x_1 are reduced without cancellation. (6.2.2)

Let Δ be an alphabet of cardinality much greater than that of Σ. Let $g: (\Delta^{\pm1})^* \longrightarrow (\Sigma^{\pm1})^*$ be a morphism, mapping every letter to a letter or to the empty word and such that

iii) $g(c^{\sigma_1}) = a^{\sigma_2} \Longrightarrow g(c^{-\sigma_1}) = a^{-\sigma_2}; \; c \in \Delta; \; \sigma_1, \sigma_2 = \pm 1;$ (6.2.3)

iv) $g(c^{\sigma}) = 1 \Longrightarrow g(c^{-\sigma}) = 1, \; c \in \Delta, \; \sigma = \pm 1.$ (6.2.4)

Fix a finite subset R (large enough) of $g^{-1}([1]_F)$ and define G = < Δ ; R >. Finally choose two words u_0 and u_1 from $(\Delta^{+1})^*$ such that

$g(u_0) \in [x_0]_{F(\Sigma)}, \; g(u_1) \in [x_1]_{F(\Sigma)}$

By the choice of R and by (6.2.3) and (6.2.4) it follows that, for any u, v in $(\Delta^{\pm 1})^*$, $u =_G v$ implies $g(u) =_F g(v)$. In particular, since $x_0 \neq_F x_1$ we have $u_0 \neq_G u_1$.

The triple (G, u_0, u_1) now constitutes the public encryption key. The encryption of a plaintext in bits, that is, a word $i_1 i_2 \ldots i_n$ in $\{0,1\}^*$ is carried out by choosing an arbitrary word $w = c_1 \ldots c_n$ where $c_j \in [u_{i_j}]_G$ $(j = 1, \ldots, n)$. This yields the cryptotext w.

The secret decryption key is the quadruple (F, x_0, x_1, g). Whenever w is a cryptotext,

$g(w) \in [x_{i_1}]_F [x_{i_2}]_F \ldots [x_{i_n}]_F$

If z is the reduced word such that $z =_F g(w)$ then by (6.2.2) z must coincide with $x_{i_1} x_{i_2} \ldots x_{i_n}$.

So given a cryptotext w, the original plain text can be recovered by the following algorithm.

1) Calculate g(w)
2) Reduce g(w) to obtain a reduced word z
3) Factorize z on elements x_0, x_1,

   say, $z = x_{i_1} x_{i_2} \ldots x_{i_n}$.

   (The factorization is unique by (6.2.1))
4) $i_1 i_2 \ldots i_n$ is the plaintext desired.

The concept of generalized parikh vector can be used for purposes of decryption here also, as explained in the case of DOL/TOL public key cryptosystems.

We illustrate this with a toy example.

Example 3.1

Let $F(\Sigma)$ be the free group with $\Sigma = \{a,b\}$. Choose $x_0 = ab$, $x_1 = ab^{-1}c$. Obviously the conditions (6.2.1) and (6.2.2) hold.

Let $\Delta = \{c_1, c_2, \ldots, c_6\}$. Define morphism $g: (\Delta^{\pm 1})^* \longrightarrow (\Sigma^{\pm 1})^*$ by

$$g(c_1) = g(c_2^{-1}) = a; \; g(c_1^{-1}) = g(c_2) = a^{-1}$$
$$g(c_4^{-1}) = g(c_6) = b; \; g(c_4) = g(c_6^{-1}) = b^{-1}$$
$$g(c_3) = g(c_3^{-1}) = g(c_5) = g(c_5^{-1}) = 1$$

Obviously g satisfies the conditions (6.2.3) and (6.2.4).

Choose $R = \{c_6c_3^{-1}c_4,\ c_4^{-1}c_5c_2^{-1},\ c_6^{-1}c_5c_4^{-1},\ c_2c_3c_2^{-1}c_5\}$

It is easy to see that $R \subseteq g^{-1}([1]_F)$.

Define $G = \langle \Delta ; R \rangle$ and choose $u_0 = c_1c_4^{-1}$, $u_1 = c_2^{-1}c_4c_1$.

Evidently $g(u_0) = ab = x_0$, $g(u_1) = ab^{-1}a = x_1$.

It is not difficult to verify the following derivations in G:

$$u_0 = c_1c_4^{-1} \overset{*}{\Longleftrightarrow} c_5c_2^{-1}c_6c_3^{-1} \text{ and } c_5c_2^{-1}c_1^{-1}c_6c_4c_2^{-1}c_6c_3^{-1}$$
$$u_1 = c_2^{-1}c_4c_1 \overset{*}{\Longleftrightarrow} c_3c_2^{-1}c_5c_6^{-1}c_5c_1 \text{ and } c_3c_2^{-1}c_6c_4c_6^{-1}c_5c_1.$$

Consider the plaintext 1001. One possible encryption is

$$w = c_3c_2^{-1}c_6c_4c_6^{-1}c_5c_1c_5c_2^{-1}c_6c_3^{-1}c_5c_2^{-1}c_1^{-1}c_6c_4c_2^{-1}c_6c_3^{-1}c_3c_2^{-1}c_5c_6^{-1}c_5c_1.$$

Then, the plaintext can be recovered from w as follows:

1) $g(w) = abb^{-1}b^{-1}aabaa^{-1}bb^{-1}abab^{-1}a$
2) $z = ab^{-1}aababab^{-1}a$
3) $z = x_1x_0x_0x_1$
4) 1001 is the plaintext desired.

Comparison of PKCs

In [19] a PKC based on word problem for finitely presented groups is given. The idea of this PKC is as follows:

A finitely presented group G with decidable word problem is chosen. Two words w_1 and w_2 which are not related in G are selected. A finitely presented group G′ is obtained by adding new relators to G so that G′ may have undecidable word problem. (G', w_1, w_2) is the public encryption key. Cryptotext for a bit 0 (or 1) is a word x_1 (or x_2) obtained from w_1 (or w_2) by applying the relators in G′.

In this system

(i) encryption is given only for a single bit and if a word is encrypted together without giving a blank in between letters then decryption is not possible.

(ii) In [14] a type of cryptanalytic attack under which this system might break is pointed out. The method is to find a finitely presented group G" in which word problem is solvable by adding new relators to G′. Hence, even if G is not known, one can get the plain text using G".

In the PKC presented in this paper, we have imposed the conditions (6.2.1) and (6.2.2), so that it is possible to encrypt and decrypt a word, not necessarily a single letter. These conditions make sure that given the cryptotext w there is only one decomposition for $z =_F g(w)$ as $z = x_{i_1} \ldots x_{i_n}$ and due to the algorithm in [3] this decomposition can be obtained.

Again, because of the trapdoor g used here, adding new relators will not be of any help. Therefore the attack which might break the system [19], mentioned earlier, will not help in this case.

ACKNOWLEDGEMENT

We gratefully acknowledge the help of Mr. C.R. Boyd, Mr. N.G. David, Miss L. Revathi and Miss Yamini Jacob.

REFERENCES:

[1] Aho, A.V. and Corasick, M.J., Efficient string matching: An aid to bibliographic search, Communications of the ACM, **18**, 6, 338-340 (1975).

[2] Apostolico, A. and Giancarlo, R., Pattern matching machine implementation of a fast test for unique decipherability, Information Processing Letters, **18** 155-158 (1984).

[3] Berstel, J. and Perrin, D., "The Theory of Codes," Academic Press, New York (1985).

[4] Book, R.V., Confluent and other types of Thue systems, Journal of the ACM, **29**, 171-182 (1982).

[5] Diffie, W. and Hellman, M.E., New directions in Cryptography, IEEE Transaction on Information Theory, **IT-22**, 6, 644-654 (1976).

[6] Eilenberg, S., "Automata, Languages and Machines", Vol. A, Academic Press, (1974).

[7] Harrison, M. "Introduction to Formal Language Theory" Addison-Wesley, Reading, Mass., (1978).

[8] Landweber, L.H., Decision problem for w-automata, Mathematical Systems Thoery, **3**, 376-384 (1969).

[9] Nivat, M., Infinite words, infinite trees and infinite computations, Mathematical Centre Tracts, **109**, 1-52 (1979).

[10] Novikov, P.S., On the algorithmic unsolvability of the word problem in group theory, Trudy Math. Inst. Stelkov, **44**, 143 (1955).

[11] Parikh, R.J., On context-free languages, Journal of the ACM, **13**, 570-581 (1966).

[12] Rozenberg, G. and Salomaa, A., "The Mathematical Theory of L-systems," Academic Press, New York, (1980).

[13] Salomaa, A., Computation and Automata, Cambridge University Press, (1986).

[14] Salomaa, A. and Yu, S., On a public key cryptosystem based on iterated morphisms and substitutions, Theoretical Computer Science, **48**, 283-296 (1986).

[15] Siromoney, R. and Dare V.R., A generalization of the parikh vector for finite and infinite words, Foundations of Software Technology and Theoretical Computer Science, Proceedings (Ed.S.N. Maheswari) Lecture Notes in Computer Science, **206**, Springer-Verlag, Berlin, 290-302 (1985).

[16] Siromoney, R., Abisha, P.J., Do Long Van and Subramanian, K.G., Public key cryptosystems based on word problems, TR MATH-17/87, Department of Mathematics, Madras Christian College.

[17] Siromoney, R. and Siromoney, G., A public key cryptosystem that defies cryptanalysis, Bulletin of EATCS, **28**, 37-43 (1986).

[18] Subramanian, K.G., Siromoney, R. and Abisha, P.J., A DOL/TOL public key cryptosystems, Inform. Proc. Letters, **26**, 95-97 (1987/88).

[19] Wagner, N.R. and Magyarik, M.R., A public key cryptosystem based on word problem, Advances in Cryptology, Proceedings, (Eds. G.R.Blakley and D.Chaum) Lecture Notes in Computer Science **196**, 19-35 (1985).

MAP SYSTEMS WITH HANDLES

Gift Siromoney
K.G. Subramanian
and
Rani Siromoney

Madras Christian College
Tambaram
Madras 600 059, INDIA

ABSTRACT

Map-generating systems depicting biological growth by binary cell division have been introduced by Lindenmayer and Rozenberg [5]. We have proposed in [21] a generalization in which each cell of a map may divide into finitely many cells at any instant of time. A few additional features introduced in this system enable us to describe the pattern of venation found on the wings of a butterfly. In this revised version, we show that this generalized map-generating systems with handles are suitable for describing fractal images and we establish hierarchy and decidability results.

1. INTRODUCTION

Formal Language theory has been an extensive area of research for more than two decades. Extensions to two or higher dimensions, both theoretical studies and practical applications which utilize syntactic techniques of language theory have been successfully done. Introduction and study of models generating or recognizing arrays corresponding to digitized pictures has been one area [15, 20]. Another extensively studied extension is that of graph-rewriting systems [2]. A third area is the introduction of map generating systems. Not too many models are developed in this direction since there are several difficulties to be overcome, if the model is to prove useful as well as elegant, and simple for implementation.

The earliest model developed by Rosenfeld [16] describes the generation of maps which are translatable into multigraphs. This model is quite general in nature.

Motivated by the L systems introduced to model the growth of filamentous organisms, there have been map generating models in two dimensions to describe biological growth [1, 5, 7, 8, 11, 12, 13, 18]. A feature common to all these models is that, growth (i.e. rewriting) takes place in parallel and is binary (i.e. each cell divides into atmost two cells). Some of these models also avoid holes inside a cell but allow intersection of two cells at a point. An additional feature of the Lindenmayer models [5] is that provision is made for the growth of walls, by allowing wall productions (Walls are also called edges). These are well-motivated models depicting biological growth and are found suitable to model real-life situations and well-suited for implementation. In general, graph rewriting systems which depict maps, show adjacency relations which reflect neighbourhood constraints. They do not normally reflect geometrical details. The map models of Lindenmayer preserve geometric relations as well. Lindenmayer has given a lucid introduction and compact survey of parallel map generating systems in [6].

In [21], we have introduced a new model for the generation of maps. This generalizes the ideas presented in [5], by allowing division of a cell into finitely many cells instead of binary division. In this paper, we show that an advantage of this extension is that we obtain families of maps which properly include the map families with unoriented walls of [5], which are now called sc-systems (singly labelled cyclic controlled BPMOL systems). It is known that it is decidable whether an arbitrary sc-system is edge insertion deterministic. In the case of map systems introduced here, we have a similar result, namely, that it is decidable whether the map system is deterministic with regard to insertion of a map with handles.

Recently, methods of generation of fractal images using matrix-valued homomorphisms have been considered [17]. The map systems proposed here are found suitable for generating images of fractals and fractal-like objects. In using map systems, we treat cells of maps depicting fractal images, as rectangular regions.

We have introduced this model since a country may divide into several smaller regions and boundaries also divided. The former is taken care of by the fact that one cell is allowed to split into finitely many cells and the latter by wall productions and these may reflect the changes that take place in geographical maps depicting countries. This model seems to be of biological significance as well, since the patterns found on the wings of insects [14] can be described by this model which has additional features to describe a region divided into finitely many subregions and star-like patterns.

Of special interest are patterns of venation (Fig.1) on butterfly wings [3, 19, 22]. In many species, both the forewings and the hindwings have a complete cell from which veins radiate towards the border. Some veins are forked and in some, two veins meet on the cell border.

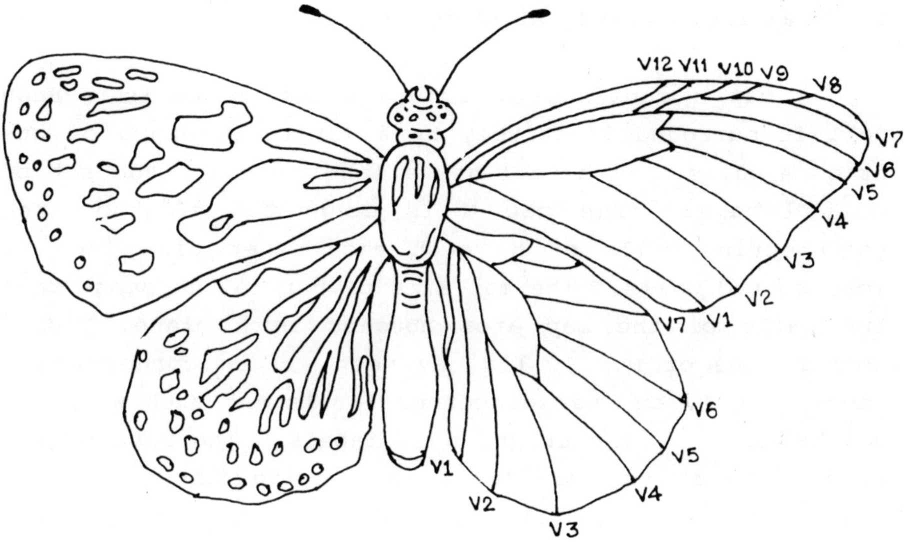

Figure 1. Patterns of venation on the wings of the butterfly Danais limniace commonly found in Madras

In some species, in the hindwing, a vein called precostal vein, does not reach the outer border but remains as an appendage to the cell. The concept of a map with handles is well-suited to describe the wing pattern and the concept of a star in the center can be used to describe the forked veins found in some species.

2. THE PROPAGATING MAP SYSTEMS

A map M consists of a finite set of cells. Each cell is surrounded entirely by a finite sequence of one or more walls. Each cell has a label $a \in \Sigma$, the set of cell labels. The map M is connected so that the neighbouring cells of M touch each other along one or more shared walls. The map M is planar in the sense that the cells of the map are embedded in a plane. At a corner, one or more walls may meet. Each corner has a label $x \in \Gamma$, the set of corner labels and each wall has a label $A \in \Delta$, the set of wall labels. The rest of the plane outside the map M is the environment, which we label with $\infty \notin \Sigma \cup \Gamma \cup \Delta$. We say that M is a map over (Σ, Δ, Γ).

The boundary of a cell in a map M is a finite sequence of consecutive walls, enclosing a cell. We write the boundary of a cell in the form $x_1A_1x_2A_2 \ldots x_nA_nx_1$, where the boundary consists of n consecutive corners labelled $x_1, x_2, \ldots, x_n$ such that A_i is the wall joining the corners labelled x_i and x_{i+1}, $i = 1, 2, \ldots, n-1$. The boundary of the map M is also a finite sequence of walls, enclosing all the cells of the map. We note that every wall in this boundary is adjacent to a cell or the environment. We specify the boundary or part of the boundary of a cell or a map, in the anti-clockwise direction, viewed from the centres of the cells. In particular, if the boundary of a map or a cell is a single wall with no corners in it, we mention only the label of the wall.

A map with handles, MH, is a map M together with end points (i.e. corners at which only single walls are incident) adjacent to the corners of the boundary of M such that for each corner of the boundary, there is atmost one end point adjacent to it. We write **M** as m(MH). The walls (handles) joining the end points with

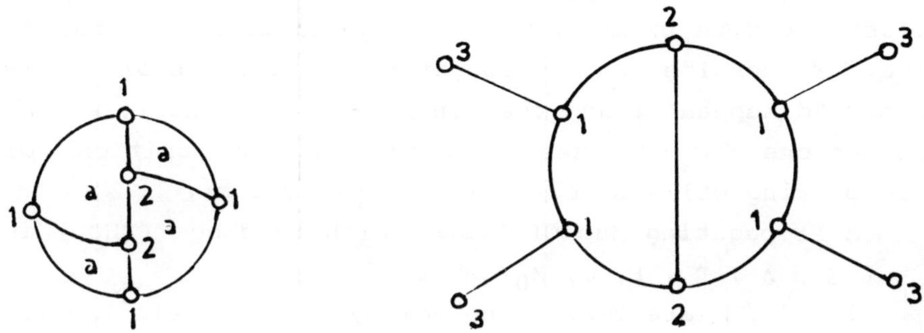

A map with four cells and six corners

A map with two cells and four handles

Figure 2

the corners of the boundary of M are embedded in the environment without crossing. A map and a map with handles are shown in Fig. 2.

A degenerate map with handles is a node labelled a together with $n (n \geqslant 1)$ end points adjacent to it (Fig. 3).

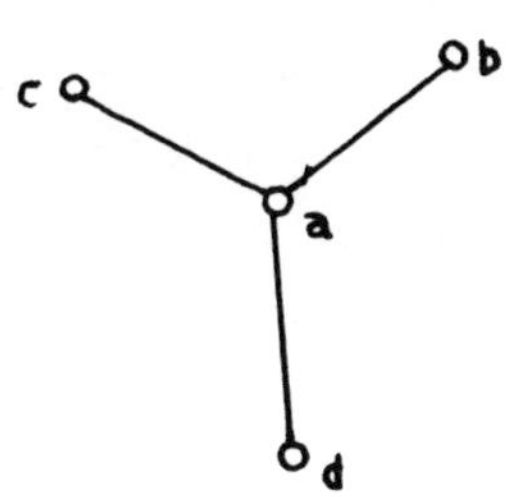

Figure 3. A degenerate map with three handles

The walls joining the end points and the node labelled a, are embedded in the environment without crossing.

We now formally define the map systems and illustrate with examples, how the generation of maps, is done. We consider only propagating (i.e. walls and cells do not "disappear") and the context-independent (i.e. the productions do not take into account the positions of neighbouring walls or cells in a map) systems.

A Propagating Map OL System with Handles (PMHOL) is $G = (\Sigma , \Delta , \Gamma , P, Q, M_0)$ where

i) Σ , Δ , Γ are finite, non-empty sets of cell labels, wall labels, and corner labels respectively;

ii) P, Q are finite, non-empty sets of wall productions and cell productions respectively;

iii) M_0 is the axiom map over (Σ , Δ , Γ).

A wall production in P is of one of the following forms: (P1) $xAy \longrightarrow xA_1z_1A_2z_2 \ \ldots \ A_{n-1}z_{n-1}A_ny$ and $yAx \longrightarrow yA_nz_{n-1}A_{n-1} \ \cdots \ z_2A_2z_1A_1x$ where $A, A_i \ \varepsilon \ \Delta$, for $i = 1, 2, \ldots, n$; $x, y, z_j \ \varepsilon \ \Gamma$, for $j = 1, 2, \ldots, n-1$. i.e., a wall production with splitting (Fig. 4). If we introduce directions ($\longrightarrow, \longleftarrow$), then instead of two types of rules for xAy and yAx, we need to have only one.

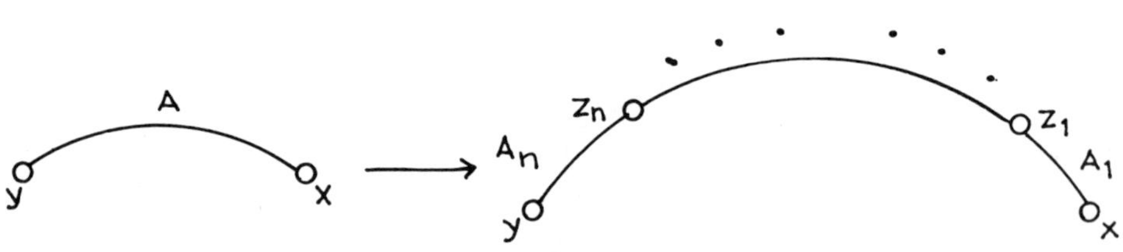

Figure 4. Wall production with splitting

(P2) $xAy \longrightarrow xAy$ and $yAx \longrightarrow yAx$, where $A \in \Delta$ and $x, y \in \Gamma$ i.e. a wall production without any change. In particular, if A is the label of a wall with no corner in it, we write A instead of xAy in the rules P_1 and P_2.

A cell production in Q is of one of the following forms:

(Q1) $a \longrightarrow b$, $a, b \in \Sigma$

(change in labelling without any splitting)

(Q2) $a \longrightarrow (MH, < K_1, u_1; K_2, u_2; \ldots; K_n, u_n >, < b_1, \ldots, b_n >)$, where MH is a map with n handles (walls) $u_iA_ix_i$ $(i = 1, 2, \ldots, n)$ whose end points are labelled $u_1, u_2, \ldots, u_n$ from Γ, so that the corners labelled $x_i \in \Gamma$ $(i = 1, 2, \ldots, n)$ divide the boundary of m(MH) into n consecutive sequences of walls, traced in the anti-clockwise direction; each K_i $(i = 1, 2, \ldots, n)$ consists of words of the form $y_1B_1y_2B_2 \ldots y_rB_ry_{r+1}$ $(r \geqslant 1)$ where $y_j \in \Gamma$ for $j = 1, 2, \ldots, r+1$ and $B_i \in \Delta$, for $i = 1, 2, \ldots, r$ (i.e. rule to rewrite a cell with a map with handles; Fig. 5).

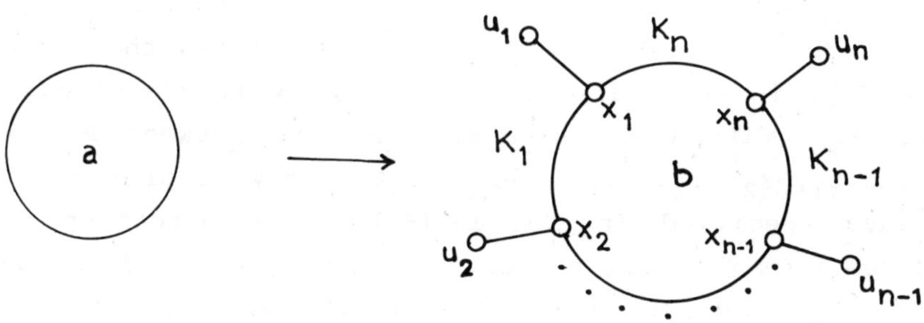

Figure 5. Rewriting rule using a map with handles

(Q3) a $\longrightarrow$ (M, < K_1, x_1; K_2, x_2; ...; K_n, x_n >, < b_1, ..., b_n >) where M is a map over (Σ , Δ, Γ) and x_1, ..., x_n are labels of n corners of the boundary of the map M as in production (Q2). K_i's are as in production (Q2) (i.e. rule to rewrite a cell with a map without handles; Fig.6).

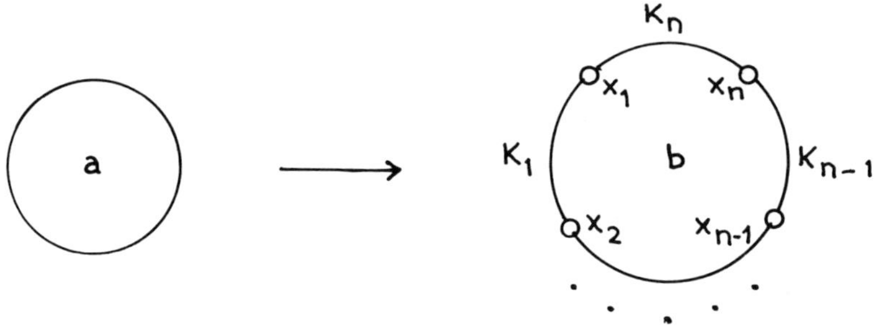

Figure 6. Rewriting rule using a map without handles

A direct derivation step in a PMHOL system G consists of two stages.

Given a map M, in the first stage, every wall in M is rewritten using a wall production, thus resulting in a map $\bar{M}$. The application of the wall production of type (P1) is that the wall labelled A and joining the corners x and y, is split into n consecutive walls labelled A_1, ..., A_n with the consecutive corners between x and y being z_1, z_2, ..., z_n. We note that a wall of a cell is always specified in the anti-clockwise direction when viewed from the cell center. The application of the wall production of type (P2) means that the wall labelled A and joining the corners x and y remains the same. We require at least one wall production for every wall label, joining two labelled corners.

In the second stage, every cell in M is rewritten using cell productions, resulting in the map M.

In applying a production of type (Q1), the cell with label a changes its label into b, without any other change.

In applying a production of type (Q2), the cell labelled a is rewritten by placing the map with handles, MH, inside the cell and the handles are joined to the corners of the boundary of the cell as indicated in the rule. In other words, if there exist n words w_i = $y_{i1}B_{i1}y_{i2}B_{i2} \cdots y_{ir_i}B_{ir_i}y_{i,r_i+1} \varepsilon K_i$, for i = 1, ..., n so that $y_{i1} = u_i$ (i = 1, 2, ..., n), $y_{i,r_i+1} = y_{i+1,1}$ (i = 1, ..., n-1) and $y_{n,r_n+1} = y_{11}$, and so that $w_1'w_2'$ $...w_n'$ is the boundary of the cell labelled a (read in the anticlockwise direction), where w_i' is obtained from w_i by leaving out the last letter y_{i,r_i+1} from w_i, for i = 1, 2, ..., n, then the corner u_i of the handle u_ix_i of MH and the corner y_{i1} of the boundary of the cell labelled a are identified into a single corner with the common label $u_i = y_{i1}$ (i = 1, ..., n). The resulting

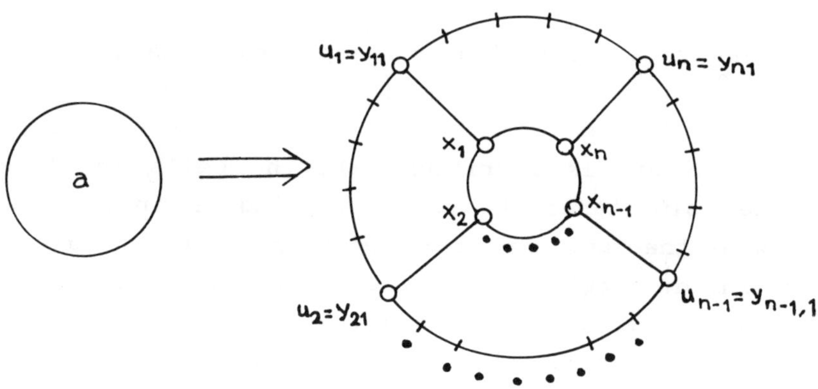

Figure 7. Rewriting by a map with handles

cells in between the handles $u_i x_i$ and $u_{i+1} x_{i+1}$ ($i = 1, \ldots, n-1$) and the cell in between $u_n x_n$ and $u_1 x_1$ are given the labels $b_1, \ldots, b_n$ respectively (Fig. 7). The application of the cell production of type (Q3) is similar. The map M is placed inside the cell with label a. The only difference is that the corners y_{i1} of the boundary of the cell labelled a should be the same as the labels x_i, of the boundary of M, for $i = 1, \ldots, n$. y_{i1} and x_i are identified resulting in a single corner with common label $y_{i1} = x_i$ ($i = 1, \ldots, n$). The resulting cells are labelled $b_1, b_2, \ldots, b_n$ as before (Fig. 8).

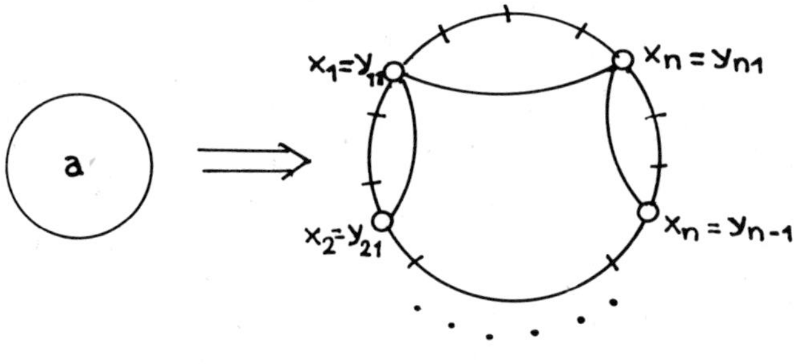

Figure 8. Rewriting by a map without handles

When a map is rewritten, all the cells in it are rewritten simultaneously i.e. rewriting is in parallel. In view of the fact that a map with or without handles is placed inside a cell region during the rewriting process, the planarity of the map is maintained. This enables the system to generate a sequence of nested maps as well.

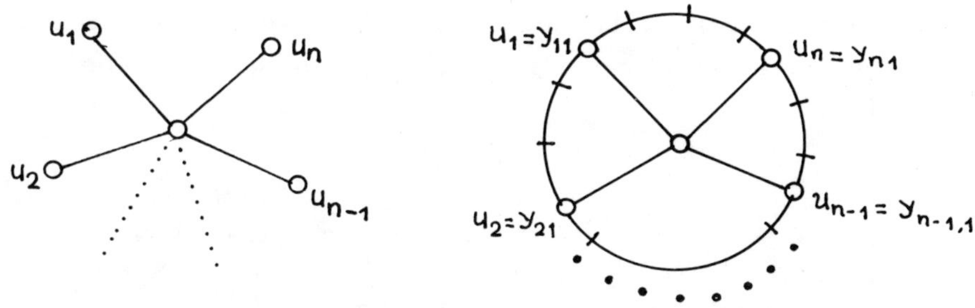

Figure 9. Degenerate map with n handles and rewriting with degenerate map

We also allow MH in (Q2) to be a degenerate map with only n handles, all of them meeting in a corner. In applying a production of this type, the end points of the handles, labelled u_i are identified with the corners y_{i1} ($i = 1, \ldots, n$) as described earlier (Fig. 9).

In particular, when MH is just a single handle with its end points labelled u_1, u_2, then the rule (Q2) is of the form:

(Q4) $a \longrightarrow (\ MH, < K_1,\ K_2 >, < b_1,\ b_2 >)$

A production of this type is applicable to a cell with label a if there exist words

$$w_1 = y_{11}B_{11}y_{12}B_{12} \cdots y_{1r_1}B_{r_1}y_{1,r_1+1} \text{ in } M_1$$

and

$$w_2 = y_{21}B_{21}y_{22}B_{22} \cdots y_{2r_2}B_{r_2}y_{2,r_2+1} \text{ in } M_2$$

so that $y_{2,r_2+1} = y_{11} = u_1$, $y_{1,r_1+1} = y_{21} = u_2$ and $w_1'w_2'$ is the boundary of the cell with label a where w_i' ($i = 1, 2$) is obtained from w by leaving out the last letter y_{i,r_i+1} from w_1. In applying this type of production, the corner of the handle, labelled $u_1(u_2)$ is identified with the corners labelled $y_{11}(y_{21})$. The resulting corner is given the common label $u_1 = y_{11}(u_2 = y_{21})$.

The resulting cell with boundary $w_1^! u_2 u_1$ is given label b_1 and the cell with boundary $u_1 u_2 w_2^!$ is given label b_2 (Fig. 10).

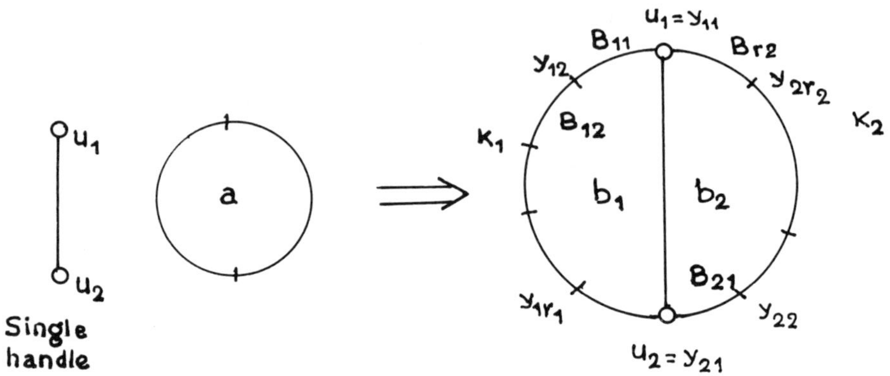

Figure 10. Rewriting by a single handle

The map language generated by a PMHOL G is the set of all maps derived from the axiom map M_0, using the productions of G.

We now illustrate with examples.

Example 2.1 Let $G_1 = (\Sigma_1, \Delta_1, \Gamma_1, P_1, Q_1, M_{01})$ be a PMHOL system, where $\Sigma_1 = \{ a,b \}$, $\Gamma_1 = \{ 1,2,3 \}$, $\Delta_1 = \{ A,B,C \}$ and the axiom M_{01} is given in Figure 11.

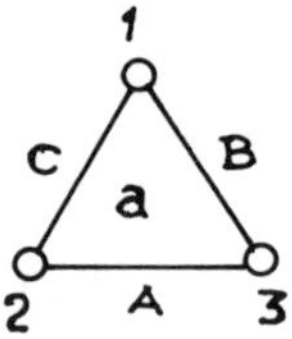

Figure 11. Axiom M_{01}

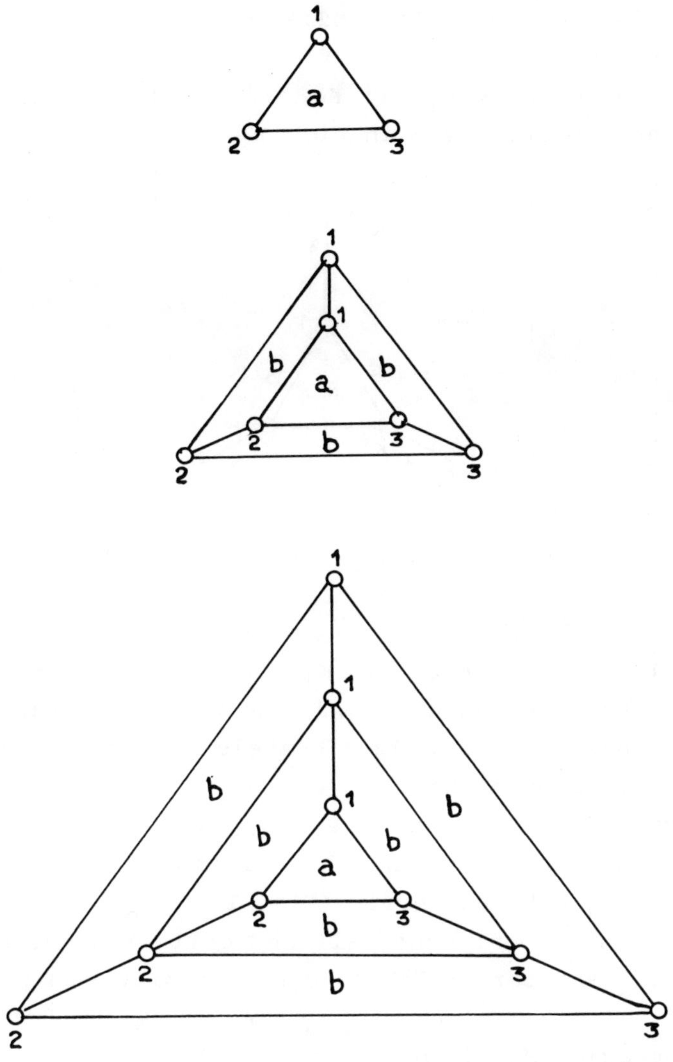

Figure 12. First three members of map language of example 2.1

P_1 consists of the wall productions:

$xzy \longrightarrow xzy$ and $yzx \longrightarrow yzx$, for $x,y \in \Gamma_1$ and $z \in \Delta_1$

Q_1 consists of the cell productions:

i) $b \longrightarrow b$

ii) $a \longrightarrow (MH_1, < K_1, 1; K_2, 2; K_3, 3 >, < b, b, b >)$
where MH_1 is given in Fig. 13.

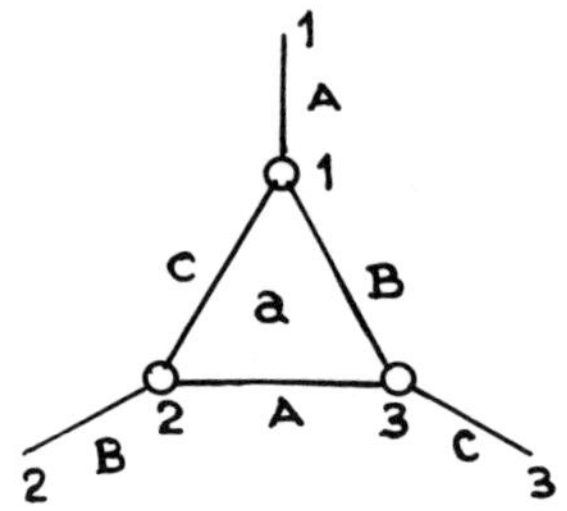

Figure 13. MH_1 of example 2.1

$K_1 = \{ 1C2 \}$, $K_2 = \{ 2A3 \}$, $K_3 = \{ 3B1 \}$
G_1 generates the language L_1. The first three members of L_1 are shown in Fig. 12. Labels of walls have been omitted for convenience.

Example 2.2 We give a map generating system to generate a map resembling the venation pattern found on the forewing of a butterfly (Fig. 1).

We mention only the wall and cell productions. The wall, cell and corner labels can be easily known from the rules.

The axiom M_{02} is given in Fig. 14.

The wall productions are as follows:

$v_0A_1v_2 \longrightarrow v_0Av_1Av_2$, $v_{11}A_2v_0 \longrightarrow v_{11}Av_{12}Av_0$
$v_7A_3v_{11} \longrightarrow v_7Av_8Av_9Av_{10}Av_{11}$,
$x_0B_1v_0 \longrightarrow x_0Ay_1Ay_2Av_0$,
$x_7B_2v_7 \longrightarrow x_7Ay_3Ay_4Ay_5Av_7$, $xAy \longrightarrow xAy$, for any two corner labels x,y.

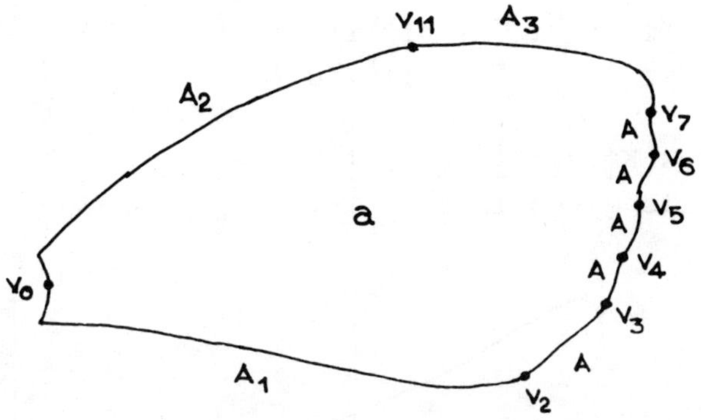

Figure 14. Axiom M_{02}

The cell productions are as follows:

$a \longrightarrow (MH_1, < K_1, v_0; K_2, v_2; K_3, v_3; K_4, v_4; K_5, v_5; K_6, v_6; K_7, v_7; K_8, v_{11} >, < b_1, b, b, b, b, b, b_1, b_1 >)$

where MH_1 is given in Fig. 15.

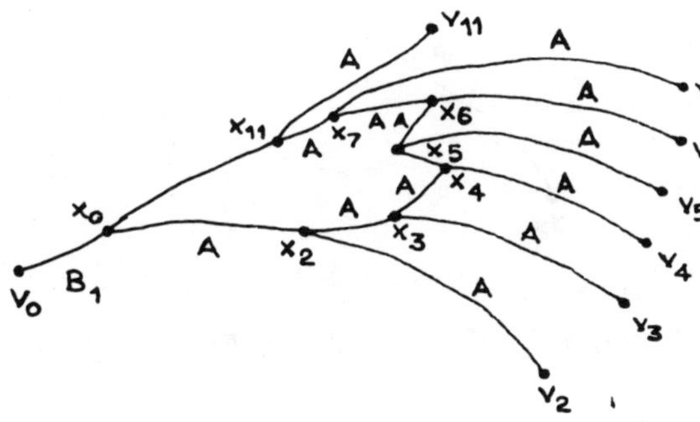

Figure 15. MH_1 of example 2.2

$K_1 = \{ v_0A_1v_2 \}$, $K_i = \{ v_iAv_{i+1} \}$, for i = 2, 3, 4, 5, 6;
$K_7 = \{ v_7Av_{11} \}$, $K_8 = \{ v_{11}A_2v_0 \}$
$b \longrightarrow b$
$b_1 \longrightarrow (MH_2, < K_1^1, y_1; K_2^1, v_1 >, < b, b >)$
where MH_2 is given in Fig. 16.

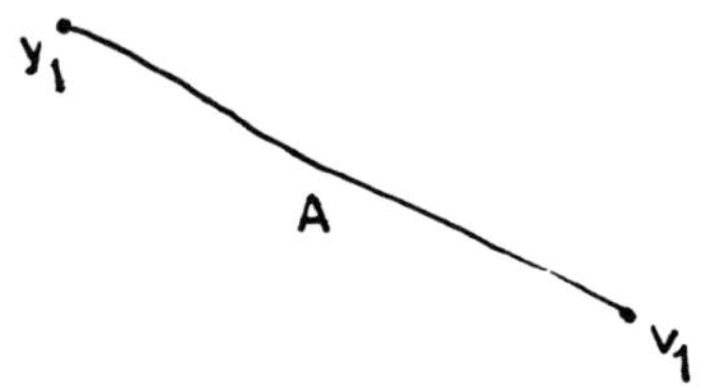

Figure 16. MH_2 of example 2.2

$K_1^1 = \{ y_1Ay_2Av_0Av_1 \}$, $K_2^1 = \{ v_1Av_2Ax_2Ax_0Ay_1 \}$
$b_1 \longrightarrow (MH_3, < K_1^2, v_{12}; K_2^2, y_2 >, < b, b_1 >)$
where MH_3 is given in Fig. 17.

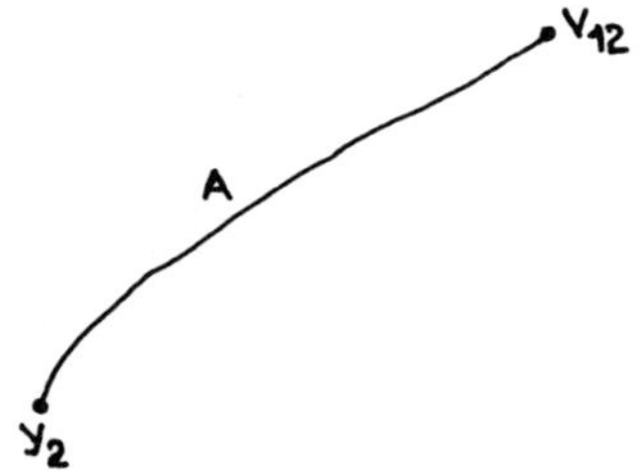

Figure 17. MH_3 of example 2.2

$K_1^2 = \{ v_{12}Av_0Ay_2 \}$, $K_2^2 = \{ y_2Ay_1Ax_0Ax_{11}Av_{11}Av_{12} \}$
$b_1 \longrightarrow (MH_4, < K_1^3, v_{10}; K_2^3, y_3 >, < b, b_1 >)$
where MH_4 is given in Fig. 18.

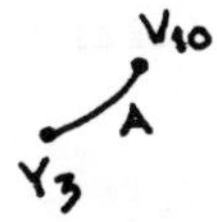

Figure 18. MH_4 of example 2.2

K_1^3 = { $v_{10}Av_{11}Ax_{11}Ax_7Ay_3$ },
K_2^3 = { $y_3Ay_4Ay_5Av_7Av_8Av_9Av_{10}$ }
$b_1 \longrightarrow$ (MH_5, < K_1^4, v_9; K_2^4, y_4 >, < b,b_1 >)
where MH_5 is given in Fig. 19.

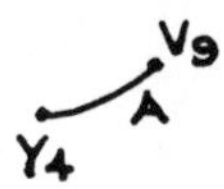

Figure 19. MH_5 of example 2.2

K_1^4 = { $v_9Av_{10}Ay_3Ay_4$ },
K_2^4 = { $y_4Ay_5Av_7Av_8Av_9$ }
$b_1 \longrightarrow$ (MH_6, < K_1^5, v_8; K_2^5, y_5 >, < b,b >)
where MH_6 is given in Fig. 20.

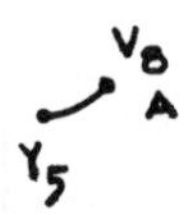

Figure 20. MH_6 of example 2.2

K_1^5 = { $v_8Av_9Ay_4Ay_5$ }, K_2^5 = { $y_5Av_7Av_8$ }

Example 2.3 (Fractal Islands)

A map generating system can be given to generate the Fractal islands [17] (Fig. 25), where the cells of the maps are treated as rectangular regions. We indicate the idea behind the construction and omit formal details. The cell labels are a,b. The corner and edge labels can be given suitably. (The cell with label a is coloured white and that with label b , black). The axiom map is given in Fig. 21.

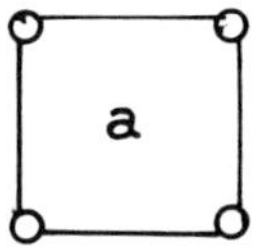

Figure 21.

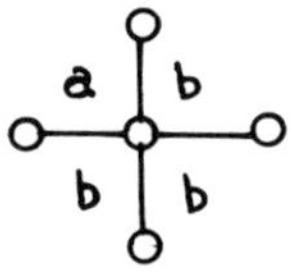

Figure 22.

The maps with handles that can be used in rewriting a cell with label a is given in Figure 22. and that with label b is given in Fig. 23, where we have indicated the labels to be given in the map with handles, for the regions after rewriting.

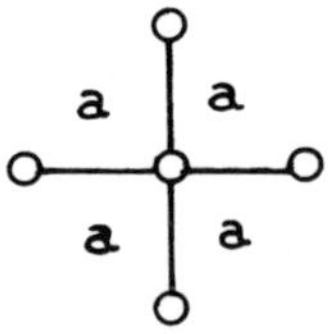

Figure 23.

For instance, the idea behind the generation of a map from the axiom is shown in Fig. 24.

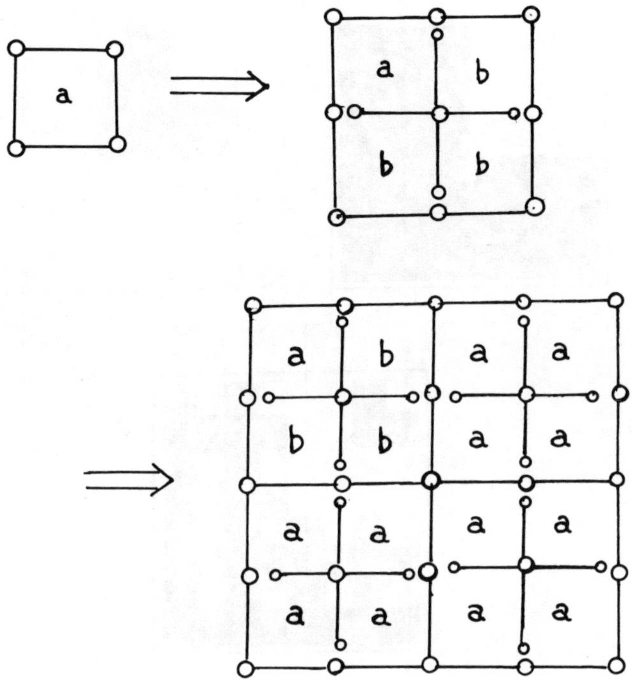

Figure 24.

The first three members of the fractal islands are shown in Fig. 25.

Example 2.4 (Sierpinski Carpet)

A map generating system can be given to generate the Sierpinski Carpet (Fig. 29) [17] using ideas similar to example 2.3. Here again the axiom map is given in Fig. 26 and the maps with handles that are needed to rewrite a cell with label a is given in Fig. 27, and to rewrite a cell with label b is given in Fig. 28. The first three members of Sierpinski carpet are given in Fig. 29.

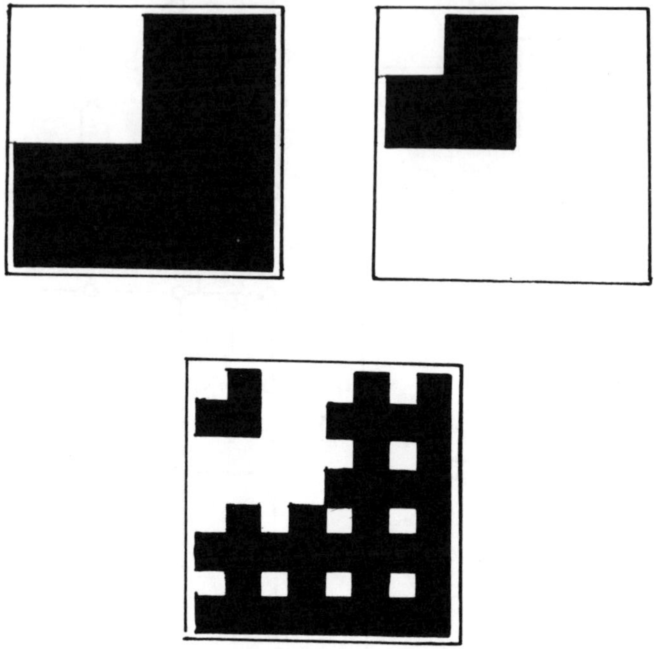

Figure 25. Fractal Islands

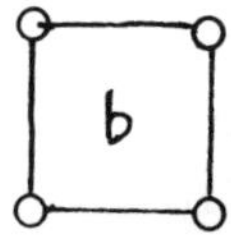

Figure 26.

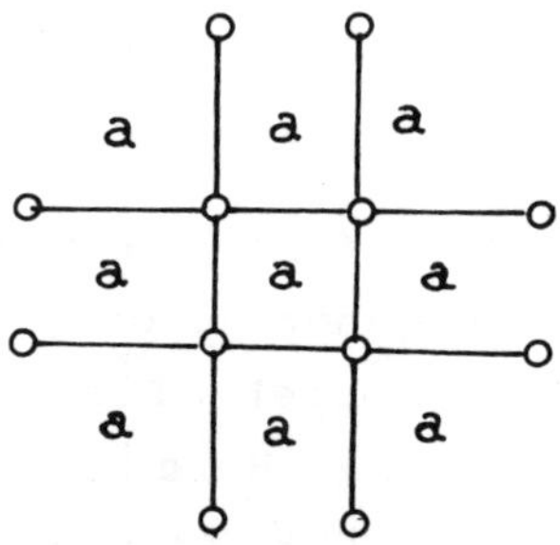

Figure 27.

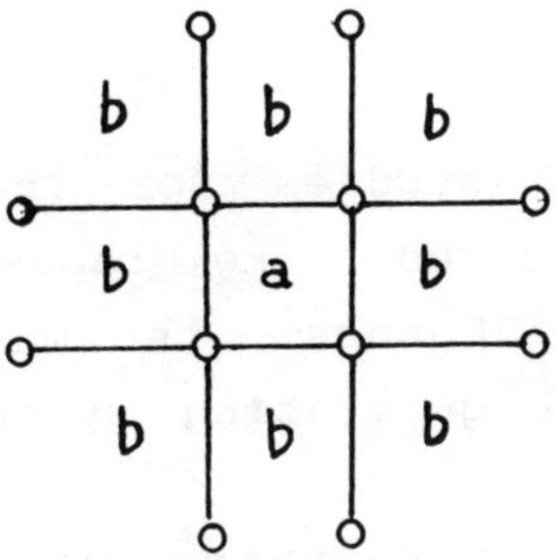

Figure 28.

Figure 29. Sierpinski carpet

3. COMPARISON

There are several studies for the generation of multi-dimensional structures, like graphs or maps, extending L-system models. Of these, the models proposed in [1] deal with parallel generating systems transforming maps.

The characteristic features of the generation process in [1] are that (i) only binary cell divisions are allowed (ii) every map generated is such that no cell has a number of neighbours exceeding a certain number specified (iii) there is a fixed 'interface' rule that decides the relative positions of the corners of the newly created walls and (iv) the generation process is context-dependent in the sense that cell division depends not only on the label of the cell but also on the labels of its neighbours and their configurations.

The map generating model of [5] generates maps with cell and wall labels. In the first stage of rewriting, each wall is subject to rewriting and in the second stage, new walls are spanned on the structure of walls and corners obtained in the first stage. But this model is less context-dependent than the model of [1]. Also, this model does not impose a fixed bound on the number of walls of a cell or a fixed 'interface' rule. These aspects are similar to those in [5]. But we have allowed division of a cell into finitely many cells unlike the binary cell division in [1] or [5]. This is a generalization of the model in [5].

Recently, parallel map generating systems with edge label control (with singly or doubly labelled edges) have been classified, compared, and decidability and hierarchy results have been established in [4]. Decision problems relating to determinism have also been examined in [9]. Map systems which need not be binary or propagating are also introduced in [10] and possibilities of future research in this direction pointed out.

4. DETERMINISTIC MAP SYSTEMS

A map system is said to be deterministic if there is a single sequence of maps generated by the system. Clearly, non-determinism in wall rewriting can be easily found by inspecting the wall productions. On the other hand, non-determinism may arise in inserting a map with handles in a cell. That this feature is decidable is brought out by the following theorem.

Theorem 4.1

It is decidable whether an arbitrary PMHOL system, is deterministic or not with regard to insertion of a map with handles, in a cell.

Proof

The labelled walls surrounding a cell in a map read in the anti-clockwise direction give rise to a word, called circular word, of the form

$$w = x_1A_1x_2A_2 \ldots x_nA_nx_1$$

where x_i are the corners of the walls and A_i are the labels of the walls, joining the corners x_i and x_{i+1}.

Let G be a PMHOL system with the set Q of cell productions. For G to be deterministic, there should be atmost one cell production for a cell label. This can be checked easily. But if a rule is applicable to rewriting a cell, the insertion of the map with handles in the rule, should be possible in only one way.

The basic idea is that there should be atmost one factorization of the circular word $w = x_1A_1 \ldots x_nA_nx_1$ in the form $y_1u_1, y_2u_2, \ldots, y_mu_m$ so that the corners $y_1, \ldots, y_m$ match with the corners of the handles of the map which rewrites the cell. It is easy to note that there are only finitely many such factorizations of w and hence the theorem follows.

We next prove that the PMHOL systems properly include the (unoriented) sc-systems.

Theorem 4.2

The set of all unoriented map sequences generated by deterministic sc-systems is properly included in the set of all map sequences generated by deterministic PMHOL systems.

Proof

Inclusion is obvious. Proper inclusion can be seen as follows:

Consider $M = (\Sigma, \Delta, \Gamma, P, Q, M_o)$ where $\Sigma = \{ a,b,c,d \}$, $\Gamma = \{ 1,2,3 \}$, $\Delta = \{ A,B,D \}$ and the axiom M_o is given in Fig. 30.

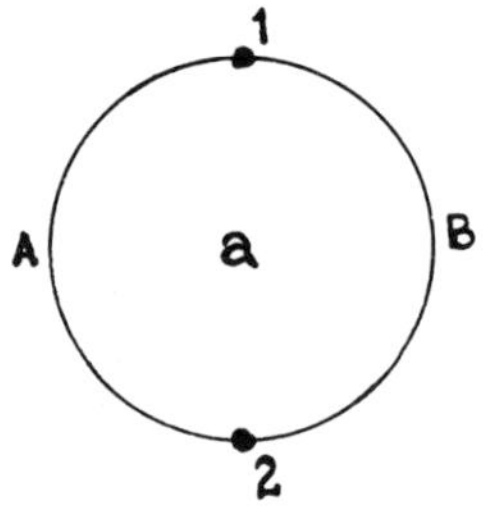

Figure 30.

P consists of the wall productions:

$2B1 \longrightarrow 2B3B1$, $2B3 \longrightarrow 2B3B3$, $3B3 \longrightarrow 3B3B3$, $3B1 \longrightarrow 3B3B1$ and the corresponding 'reversed' rules.

(i.e. $1B2 \longrightarrow 1B3B2$ etc.)

Q consists of the cell productions:

$d \longrightarrow d$

$a \longrightarrow (MH_1, < \{ 1A2 \}, 1; \{ 2B1 \}, 2 >, < b,d >)$

$b \longrightarrow (MH_2, < \{ 1A2 \}, 1; \{ 2D1 \}, 2 >, < b,c >)$

$c \longrightarrow (MH_3, < \{ 1A2 \}, 1; \{ 2D1 \}, 2 >, < c,c >)$

where MH_1, MH_2 and MH_3 are given in Fig. 31.

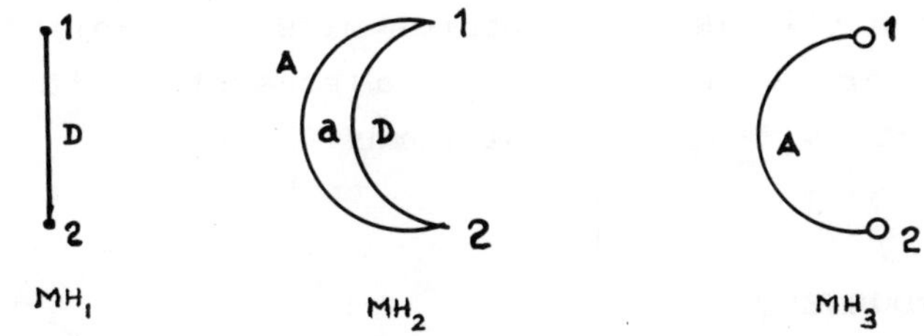

Figure 31.

The first three members of the map language are shown in Fig. 32.

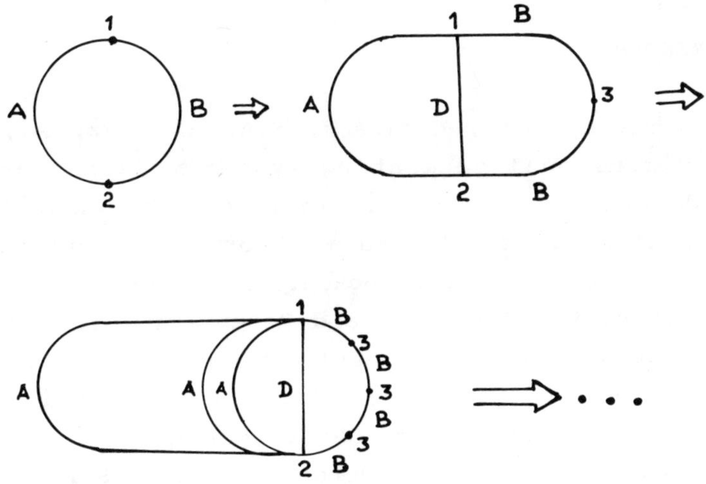

Figure 32.

The circular words are

{ 1A2A1 , 1A2D1 , 2B3, 3B1 } { $(3B)^n3$ / $n \geq 0$ }

Thus the map system M generates maps with an infinite set of circular words whereas in a sc-system, there can be only finitely many circular words.

ACKNOWLEDGEMENT

We gratefully acknowledge the help of Mr. C.R.Boyd, Mr. N.G.David, Ms L.Revathi and Ms D.Sujila in the preparation of the paper

REFERENCES

[1] Carlyle, J.W., Greibach, S.A. and Paz, A., A two-dimensional generating system modeling growth by binary cell division, in Proc. 15th Ann. Symp. on Switching and Automata Theory, New Orleans, IEEE Computer Soc., Long Beach., 1-12 (1974).

[2] Claus, V., Ehrig, H. and Rozenberg, G., Eds., Graph Grammars and their application to Computer Science and Biology, Lecture Notes in Computer Science, **73**, Springer-Verlag, Berlin (1979).

[3] Dayanandan, P., Gladstone, M. and Siromoney, G., Butterflies of Tambaram, The Madras Christian College Magazine, **47** (1978).

[4] de Boer, M.J.M. and Lindenmayer, A., Map OL-Systems with edge label control: comparison of marker and cyclic systems, Graph Grammars and Their Applications to Computer Science VII, (Ehrig, H., Nagl, M., Rozenberg, G. and Rosenfeld, A., Eds.) Lecture Notes in Computer Science, **291**, 378-392 (1986).

[5] Lindenmayer, A. and Rozenberg, G., Parallel generation of maps, in [2], 301-316 (1979).

[6] Lindenmayer, A., An Introduction to parallel map generating systems, Graph Grammars and Their Applications to Computer Science VII, (Ehrig, H., Nagl, M., Rozenberg, G. and Rosenfeld, A., Eds.) Lecture Notes in Computer Science, **291**,27-40 (1986).

[7] Mayoh, B.H., Multidimensional Lindenmayer organisms, in L Systems (Rozenberg, G. and Salomaa, A., Eds.), Lecture Notes in Computer Science, **15**, Springer-Verlag, Berlin, 302-326 (1974).

[8] Mayoh, B.H., Another model for the development of multi-dimensional organisms, in "Automata, Languages, Development", (Lindenmayer, A. and Rozenberg, G., Eds.), North-Holland, Amsterdam, 469-485 (1976).

[9] Nakamura, A., Lindenmayer, A. and Aizawa, K., Some systems for map generation, in "The Book of L," (Rozenberg, G. and Salomaa, A., Eds.) Springer-Verlag, Berlin, 323-331 (1985).

[10] Nakamura, A., Lindenmayer, A. and Aizawa, K., Map OL systems with markers, Lecture Notes in Computer Science, **291**, 479-495 (1986).

[11] Nyrup, K. and Mayoh, B.H., Map Grammars: Cycles and the algebraic approach, in [2], 301-316 (1979).

[12] Paz, A., Multidimensional parallel rewriting systems, in "Automata, Languages, Development", (Lindenmayer, A. and Rozenberg, G., Eds.), North-Holland, Amsterdam, 509-515 (1976).

[13] Paz, A. and Raz, Y., Complexity of pattern generation by map L-systems, in [2], 367-378 (1979).

[14] Richards, O.W. and Davies, R.G., "A General Text-book of Entomology", The English Language Book Society (1965).

[15] Rosenfeld, A., "Picture Languages," Academic Press, New York (1979).

[16] Rosenfeld, A. and Strong, J.P., A grammar for maps, in Software Engineering (J. Tou Ed.), Vol.2, Academic Press, New York, 227-239 (1971).

[17] Shallit, J., Two methods for the generation of fractal images, University of Chicago Technical report 87-010, June 1987.

[18] Siere, P.L.J., Rozenberg, G. and Lindenmayer, A., Cell division patterns: Syntactical description and implementation, Computer Graphics and Image Processing, **18**, 329-346 (1982).

[19] Siromoney, G., Butterflies of Tambaram, The Madras Christian College Magazine, **32** (1963).

[20] Siromoney, R., Array Languages and Lindenmayer systems - a survey, in "The Book of L", (Rozenberg, G. and Salomaa, A., Eds.) Springer-Verlag, Berlin (1985).

[21] Siromoney, G., Subramanian, K.G. and Siromoney, R., A map-generating system, Proceedings of the Third Conference on Foundations of Software Technology and Theoretical Computer Science, Bangalore, 145-170 (1983).

[22] Wynter-Blyth, M.A., Butterflies of the Indian Region, The Bombay Natural History Society, Bombay (1957).

CRYPTOSYSTEMS FOR TAMIL

Rani Siromoney
Department of Mathematics

and

M. Chandrasekaran
Abdul Huq
Department of Statistics

Madras Christian College
Tambaram Madras 600 059

Abstract

In 1961, Siromoney had written a popular scientific article on cryptography in Tamil making use of his work on information theory. Shannon's definition of perfect secrecy and the role played by frequency distributions in breaking cryptosystems, based on natural languages, are well-known. Details of the database required for such cryptanalytic attacks in Tamil, based on Siromoney's work in the early sixties, are discussed. Methods which make use of this database for breaking substitution ciphers are given. A stream cipher for Tamil is constructed on the basis of cellular automata which are powerful models of parallel computation.

1. INTRODUCTION

At the memorial meeting held on 24th March 1988 to honour the memory of Professor Gift Siromoney, one of his friends and research associates with a similar "wide spectrum" of interests, said that he was always "ahead of you". How very true is this statement is reflected in this article, which has been inspired by a manuscript entitled "Cryptography in Tamil" that he had written for a popular science magazine in 1961.[13)]

Down the centuries, cryptosystems have been used mainly by diplomatic and military circles followed by amateurs. Recently there has been an explosive increase in cryptological studies due to the need for security in communication and storage of sensitive data in computer networks.[1,4)]

The need for applying modern techniques to Tamil studies was keenly felt by Siromoney as early as 1959 and work on Tamil using information theory was started then. Choosing a large random sample and using a hand calculator, he made a study of the proportions of different letters of the alphabet in the language. Results based on statistical analysis were applied to improve the standard keyboard of Tamil typewriter and for the invention of a keyboard for a teleprinter in Tamil. One may compare this with the fact that the first teleprinter in Tamil was introduced in the State of Tamil Nadu much later - again an instance of "far ahead of you" - a pioneer in several fields of research.

Tamil, one of the national languages of the Indian Union, is the official language of Tamil Nadu. It is spoken by about fifty million people, some of whom live in Sri Lanka, Malaysia and Singapore. As one of the ancient languages of India, it has a history of more than two thousand years and a literature comparable to the best in the world.

Compared to other Indian languages, Tamil has a relatively small number of pure consonants and vowels. Its alphabet has thirty basic letters, of which eighteen are consonants and twelve are vowels. The short and long vowels are reckoned as distinct letters. In addition, there are 18 $\times$ 12 = 216 combinations of consonants and vowels, each one of these representing a distinct sound. There is also one special auxiliary symbol called aitham and this brings the total to 247.

In the calculation of the proportions of different letters of the alphabet and the one-gram entropy, and in the construction of Huffman code, Siromoney[14)] considered a restricted set of thirty letters (eighteen consonants and twelve vowels), since every other letter except the special symbol can be expressed as a combination of these basic letters. A large sample was taken from the prose works published in Tamil Nadu during 1946 - 57 using random sampling methods. His estimates of the maximal entropy $H_0 = \log_2 n$ and the one-gram entropy $H_1 = -\sum p_i \log_2 p_i$ (where n is the number of letters and p_i is the relative frequency of the i-th letter) were 4.91 bits and 4.34 bits respectively.Similar investigation was done on the basis of samples of Tamil poetry taken from six different works belonging to periods ranging from the beginning of Christian era to the modern period. While all these analyses have been based on a thirty-letter alphabet for Tamil, Siromoney has also obtained unigram frequencies of the 247 letters.[15)]

These details are included here in view of the fact that apart from being useful in the cryptanalytic attack against various classical cryptosystems, we find that Salomaa[12)] has emphasized recently the need for a clear understanding of the significance and advantages of using a natural language, specially, if it is less-known than English such as Chinese or Finnish. Perhaps, we could add Tamil too to this list since so much work has been done by Siromoney for Tamil. It has also been pointed out that the distribution of letters depends very much on the type of text: ordinary prose, slang, technical, telegrahic etc., and that no table can conceivably take into account all types of texts. It is of interest to mention here that details relating to different kinds of texts were collected recently and are available with the authors. With a 247 letter alphabet for Tamil, large samples were taken from books on religion, philosophy, law, children's literature and Tamil prose as well as from newspapers.

For modern languages, translators may be found to cryptanalyse the message very easily. But a prehistoric language with a script like the Indus script which has challenged scholars at decipherment may prove a better candidate for a cryptosystem. Only difficulty is that, since there is no agreement between scholars regarding the meaning of the different signs, more problems will be created. But the positional frequencies of the signs as well as the distribution of pairwise combinations have been worked out[5)] and used to get a greater understanding of the structure of the Indus language.[3,16)] If there is an indication that these may prove useful in cryptographic studies, then we already have the database to work with.

Normally, in most of the well-known cryptosystems, the message is first encoded numerically. It should be noted that the statistical properties inherent in the natural language carry over to the encoded language too. Hence statistical studies of natural languages will remain relevant in this context.

Having introduced, in this section, various details regarding Tamil and cryptography, in general, we review the basic terminology relating to cryptosystems and outline a few classical cryptosystems in the next section. These systems are vulnerable to "ciphertext-only" attacks using frequency distributions. In the third section the database required for such cryptanalytic attacks is described. Such a database is created in continuation of the work done by Siromoney in the early sixties. Two methods for breaking substitution ciphers in Tamil are presented in the fourth section. In the last section, a stream cipher for Tamil is constructed based on a cellular automaton.

2. SIMPLE CRYPTOSYSTEMS VULNERABLE TO STATISTICAL ANALYSIS

Messages may be communicated via an insecure channel such as a telephone line subject to wire tapping by an eavesdropper, or data may be stored in an information system. Such messages are referred to as the plaintext (or cleartext) which are encrypted by the sender and the resulting cryptotext (or ciphertext) sent via the channel. The receiver then decrypts the cryptotext back to the plaintext. The process of converting a plaintext to a ciphertext is called enciphering or encryption and the reverse process is called deciphering or decryption.

A cryptosystem specifies several (often, infinitely many) keys. Each key K determines an encryption function e_K and a decryption function d_K. Cryptotext C is obtained from plaintext w using the key e_K i.e., $e_K(w) = C$. Conversely, $d_K(C) = w$. Thus $d_K(e_K(w)) = w$. In this case, d_K is the inverse of e_K. Each K determines mappings e_K

and d_K between plaintext-space Σ^* for some alphabet Σ and the cryptotext-space Δ^*, for some alphabet Δ. The plaintext may be from a subspace consisting of the set of all meaningful sentences in natural language. Thus an enciphering function transforms a plaintext message into a ciphertext message and the deciphering function recovers the plaintext from the ciphertext. Any such set-up is called a cryptosystem. Breaking the code without the knowledge of the key is known as cryptanalysis.

The cryptanalyst is the eavesdropper who tries to decipher the encrypted message. Five possible initial set-ups are known: cryptotext-only, known-plaintext, chosen-plaintext, chosen-cryptotext, encryption-key-only, the last two relevant only to modern public-key cryptosystems. Normally, it is assumed that the cryptanalyst knows the cryptosystem used. One has only to find out the key.

The plaintext and ciphertext are broken up into message units which might be a single letter, a pair of letters (digrams, which by the terminology of cryptography, may be called a digraph), a triple of letters (trigraph) or a block of several letters.

If the message unit is taken to be a single letter in an N-letter alphabet labelled by the integers 0, 1, ..., N-1, the enciphering function f may be defined by the rule $C = f(p) \equiv P + b \mod N$. As a special case, when $N = 26$ and $b = 3$, we obtain Julius Caesar's system, the oldest of all the cryptosystems. It is to be noted that the translations induced by the cryptosystem Caesar and its basic variations are all letter-to-letter morphisms.

Simple substitution ciphers are easy to break in a ciphertext-only attack using single letter frequency distributions. When one knows the frequencies of occurrence of various letters of the alphabet in the plaintext, by noting the most frequently occurring letter in the ciphertext, it is easy to guess the key. This is illustrated in the next section with reference to Tamil.

An improvement is to use an affine map $C \equiv aP + b \mod N$ where a and b are fixed integers and form the key. Here again, the key can be found easily by making use of frequently occurring letters of the alphabet. Sometimes, the plaintext and ciphertext message units may be two-letter blocks and a cryptosystem may be designed on the basis of an affine transformation. In this case, known frequency of digraphs in the language used for the plaintext is helpful in breaking the system and retrieving the key.

The cryptosystem playfair encrypts pairs of letters. The rules governing the encryption may be expressed in terms of productions of the form AB —> CD and hence the system is typically context-sensitive.

Instead of having to remember a 5 X 5 square of letters, generally a keyword is specified. In the earlier years, playfair was considered safe since statistical analysis based on the frequency of single letters did not work. But with the availability of information about the frequency of digrams, trigrams etc., the situation has changed and the cryptosystem is vulnerable to ciphertext-only attacks.[11)]

There are other monoalphabetic variants of Caesar cipher and polyalphabetic substitutions where a letter may be encrypted differently in different parts of the plaintext alphabet. The well-known Vigenere's ciphers are keyword - controlled Caesar ciphers in which statistical frequencies get distorted. Hence cryptanalysis is by Kasiki's technique of finding repetitions of the same word w as long as possible, since the length of the keyword is likely to divide the distance between the two occurrences of w.

We conclude this section with an example in Tamil for a substitution cipher which is one of the well-known classical cryptosystems that Siromoney had illustrated in his manuscript. As explained earlier, each vowel-consonant is taken as two letters - a consonant followed by a vowel. Consider the message

y ā t u m ū r ē y ā v a r u m k ē ḷ i r

which means " Every country is my country; every man is my kinsman ", favourite lines of Siromoney. Caesar cipher, which substitutes every letter of the plaintext alphabet by the letter three positions down in the alphabet, produces the cryptotext:

v u n ē l ai l̤ ō v u r̤ ī l̤ ē l n̄ ō a ū l̤

3. DATABASE FOR CRYPTANALYSIS OF MESSAGES IN TAMIL

Analysis of several cryptosystems require an exhaustive statistical database. Value of unigram and digram frequencies of letters in this regard has been recognised for a long time. Methods based on combinations of higher order (usually referred to as n-grams) have also been proposed. Such statistics will enable us in the computation of useful measures like the rate of language, conditional entropy and unicity distance. As early as 1963, Siromoney compiled unigram frequencies for thirty basic letters which are presented in Table 1 (the frequencies are relative to a total of 1000).

We note that even unigram frequencies are adequate to compromise certain cryptosystems. Caesar cipher is one such simple system. Assume that we have a long message which we know was encrypted using a Caesar cipher in Tamil. From Table 1, we observe that $\underline{a}$ is the most frequently occurring letter. It is thus reasonable to assume that the most frequently occurring letter in the ciphertext is the encryption of $\underline{a}$. If we find that the most common letter in the ciphertext is $\underline{\bar{e}}$, we infer that the transformation takes $\underline{a}$ = 1 to $\underline{\bar{e}}$ = 8 i.e., 8 = 1 + k mod 30, leading to k = 7. Thus to decipher the ciphertext every letter in it has to be shifted seven positions backwards.

Another application of unigram statistics is in message compression which can be achieved using Huffman code. Although message compression cannot replace encryption, it can enhance data security. Siromoney[14) obtained Huffman code as well as telegraphic codes for letters in Tamil. (We note that telegraphic codes are also used to encrypt messages.) Table 1 shows these two codes and the decoding tree corresponding to the Huffman code can be constructed (Fig. 1).

In the next section, we demonstrate how digram frequencies can be used in cryptanalysis. While the unigram and digram statistics have already been compiled for Tamil, work is in progress to collect data on n-grams.

4. METHODS FOR BREAKING SUBSTITUTION CIPHERS IN TAMIL

We have noted that simple substitution ciphers are vulnerable to a "ciphertext-only" attack, using single letter frequency distributions. By comparing the letter frequencies in a given ciphertext with the expected frequencies, a cryptanalyst can match the ciphertext letters with plaintext letters. Use of digram and trigram distributions will lead to better results. Ciphers based on shifted alphabets are also easy to solve, since there is a constant distance between each ciphertext letter and its corresponding plaintext letter. Ciphers based on affine transformations can be compromised as well, even though they appear more difficult to break.

Two automatic methods for breaking substitution ciphers are presented here. It is to be noted that we are concerned with "ciphertext-only" attack.

Let Σ be an alphabet consisting of letters in Tamil. Formally, a substitution cipher is a code in which every letter of Σ in the message $M = m_1\ m_2\ \ldots\ m_n$ is replaced consistently by another letter to give the coded message

$C = c_1\ c_2\ \ldots\ c_n$. A key for subtitution cipher is a transformation $k:\Sigma \longrightarrow \Sigma$ such that $M=k(c_1)\ k(c_2)\ \ldots k(c_n)$. To decrypt such messages, manual methods primarily based on the unigram and digram frequencies are well-known.

Both the methods discussed here are iterative in nature and such procedures start with an initial key, the choice of which is left to the cryptanalyst. One can choose a random key but the methods work better (i.e., converge faster) if unigram frequencies are used to obtain the initial key. A more powerful digram frequency analysis is made to improve the key successively.

<u>Method 1</u>: Relaxation algorithms are iterative parallel classification algorithms, originally introduced in image processing.[9)] Algorithms of this type have also been designed for use in cryptography. We present here a relaxation algorithm that is an adaptation of a procedure developed and implemented by Peleg[8)] in image processing and by Peleg and Rosenfeld[10)] in cryptography.

Let $X_i (i = 1,2,\ldots,n)$ be the random variable corresponding to every ciphertext letter $c_i \in \Sigma$ with an associated probability vector, specifying the probabilities of c_i being different plaintext letters. As discussed earlier, an initial key can be constructed on the basis of unigram frequencies. The probability vectors of these key letters $P_i^{(0)} : \Sigma \longrightarrow [0,1]$ are estimated for every random variable X_i. Digram frequencies of plaintext letters obtained from a large sample of ordinary Tamil texts are used to update these vectors.

Let $P_i(X_i = \alpha) = \text{Prob}(X_i = \alpha / P_i)$ be the conditional probability that the cipher letter c_i is α

given that the probability vector associated with c_i is P_i. Also let $P_i^{(k)}$ be the updated probability vector P_i at the k-th iteration. The procedure for obtaining $P_i^{(k+1)}$ from $P_i^{(k)}$ is described below.

$$\text{Define} \quad r_{ij}(\alpha,\beta) = \frac{\text{Prob}(X_i = \alpha,\ X_j = \beta)}{\text{Prob}(X_i = \alpha)\ \text{Prob}(X_j = \beta)}$$

These r_{ij}'s are the coefficients which are used in updating the probabilities P_i. We note that $r_{ij}(\alpha,\beta)$ remains constant during the entire updating process as they are computed on the basis of unigram and digram frequencies obtained from a sample of Tamil texts.

$\text{Prob}(X_i = \alpha / P_i, P_j)$ at the (n+1)-st iteration is given by

$$P_{ij}^{(n+1)}(X_i=\alpha) = \frac{\sum_{\beta\in\Sigma} P_i^{(n)}(X_i=\alpha)\ P_j^{(n)}\ (X_j=\beta)\ r_{ij}(\alpha,\beta)}{\sum_{\lambda\in\Sigma}\sum_{\beta\in\Sigma} P_i^{(n)}\ (X_i=\alpha)\ P_j^{(n)}(X_j=\beta)\ r_{ij}^{(\alpha,\lambda)}}$$

where $P_i^{(0)}$ is the initial estimate for the probability distribution of X_i.

$\text{Prob}(X_i = \alpha / P_i)$ at the (k+1)-st iteration is obtained from $P_i^{(k+1)}(X_i=\alpha) = \sum W_j\ P_{ij}^{(k+1)}(X_i=\alpha)$, where the summation is over all j's for which the pairs c_ic_j occur in the ciphertext and W_j's are weights such that

$\sum W_j = 1$. Peleg[8] has shown that a simple average with equal weights given to all the letters occurring next to c_i produce good results.

For every iteration, a key $K^{(n)}$ is constructed from $P^{(n)}$ such that $K^{(n)}(\alpha) = \beta$ if $P_\alpha{}^{(n)}(\beta)$ is the maximal element in $P_\alpha{}^{(n)}$. We note that the number of elements in $K^{(n)}$ which agrees with K usually increases with the number of iterations performed. The iteration process is terminated when the difference between $P_i{}^{(k+1)}$ and $P_i{}^{(k)}$ becomes negligible.

Method 2: The basic idea of this method is to make repeated pairwise changes to the initial key, leading to a final key close or equal to the actual key.[7] At every iteration, the plain letters assigned to two randomly selected cipher letters are interchanged and digram frequencies are computed. If the new digram frequencies based on these changes is closer to the standard digram frequencies the key is changed.

Performance of the procedure can be assessed in terms of the following measures :

(i) percentage of letters of the key correctly recovered

(ii) percentage of plaintexts correctly recovered.

While the computation of the first one is straightforward, that of the second is as follows:

With SM denoting the event of successfully recovering the coded message, let $p_\alpha(SM)$ be the probability that at least α percent of the plaintext is recovered as the result of cryptanalysis. It is customary to take α to be 90.

By deliberately introducing randomness in the choice of key letters to be interchanged, we can ensure that the probability of repeated analyses of a given cryptotext producing the same path to a solution is low. In that case successive iterations of the algorithm can be considered statistically independent events and therefore the probability of success can be improved by increasing the number of trials. We assume that the number of trials is decided in advance and the probability of success at each trial is constant. Thus the distribution of the number of successful trials is given by the binomial distribution. It follows that if x is the number of successful attacks in n trials, x/n can be used as an estimate of $p_\alpha(SM)$ where x/n follows binomial distribution.

Confidence limits for $p_\alpha(SM)$ can be obtained as

$$\text{Prob}(\ a \leq p_\alpha(SM) \leq b\ ) = r$$

where $a = x / (\ x + (\ n - x + 1)\ F_r)$

$b = (x+1) F'_r \ / \ ((n + x) + (x + 1)\ F'_r)$

r = chosen level of confidence

F_r and F'_r are distributed as F variates with $[2(n-x+1),2x]$ and $[2(x+1),2(n-x)]$ degrees of freedom respectively.[2)]

For better results trials can be grouped. Let $p_\alpha(SM,m)$ be the probability that at least α percent of the plaintext is recovered in at least one out of m repeated trials of the analysis. Then $p_\alpha(SM,m)$ can be approximated from $p_\alpha(SM)$ as

$$p_\alpha(SM,1) = p_\alpha(SM) \quad \text{and}$$

$$p_\alpha(SM,m) = 1 - (1 - p_\alpha(SM,1))^m$$

Although the two methods presented here are simple in structure, they have been successfully used to break substitution ciphers. Only unigram and digram frequencies of letters of Tamil alphabet are required to implement them. While unigram statistics are useful in choosing a good intial key, the updating procedure is based on the digram frequencies. As mentioned earlier, data on these have been computed from a random sample of long Tamil texts.

5. STREAM CIPHER BASED ON CELLULAR AUTOMATA

The weakness of many of the classical systems is due to the fact that the same key is repeated several times. By simple modifications, most of these could be made secure. If the key length is permitted to be as long as the message itself, a perfectly secure stream cipher can be constructed. In a Vernam cipher, the plaintext which is a binary sequence is superimposed by a binary key sequence via addition modulo 2. When the key sequence is generated at random, the transmitter and the receiver apply it only once and the cipher is theoretically unbreakable. Such a system is called a one-time pad and is constructed as follows. Let M be the plaintext message $m_1\ m_2\ \ldots\ m_n$ where each m_i is expressed as a binary digit. The key is a random sequence of binary digits $K = k_1\ k_2\ \ldots\ k_n$. Encryption is done as $M \oplus K = C$ and the decryption as $C \oplus K = M$ where $\oplus$ is the XOR operator defined as

$$(a+b) \bmod 2 = a \oplus b = \begin{cases} 0 & \text{if } a = b \\ 1 & \text{if } a \neq b \end{cases}$$

where a and b are binary digits. Subtraction is as follows:

$$(a-b) \bmod 2 = (a+b-2) \bmod 2 = (a+b) \bmod 2 = a \oplus b$$

The operator $\oplus$ is extended pairwise to bit strings and we can write $C = M \oplus K$ to denote the sum of (or difference between) M and K.

We now construct a stream cipher for Tamil using cellular automata, a brief discussion of which is presented first.

Cellular automata have been used as models of computation and also investigated extensively in studies of the origin of randomness in physical sciences. The one dimensional cellular automaton consists of a linear array of sites, each site carrying a value in $\{0, 1, \ldots, k-1\}$. The value a_i of the site at each position i is updated in discrete time steps according to an identical deterministic rule depending on r sites in the neighbourhood

$$a_i^{(t+1)} = \phi[\, a_{i-r}^{(t)}, a_{i-r+1}^{(t)}, \ldots, a_{i+r}^{(t)}]$$

If we consider the patterns generated by cellular automata growing from simple seeds consisting of a few non-zero sites, some local rules give rise to simple behaviour, while others produce complicated patterns.[6] Different initial states with a specific cellular automaton rule yield patterns that differ in detail, but are similar in form and statistical properties. Different cellular automaton rules yield very different patterns. An extensive empirical study suggests that the patterns take on four qualitative forms, (i) disappears with time, (ii) evolves to a fixed finite size, (iii) grows indefinitely at a fixed speed (iv) grows and contracts irregularly.[17] Most cellular automaton rules have the important feature of irreversibility: several different configurations may evolve to a single configuration, and with time, a contracting subset of possible configurations appears.

In particular, when k=2, each cell of the cellular automaton has a value a_i equal to 0 or 1. The values are updated according to the rule

$$a_i^{(t+1)} = a_{i-1}^{(t)} \text{ XOR } (a_i^{(t)} \text{ OR } a_{i+1}^{(t)})$$

or equivalently,

$$a_i^{(t+1)} = (a_{i-1}^{(t)} + a_i^{(t)} + a_{i+1}^{(t)} + a_i^{(t)}\, a_{i+1}^{(t)}) \bmod 2$$

A stream cipher based on this simple one-dimensional cellular automaton is discussed by Wolfram.[18] The initial state of the register is used as a seed or key. The values $a^{(t)}$ attained by a particular cell can then serve as a random sequence which shows no statistical regularities for sequences of length upto 2^{19}. Ciphertext $C = c_1\ c_2\ \dots\ c_n$ can be obtained from binary plaintext $P = m_1\ m_2\ \dots\ m_n$ as $c_t = m_t \oplus a^{(t)}$, $t = 1, ?, \dots, n$, and the plaintext can be recovered by repeating the same operation only if the sequence $a^{(t)}$ is known.

In order to construct the stream cipher for Tamil, the thirty-letter alphabet as explained in the earlier sections is considered. The plaintext over the thirty letter alphabet is converted into a sequence of bits, making use of Huffman code (see Table 1), which assigns shorter sequences to more frequent letters in an unambiguous manner. Thus maximum efficiency and unique decipherment are ensured. Now the random key sequence in bits, generated by the cellular automaton as explained above, is added modulo 2 to the plaintext message in bits. This stream cipher is secure. Encryption and decryption are fairly straightforward and easy since this cellular automaton can be implemented efficiently on an integrated circuit.

The security of such a cryptosystem relies on the difficulty of finding the seed from a time sequence of cell values and this problem is known to be in the class **NP**. In other words, no systematic algorithm for its solution is currently known that takes less than exponential time. No statistical regularities have been found in sequences shorter than the cycle length.

Alternatively, the alphabet can be taken to consist of all the 247 letters. Numerical equivalents for the 19 x 13 letters are given as follows: The first twelve letters listed in the first column of Table 1, which represent vowels, are given numbers sequentially from 1 to 12. Similarly, the next eighteen letters in the Table, which represent consonants, are numbered 1 through 18 sequentially. A zero is included in both the lists.

Each letter of the alphabet can now be represented by a pair (i,j), i = 0, 1, ..., 18, j = 0, 1, ..., 12. The pair (0,0) represents the auxiliary symbol <u>aitham</u>. The pairs (0,j), j = 1, 2, ..., 12 represent the set of all vowels. The pairs (i,0), i = 1, 2, ..., 18 represent the set of all consonants. The pair (i,j), i=1, 2, ..., 18, j = 1, 2, ..., 12 represents the consonant-vowel combination i+j. For example, the pairs (0,1), (1,0) and (1,1) stand for <u>a</u>, <u>k</u> and <u>ka</u> respectively.

This is a simple way of conversion, to ensure that we get the first coordinate of the pair to run through values 0 to 18 and the second coordinate of the pair to run through the values 0 to 12. It helps us to use computation in the Galois fields GF(19) and GF(13). We can now select two cellular automata-one to encrypt the first coordinate and the other for the second coordinate.

As before, each cellular automaton consists of N sites arranged around a circle (so as to give periodic boundary conditions). The values of the sites at time step t are denoted by $a_0^{(t)}, \ldots, a_{N-1}^{(t)}$. The possible site values are taken to be elements of Z_k (the residue class modulo k), in which case site values are conveniently represented as integers modulo k. For the construction of the cryptosystem for Tamil, we choose two cellular automata- one with k = 19 and the other with k = 13.

The complete configuration of a cellular automaton is specified by the values of its N sites and represented by a characteristic polynomial $a^{(t)}(x) = \sum_i a_i^{(t)} x^i$, where the value of site i is the coefficient of x^i and all coefficients are elements of $\mathbf{Z}_k$, k=19 or k=13. Configurations are referred to by their corresponding characteristic polynomials. Thus each plaintext message over a 247 - letter alphabet in Tamil is considered as a sequence of pairs (i,j), i=0, 1, ..., 18, j=0, 1, ..., 12 and represented by a pair of characteristic polynomials (A(x), B(x)), A(x) with coefficients in $\mathbf{Z}_{19}$ and B(x) with coefficients in $\mathbf{Z}_{13}$.

The register size N is chosen to be very large so as to include all possible plaintext lengths or, as is customary, the plaintext message may be divided into blocks of length less than or equal to N. There are two possibilities open. Additive cellular automata, in which the value of a site is given by a linear combination (in $\mathbf{Z}_k$) of the values at sites on the previous time step, are selected and the irreversibility of the cellular automata is then exploited for choice of the key, encryption and decryption procedures. Alternatively, very general "non-additive" cellular automata (such as the one chosen earlier for the stream ciphers) in which the value of site i at time t, $a_i^{(t)}$, is an arbitrary function over $\mathbf{Z}_k$, not reducible to linear form, may be selected. The choice of the cellular automata over Z_{19} and Z_{13} should be such that the random sequence formed by the values of $a_i^{(t)}$ obtained from a particular cell i, shows no statistical regularities. Then two random sequences of keys namely $k_1\ k_2 \ldots$ over $\mathbf{Z}_{19}$ and $k_1'\ k_2' \ldots$ over $\mathbf{Z}_{13}$ are generated and applied to the sequence of pairs (m_i, m_i') of the plaintext. The cryptotext is the sequence of pairs (c_i, c_i') where $c_i = (m_i + k_i) \bmod 19$, $c_i' = (m_i' + k_i') \bmod 13$. The sequence of plaintext pairs is obtained easily by taking $m_i = (c_i - k_i) \bmod 19$ and $m_i' = (c_i' - k_i') \bmod 13$. This is possible only if the keys (which are random sequences) are known. Thus the system is secure and encryption and decryption are simple and efficient, based directly on the plaintext message in Tamil.

This has opened up a new area of application of cellular automata to the development of cryptosystems in Tamil. We have made only a small beginning and further work needs to be done in the choice of the arbitrary cellular automata, the corresponding analysis and its suitability for use in cryptosystems.

6. CONCLUSION

Based on Tamil studies initiated by Siromoney in the early sixties, we have given methods of breaking cryptosystems of the substitution type. Frequency distributions are useful in such cryptanalytic attacks and details of the required database are discussed. A stream cipher for Tamil, making use of a thirty-letter alphabet, based on a cellular automaton is constructed. For the 247 (19×13) - letter alphabet, methods of constructing cryptosystems based on cellular automata over $\mathbf{Z}_k$, the field of integer modulo k, $k = 19$, $k = 13$ are indicated. This opens up an interesting and challenging area of research and further work needs to be done in the construction of safe and efficient cryptosystems for Tamil.

REFERENCES

1. Denning, D.E.R., "Cryptography and Data Security", Addison-Wesley, Reading (1983).

2. Gallagher, R., "Information Theory and Reliable Communication", Wiley, New York (1968).

3. Huq, A., "Computer Analysis of the Indus Script", Ph.D. Thesis, University of Madras (1988).

4. Koblitz, N., "A Course in Number Theory and Cryptography", Graduate Texts in Mathematics, Springer-Verlag, New York (1987).

5. Mahadevan, I., "The Indus Script: Texts, Concordance and Tables", Memoirs of the Archaeological Survey of India, No.77, New Delhi (1977).

6. Martin, O., Odlyzko, A.M. and Wolfram, S., "Algebraic properties of cellular automata", Communications in Mathematical Physics, 93, pp. 219-258 (1984).

7. Matyas,S.M. and Meyer, C.H., "Cryptography: A New Dimension in Computer Data Security ", A guide for the design and implementation of secure systems, Cryptography Competency Center, IBM Corporation, Kingston, New York (1982).

8. Peleg,S., "A new probabilistic relaxation scheme", TR-711, University of Maryland, College Park (1978).

9. Peleg, S., and Rosenfeld, A., "Determining compatibility coefficients for curve enhancement relaxation procedure", IEEE Transanctions on Systems, Man and Cybernetics, SMC-8 pp. 548-555 (1978).

10. Peleg,S. and Rosenfeld, A.,"Breaking substitution ciphers using a relaxation algorithm", Communications of the Association for Computing Machinery, 22, pp. 598-605 (1979).

11. Salomaa,A., "The formal language theory column", Bulletin of the European Association for Theoretical Computer Science,No.33, pp. 42-53 (1987).

12. Salomaa,A., "The formal language theory column", Bulletin of the European Association for Theoretical Computer Science, No.35, pp. 92-97 (1988).

13. Siromoney, G., "Cryptography in Tamil", (in Tamil), Unpublished manuscript (1961).

14. Siromoney,G., "Entropy of Tamil prose", Information Control, 6, pp. 297-300 (1963).

15. Siromoney,G., "On Certain Applications of Information Theory", Ph.D Thesis, University of Madras (1964).

16. Siromoney,G., and Huq, Abdul, "Segmentation of Indus Texts: a dynamic programming approach", Computers and the Humanities, 22, pp. 11-21 (1988).

17. Wolfram,S., "Cellular automata as models of complexity", Nature, 311, pp. 419-424 (1984).

18. Wolfram,S.,"Cryptography with cellular automata", Proceedings of Advances in Cryptology, CRYPTO'85, Lecture Notes in Computer Science, 218, Williams, H.C. (Ed.), pp. 429-432 (1985).

Table 1. Details of Tamil letters and their corresponding codes

LETTER	TRANS-LITERATION	RELATIVE FREQUENCY	HUFFMAN CODE	TELEGRAPHIC CODE
அ	a	150	101	·
ஆ	ā	47	0100	· —
இ	i	78	1101	· ·
ஈ	ī	4	01111010	— · — —
உ	u	77	1100	— —
ஊ	ū	4	011110111	— — · —
எ	e	17	011111	· — — —
ஏ	ē	13	010101	· — · —
ஐ	ai	27	01100	· · · ·
ஒ	o	10	000100	· — — ·
ஓ	ō	7	0111100	— · — ·
ஔ	au	0	0111101100	· — · ·
க்	k	79	1110	—
ங்	ṅ	6	0101000	· · — —

Table 1. (contd.)

LETTER	TRANS-LITERATION	RELATIVE FREQUENCY	HUFFMAN CODE	TELEGRAPHIC CODE
ச்	c	22	00011	. . . —
ஞ்	ñ	1	0111101101	. . — .
ட்	ṭ	36	10001	. — —
ண்	ṇ	11	000101	— . . —
த்	t	71	1001	— .
ந்	n	21	00000	— . . .
ப்	p	44	0010	— — —
ம்	m	42	11111	. — .
ய்	y	29	01101	. . —
ர்	r	45	0011	. . .
ல்	l	31	01110	— — .
வ்	v	35	10000	— . —
ழ்	l̤	7	0101001	— — . .
ள்	ḷ	21	00001	— — — .
ற்	r̤	27	01011	— — — —
ன்	n̤	38	11110	— . .

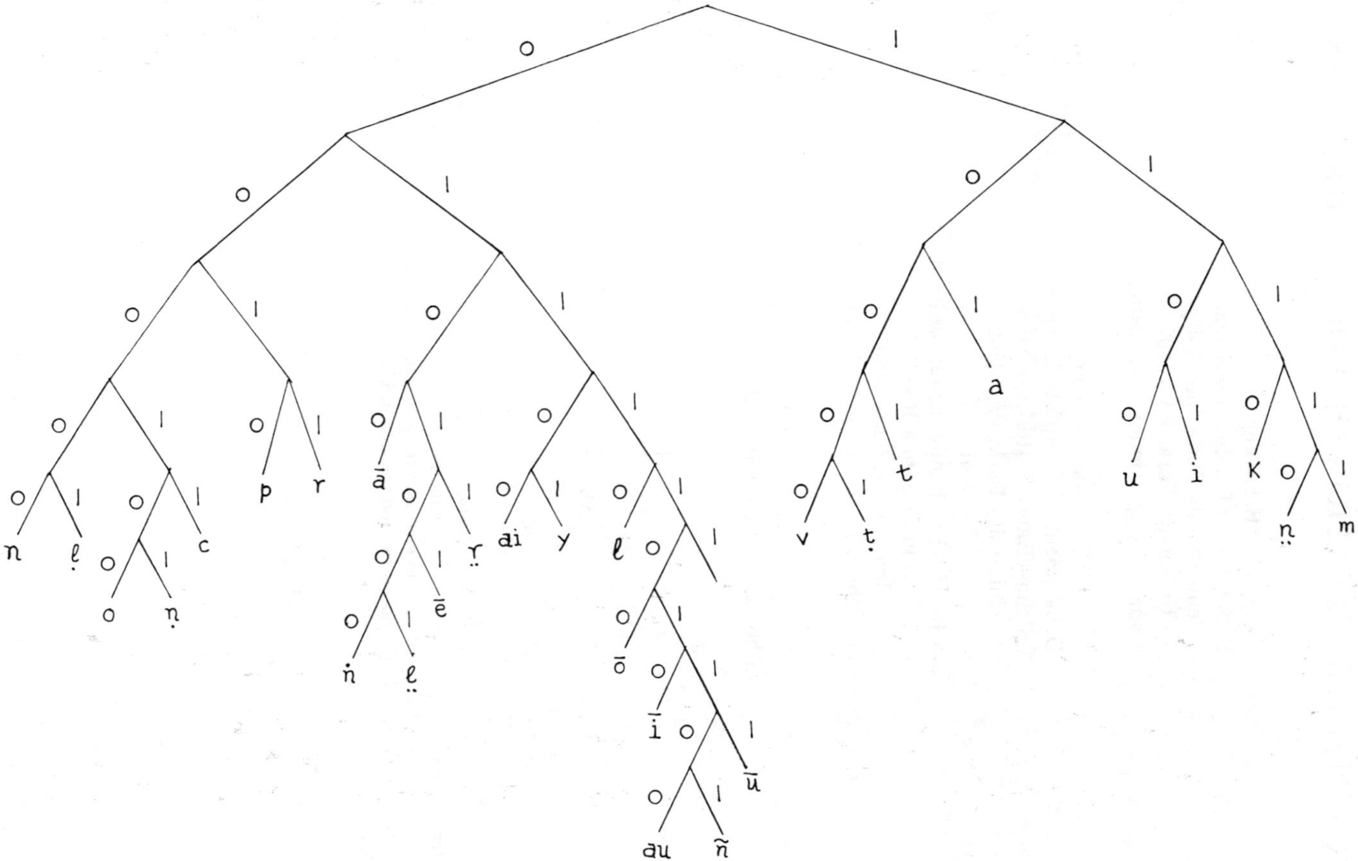

Fig. 1. Huffman decoding tree

PROVING TERMINATION OF LOGIC PROGRAMS

Bal Wang
Department of Computer Science
Pennsylvania State University
University Park, PA 16802
e-mail: wang@gondor.cs.psu.edu

R.K. Shyamasundar
Department of Computer Science
Pennsylvania State University
University Park, PA 16802
and
Tata Institute of Fundamental Research
Homi Bhabha Road
Bombay 400 005, India
e-mail: shyam@shire.cs.psu.edu or shakti!uunet!tifr!root

in honour of Professor Gift Siromoney

Abstract

In this paper, we provide an approach for proving the termination of logic programs. First, we introduce U-Graphs as an abstraction of logic programs and establish that SLDNF derivations can be realized by instances of paths in the U-graph. Such a relation enables us to confine ourselves to U-graphs for establishing the *universal termination* of logic programs. In our method, we associate pre- and post-assertions to the nodes of the graph and *ordered assertions* to selected edges of the graph. With this as the basis, we develop a method for establishing the termination in a simple way.

1 Introduction

One of the most important features of logic programming is its declarative semantics. In other words, one can consider the programs to be self-specifying as they are non-procedural, and hence do not need elaborate correctness proofs. However, certain properties of logic programs are inexpressible in terms of their declarative semantics. For example, the programmers use informal reasoning of programs such as form of procedure calls, success patterns of terms etc. These properties are inexpressible in terms of the declarative semantics [DM88]. However, the termination of logic programs needs a formal correctness proof whether one considers the logic programs to be self-specifying or not. In other words, what is needed for logic programming is the development of a sound methodology for developing correct logic programs. Though this problem has been dealt by researchers under various topics such as transformation-, modular- and verification of logic programs, there has not been a significant development that leads to a methodology for the development of logic programs.

When considering termination, there are two possible interpretations. One interpretation is that a program terminates iff it either fails finitely or produces a successful derivation. This is referred to as *existential termination*. An alternative necessary and sufficient criterion for termination is that all program derivations are finite. This is referred to as *universal termination* [VaP86].

In other words, the above definitions correspond to finding one and every solution of a program respectively. A property of universal termination is that it is sensitive only to the computation rule (i.e., subgoal selection rule) unlike the former which depends on the clause selection rule (i.e., search rule). Francez et al. [FGKP85] formulate proof rules for proving the *existential* termination of Prolog programs based on the notion of parameterized invariants for guarded commands. Basically, they seek for a well-founded variant function that is decreasing on the sequence of computation states. This approach appears to be unduly complicated, as one has to use the proof rules for describing the execution behavior of the interpreter to reason about the termination of the program. The proofs of even very simple programs become very complex with such an approach.

Floyd [Flo67] established the fundamental connection between termination proofs of programs and well-founded sets. From Floyd's connection, it follows that any method of showing termination [1] involves the discovery of a well-founded set with respect to a given set of initial assertions. In this paper, we show how the discovery of well-founded ordering can be localized by considering the structure of the U-graph of a program and thus, leading to a simple method. The basis of the method can be informally captured as follows: Let $A_0 \leftarrow A_1, A_2, ..., A_n$ be a clause of the given program. When this clause is used in a SLDNF derivation, it corresponds to replacing the current subgoal unifying with A_0 with mgu θ by the set of goals $(A_1, ..., A_n)\theta$. Thus, in order to prove universal termination, we have to show that all the subgoals $A_1\theta, ..., A_n\theta$ terminate. That is, each subgoal can give rise to only a finite SLDNF tree (irrespective of whether the goal succeeds

[1] irrespective of whether the program is deterministic, nondeterministic, backtracking etc.

or fails). If a subgoal, say A_i, is not recursive, then the termination can be guaranteed in an easy way. However, if it is recursive, we have to show that there is a bound on the number of subgoals it can give rise to. Recursive predicates can be identified by looking at cycles of the graph. To establish this property ordered assertions are provided for a selected set of signed edges that belong to cycles of the U-graph. Using this set of assertions, we describe a method of showing the termination of logic programs relative to the pre- and post-assertions of the nodes of the U-graph. The reasons as to why we do not need assertions for every signed-edge and why there is no need for providing ordered assertions for the u-edges of the graph will become clear after we describe the method. In short, we are able to establish the termination by using ordered assertions on parts of the cycles of the U-graph. Such an approach has two advantages: first, the effort of finding a well-founded order is localized and second, the localization property enables us to use some of the techniques of term-rewriting [2] (cf. [Der85]), for arriving at ordered assertions. In short, our approach provides a methodology for establishing the universal termination of logic programs in a simple way. Note that universal termination is important as even in deductive databases backtracking for the next solution is used very often. In other words, the method based on the U-graph formulation provides a nice simple method for proving the termination of logic programs.

The paper is organized as follows: We introduce U-graphs in section 2; section 3 introduces the specification language of assertions. The method is described with an example in section 4. In section 5, we establish the formal correctness of the method followed by a discussion of the method.

2 U-graphs

In this section, we introduce the main tool, U-graph, for analyzing logic programs. Later we also establish the relationship between U-graphs and SLDNF derivations by introducing *g-tree* which connects a path in the U-graph and a sub-derivation of a given SLDNF derivation.

In the literature various classes of normal programs (cf. [Lly87]) are abstracted by signed dependency graphs. In the signed dependency graph, only predicate symbols are considered as vertex set and the set of edges are those pairs $< p, q >$, where p is the predicate symbol of a clause C and q is the predicate symbol of a literal occurring in the body of C. In a sense, the relation is obtained by removing the arguments of each literal in each clause of normal programs. The construct is a succinct abstraction to characterize normal programs. However, it discards too much information which is useful to characterize normal programs in a more precise way. In this section, we introduce U-graphs as an abstraction of a normal program that has more information than the signed dependency graph abstraction.

[2] Conditional narrowing of logic programs does not permit in general the techniques of termination of term-rewriting systems to be used for establishing the termination of logic programs.

Without loss of generality, we assume that there are no common variables between any two clauses in a given normal program. In any clause C, we consider the head and the literals in the body of C as distinct literals; we resort to subscripting the literals whenever one literal appears more than once in the clause. For example, consider the clause
$p(s(X)) \leftarrow p(s(X)), \neg p(X)$
In this clause, all literals have the same predicate symbol p, and there are two identical literals. In order to distinguish them, we subscript the whole clause as follows:
$p_h(s(X)) \leftarrow p_{b,1}(s(X)), \neg p_{b,2}(X)$
If the context is clear, we omit the subscripts.

Definition 1(U-graph): Given a normal program P, the *U-graph* U(V,E) of P is a directed graph, where the set of vertices V is the bag of all atoms occurring in P, and edge $< A, B > \in$ E if either
(1) there is a clause of the form $A \leftarrow ...B, ...,$ (or $A \leftarrow ..., \neg B, ...$); in this case, the edge is signed by +1 (or -1) and we call it a positive (or negative) edge, or
(2) there are two clauses C_1, C_2 such that A (or ¬A) occurs in the body of C_1, B is the head of C_2, and A unifies to B; in this case the edge is signed by the mgu of A and B and is called an u-edge.

Given a normal program P, let V_H denote the set of all heads in all clauses in P, and V_B denote all atoms occurring in the bodies of all clauses in P. Clearly, $V = V_H \cup V_B$.

Remarks:

1. All in-edges of a vertex in V_H (V_B) must be from some vertices in V_B (V_H), and all out-edges of a vertex in V_B (V_H) must be leading to vertices in V_H (V_B). Hence, every path in a U-graph consists of vertices in V_H and V_B alternately.
2. Each cycle has even length.
3. In fact, a vertex A in V represents a set of variant of A without any common variable. If $H_1, B_1, ..., H_n$ is a path in the U-graph, and $H_{i_1}, ..., H_{i_k}$ correspond to some vertex H $\in V_H$, say the head of clause C, then for all $1 \leq j \leq k$, H_{i_j} are variants of H, and B_{i_j} is obtained by applying the renaming substitution σ, such that $H\sigma = H_{i_j}$ (by (1), B_{i_j} is in the body of clause C).
4. The notion of U-graphs has some resemblence to the notion of *connection graphs* [Nil82]. It may be noted that the purpose of connection graphs is to provide a template for generating the AND/OR solution tree for the problem on hand; however, the purpose of the U-graphs is to capture the static information of the logic program as far as possible.

Example: Let P be a normal program defined by
p(f(X)) ← q(X, Y), r(s(X))
q(s(X), X) ← ¬ p(X), r(X)
r(a) ←
r(s(X)) ← ¬r(X)

The U-graph of P is shown in Figure 1.

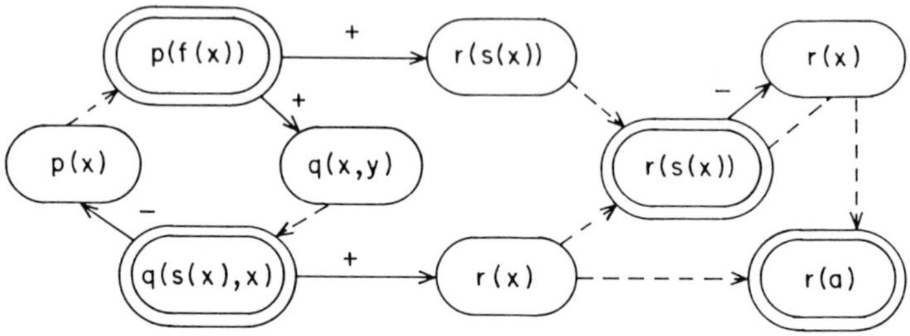

Figure 1

It may be noted that if there are no u-edges, then the graph would be acyclic. In other words, there would be only finite SLDNF derivations.

Before describing the method, we introduce the specification language of assertions on the lines of the language in [DM88].

3 Specification Language for Assertions

Our method of establishing termination requires assertions for the nodes of the program. The specification language for the assertion is defined below.

Definition 2(The Specification Language for Assertions):

1. *Variables*:

   a We use variables for representing the variable corresponding to each of the arguments of a literal. We use the notation i.A and A.i to represent the variable corresponding to the ith argument of the atom A at invocation, and after invocation respectively.

   b Terms *T, U, V*,...

2. *n-ary function symbols* (n $\geq$ 0):

   a n-ary function symbols of the object languages.

   b variables of the object language: X, Y, Z,... (n=0).

   Note that the interpretation of a function symbol corresponding to (a) and (b) is the function symbol itself.

3. *Terms*: standard definition.

4. *Predicate Symbols*: =, var, ground, $\lhd$, $\approx$,... The interpretation of these predicates is given below:

   - = term equality.
   - var(T) iff T is a (object language) variable.
   - ground(T) iff T is a (object language) ground term.
   - T$\lhd$ U iff T is a proper sub-term of U.
   - $T \approx$ U iff the terms T and U are variants of each other (they differ at most in the names of their variables).
   - disconnected($V_1, ..., V_n$) iff no variable occurs in more than one of the terms in $\{V_1, ..., V_n\}$.
   - subterm(T, U, I) iff T $\lhd$ U and I is the corresponding selector (assuming any fixed way of assigning selectors to subterm occurrences).

5. Logical *connectives* and *quantifiers*: *true*, *false*, $\wedge$, $\vee$, $\Rightarrow$,...

6. *formulas*: standard definition.

For any node in the U-graph corresponding to a literal, say A, an assertion $< F^b, F^a >$ can be attached with the interpretation that F^b is the pre-assertion and F^a is the post-assertion. Note that F^b is a formula which contains only the variables of the form i.A where i ranges over all the argument positions of A. However, F^a is a formula containing variables of the form i.A or A.i where i ranges over all the argument positions of A.

(8) For any signed edge $< A, B >$, an *ordered assertion* $< w_{(AB)}, w_B >$ can be attached, where $w_{(AB)}$ and w_B are partial mappings from the set of all substitutions to a well-founded ordered set W with least element 0, such that if $w_{(AB)}(\theta) > 0$ for some substitution θ, then there is some substitution δ such that $w_B(\theta\delta)$ is defined.

Note: It must be noted that certain characteristics of the program cannot be represented in the U-graph. For instance, the relations of shared variables among the literals in the body of a clause is not available in the U-graph. However, the assertion language is rich enough to carry this information without any loss. If a signed edge $< A, B >$ is applied in a derivation, i.e., Bθ becomes the selected subgoal, for some substitution *theta*, it is only then that the assertion attached to A becomes applicable. With this as the basis, one can find a proper ordering of the literals in the body of a clause based on the generator-consumer concept to fit the computation rule used by an interpreter.

Notation: Let A be a vertex in V, $< A, B_1 >, ..., < A, B_n >$ be the out-edges of A, and $< F^b, F^a >, < F_1^b, F_1^a >, ..., < F_n^b, F_n^a >$ be the assertions attached to A, $B_1, ..., B_n$ respectively, then we call the ordered set $\{ < F^b, F^a >, < F_1^b, F_1^a >, ..., < F_n^b, F_n^a > \}$ the *A-set* of A.

Having described the specification language of assertions, we describe the method of proving termination in the following section.

4 Method for Proving the Termination of Logic Programs

Let U be the U-graph of the given logic program P. In the following definition, we consider the properties to be satisfied by the assertions attached to the nodes of the U-graph for consistency.

Definition 3: Let A $= p(t_1, ..., t_n)$ be an atom with attached assertion $< F^a,\ F^b >$, and θ be a substitution. The function *val* takes formulas F^b and θ to the truth value of $F^b[1.A/t_1\theta, ..., n.A/t_n\theta]$, and takes formula F^a and θ to the truth value of $F^a[1.A/t_1\theta, ..., n.A/\theta, A.1/t_1\theta\delta, ..., A.n/t_n\theta\delta]$ where δ is an answer of $goal \leftarrow A\theta$. Here, we use the usual substitution notation $F[x_1/s_1, ..., x_n/s_n]$ to stand for the substitution of free variables x_i by s_i.

In the following definition, we consider the properties to be satisfied by the assertions attached to the nodes of the U-graph for consistency. Thus, the definition considers the whole clause.

Definition 4: Given a normal program P with U-graph U(V, E), let A_0 be a vertex in V_H, $< A_0, A_1 >, ..., < A_0, A_n >$ be the out-edges of A_0. The A-set $\{ < F_0^b, F_0^a >, < F_1^b, F_1^a >, ..., < F_n^b, F_n^a > \}$ of A_0 is said to be a *consistent* with order $< i_1, ..., i_n >$ if $< i_1, ..., i_n >$ is a permutation of $< 1, ..., n >$ such that, for any substitution θ

$$val(F_0^b, \theta) \wedge (\wedge_{j=1}^{k-1} val(F_{i_j}^a, \theta\delta_1...\delta_{j-1})) \Rightarrow val(F_{i_k}^b, \theta\delta_1...\delta_{k-1}) \tag{1}$$

where $\delta_1, ..., \delta_{k-1}$ are the answer substitutions of the subgoals $A_{i_1}\theta, ..., A_{i_{k-1}}\theta\delta_1...\delta_{k-2}$, and

$$val(F_0^b, \theta) \wedge (\wedge_{i=1}^{n} val(F_i^a, \theta\delta)) \Rightarrow val(F_0^a, \theta\delta) \tag{2}$$

where $\delta = \delta_1...\delta_n$.

Note: If n $= 0$, i.e., $A_0 = p(t_1, ..., t_n)$ is the head of a unit clause, then formula (2) corresponds to

$$val(F_0^b, \theta) \Rightarrow val(F_0^a, \theta) \tag{3}$$

and there is no condition corresponding to (1).

Essentially, relation (1) shows that if the subgoal A_j in the clause depends on the variables of some subset of the literals in the clause, say $\{A_0, A_{i_1}, ..., A_{i_m}\}$ then the pre-assertion of A_0 after unification (say through θ) with the goal together with the post-assertions of A_{i_k} for $1 \leq k \leq m$ should imply the pre-assertion of A_j. with respect to θ. The permutation order can be understood in an easy way if we consider the special case of moding of the clauses or program [3]. In the case of moding, we have to make sure that there is partial ordering of the subgoals. The checking for acyclicity of the moding can be achieved as a special case of (1). If it is a Prolog clause then (1) becomes

$$val(F_0^b, \theta) \wedge (\wedge_{j=1}^{k-1} val(F_j^a, \theta\delta_1...\delta_{k-1})) \Rightarrow val(F_k^b, \theta\delta_1...\delta_{k-1})$$

Relation (2) shows that the pre-assertion of A_0 and the post-assertions of all the subgoals A_i in the body of the clause whose head is A_0 with respect to θ and δ should imply the post-assertion of the head of the clause with respect to θ and δ. Note that θ can be considered as the answer substitution from the body.

In the following, we consider the assertions attached to the edges of the graph. As mentioned already, assertions are attached to only signed edges. No assertion is attached to a unification edge.

Definition 5: Let A_0 be a vertex in V_B, and $\{< A_0, A_1 >, ..., < A_0, A_n > \}$ be the set of all out-edges of A_0. We say that the A-set $\{ < F_0^b, F_0^a >, < F_1^b, F_1^a >, ..., < F_n^b, F_n^a > \}$ of A_0 is *safe* if for all substitutions θ, there exist $A_{i_1}, ..., A_{i_k}$, $k \geq 1$, which are unifiable to $A_0\theta$ with mgu $\theta_1, ..., \theta_k$, for some subset $\{i_1, ..., i_k\}$ of $\{1, ..., n\}$, then

$$\forall j, val(F_0^b, \theta) \Rightarrow val(F_{i_j}^b, \theta_j), \tag{4}$$

Let $\delta_1, ..., \delta_k$ be the answer substitutions that are passed back to the goal by the head of the clause (after success). Then,

$$\forall j, val(F_{i_j}^a, \delta_j) \Rightarrow val(F_0^a, \theta\delta_j) \tag{5}$$

The relation (4) corresponds to saying that after unifying the subgoal $A_0\theta$ with the heads of clauses, the pre-assertion of A_0 should imply the pre-assertions of the heads of clauses which with respect to their mgu's. In other words, this condition corresponds to the *enablement* of the input clauses. The relation (5), corresponds to saying that the values consistently passed by the heads of the clauses to the subgoals satisfy the post-condition of the subgoals with respect to the underlying unification θ.

Definition 6 (Safety of Ordered Assertions): Let $A_1, B_1, ..., A_n, B_n, A_1$ be a simple cycle in the graph, where $A_i \in V_H$, $B_i \in V_B$, for all $1 \leq i \leq n$. Let $< w_{(A_i\ B_i)}, w_{B_i} >$ be the ordered assertion attached to signed edge $< A_i, B_i >$, for all $1 \leq i \leq n$.
We say that the set of ordered assertions is safe if

1. Let $< A_i, D_1 >, ..., < A_i, D_m >$ be the out-edges of A_i with consistent A-set $\{< F_0^b, F_0^a >, < F_1^a, F_1^b >, ..., < F_m^b, F_m^a >\}$ with order $< r_1, ..., r_m >$, $B_i = D_{r_k}$. Let

[3]Moding can be represented by using pre-assertions specifying the arguments that are grounded.

$\delta_1, ..., \delta_{k-1}$ be the answer substitutions of subgoals $D_{r_1}(\theta)$, $D_{r_2}(\theta\delta_1)$,..., $D_{r_{k-1}}(\theta\delta_1...\delta_{k-2})$, respectively.

1.a If for all substitutions θ and for all $< A_i,\ B_i >$, then
$val(F_0^b, \theta) \wedge (\wedge_{j=1}^{k-1} val(F_{r_j}^a, \theta\delta_1...\delta_{j-1}) \wedge (w_{(A_i B_i)}(\theta) > 0)$
$\Rightarrow w_{(A_i B_i)}(\theta) \geq w_{B_i}(\theta\delta_1...\delta_{k-1})$.

1.b There is an i, $1 \leq i \leq n$,
$val(E^b, \theta) \wedge (w_{(A_i B_i)}(\theta) > 0) \Rightarrow w_{(A_i B_i)}(\theta) > w_{B_i}(\theta\delta_1...\delta_{k-1})$.
In this case, we call $< A_i, B_i >$ a *strictly decreasing edge.*

1.c If $w_{(A_i\ B_i)}(\theta) = 0$, and $< A_i, B_i >$ is a strictly decreasing edge, then there must be an h, $1 \leq h \leq k$, such that $D_{r_h}\theta\delta_1...\delta_{h-1}$ fails to unify to any vertex in V_H.

2. Let H $\in V_H$ be a vertex unifiable to $B_i\theta$ with mgu δ, for some substitution θ and $< H, D_1 >, ..., < H, D_m >$ be the out-edges of H with a safe A-set with order $< r_1, ..., r_m >$.
If $w_{B_i}(\theta) \geq 0$ then $w_{B_i}(\theta) \not< w_{(HD_i)}(\theta\delta)\ \forall D_i \ni B_i, H$, and D_i are in the same SCC.

Intuitively, (1.a) and (1.b) say that for each simple cycle, if the least element of the order assertions has not yet reached then no edge in the cycle increases order (on the well-founded set W), and there must be an edge in each cycle that strictly decreases the order. Condition (2) says that after unification, the order should not be increased and (1.c) says that when the order reaches the least element of W then derivations cannot have input clauses which carry strictly decreasing edges.

Definition 7: Given a normal program P and a *goal* $\leftarrow A_1, ..., A_m$, we construct the *extended program* $P' = P \cup \{Goal \leftarrow A_1, ..., A_m\}$, where *Goal* is a new predicate symbol having the join of all the variables as the set of arguments. The U-graph for the extended program is referred to as the extended U-graph.

4.1 Steps of the Method

As mentioned above, we denote $(W, <)$ as a well-founded set, and 0 as a generic name for representing the zero elements in W.

Let P be the given logic program P, $\leftarrow A_1, ..., A_m$ be the normal goal. Let P' be the extended program of P, $\leftarrow$ *goal* U(V, E) be the extended U-graph.
Given
1. the pre- and the post-assertions of the subgoals of the given goal,
2. the assertions at the nodes of V,
3. the ordered assertions for selected signed cyclic-edges of U,
the method establishes [4],
$\models \{true\} \leftarrow Goal\{true\}$

[4]Here, the assertion *true* corresponds to either success or failure using the computation rule satisfying the pre-assertions of the clause

provided the following conditions are satisfied:
1. The A-set of each vertex in V_B is safe.
2. The A-set of each vertex A in V_H is consistent.
3. The set of ordered assertions is safe.

The explanation for the safety and consistency of the assertion has already been given through definitions 4-5. The crucial step is the third step which establishes that the computation descends through well-founded chain. That is, if there is a cycle then there must be a signed edge $< A, B >$ in the cycle with ordered assertion $< w_{(AB)}, w_B >$ such that
$val(E^b, \theta) \wedge (w_{(A_iB_i)}(\theta) > 0) \Rightarrow w_{(A_iB_i)}(\theta) > w_{B_i}(\theta\delta_1 ... \delta_{k-1})$
where $< F_B^b, F_B^a >$ is the assertion attached to B. The above relation shows that choosing this direction corresponds to climbing down the well-founded chain. Further, it can be observed from the U-graph definition and steps 1 and 2 of the method, that at a vertex with nonzero number of outgoing edges and $w \neq 0$, the subgoal unifies to at least one head of some clause without increasing the order. From the above informal argument, one can infer the existence of a global well-founded ordering. As we are not considering the search rule, it should be clear that we establish universal termination.

If we have to use the above method for prolog programs, we need to check for the left-to-right depth-first search condition. That is, if one is considering the i-th clause of head, then one need to establish that all the i-1 clauses, which are prior to the i-th clause in the textual order, fail finitely. These aspects are discussed in [WS89a]. The definitions look complicated as we have adopted a the approach of establishing the termination of programs. Even though the definitions look complicated, the method is quite simple and practical. In fact, the definitions become quite simple if we adopt the transformational approach of transforming the program to a set of term-rewriting systems[5]. Such a transformational approach is discussed in [WS89a]. The method is illustrated by the permutation program given below.

[5]This was pointed out by Prof. Deepak Kapur of SUNY,Albany.

Example: Consider the following program Permute given below:

permute([ ],[ ]) ←
permute(T, [H | P]) ← remove(T, H, R),permute(R, P)
remove([H | L], H, L) ←
remove([B | C], D, [B | E]) ← remove(C, D, E)

Consider a goal, ← permute(s,t). The extended U-graph of Permute is shown in Figure 2.

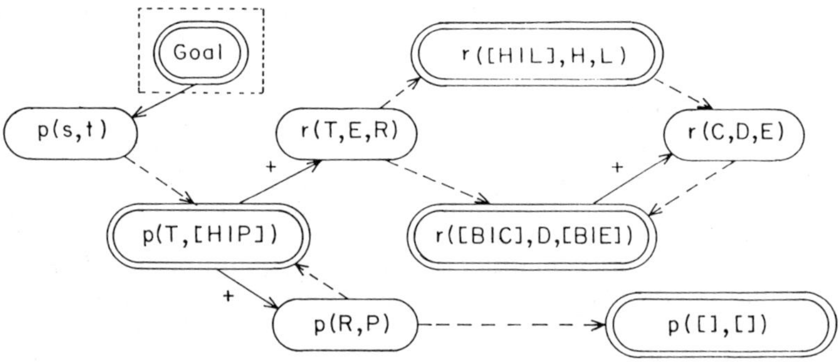

Figure 2

The assertions associated with the various nodes (using A as the general name of the node) are given below:

1. $A = Goal :< F^b, F^a >=< true, true >$
2. $A = permute(s,t) :< F^b, F^a >=< ground(1.A), true >$
3. $A = permute(T,[H|P]) :< F^b, F^a >=< ground(1.A), true >$
4. $A = r(T,H,R) :< F^b, F^a >$ *where*

$F^b = ground(1.A), F^a = [ground(A.1) \wedge ground(A.3) \wedge (A.3 \prec A.1)]$

5. $A = p(R, P) :< F^b, F^a >=< ground(1.A), true >$

6. $A = p([\,],[\,]) :< F^b, F^a >=< true, true >$

7. $A = r([B|C], D, [B|E]) :< F^b, F^a >$ *where*
   $F^b = ground(1.A), F^a = [ground(A.1) \wedge ground(A.3) \wedge (A.3 \prec A.1)]$

8. $A = r([H|L], H, L) :< F^b, F^a >$ *where*
   $F^b = ground(1.A), F^a = [ground(A.1) \wedge ground(A.3) \wedge (A.3 \prec A.1)]$

9. $A = r(C, D, E) :< F^b, F^a >$ *where*
   $F^b = ground(1.A), F^a = [ground(A.1) \wedge ground(A.3) \wedge (A.3 \prec A.1)]$

In the above equations, $\prec$ corresponds to subsequence ordering. Let the well-founded set W be the set of natural numbers. For the two edges involved in cycles, the ordered assertions are given below:

1. $< A, B >=< p(T, [H|P]), p(R, P) >: < w_{(AB)}, w_B >=< size(1.A), size(1.B) >$

2. $< A, B > = < r([B|C], D, [B|E]), r(C, D, E) >$ where $w_{(AB)} = size(1.A)$, $w_B = size(1.B)$, and size(T) is the number of (function and constant) symbols occurring in a ground term T.

It is not difficult to see that the A-set of $permute(T, [H|P])$ and $remove([B|C], D, [B|E])$ are consistent with order $< 1, 2 >$ and $< 1 >$, respectively. All A-sets of vertices in V_B are safe, and the set of ordered assertions is also safe. Therefore, if the first parameter of the $goal \leftarrow permute(s, t)$ is ground, i.e. if $val(F^b, \epsilon)$ is true, then the program terminates by a computation follows from the orders associated with the A-sets of the heads of all non-unit clauses.

It may be noticed that each A-set of a vertex H corresponds to a set of assertions of a clause whose head is H.

5 Formal Correctness of the Method

Before showing the correctness of the method, we establish the relationship between U-graphs and SLDNF derivations by introducing g-trees which connects a path in the U-graph and a sub-derivation of a given SLDNF derivation. Note that we are considering SLDNF derivations rather than SLD derivations as the latter can be obtained as a special case of the former.

5.1 G-trees and U-graphs

SLDNF derivations as defined in [Lly87] discard too much information particularly when the tree is nonterminating (note that there will be no information about the lemma trees). We would like to capture the totality of the SLDNF derivations along with the lemma trees in terms of the instances of paths in the U-graph.

It may be noted that in the U-graph there is no edge that corresponds to a literal in the body of a clause and the head of a clause having the same predicate symbol that are not unifiable. No information is lost by doing so for establishing the relationship between U-graphs and SLNDNF-derivations is captured by the following straightforward lemma.

Lemma 1: Given two atoms A and B, A and B are not unifiable if and only if Aθ and B are not unifiable, for any substitution such that lvar(θ) $\cap$ var(B) = ϕ [6].

Proof:
if: trivial, by letting θ be the identity substitution.
only if: suppose there is a substitution δ such that
lvar(δ) $\cap$ var(B) = ϕ,
and Aδ and B are unifiable with mgu σ. As all the variables occurring in δ are not in B,
B = Bδ
A$\delta\sigma$ = Bσ = B$\delta\sigma$.
The last equation implies that A and B are unifiable, contradicting the hypothesis.

Definition 8: We say that A^h is an instance of literal A, (where the superscript h stands for Herbrand universe) if there is a substitution θ such that A^h = Aθ. Similarly, we say that H_1^h, $B_1^h, ..., H_n^h$ is an *instance* of a path H_1, $B_1, ..., H_n$ with substitutions $\theta_1, ..., \theta_n$ in the U-graph of a given normal program, if $H_i^h = H_i\theta_i$, $\forall 1 \leq$ i $\leq$ n, and $B_i^h = B_i\theta_i$, $\forall 1 \leq$ i $\leq$ n, $B_j^h\theta_{i+1} = H_{j+1}^h, \forall 1 \leq$ j $\leq n-1$.

Definition 9: Let P be a normal program with U-graph U, and G be a normal goal. If P $\cup$ { G } has an SLDNF derivation $G_0 = G$, G_1, $G_2, ...$ with input clauses $C_1, C_2, ...$, and mgu's θ_1, $\theta_2, ...$. We say that a derived goal G_i is obtained by *applying* u-edge $< B, H >$ in U, if $B\theta_1...\theta_{i-1}$ is the selected subgoal of G_{i-1}, and H is the head of input clause C_i. We say that $G_0, G_1, G_2, ...$ is obtained from an instance $H_1^h, B_1^h, ..., H_n^h$ of path $H_1, B_1, ..., H_n$, if H_i is the head of input clause C_i, and B_j^h is the selected subgoal of G_j, for all 1 $\leq$ i $\leq$ n, 1 $\leq$ j $\leq n-1$.

For establishing the relationship between U-graphs and SLDNF derivations, we will first extend an SLDNF derivation as follows.

Definition 10 (Extended SLDNF Derivation): Let SD be an SLDNF derivation of P $\cup$ G which consists of a sequence of goals $G_0 = G$, G_1, $G_2, ...$, a sequence of input clauses C_1, $C_2, ...$, and a sequence of substitutions θ_1, $\theta_2, ...$. An *extended SLDNF derivation*

[6] Here, lvar(θ) denotes all variables replaced by substitution θ and var(B) denotes all variables occuring in literal B.

SD^d of SD consists a sequence of goals $G'_0 = G, G'_1, G'_2, ...$, a sequence of input clauses $C'_1, C'_2, ...$, and a sequence of substitutions $\theta'_1, \theta'_2, ...$, such that
(1) If SD is infinite then SD^d and SD are the same, i.e., $G'_i = G_i$, $C'_i = C_i$, and $\theta'_i = \theta_i$, for i $\geq$ 1.
(2) If SD is finite and SD either succeeds or fails then, similar to (1), SD^d and SD are the same.
(3) SD is finite and SD neither succeeds nor fails; in this case, either there are infinitely many lemma trees or there is an infinite lemma tree.

(i) *infinitely many lemma trees*: In this case, let $LT^{(1)}$, $LT^{(2)}, ...$ be the infinite sequence of lemma trees, and $SD^{(i)} \equiv G_0^{(i)}, G_1^{(i)}, ..., G_{n_i}^{(i)}$ be the branch in $LT^{(i)}$ such that the selected subgoal in $G_{n_i}^{(i)}$ is the root of $LT^{(i+1)}$. Then SD^d is the concatenation of SD and $SD^{(1)}$, $SD^{(2)}, ...$

(ii) *there is an infinite lemma tree*: In this case, Let $LT^{(1)}, ..., LT^{(m)}$ be the lemma trees generated before reaching the infinite lemma tree $LT^{(m+1)}$. Similar to (i), let $SD^{(i)} \equiv G_0^{(i)}, G_1^{(i)}, ..., G_{n_i}^{(i)}$ be the branch in $LT^{(i)}$, $1 \leq$ i $\leq$ m, such that the selected subgoal in $G_{n_j}^{(j)}$ is the root of $LT^{(j+1)}$, for $1 \leq$ j $\leq m$, and $SD^{(m+1)}$ be a infinite branch in $LT^{(m+1)}$. Then SD^d is obtained by concatenating SD, $SD^{(1)}, ..., SD^{(m+1)}$.

We say that an SLDNF derivation is an *inconclusive* SLDNF derivation if it neither succeeds nor fails.

Intuitively, if SD is either a success or a failure SLDNF derivation, then an extended derivation of SD is identical to SD. However, if SD is an infinite or inconclusive derivation, then an extended SLDNF derivation is a collection of derivations in the main and lemma trees that cause inconclusion.

Definition 11 (G-tree): Let SD^d be an extended SLDNF derivation of P $\cup$ $\{G\}$ which consists of a sequence of goals $G_0 = G$, G_1, $G_2, ...$, a sequence of input clauses C_1, $C_2, ...$, and a sequence of substitutions θ_1, $\theta_2, ...$ We define the *g-tree* of SD^d, denoted by $GT(SD^d)$, as follows. The root of the $GT(SD^d)$ is G_0 and $< G_0, G_1 >$ is an edge in $GT(SD^d)$. $< G_i, G_j >$ is an edge in $GT(SD^d)$, i $>$ 0, if the selected subgoal of G_j is from the input clause C_{i+1}. $< G_0, G_j >$ is an edge if the selected subgoal of G_j is from the top level goal G ($=G_0$).

The purpose of introducing g-trees is to establish a relationship between an SLDNF derivation and a path in a U-graph. In general, a subsequence of goals of a derivation does not correspond to an instance of a path in U-graph. However, each branch $G_{i_0} = G_0, G_{i_1}, G_{i_2}, ...$ in a g-tree is obtained along (corresponds to) an instance H_1^h, $B_1^h, ...$ of a path $H_1, B_1, ...$, where H_i is the head of input clause C_{i_k}, and B_i^h is the selected subgoal of G_{i_k}, for all k $\geq$ 1.

Lemma 2: Let G_0, G_{i_1}, $G_{i_2}, ...$ be a branch in the g-tree of a given extended SLDNF derivation. If the head of input clause C_{i_j+1} is H_j^h, and the selected subgoal of $G_{i_{j+1}}$ is B_j^h, for j $\geq$ 1, then H_1^h, B_1^h, H_2^h, $B_2^h, ...$ is an instance of a path in the U-graph.

Proof: Trivial, by definition.

Lemma 3: There is an inconclusive SLDNF derivation if and only if there is an infinite extended SLDNF derivation.

Proof: Trivial, by definition.

Lemma 4: If there is an inconclusive SLDNF derivation, then there is an infinite branch in the g-tree of SD.

Proof: By the above lemma, we can conclude that if there is an inconclusive SLDNF derivation, then there is an infinite extended SLDNF derivation. Let SD^d consisting of a sequence of goals G_0, $G_1, \ldots$ be a infinite extended SLDNF derivation. First, we know that for all i, i ≥ 1, G_i must be a node in the $GT(SD^d)$; hence $GT(SD^d)$ contains infinite nodes. Secondly, since each goal in the sequence $G_0, G_1, \ldots$ is obtained by using one input clause only, by definition of g-tree, each node in the $GT(SD^d)$ has bounded number of children. By Konig's lemma, an infinite tree with bounded children for each node must have an infinite branch.

By lemma 2, we know that if an extended SLDNF derivation is infinite then there must be an instance of an infinite path in U-graph. In other words, if there is no such infinite instance path (all possible instance paths that could be found are finite) then there is no possible infinite extended SLDNF derivation. The connection between success and finite failure SLDNF derivations and their g-trees follow from the definition in a natural way. The following theorem captures inconclusive SLDNF derivations in terms of U-graphs.

Theorem 1: Let P be a normal program and G be a goal. P $\cup\{G\}$ has an inconclusive SLDNF derivation if and only if there is an instance H_1^h, $B_1^h, \ldots$ of an infinite path PA $\equiv H_1$, $B_1, \ldots$ in the U-graph of P, such that there is a subgoal A in G, A and H_1 are unifiable, and H_1^h is an instance of A.

Proof:
(only if): By lemma 2, if there is an inconclusive SLDNF derivation then there is an infinite branch in the g-tree. Together with the fact that each branch in the g-tree corresponds to an instance of a path in the U-graph, the result follows.
(if): It is clear that if there is an instance of path H_1, $B_1, \ldots$, with $\theta_1, \theta_2, \ldots$, for some subsitutions θ_i, i ≥ 1, then there is an instance of a path with $\delta_1, \delta_2, \ldots$, where δ_i is the mgu of $B_{i-1}\delta_{i-1}$ and H_i. Let R be a computation rule which selects the subgoals along the path PA, i.e., A is selected in G_0, the clause with the head H_i is the input clause C_i, and $B_i\theta_i$ is selected in G_i, i ≥ 1, where θ_i, i ≥ 1, are mgu's of $B_{i-1}\theta_{i-1}$ and H_i. We can easily see that there is an infinite extended SLDNF derivation, and hence there is an inconclusive SLDNF derivation (lemma 3).

Definition 12: Given a normal program P with U-graph U(V, E), let **F** be the set of assertions attached to all vertices in U. We say that a computation rule is a *safe* rule if R selects the subgoal $A\theta$ with assertion $< F^a, F^b >$ only if $val(F^b, \theta)$ is true.

Theorem 2: Given a normal program P and a goal $\leftarrow A_1, ..., A_n$, let P' is the extended program, i.e. $P' = P \cup \{Goal \leftarrow A_1, ..., A_n\}$, with extended U-graph U(V, E). If

1. There is a set **F** of assertions attached to all vertices in V, such that

   a for each A-set of a vertex A $\in V_H$ is consistent, and

   b for each A-set of a vertex A $\in V_B$ is safe.

2. There is a safe set of ordered assertions attached to all signed edges involved in cycles.
   then P $\cup\{\leftarrow Goal\}$ has finite SLDNF tree via a consistent computation rule with respect P and **F**.

Proof: It is easy to see that following the method discussed above and the consistent computation rule, the pre-condition of selected subgoal of any possible SLDNF derivations always satisfied, and hence by the safety of ordered assertions, there is a well-founded ordering over all instances of paths in every strongly connected component. Now, suppose there is no finite SLDNF tree; then by definition there must be an infinite extended SLDNF derivation, say $G_0 = G,\ G_1, ...$.
Claim: There is no such infinite SLDNF derivation. In the first step, we establish the g-tree for this infinite extended SLDNF derivation $G_0,\ G_1, ...$ By lemma 4, we know that there must be an infinite branch in the g-tree. Further, we know that this infinite branch corresponds to an instance of an infinite path in the U-graph. Because each A-set of a vertex is safe and if in each step of the derivation, the assertion attached to each vertex is always satisfied, there cannot be an instance of a infinite path in the U-graph (otherwise, W is not a well-founded set).

6 Discussion

In the preceding sections, we have described a method for showing the termination of logic programs using U-graphs. As we are not considering the search rule, it should be clear that we establish universal termination. The method is simple and allows us to concentrate only on those portions that are not easily amenable for intuition. It must be noted that the formal specification of the method looks long, the method is really simple. Each condition can be checked easily. In fact, as already remarked, the definitions become simple if we use the transformational approach. As opposed to the transformational approach, the method described provides good comparison between the termination proofs of imperative programs and logic programs. The U-graph abstraction allows us to localize the task of finding the well-founded set and we can use some of the techniques of [Der85] for arriving at the ordered assertions. It is interesting to see that from the analysis of the two cycles in Figure 3, we can have two set of ordered assertions. The first set as given above corresponds to a goal $\leftarrow perm(s,t)$, where s is a ground term, which has a finite SLD-derivation by Prolog computation rule. The second set can be derived by considering the goal ← $perm(s,t)$, where t is aground term. In this case, we can find that we have a different order to keep the consistency of clause

permute(T,[H|T]) ← remove(T,H,R), permute(R,P)

and hence, we need different computation rule to achieve termination. The disjointness of the program clauses can be easily observed as illustrated by the program and its U-graph below:

p(X) ← p(f(X))

p(a) ←

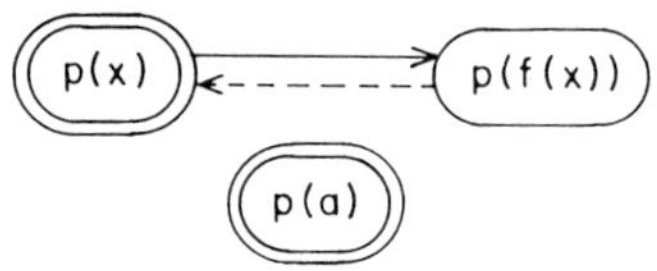

Figure 3

Another advantage of the method is that pre-assertion for the predicates can be distributed which is very helpful in understanding of the program. Further, we can even check through the pre-assertions to see whether the logic program can be transformed to a functional program; for instance, conditions given by Reddy [Red84] for the transformation of logic programs to functional programs can be easily derived in a natural way. In fact, we are trying to use U-graphs for annotating logic programs. The annotations easily leads to parallel implementations, efficient implementations etc. Our initial investigation for the verification of logic programs is quite encouraging. As the U-graph has unification information, we are exploring the methods of verification of Prolog programs that uses extensions of execution models as in [KS87]. Our study shows that termination property of logic programs is very fundamental in the study of logic programs. Recently, we have considered [WS89b] the termination property to show how one can arrive at classes of normal programs that are complete under SLDNF resolution using Herbrand models.

7 References

[Der85] Dershowitz,N. (1985) *Computing with Rewrite Systems*, *Information and Control*, 65, 122-157.

[DM88] Drabent, W. and J. Maluszynski (1988) *Inductive Assertion Method For Logic Programs*, *Theoretical Computer Science*, 59, pp. 133-155.

[Flo67] Floyd,R.M.(1967) *Assigning Meanings to Programs*, *Proc. AMS Symposium* *on Applied Mathematics*, 19, Providence, RI.

[**FGKP85**] Francez, N., O. Grumberg, S. Katz and A. Pnueli (1985) *Proving Termination of Prolog Programs*,*Proc. Logics of Programs*, LNCS, Vol. 193, Springer Verlag, 1985.

[**KS87**] Kanamori, T., and H. Seki (1987) *Verification of Prolog programs using an extension of execution*, LNCS, 225, 1987.

[**Lly87**] Llyod, J. (1987) **Foundations of Logic Programming**, Revised New Edition, Springer-Verlag, 1987.

[**Nil82**] Nilsson, N.J. (1982) **Principles of Artificial Intelligence**, Springer-Verlag, Berlin.

[**Red84**] Reddy, U.R.(1986) *Transformation of Logic Programs into Functional Programs*, *IEEE Symposium on Logic Programming*, 1984, pp. 187-197.

[**VP86**] Vasak, T., and J. Potter (1986) *Characterization of Terminating Logic Programs*, *Conference on Logic Programming*, pp.140-147.

[**WS89a**] Wang, Bal, and R.K. Shyamasundar (1989) *Termination of Logic Programs*, Internal Report, Pennsylvania State University, February 1989.

[**WS89b**] Wang, Bal, and R.K. Shyamasundar (1989) *Negation as Finite Failure: Completeness of SLDNF Resolution*, Internal Report, Pennsylvania State University, December 1989.

NEW APPROACH FOR ARRAY GRAMMATICAL INFERENCE

P.S.P. Wang and H.J.Lin

College of Computer Science and Mathematics Department
Northeastern University
Boston M A 02120

ABSTRACT

The basic concept of grammatical inference for two-dimensional arrays is presented. Some algorithms for inferring two-dimensional array grammars are constructed. Some approaches simulate derivation processes of a subclass of array grammars known as context-free (type-2) array grammars (CFAGs). Furthermore, another approach simulates derivation processes of a subclass of context-sensitive (type-1) array grammars (CSAGs) for the sample of arrays with loops in their patterns. This class of languages is especially useful for generating and recognizing line-drawing patterns. Several examples are illustrated. Finally, some future research topics such as algorithm improvement, optimization, implementation , applications to pattern recognition, unsupervised clustering analysis, and artificial intelligence problems are proposed.
Keywords: Array grammar, parsing, pattern recognition, top-down approach, two-dimensional grammatical inference.

1. INTRODUCTION

Recently, there is a growing interest in the study of grammars whose languages are sets of arrays rather than strings. Such study has significant applications in imaging technology, pattern recognition, and data processing of two-dimensional patterns [9,10,13,14, 16,17,20,24]. Some fundamental properties and principles of array grammars such as parallelism [12,15,18,19], Chomsky Normal Form (CNF) [3,16], array recognizers [3,12,14,15], hierarchical structure and pumping lemma [22] have been investigated.

However, the basic principles of two-dimensional grammatical inference for arrays remain largely unknown. Because of this, the new approach for clustering analysis proposed in [16] is basically supervised in that the grammars of given input sample patterns must be given a priori. The array grammar approach introduced in [16] is shown better than other approaches in the literature such as tree grammar [8]. It would be even better and desirable if the clustering analysis using array grammars in [16] could be unsupervised. We need to explore studies on grammatical inference techniques for array languages. Historically speaking, grammatical inference is one of the most difficult and most intriguing problems associated with the linguistic approach to pattern recognition. The one-dimensional grammatical inference has been studied in [4,6,7]. However, comparatively few studies have been done for two-dimensional grammars. This is probably due to the fact that a reasonable grammar for a two-dimensional language is very difficult to obtain by natural extension of one-dimensional grammars. For instance, in the string case when a one-dimensional rule, say $A \longrightarrow BCD$, is applied to a sentential form $\alpha A\beta$, we get $\alpha BCD\beta$. This can be done by either pushing α to the left or pushing β to the right. When the application of a rule is extended to the two-dimensional case we are immediately in trouble. For example, if we apply the rule

```
                                                          X
     B                          XXX               XXX     XBX     XXX
A ->     to the sentential form YAY we may obtain YBY or YCDY or YBY or ...
     CD                         ZZZ               ZCDZ    ZZZ     ZCD
                                                   Z               ZZ
```

The shearing effect occurs and what we really want might be totally distorted. Therefore, isometric grammars [12,17] which overcome such a disadvantage have been developed. The principal objective of this research is to explore some methods for the grammatical inference of array patterns. The greatest application of inference technique has been in the area of pattern recognition and clustering analysis [5,13,16]. In section 2, some basic notations and definitions of array grammar are introduced. The concept of grammatical inference is illustrated and definitions of parsing tree and parsing window are introduced in section 3. In section 4, a technique for array grammatical inference and its algorithm for the array sample in which there might be a loop in its pattern are proposed. Finally, some future research topics are discussed in section 5. A preliminary version of this paper has been presented in [23].

2. DEFINITIONS AND NOTATIONS FOR ARRAY GRAMMARS

Each member in I^2 is of the form [x,y], called a vertex in I^2, where x and y are two elements in I; that is, two integers. A vertex p = [x,y] has two types of neighbors [12]:

(a) its four horizontal and vertical neighbors [u,v] such that $|x-u|+|y-v| = 1$ and

(b) its four diagonal neighbors [u,v] such that $|x-u| = |y-v| = 1$. We shall refer to the neighbors of type (a) as the 4-neighbors of p, and to the neighbors of both types, collectively, as the 8-neighbors of p. The former neighbors are said to be 4-adjacent to p, and the latter, 8-adjacent.

By a path π of length n from p to q in I^2 we mean a sequence of vertices $p = p_0 p_1 \ldots p_n = q$ such that p_i is adjacent to p_{i-1}, $1 \leq i \leq n$. Note that this comprises two definitions in one, namely, 4-path and 8-path, depending on whether we use the definition of 4- or 8-adjacency. In this paper, we shall use the definition of 8-adjacency.

Definition 2.1

An array is connected if there is a path of non-# symbols between every pair of non-# symbols.

With the definition of 8-adjacency, neighbors of [i,j] are [i-1,j], [i-1,j+1], [i,j+1], [i+1,j+1], [i+1,j], [i+1,j-1], [i,j-1] and [i-1,j-1] in the window of [i,j] as in Figure 2.1. They are denoted as follows: [i,j]-0 = [i,j], [i,j]-1 = [i-1,j], [i,j]-2 = [i-1,j+1], [i,j]-3 = [i,j+1], [i,j]-4 = [i+1,j+1], [i,j]-5 = [i+1,j], [i,j]-6 = [i+1,j-1], [i,j]-7 = [i,j-1], and [i,j]-8 = [i-1,j-1]. We let Dir = {0,1,2,3,4,5,6,7,8}, the set of eight directions, and for every d ϵ Dir, let $\bar{d}$ be the opposite direction of d. For example, $\bar{1}$=5, $\bar{6}$=2, and $\bar{0}$ = 0; thus [i,j]-$\bar{1}$ = [i,j]-5 = [i+1,j] and [i,j]-$\bar{6}$ = [i,j]-2 = [i-1,j+1]. [i,j]-d are called the neighbor-d of the window of [i,j] or the neighbor-d of [i,j].

$i-1,j-1$	$i-1,j$	$i-1,j+1$
$i,j-1$	i,j	$i,j+1$
$i+1,j-1$	$i+1,j$	$i+1,j+1$

Figure 2.1
A window on position $[i,j]$

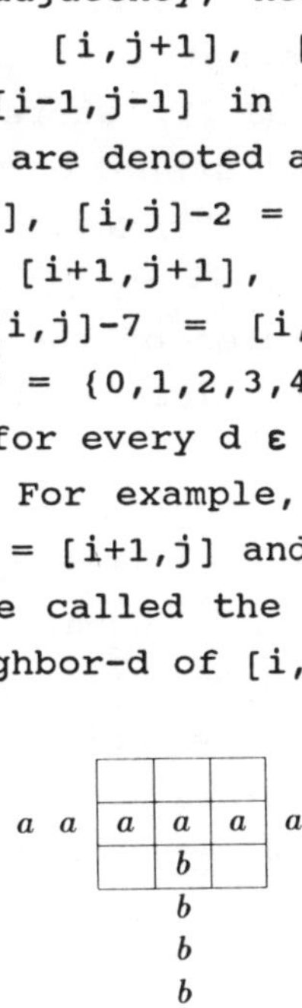

Figure 2.2
A T-shaped array t composed of a's and b's

When we place the window upon an array square of a given array composed of the alphabet. For example, as the array t shown in Figure 2.2, we assume that the window is on the array square of [i,j], and the symbols in [i,j], [i,j]-3, and [i,j]-7 are all a's, the symbol in [i,j]-5 is b, and symbols in [i,j]-1, [i,j]-2, [i,j]-4, [i,j]-6, [i,j]-8 are all #'s. We express the situation of the window on [i,j] of this array as follows: t([i,j]) = t([i,j]-3) = t([i,j]-7) = a, t([i,j]-5)=b, and t([i,j]-1) = t([i,j]-2) = t([i,j]-4) = t([i,j]-6) = t([i,j]-8) = #. In this paper, the window is always placed (or defined) on an array square in which the symbol is not #. For a window on [i,j], if t([i,j]-d) = # for every d, then this window is called a single window.

Definition 2.2: [17,20]

An isometric array grammar is a quintuple G = (N,T,P,S,#), where N is a nonempty finite set of nonterminal symbols, T is a nonempty finite set of terminal symbols, $N \cap T = \phi$, $S \in N$ is the start symbol, $\# \notin N \cup T$ is the blank symbol, and P is a set of rewriting rules of the form $\alpha \longrightarrow \beta$, where α and β are geometrically identical over $N \cup T \cup \{\#\}$ and α are not all #'s.

We say that array x directly generates array y, denoted $x \Longrightarrow y$; if there is a rewriting rule $\alpha \longrightarrow \beta$, x contains α as a subarray and y is identical to x except that the subarray α is replaced with the corresponding symbols of the array β. Let $\overset{*}{\Longrightarrow}$ be the reflexive transitive closure of $\Longrightarrow$. The language generated by an array grammar G, denoted by L(G), is the set of all arrays of terminal symbols and #'s that can be generated from the starting symbol S in the field of #'s.

Definition 2.3: [3,20]

Let G = (N,T,P,S,#) be an isometric array grammar:

(1) G is of type 0 (isometric, IAG) if there are no restrictions on P;

(2) G is of type 1 (monotonic, IMAG) if both sides of each rule are connected and the image of each left-side symbol is in N ∪ T; that is, #'s cannot be created;

(3) G is of type 2 (context-free, ICFAG) if it is monotonic and the left side of each rule contains exactly one nonterminal symbol in a field of #'s;

(4) G is of type 3 (regular, IRAG) if every rewriting rule is of the form:

```
                                 #    B  A    a  A     a  #     B    A    a
A -> a, #A -> Ba, A# -> aB,        ->          ->          ->         ->        ->
                                 A    a, #    B, #     B, A     a, #      B ,
```

```
    #     B   where A and B are nonterminal symbols and a is a terminal
or      ->
    A     a ,  symbol.
```

Let IAL, IMAL, ICFAL, and IRAL denote the isometric, monotonic, context-free, and regular array languages, respectively.

Example 2.1:

Let G = ({S,A,B},{a},P,S,#) be an array grammar generating T-shaped arrays composed of a's in the field of

```
                                    A    a
#'s, where P = {S# -> aS, S# -> AB,    ->     B# -> aB,  A -> a, B -> a}.
                                    #    A,
```

```
          aaaaa
The array   a    is generated by G as follows:
            a
```

```
S##    aS#    aaS#    aaAB    aaaB    aaaB    aaaB#    aaaaB    aaaaa
### => ### => #### => #### => ##A# => ##a# => ##a## => ##a## => ##a##
###    ###    ####    ####    ####    ##A#    ##a##    ##a##    ##a##.
```

For more examples of array languages, please refer to [1,23].

In fact, an ICFAG (Isometric Context-Free Array Grammar), as defined in Definition 2.3, is essentially not "context-free"; for example when the production rule of an ICFAG is applied in a generating procedure, it must be checked whether the symbols to the right of and below "A" are #'s. Thus, the rule is still "sensitive" to #'s. For this reason, the properties of one-dimensional or string context-free grammars can not be directly extended to those of two-dimensional or array context-free grammars.

It is easy to prove that for any ICFAG G = (N,T,P,S,#) with the definition of 8-adjacency, there exists another ICFAG G' = $(N',T,P',S',\#)$ equivalent to G; that is, $L(G') = L(G)$, such that every production rule

in G' is of the form $\begin{matrix} L_8 & L_1 & L_1 \\ L_7 & A & L_3 \\ L_6 & L_5 & L_4 \end{matrix} \rightarrow \begin{matrix} R_8 & R_1 & R_2 \\ R_7 & R & R_3 \\ R_6 & R_5 & R_4 \end{matrix}$,

called the 9-point normal form, where $A \in N'$, L_i's $\in \{\#,*\}$, $R \in N' \cup T'$, and R_i's $\in \{\#,*\} \cup N' \cup T'$.

Throughout this paper, the context-free grammars are of the 9-point normal form with the definition of 8-adjacency.

3. PARSING TREE AND WINDOWS

In the inference process, the given array sample is parsed by moving a window square by square, and each array square can be parsed only once. This parsing can be illustrated by a tree, called the parsing tree. During the parsing process, if the window parses from $[i_1,j_1]$ to $[i_2,j_2]$, then $[i_1,j_1]$ is said to be the ancestor of $[i_2,j_2]$ and $[i_2,j_2]$ is said to be a descendant of $[i_1,j_1]$. Since the window parses the array square by square, $[i_1,j_1]$ and $[i_2,j_2]$ are neighbors of each other; that is, $[i_1,j_1]=[i_2,j_2]-d$, for some $d \in$ Dir. It can be stated that the ancestor of $[i_2,j_2]$ is its neighbor-d and it can be denoted that dir($[i_2,j_2]$) = d. If the window is on the position [i,j] of a sample array smp and [i,j]-d is a neighbor of [i,j] which has not been parsed and smp([i,j]-d) $\neq$ #, then the window will parse

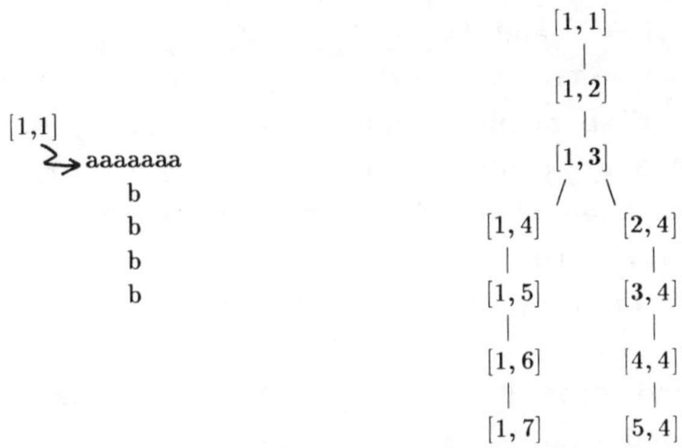

(a) array t (b) parsing tree of t

Figure 3.2

from [i,j] to [i,j]-d. If there are more than one such neighbor then the window will parse from [i,j] to each one. For example, in Figure 3.2.a, the parsing for the array t is illustrated by the parsing tree shown in Figure 3.2.b, where we let the upper-left corner be the starting point with coordinates [1,1]. The window parses from [1,1] to [1,2], from [1,2] to [1,3], then from [1,3] to [1,4], from [1,4] to [1,5], from [1,5] to [1,6], from [1,6] to [1,7], and then it moves back to [1,3] (but does not read the symbol of [1,3]), and then continues to parse from [1,3] to [2,4], from [2,4] to [3,4], from [3,4] to [4,4], from [4,4] to [5,4]. Nodes [1,7] and [5,4] having no descendant are called leaves of the tree.

To avoid repeatedly parsing the array squares, we need to make restrictions on the motion of the window. This is discussed as follows:

If α and β are two connected array squares of a sample array smp, with $\alpha = [i_1, j_1]$ and $\beta = [i_2, j_2]$, assuming that α is the ancestor of β, then there are two possible cases:

(1) $|i_1 - i_2| = 1$ and $|j_1 - j_2| = 1$,

(2) $|i_1 - i_2| = 1$ and $|j_1 - j_2| = 0$, or $|i_1 - i_2| = 0$ and $|j_1 - j_2| = 1$.

In case 1, if we assume that $i_2 = i_1$ and $j_2 = j_1 + 1$ as in Figure 3.3.a; that is, α is the neighbor-8 of β or $dir(\beta) = 8$, then the intersection of neighbors of α and neighbors of β are θ_1 and θ_2. If $smp(\theta_1) \neq \#$ and $smp(\theta_2) \neq \#$ then, by assuming that θ_1 and θ_2 both are not ancestors of α or β, the window will move from α to θ_1 and θ_2, and from β to θ_1 and θ_2. Thus, the array squares θ_1 and θ_2 are parsed twice. To avoid this duplication, we give priority to the ancestor α; that is, let the window move from α but not from β to θ_1 and θ_2. To do this, we replace $smp[\theta_1]$ and $smp[\theta_2]$ with #'s in the window of β; thus the ancestor of θ_1 and θ_2 is α. Similarly, in case 2, if $i_2 = i_1$ and $j_2 = j_1 + 1$; that is, α is the neighbor-7 of β or $dir(\beta) = 7$, as in Figure 3.3.b, then the intersections of neighbors of α and neighbors of β are θ_1, θ_2, θ_3 and θ_4. Thus, the contents of $\theta_1, \theta_2, \theta_3$ and θ_4 in the window of β are all replaced with #'s. Therefore, if a window is on an array square β, then the contents of some neighbors in the window of β will be replaced with #'s according to the value of $dir(\beta)$.

(a) $i_2 = i_1 + 1, j_2 = j_1 + 1$ (b) $i_2 = i_1, j_2 = j_1 + 1$

Figure 3.3
windows of two connected array squares
$\alpha = [i_1, j_1]$ and $\beta = [i_2, j_2]$

For simple discussions, we define a "set function" denoted by SF, which is a mapping from Dir to 2^{Dir} as follows: SF(0) = ϕ, SF(1) = {1,2,3,7,8}, SF(2) = {1,2,3}, SF(3) = {1,2,3,4,5}, SF(4) = {3,4,5}, SF(5) = {3,4,5,6,7}, SF(6) = {1,7,8}, SF(7) = {1,5,6,7,8}, and SF(8) = {1,7,8}. Thus, if dir(β) = i, then, for every d ε SF(i), the content of the neighbor-d in the window of β will be replaced with #. This is shown in Figure 3.4. After replacing the contents of such neighbors as mentioned above in the window of β , the new window is called the primary window of β. Thus the primary window on the array square [i,j], denoted by priW([i,j]), is defined as follows:

$$priW([i,j]) = \begin{array}{|c|c|c|} \hline w(i,j,8) & w(i,j,1) & w(i,j,2) \\ \hline w(i,j,7) & w(i,j,0) & w(i,j,3) \\ \hline w(i,j,6) & w(i,j,5) & w(i,j,4) \\ \hline \end{array} \text{ , where}$$

$$w(i,j,d) = \begin{cases} \# & \text{if } d \in SF(dir[i,j]) \\ smp([i,j]-d) & \text{otherwise.} \end{cases}$$

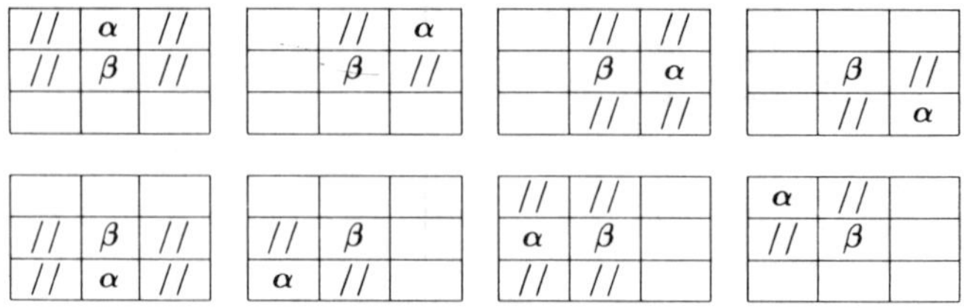

Figure 3.4
The contents of the shaded array squares in the window of β whose ancestor is α are erased

If the parsing process is according to the primary window of each array square, then the array square is treated as the "unique" ancestor of all the non-# neighbors in its primary window. As in Figure 3.5, if the L-shaped array 1 is parsed, starting from the upper-left corner with the given coordinates [1,1], then

priW([4,1]) = 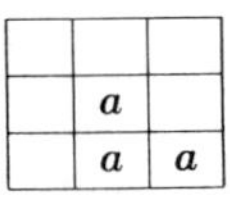 and priW([5,1]) = 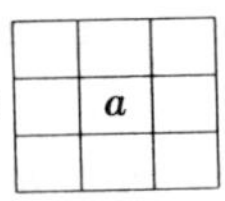

since [4,1] is the ancestor of [5,1]. Thus, if the parsing is according to the primary window, then the parsing track for the array 1 is as in Figure 3.6.a. However, the parsing track shown in Figure 3.6.b might be desired and it is more natural.

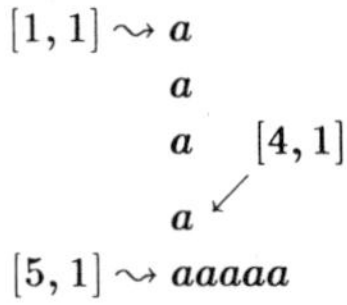

Figure 3.5
array 1

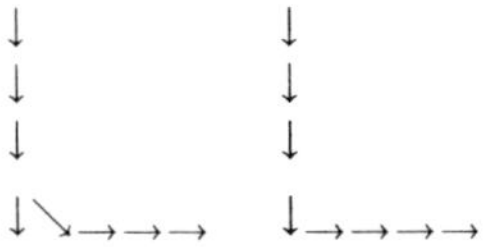

(a) (b)

Figure 3.6
parsing tracks for array 1

To get the more natural parsing track, the primary window is modified to a newly defined "true window", which is shown as follows:

For a primary window

a_8	a_1	a_2
a_7	a_0	a_3
a_6	a_5	a_4

on $[i,j]$, where $a_0 \in \Sigma$ and $a_j \in \Sigma \cup \{\#\}$

for $1 \leq j \leq 8$. Neighbors on the corners, [i,j]-2, [i,j]-4, [i,j]-6, and [i,j]-8, are called the corner neighbors of [i,j]. For any non-# corner neighbor [i,j]-d (that is, d ϵ {2,4,6,8}),

$$\text{define } < d-1 >= \begin{cases} 8 & \text{if } d=1 \\ d-1 & \text{otherwise,} \end{cases}$$

$$\text{and } < d+1 >= \begin{cases} 1 & \text{if } d=8 \\ d+1 & \text{otherwise,} \end{cases}$$

and let x = < d-1 > and y = < d+1>. If $a_x \neq$ # then assign a_d into the primary window of [i,j]-x, and erase a_d from the primary window of [i,j]. Otherwise, if $a_y \neq$ # then assign $a_d$into the primary window of [i,j]-y and erase a_d from the primary window of [i,j]. To state the job of the assignment as mentioned above, we will define a function "assign" from I^2 to 2^{I^2}. For example, if a_d is assigned into the primary window of [i,j]-x, then we state that assign ([i,j]-x) := assign ([i,j]-x) $\cup$ {[i,j]-d}. The initial value of the function "assign" of each array square is an empty set. After the modification shown above, the modified primary window is called the "true window", which is shown as follows:

Definition 3.1:

The true window of an array square [i,j] in a sample array smp, denoted by TW([i,j]), is a window

$tw(i,j,8)$	$tw(i,j,1)$	$tw(i,j,2)$
$tw(i,j,7)$	$tw(i,j,0)$	$tw(i,j,3)$
$tw(i,j,6)$	$tw(i,j,5)$	$tw(i,j,4)$

on $[i,j]$, where $tw(i,j,0) = w(i,j,0)$;

$$\text{for } d \in \{1,3,5,7\},\ tw(i,j,d) = \begin{cases} w(i,j,d) & \text{if } [i,j]\text{-}d \notin assign([i,j]) \\ smp([i,j]\text{-}d) & \text{if } [i,j]\text{-}d \in assign([i,j]); \end{cases}$$

and for $d \in \{2,4,6,8\}$, by letting $x =< d-1 >$ and $y =< d+1 >$,

$$tw(i,j,d) = \begin{cases} \# & \text{if } [i,j]\text{-}d \notin assign([i,j]) \\ w(i,j,d) & \text{otherwise.} \end{cases}$$

Example 3.1:

If an E-shaped array e is parsed from the upper-left corner of the given coordinates [1,1], as in Figure 3.7.a, then the array square of [3,1] is the ancestor of [4,1], and the intersection of their neighbors is [4,2]; thus,

priW([3,1]) =

	a	
	a	a

priW([4,1]) =

	a	
	a	

To find the true windows of [3,1] and [4,1], we assign the terminal symbol of [3,1]-4, the neighbor of priW([3,1]), into the primary window of [4,1]. Therefore,

TW([3,1]) =

	a	
	a	

and TW([4,1]) =

	a	a
	a	

A complete parsing tree with the true windows on each array square for the array e is shown in Figure 3.7.b.

Definition 3.2:

The parsing window of an array square [i,j] in a sample array, denoted by PW([i,j]), is a window

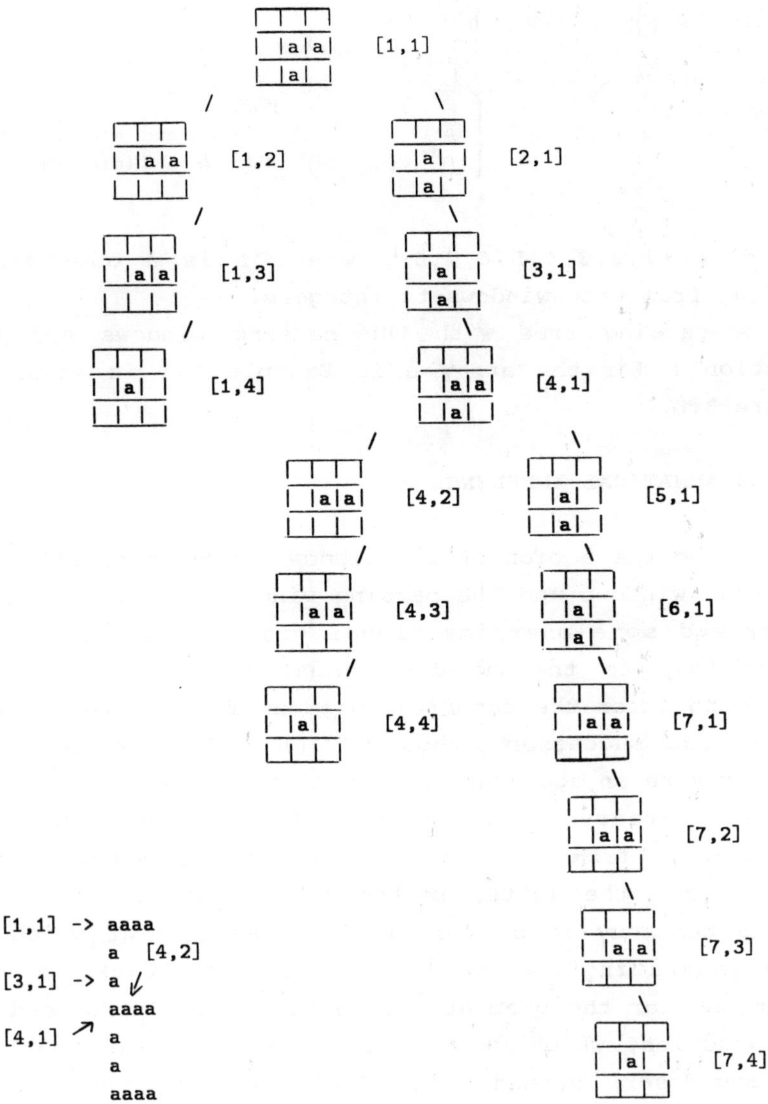

(a)

array e

(b)

A parsing tree with true windows for array e

Figure 3.7

$pw(i,j,8)$	$pw(i,j,1)$	$pw(i,j,2)$
$pw(i,j,7)$	$pw(i,j,0)$	$pw(i,j,3)$
$pw(i,j,6)$	$pw(i,j,5)$	$pw(i,j,4)$

on $[i,j]$, where

$$pw(i,j,d) = \begin{cases} F & \text{if } d = dir \\ \# & \text{if } d \neq dir \text{ and } tw(i,j,d) = \# \\ f(TW([i,j]-d)) & \text{if } d \neq dir \text{ and } tw(i,j,d) \neq \#, \end{cases}$$

for d ϵ {1,2,3,4,5,6,7,8}, where f is a one-to-one mapping from true windows to integers.

A parsing tree with the parsing windows and the function f for the array e in Example 3.1 is shown in Figure 3.8.

4. GRAMMATICAL INFERENCE

Since the motion of the window can be controlled by the true windows and the parsing windows, it is possible to extend some one-dimensional grammatical inference methodology to the two-dimensional case, such as the method to infer the canonical grammar for a given sample [5] and the successor method (SM) [11]. The former method will provoke an aggregation of nonterminal symbols of the grammar inferred from the sample which has too many elements or from the sample which has elements of too large size; the latter method is faster but it has a strong tendency to produce an inferred grammar which is "overgenerating". To reduce this drawback, a new technique for the grammatical inference is introduced in this section, which we call the BCS (Between Canonical and Successor) method since the language generated by this inferred grammar is between the language generated by the canonical grammar and the language generated by the SM-inferred grammar.

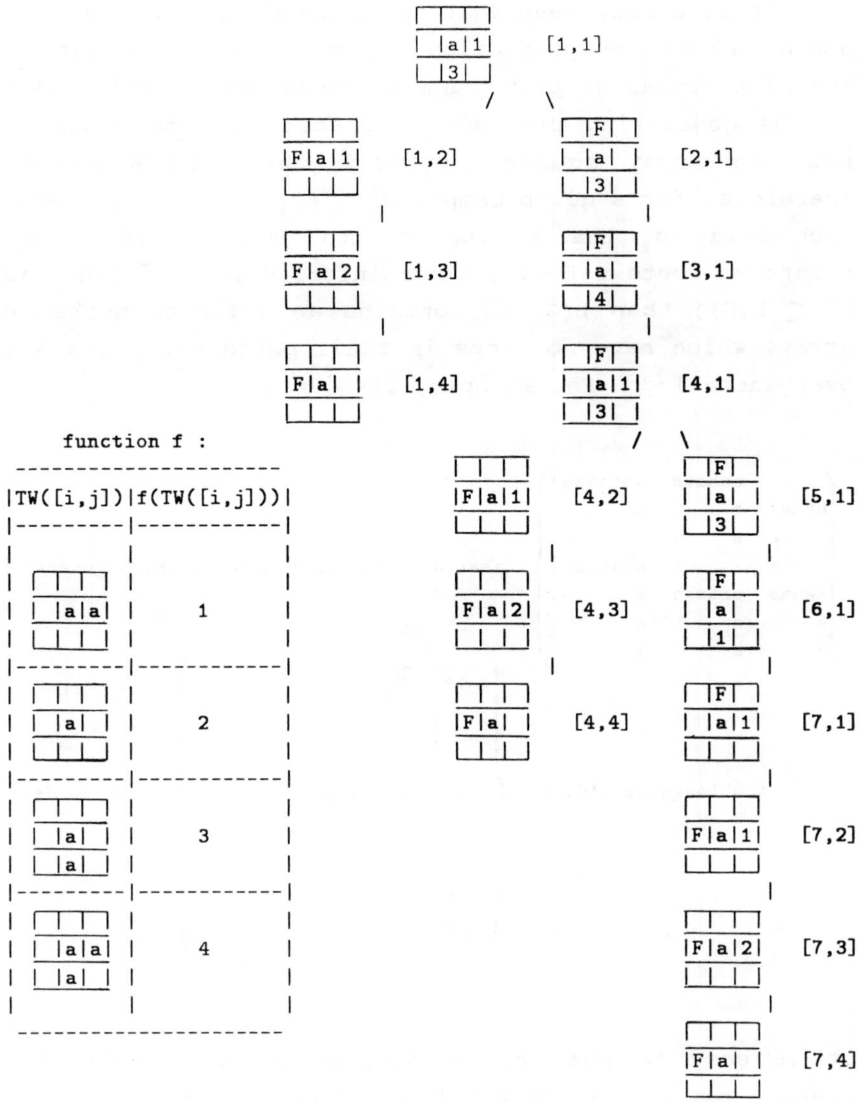

Figure 3.8. A parsing tree with parsing windows for the array e

It is easily seen that any context-free grammar with useful recursive production rules cannot generate an infinite number of patterns with loops exclusively, since in the generating procedure, it does not know where to meet an array square in which there is a symbol. Therefore, for a given sample $S^+ = \{s_1, s_2, \ldots, s_n\}$, where each array s_i has a loop in its pattern, if G is a recursive context-free grammar inferred from S^+ (that is, $S^+ \subseteq L(G)$) then $L(G)/S^+$ contains an infinite number of arrays which have no loops in their patterns. Thus G is overgenerating. For example, if S^+ =

```
{        aaaaaa  aaaaaaa }
 aaaaa   a    a  a     a
 a   a   a    a  a     a
 a   a   a    a  aaaaaaa     then an inferred grammar G which generates
 aaaaa   aaaaaa  a
 a       a       a
 a     , a     , a       ,
```

```
                           m
                        ______
                        aa...a  |
                        .    .  |
                        .    .}n|
                        .    .  |
the language L(G) =   { a....a  | m, n, p >= 2 }  might be desired.
                        a       |
                        .       |
                        . }p    |
                        .       |
                        a       |
```

It is easy to see that G must be a context-sensitive grammar but not a context-free grammar. Thus, to infer such a sample we need an approach to infer a context-sensitive grammar. In this section, we develop an approach which simulates derivation processes of context-sensitive (type-1) array grammars.

Let A be an array with a loop; then, as in the previous sections, a parsing will repeatedly scan the loop, and never stop. Thus, to parse such kind of arrays, we need a new approach to avoid the endless parsing. It is easy to see that a repeated parsing always starts at the array square which has more than one non-# neighbor which has not been parsed in its parsing window. For example, as in Figure 4.1.a, a P-shaped array is parsed from the upper-left corner [1,1]; then the repeated parsing will start at the point of [4,1], which has two neighbors in its parsing window (see Figure 4.1.b). Such points from which the repeated parsing starts are called the entering points. If we could avoid the starting of repeated parsing at entering points, then we could avoid all the repeated parsing occurring. To do this, we record all the array squares which have more than one non-# neighbor, and the neighbors which have not been parsed in their parsing windows. Thus the motion of the window can be controlled so that it can only parse the non-# neighbors which have not been parsed yet.

For example, if a P-shaped array (in Figure 4.1.a) is parsed and the upper-left corner is the starting point of coordinates [1,1], then as in Figure 4.1.c, the window will parse from [1,1] to [1,2], from [1,2] to [1,3], from [1,3] to [1,4], from [1,4] to [1,5], from [1,5] to [2,5], from [2,5] to [3,5], from [3,5] to [4,5], from [4,5] to [4,4], from [4,4] to [4,3], from [4,3] to [4,2], and from [4,2] to [4,1], then stop because [4,1] has two non-# neighbors in its parsing window, and move back to [2,1], and parse from [2,1] to [3,1], from [3,1] to [4,1], and then stop. In the pattern, the array square [4,1] has three non-#neighbors, which are [4,1]-1 (=[3,1]), [4,1]-3 (=[4,2]), and [4,1]-5 (=[5,1]); but up to now, [4,1]-1 and [4,1]-3 have been parsed. Thus [4,1]-5(=[5,1]) is

```
[1,1]
  ↘aaaaa
   a   a
   a   a
  ↗aaaaa
[4,1] a
      a
```

(a)
a P-shaped
array p

(b)

```
        [1,1]
        /   \
   [1,2]     [2,1]
     |         |
   [1,3]     [3,1]
     |         |
   [1,4]     [4,1]
     |
   [1,5]
     |
   [2,5]
     |
   [3,5]
     |
   [4,5]
     |
   [4,4]
     |
   [4,3]
     |
   [4,2]
     |
   [4,1]
```

(c)
an incomplete parsing
tree for array p

Figure 4.1

the only one which can be parsed from [4,1], and so the window parses from [4,1] to [5,1], and from [5,1] to [6,1] (see Figure 4.2). Since the window moved from [4,3] to [4,2] and from [2,1] to [3,1], [4,2] and [3,1] are assigned to be neighbors of [4,3] and [2,1], respectively. Thus there is only one non-# neighbor in the true window of [4,1] and TW([4,1]) =

	a	
	a	

.

The parsing tree with parsing windows and the function f for the array p is shown in Figure 4.3. An algorithm for the grammatical inference based on the BCS method is shown in Algorithm 4.1.

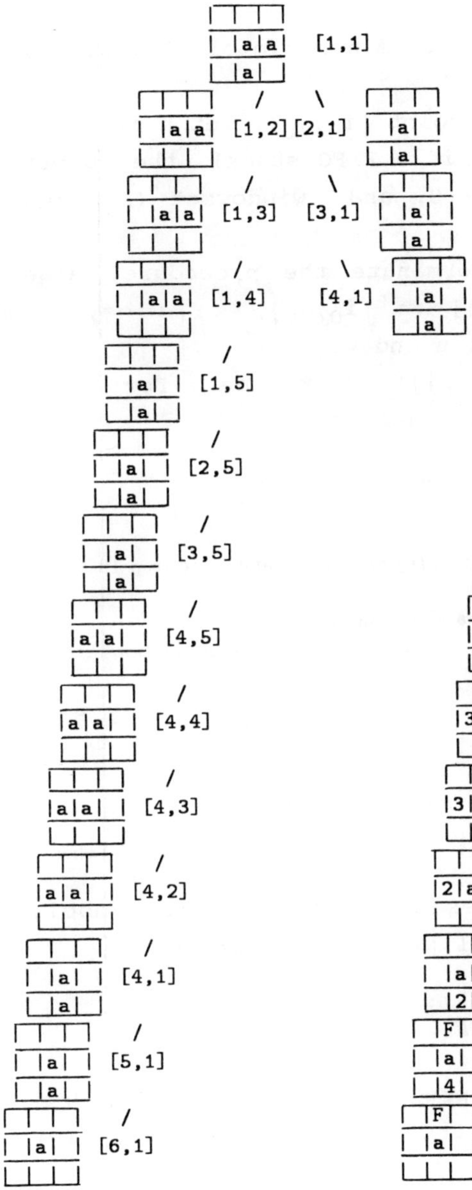

Figure 4.2 A parsing tree with true windows for array p

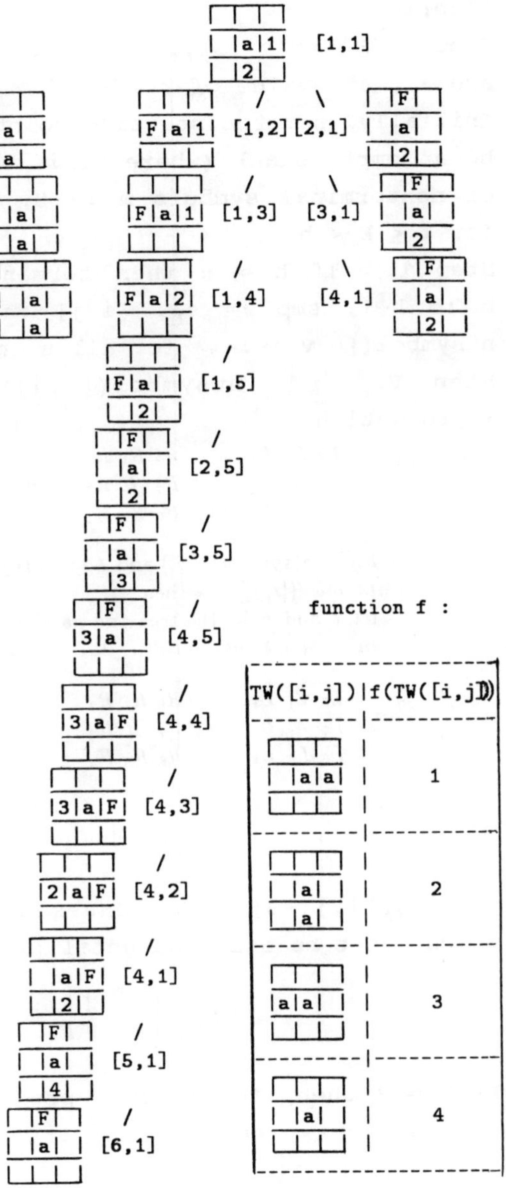

Figure 4.3 A parsing tree with parsing windows for array p

Algorithm 4.1:

Input: $S^+ = \{s_1, s_2, \ldots, s_n\}$, terminal symbols $A_1, A_2, \ldots,$ and A_t, and value of rt.

Initially, set the starting point $[i_0, j_0]$, let h := 0, ST be an empty stack (where ST is a FIFO stack), the number of nonterminal symbols m := 0, and windowset $(A_k) := \phi$ for $1 \le k \le h$.

Step 1. If h = n then terminate the procedure, else h := h+1, smp := s_h, [i,j] := $[i_0, j_0]$, Y := *, and ntsymbol([u,v]) := * for all u and v.

Step 2. If ntsymbol([i,j]) ≠ * then for every Y-production

$$\begin{matrix} L_8 & L_1 & L_1 \\ L_7 & Y & L_3 \\ L_6 & L_5 & L_4 \end{matrix} \;\rightarrow\; \begin{matrix} R_8 & R_1 & R_2 \\ R_7 & R & R_3 \\ R_6 & R_5 & R_4 \end{matrix}\text{ , if } R_d = \beta([i,j]) \text{ then}$$

let $R_d := ntsymbol([i,j])$ and $L_d := ntsymbol([i,j])$, and go to step 10.

If $ntsymbol([i,j]) = *$ then

let T and P be the true and parsing windows of $[i,j]$, respectively;

$m := m + 1$; $ntsymbol([i,j]) := A_m$ and construct one production

$$\begin{matrix} L_8 & L_1 & L_1 \\ L_7 & A_m & L_3 \\ L_6 & L_5 & L_4 \end{matrix} \;\rightarrow\; \begin{matrix} R_8 & R_1 & R_2 \\ R_7 & R & R_3 \\ R_6 & R_5 & R_4 \end{matrix}\text{ , where } R = smp([i,j]),$$

$$R_d = \begin{cases} \beta([i,j]-d) & \text{if } neighbor\text{-}d \text{ of } T \neq \# \\ * & \text{otherwise,} \end{cases} \qquad \text{where}$$

$\beta([i,j]-d)$ is an unassigned nonterminal symbol, which won't be assigned until [i,j]-d is scanned,

$$\text{and } L_d = \begin{cases} \# & \text{if } R_d \neq * \\ * & \text{if } R_d = *, \end{cases}$$

If Y ≠ * then, for every Y-production which has $\beta([i,j])$ as an array square in its right-hand side, let $\beta([i,j]) := A_m$.

Let sr := 0 and Y := A_m.

Step 3. If sr $\le$ 8 then go to step 10, else let sr := sr + 1.

Step 4. If neighbor-sr = # in T then go to step 3.

Step 5. Find a maximal value mx, such that in the sequence $x_1, x_2, \ldots, x_{mx}$, with x_1 = [i,j]-sr, x_{r+1} is the unique descendant of x_r for $1 \le r \le mx - 1$ and x_r is not an entering point for $2 \le r \le mx - 1$, and if mx > 1 then ntsymbol(x_1) = *. Let T_t and P_t be the true and parsing windows of x_t, respectively, for $1 \le t \le mx$, and let q := 1 and Y' := Y.

Step 6. If q = mx then

if T_{mx} is not single then push (x_q,Y') into ST and go to step 3.

Step 7. Find a maximal value of k(= 1 or > rt), and let q' := q / k such that q'$\le$ mx and $T_q = T_{q+1} = \cdots = T_{q'-1}$, and construct the production rules as follows:

(a) If k = 1 then only one production rule is constructed:

which is $\begin{matrix} L_8 & L_1 & L_1 \\ L_7 & \alpha & L_3 \\ L_6 & L_5 & L_4 \end{matrix} \rightarrow \begin{matrix} R_8 & R_1 & R_2 \\ R_7 & R & R_3 \\ R_6 & R_5 & R_4 \end{matrix}$, where α will be determined in step 8, $R = smp(x_q)$,

$$R_d = \begin{cases} \beta(x_{q'}) & \text{if } neighbor\text{-}d \text{ of } T_q \ne \# \text{ and } T_{q'} \text{ is not single} \\ smp(x_{q'}) & \text{if } neighbor\text{-}d \text{ of } T_q \ne \# \text{ and } T_{q'} \text{ is single} \\ * & \text{otherwise,} \end{cases} \quad \text{and } L_d = \begin{cases} \# \text{ if } R_d \ne * \\ * \text{ if } R_d = *. \end{cases}$$

(b) If k $\ge$ rt then two production rules are constructed:

one is $\begin{matrix} L_8 & L_1 & L_1 \\ L_7 & \alpha & L_3 \\ L_6 & L_5 & L_4 \end{matrix} \rightarrow \begin{matrix} R_8 & R_1 & R_2 \\ R_7 & R & R_3 \\ R_6 & R_5 & R_4 \end{matrix}$, where α will be determined in step 8, $R = smp(x_q)$,

$$R_d = \begin{cases} \alpha & \text{if } neighbor\text{-}d \text{ of } T_q \ne \# \\ * & \text{otherwise,} \end{cases} \quad \text{and } L_d = \begin{cases} \# & \text{if } R_d \ne * \\ * & \text{if } R_d = *. \end{cases}$$

another one is $\begin{matrix} L_8 & L_1 & L_1 \\ L_7 & \alpha & L_3 \\ L_6 & L_5 & L_4 \end{matrix} \rightarrow \begin{matrix} R_8 & R_1 & R_2 \\ R_7 & R & R_3 \\ R_6 & R_5 & R_4 \end{matrix}$, where $R = smp(x_q)$,

$$R_d = \begin{cases} \beta(x_{q'}) & \text{if } \textit{neighbor-d} \text{ of } T_q \neq \# \text{ and } T_{q'} \text{ is not single} \\ * & \text{otherwise,} \end{cases}$$

$$\text{and } L_d = \begin{cases} \# & \text{if } R_d \neq * \\ * & \text{if } R_d = *. \end{cases}$$

Step 8. Determine nonterminal symbol for α :
Let WS := { P_q, $P_{q'}$ };
if there exists a nonterminal symbol A_x, $2 \leq x \leq m$, such that windowset(A_x) = WS and x_q is not an entering point, then let α := A_x else let m := m+1, α = A_m and windowset(A_m) := WS.
Step 9. For every Y′-production which has $\beta(x_q)$ as an array square in its right-hand side, let $\beta(x_q)$:= α .
Let Y′ := α and q := q′, and go to step 6.
Step 10. If ST is not empty then pop an element $[\tilde{i},\tilde{j},\tilde{Y}]$ from ST, let [i,j] := $[\tilde{i},\tilde{j}]$, Y := $\tilde{Y}$, and go to step 2. Otherwise, go to step 1.

By using Algorithm 4.1 and assuming that the value of rt = 3, the procedure that infers a grammar from the array p, given in Figure 4.2, is shown in Table 4.1. The inferred grammar G = ({ S, A_2, A_3, A_4, A_5, A_6, A_7 }, { a }, P, S, #), where

$$P = \left\{ \begin{array}{l} S\# \\ \# \end{array} \rightarrow \begin{array}{l} aA_2 \\ A_5 \end{array}, \quad A_2\# \rightarrow aA_2, \quad \begin{array}{c} A_2 \\ \# \end{array} \rightarrow \begin{array}{c} a \\ A_3, \end{array} \quad \begin{array}{c} A_3 \\ \# \end{array} \rightarrow \begin{array}{c} a \\ A_3, \end{array} \right.$$

$$\#A_3 \rightarrow A_4a, \quad \#A_4 \rightarrow A_4a, \quad \#A_4 \rightarrow A_6a, \quad \begin{array}{c} A_5 \\ \# \end{array} \rightarrow \begin{array}{c} a \\ A_5, \end{array}$$

$$\left. \begin{array}{c} A_5 \\ A_6 \end{array} \rightarrow \begin{array}{c} a \\ A_6, \end{array} \quad \begin{array}{c} A_6 \\ \# \end{array} \rightarrow \begin{array}{c} a \\ A_7, \end{array} \quad \begin{array}{c} A_7 \\ \# \end{array} \rightarrow \begin{array}{c} a \\ A_7, \end{array} \quad A_7 \rightarrow a \right\}.$$

x_r's	true window	parsing window	production rules	comment for variables	stack ST
initially $Y = *$ given $[i,j]$ $= [1,1]$	$\begin{array}{\|c\|c\|c\|}\hline & & \\ \hline & a & a \\ \hline & a & \\ \hline\end{array}$	$\begin{array}{\|c\|c\|c\|}\hline & & \\ \hline & a & 1 \\ \hline & 2 & \\ \hline\end{array}$	$\begin{array}{l} S\# \\ \# \end{array} \rightarrow \begin{array}{l} aR_3 \\ R_5 \end{array}$	$R_3 := \beta([1,2])$ $R_5 := \beta([2,1])$	$\sqcup$
$Y = S, sr = 3$ $x_1 = [1,2]$	$\begin{array}{\|c\|c\|c\|}\hline & & \\ \hline & a & a \\ \hline & & \\ \hline\end{array}$	$\begin{array}{\|c\|c\|c\|}\hline & & \\ \hline F & a & 1 \\ \hline & & \\ \hline\end{array}$	$q = 1$ $q' = 4$ $Y' = S$	$R_5 := \beta([1,5])$	
$x_2 = [1,3]$	$\begin{array}{\|c\|c\|c\|}\hline & & \\ \hline & a & a \\ \hline & & \\ \hline\end{array}$	$\begin{array}{\|c\|c\|c\|}\hline & & \\ \hline F & a & 1 \\ \hline & & \\ \hline\end{array}$	$A_2\# \rightarrow aA_2$	substitute $\beta([1,2]) := A_2$ in S-productions	
$x_3 = [1,4]$	$\begin{array}{\|c\|c\|c\|}\hline & & \\ \hline & a & a \\ \hline & & \\ \hline\end{array}$	$\begin{array}{\|c\|c\|c\|}\hline & & \\ \hline F & a & 2 \\ \hline & & \\ \hline\end{array}$	$\begin{array}{l} A_2 \\ \# \end{array} \rightarrow \begin{array}{l} a \\ R_5 \end{array}$		
$x_4 = [1,5]$	$\begin{array}{\|c\|c\|c\|}\hline & & \\ \hline & a & \\ \hline & a & \\ \hline\end{array}$	$\begin{array}{\|c\|c\|c\|}\hline & & \\ \hline F & a & \\ \hline & 2 & \\ \hline\end{array}$			
$x_5 = [2,5]$	$\begin{array}{\|c\|c\|c\|}\hline & & \\ \hline & a & \\ \hline & a & \\ \hline\end{array}$	$\begin{array}{\|c\|c\|c\|}\hline & F & \\ \hline & a & \\ \hline & 2 & \\ \hline\end{array}$	$q = 4$ $q' = 7$ $Y' = A_2$	$R_7 := \beta([4,5])$	
$x_6 = [3,5]$	$\begin{array}{\|c\|c\|c\|}\hline & & \\ \hline & a & \\ \hline & a & \\ \hline\end{array}$	$\begin{array}{\|c\|c\|c\|}\hline & F & \\ \hline & a & \\ \hline & 3 & \\ \hline\end{array}$	$\begin{array}{l} A_3 \\ \# \end{array} \rightarrow \begin{array}{l} a \\ A_3 \end{array}$ $\#A_3 \rightarrow R_7a$	substitute $\beta([1,5]) := A_3$ in A_2-productions	
$x_7 = [4,5]$	$\begin{array}{\|c\|c\|c\|}\hline & & \\ \hline a & a & \\ \hline & & \\ \hline\end{array}$	$\begin{array}{\|c\|c\|c\|}\hline & F & \\ \hline 3 & a & \\ \hline & & \\ \hline\end{array}$	$q = 7$ $q' = 11$ $Y' = A_3$		
$x_8 = [4,4]$	$\begin{array}{\|c\|c\|c\|}\hline & & \\ \hline a & a & \\ \hline & & \\ \hline\end{array}$	$\begin{array}{\|c\|c\|c\|}\hline & & \\ \hline 3 & a & F \\ \hline & & \\ \hline\end{array}$			
$x_9 = [4,3]$	$\begin{array}{\|c\|c\|c\|}\hline & & \\ \hline a & a & \\ \hline & & \\ \hline\end{array}$	$\begin{array}{\|c\|c\|c\|}\hline & & \\ \hline 3 & a & F \\ \hline & & \\ \hline\end{array}$	$\#A_4 \rightarrow A_4a$	$R_7 := \beta([4,1])$	
$x_{10} = [4,2]$	$\begin{array}{\|c\|c\|c\|}\hline & & \\ \hline a & a & \\ \hline & & \\ \hline\end{array}$	$\begin{array}{\|c\|c\|c\|}\hline & & \\ \hline 2 & a & F \\ \hline & & \\ \hline\end{array}$	$\#A_4 \rightarrow R_7a$	substitute $\beta([4,5]) := A_4$ in A_3-productions	$\Downarrow$

(continued) $x_{11} = [4,1]$ (entering point)	$\begin{array}{\|c\|c\|c\|}\hline \; & \; & \; \\ \hline & a & \\ \hline & a & \\ \hline\end{array}$ $\begin{array}{\|c\|c\|c\|}\hline \; & \; & \; \\ \hline & a & F \\ \hline & 2 & \\ \hline\end{array}$			$\underline{\|4,1,A_4\|}$
$Y = S, sr = 5$ $x_1 = [2,1]$	$\begin{array}{\|c\|c\|c\|}\hline \; & \; & \; \\ \hline & a & \\ \hline & a & \\ \hline\end{array}$ $\begin{array}{\|c\|c\|c\|}\hline & F & \\ \hline & a & \\ \hline & 2 & \\ \hline\end{array}$	$q = 1$ $q' = 3$ $Y' = S$	$R_5 := \beta([4,1])$	
$x_2 = [3,1]$	$\begin{array}{\|c\|c\|c\|}\hline \; & \; & \; \\ \hline & a & \\ \hline & a & \\ \hline\end{array}$ $\begin{array}{\|c\|c\|c\|}\hline & F & \\ \hline & a & \\ \hline & 2 & \\ \hline\end{array}$	$\begin{array}{c}A_5\\ \#\end{array} \to \begin{array}{c}a\\ A_5\end{array}$	substitute	$\Downarrow$
$x_3 = [4,1]$	$\begin{array}{\|c\|c\|c\|}\hline \; & \; & \; \\ \hline & a & \\ \hline & a & \\ \hline\end{array}$ $\begin{array}{\|c\|c\|c\|}\hline & F & \\ \hline & a & \\ \hline & 2 & \\ \hline\end{array}$	$\begin{array}{c}A_5\\ \#\end{array} \to \begin{array}{c}a\\ R_5\end{array}$	$\beta([2,1]) := A_5$ in S-productions	$\|4,1,A_5\|$ $\underline{\|4,1,A_4\|}$
pop $[4,1,A_4]$ $Y = A_4$ $[i,j] = [4,1]$ (entering point)	$\begin{array}{\|c\|c\|c\|}\hline \; & \; & \; \\ \hline & a & \\ \hline & a & \\ \hline\end{array}$ $\begin{array}{\|c\|c\|c\|}\hline \; & \; & \; \\ \hline & a & F \\ \hline & 2 & \\ \hline\end{array}$	$\begin{array}{c}A_6\\ \#\end{array} \to \begin{array}{c}a\\ R_5\end{array}$	$R_5 := \beta([5,1])$ $ntsymbol([4,1])$ $:= A_6$ substitute $\beta([4,1]) := A_6$ in A_4-productions	$\Downarrow$ $\underline{\|4,1,A_5}$
$Y = A_6, sr = 5$ $x_1 = [5,1]$	$\begin{array}{\|c\|c\|c\|}\hline \; & \; & \; \\ \hline & a & \\ \hline & a & \\ \hline\end{array}$ $\begin{array}{\|c\|c\|c\|}\hline & F & \\ \hline & a & \\ \hline & 2 & \\ \hline\end{array}$	$q = 1$ $q' = 3$ $Y' = A_6$		
$x_2 = [6,1]$	$\begin{array}{\|c\|c\|c\|}\hline \; & \; & \; \\ \hline & a & \\ \hline & a & \\ \hline\end{array}$ $\begin{array}{\|c\|c\|c\|}\hline & F & \\ \hline & a & \\ \hline & 4 & \\ \hline\end{array}$	$\begin{array}{c}A_7\\ \#\end{array} \to \begin{array}{c}a\\ A_7\end{array}$	substitute $\beta([5,1]) := A_7$ in A_6-productions	
$x_3 = [7,1]$	$\begin{array}{\|c\|c\|c\|}\hline \; & \; & \; \\ \hline & a & \\ \hline \; & \; & \; \\ \hline\end{array}$ $\begin{array}{\|c\|c\|c\|}\hline & F & \\ \hline & a & \\ \hline \; & \; & \; \\ \hline\end{array}$	$A_7 \to a$		$\Downarrow$
pop $[4,1,A_5]$ $Y = A_5$ $[i,j] = [4,1]$ (entering point) $ntsymbol[4,1]$ $= A_6$	$\begin{array}{\|c\|c\|c\|}\hline \; & \; & \; \\ \hline & a & \\ \hline & a & \\ \hline\end{array}$ $\begin{array}{\|c\|c\|c\|}\hline & F & \\ \hline & a & \\ \hline & 2 & \\ \hline\end{array}$		In A_5-productions modify $\begin{array}{c}A_5\\ \#\end{array} \to \begin{array}{c}a\\ R_5\end{array}$ to $\begin{array}{c}A_5\\ A_6\end{array} \to \begin{array}{c}a\\ A_6\end{array}$	$\|\underline{\qquad}\|$ $\Downarrow$ $\|\underline{\qquad}\|$

Table 4.1

5. NOISY SAMPLES

For a sample, including noisy patterns, the inferred grammar might have a complicated structure and generate a noisy language. Such an inferred grammar cannot characterize the sample well at all. If such a noisy sample can be smoothed before the grammatical inference, then the grammar inferred from the smoothed sample would represent its corresponding pattern structure (or the structure of the smoothed pattern) and would have the simpler structure.

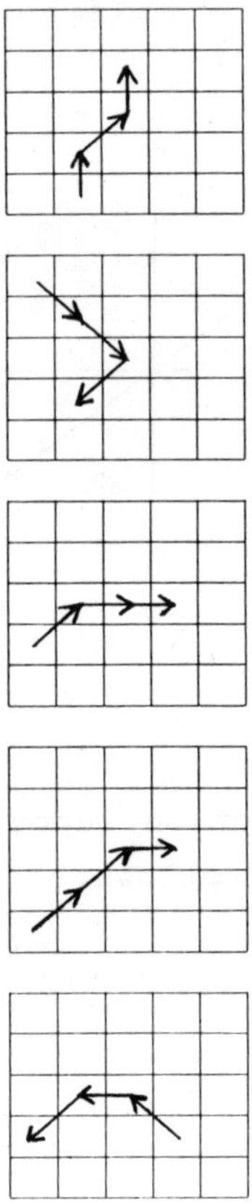

	3-primitive chain	reduced primitive
(a)	$d_1 d_2 d_1$	$\uparrow$ d_1
(b)	$d_4 d_4 d_6$	$\downarrow$ d_5
(c)	$d_2 d_3 d_3$	$\rightarrow$ d_3
(d)	$d_2 d_2 d_3$	$\nearrow$ d_2
(e)	$d_8 d_7 d_6$	$\leftarrow$ d_7

Figure 5.1
Primitive selection of a line segment

An example of hand-printed character recognition is given to demonstrate the smoothing operation.

In this section, as in [5], eight pattern primitives which are line segments with eight different orientations, $d_1 = \uparrow$, $d_2 = \nearrow$, $d_3 = \rightarrow$, $d_4 = \searrow$, $d_5 = \downarrow$, $d_6 = \swarrow$, $d_7 = \leftarrow$, and $d_8 = \nwarrow$ are selected. For example, the 3-primitive chains $d_1d_2d_1$, $d_4d_4d_6$ and $d_2d_3d_3$ are reduced to primitives d_1, d_5 and d_3, respectively. Several typical results from such data preparation are shown in Figure 5.1.

Each primitive d_i can be treated as a vector $\langle x_1, x_2 \rangle$, which is defined in Figure 5.2.

$d_1 = \langle -1, 0 \rangle,$

$d_2 = \langle -1, 1 \rangle,$

$d_3 = \langle 0, 1 \rangle,$

$d_4 = \langle 1, 1 \rangle,$

$d_5 = \langle 1, 0 \rangle,$

$d_6 = \langle 1, -1 \rangle,$

$d_7 = \langle 0, -1 \rangle,$

$d_8 = \langle -1, -1 \rangle$

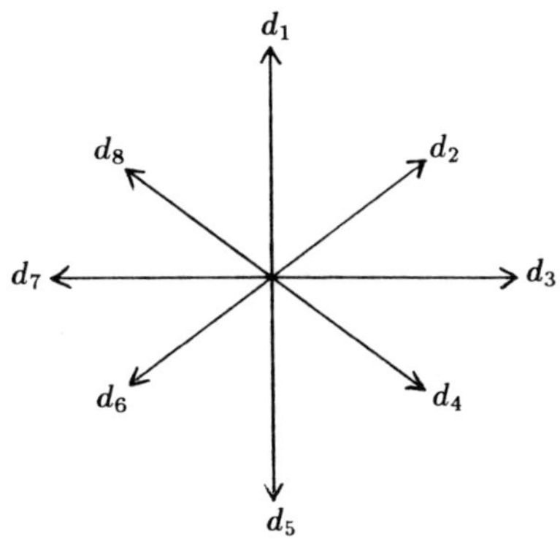

Figure 5.2

A general definition of the reduction function RED_n of the n-primitive chains is shown as follows:

Definition 5.1:

RED_n is a mapping from Dir^n to $Dir \cup \{d_0\}$, where $Dir = \{d_1, d_2, d_3, d_4, d_5, d_6, d_7, d_8\}$, $d_0 = \langle 0, 0 \rangle$, and $Dir^n = \{a_1a_2 \ldots a_n / a_i \in Dir \text{ for each } i\}$. If $a_1a_2 \ldots a_n \in Dir^n$ then $RED_n(a_1a_2 \ldots a_n) = \langle v_1, v_2 \rangle$, where, by letting $\langle u_1, u_2 \rangle = a_1 + a_2 + \ldots\ldots + a_n$,

$$\langle v_1, v_2\rangle = \begin{cases} \langle u_1/|u_1|, 0\rangle & \text{if } |u_1| - |u_2| \geq (2/3) * n, \\ \langle 0, u_2/|u_2|\rangle & \text{if } |u_2| - |u_1| \geq (2/3) * n, \\ \langle [u_1], [u_2]\rangle & \text{otherwise,} \end{cases}$$

where $[u]$ is defined as follows: $[u] = \begin{cases} u/|u| & \text{if } u \neq 0, \\ 0 & \text{if } u = 0. \end{cases}$

The value n, the length of the primitive chain, is determined according to the size of the sample. Suppose that each array in the sample is on a $m_1 \times m_2$ grid, we let n = Round((1/6)*min(m_1,m_2)). To smooth an m-primitive chain $a_1a_2 \ldots a_m$ for m > sn, it needs to be segmented into $a_1a_2 \ldots a_{sn}$, $a_{sn+1}a_{sn+2} \ldots a_{2\times sn}$, ..., and $a_{i\times sn+1}a_{i\times sn+2} \ldots a_m$ so that the length of the last line segment m-ixsn is between (1/2)n and (3/2)n (that is, (1/2)sn $\leq$ m-ixsn<(3/2)sn). If the noisy array t, shown in Figure 5.3.a, is parsed from the upper-left point then its parsing tree will be as shown in Figure 5.4. Let $m_1 = m_2 = 20$, then sn = 3 and it can be smoothed, by the segmentation as in Figure 5.3.b, to reduce a smoothed array as in Figure 5.3.b. As in Figure 5.3.c and Figure 5.4, the path $\overrightarrow{[1,1][1,2][0,3][0,4]}$ is reduced to one primitive $\overrightarrow{x_1x_2} = d_3$ and the path $\overrightarrow{[0,4][0,5][0,6]}$ is reduced to $\overrightarrow{x_2x_3} = d_3$. Thus, the path $\overrightarrow{[1,1][1,2][0,3][0,4][0,5][0,6]}$ is reduced to $\overrightarrow{x_1x_2x_3}$. The parsing tree with true and parsing windows for such a smoothed array is shown in Figure 5.5.

An algorithm, which infers a noisy array pattern by, firstly, smoothing the pattern and then constructing an inferred grammar for such a smoothed pattern, is shown in Algorithm 5.1.

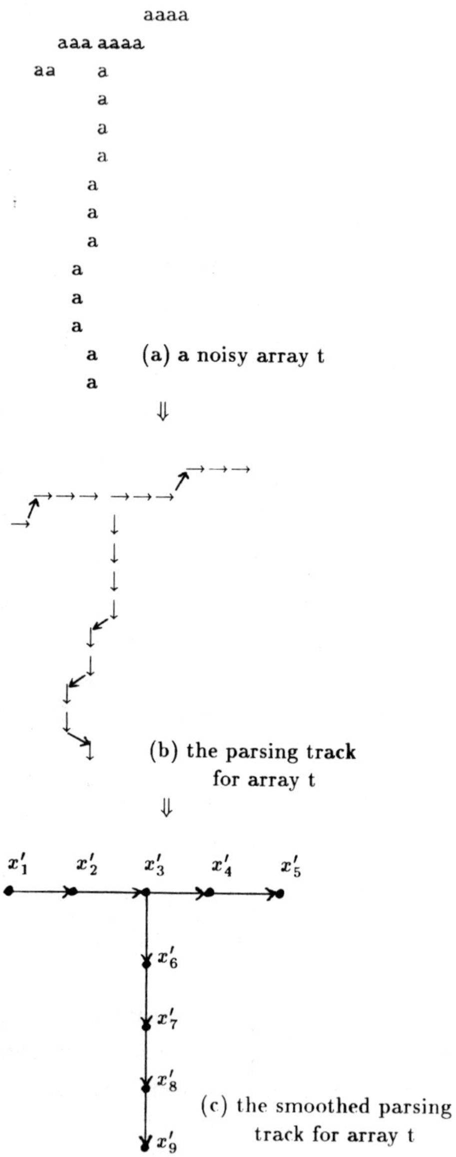

Figure 5.3. an example of smoothing processing

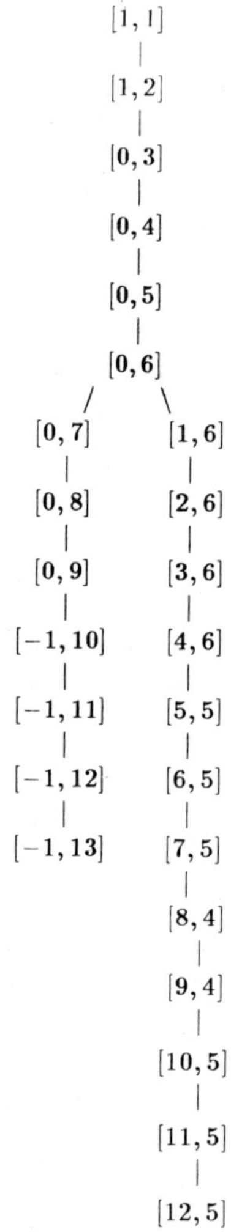

Figure 5.4. parsing tree for array t in Figure 5.3

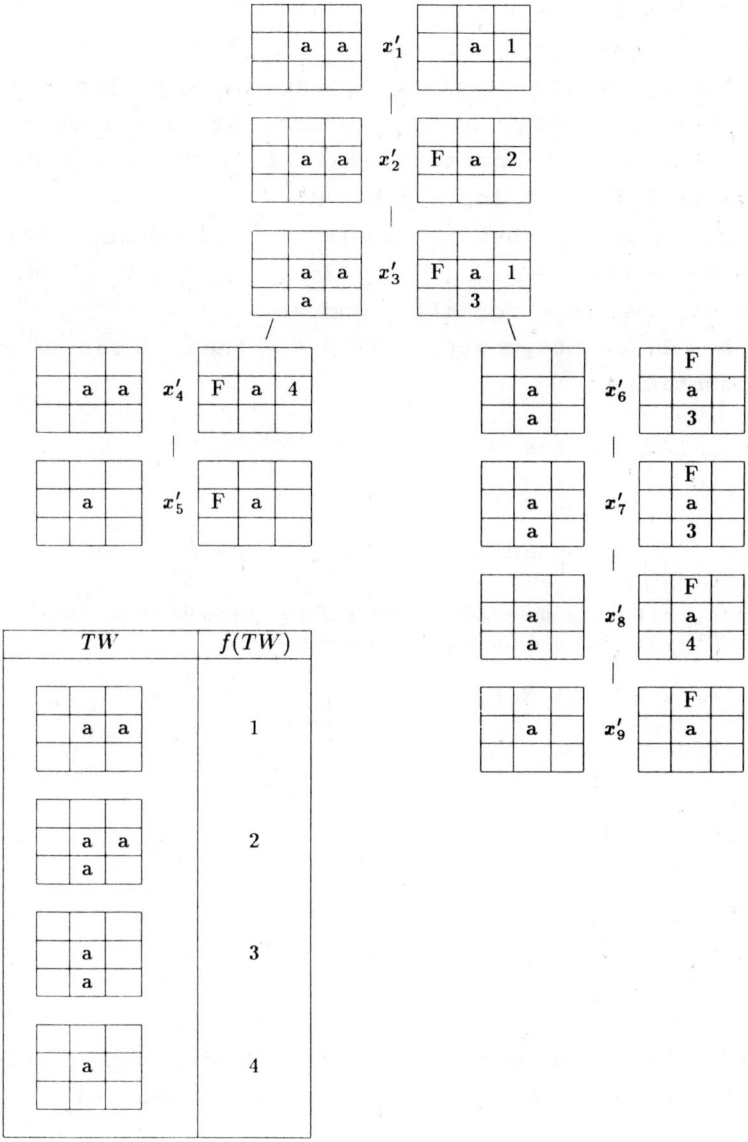

Figure 5.5. The parsing tree with true windows and parsing windows for the smoothed array t shown in Figure 5.3

Algorithm 5.1:

Input: $S^+ = \{s_1, s_2, \ldots, s_n\}$.

Initially, set the starting point $[i_0, j_0]$, let h := 0, ST := ϕ be an empty stack (where ST is a FIFO stack), the number of nonterminal symbols m := 0, and windowset(A_k) := ϕ for $1 \le k \le h$.

Step 1. If h = n then terminate the procedure, else let h := h+1, smp := s_h, [i,j] := $[i_0, j_0]$, Y := *, and ntsymbol[u,v] := * for all u and v.

Step 2. If ntsymbol([i,j]) $\neq$ * then for every Y-production

$$\begin{matrix} L_8 & L_1 & L_2 \\ L_7 & Y & L_3 \\ L_6 & L_5 & L_4 \end{matrix} \rightarrow \begin{matrix} R_8 & R_1 & R_2 \\ R_7 & R & R_3, \\ R_6 & R_5 & R_4 \end{matrix} \text{ if } R_d = \beta([i,j]) \text{ then}$$

let $R_d :=$ *ntsymbol* $([i,j])$ and $L_d :=$ *ntsymbol* $([i,j])$, and go to step 11.
If *ntsymbol* $([i,j]) := *$ then
let T and P be the true and parsing windows of $[i,j]$, respectively; $m := m+1$; *ntsymbol* $([i,j]) := A_m$; and construct one production rule

$$\begin{matrix} L_8 & L_1 & L_2 \\ L_7 & A_m & L_3 \\ L_6 & L_5 & L_4 \end{matrix} \rightarrow \begin{matrix} R_8 & R_1 & R_2 \\ R_7 & R & R_3, \\ R_6 & R_5 & R_4 \end{matrix} \text{ where } R = smp([i,j]),$$

$$R_d = \begin{cases} \beta([i,j]-d) & \text{if } neighbor\text{-}d \text{ of } T \neq \# \\ * & \text{otherwise,} \end{cases} \quad \text{where } \beta([i,j]-d) \text{ is an unassigned}$$

nonterminal symbol, which won't be assigned until $[i,j]$-d is scanned,

$$\text{and } L_d = \begin{cases} \# & \text{if } R_d \neq * \\ * & \text{if } R_d = *. \end{cases}$$

If Y $\neq$ * then, for every Y-production which has β([i,j]) as an array square in its right hand side, let β([i,j]) := A_m.

Let sr := 0 and Y := A_m.

Step 3. If sr $\le$ 8 then go to step 11, else let sr := sr + 1.

Step 4. If neighbor-sr = # in T then go to step 3.

Step 5. Find a maximal value mx, such that in the sequence $x_1, x_2, \ldots, x_{mx}$ with x_1 = [i,j]-sr, if mx > 1, then x_{r+1} must be the unique descendant of x_r for r = 1,2,...,mx-1, x_r is not an entering point for r = 2,3,...,mx-1, and if mx > 1 then ntsymbol(x_1) must be *.

Step 6. Segment $x_1 x_2 \ldots x_{mx}$ into $x_{r_1} x_{r_1+1} \ldots x_{r_2}$, $x_{r_2} x_{r_2+1} \ldots x_{r_3}, \ldots,$ and $x_{r_{(g-1)}} \ldots x_{r_g}$ to reduce $x'_1 x'_2 \ldots x'_g$, where $1 = r_1 \le r_2 \le \ldots \le r_g = mx$ (obviously, if mx = 1 then g = 1).

Let T_t be the true window and P_t be the parsing window of x'_t for $1 \le t \le g$. Let q := 1 and Y' := Y.

Step 7. If q = g then if T_g is not single or x_{r_g} is an entering point then push (x_{r_g}, Y') into ST; go to step 3.

Step 8. Find a maximal value of q' with $q < q' \le g$ such that $T_q = T_{q+1} = \ldots = T_{q'-1}$, and construct two production rules:

one is $\begin{matrix} L_8 & L_1 & L_2 \\ L_7 & \alpha & L_3 \\ L_6 & L_5 & L_4 \end{matrix} \rightarrow \begin{matrix} R_8 & R_1 & R_2 \\ R_7 & R & R_3 \\ R_6 & R_5 & R_4 \end{matrix}$, where α will be determined in step 9, $R = smp(x_{r_q})$,

$$R_d = \begin{cases} \alpha & \text{if } neighbor\text{-}d \text{ of } T_q \neq \# \\ * & \text{otherwise,} \end{cases} \quad \text{and} \quad L_d = \begin{cases} \# & \text{if } R_d \neq * \\ * & \text{if } R_d = *. \end{cases}$$

Another one is $\begin{matrix} L_8 & L_1 & L_2 \\ L_7 & \alpha & L_3 \\ L_6 & L_5 & L_4 \end{matrix} \rightarrow \begin{matrix} R_8 & R_1 & R_2 \\ R_7 & R & R_3 \\ R_6 & R_5 & R_4 \end{matrix}$, where $R = smp(x_{r_q})$,

if $q' = g$ then

$$R_d = \begin{cases} \beta(x_{r_{q'}}) & \text{if } neighbor\text{-}d \text{ of } T_{q'} \neq \# \text{ and } T_{q'} \text{ is not single} \\ * & \text{otherwise,} \end{cases}$$

if $q' \neq g$ then

$$R_d = \begin{cases} \beta(x_{r_{q'}}) & \text{if } neighbor\text{-}d \text{ of } T_{q'} \neq \# \\ * & \text{otherwise.} \end{cases}$$

And $L_d = \begin{cases} \# & \text{if } R_d \neq * \\ * & \text{if } R_d = *, \end{cases}$

Step 9. Determine nonterminal symbol for α:
Let $WS = \{P_q, P_{q'}\}$; if there exists a nonterminal symbol A_x, $2 \leq x \leq m$, such that windowset(A_x) = WS and x_{r_q} is not an entering point, then let $\alpha := A_x$ else let $m := m+1$, $\alpha := A_m$ and windowset(A_m) := WS.
Step 10. For every Y'-production which has $\beta(x_{r_q})$ as an array square in its right hand side, assign $\beta(x_{r_q}) := \alpha$. Let $Y' := \alpha$ and $q := q'$, and go to step 7.
Step 11. If ST is not empty then pop an element $[\tilde{i}, \tilde{j}, \tilde{Y}]$ from ST, let $[\tilde{i}, \tilde{j}] := [i, j]$, $Y := \tilde{Y}$, and go to step 2. Otherwise, go to step 1.

Algorithm 5.1 is tested on VAX8650/VMS using PASCAL. Some input and output are shown in Appendix 1.

The noisy array p shown in Figure 5.6.a, whose smoothed parsing track is shown in Figure 5.6.b, has the parsing tree with true windows and parsing windows shown in Figure 5.7. By using Algorithm 5.1 shown in Table 5.1, the inferred grammar for the array p is $G = (\{S, A_2, A_3, A_4, A_5, A_6, A_7\}, \{a\}, P, S, \#)$, where

$$P = \left\{ \begin{array}{c} S\# \\ \# \end{array} \rightarrow \begin{array}{c} aA_2 \\ A_5 \end{array}, \quad A_2\# \rightarrow aA_2, \quad \begin{array}{c} A_2 \\ \# \end{array} \rightarrow \begin{array}{c} a \\ A_3 \end{array}, \quad \begin{array}{c} A_3 \\ \# \end{array} \rightarrow \begin{array}{c} a \\ A_3 \end{array}, \quad \#A_3 \rightarrow A_4 a, \right.$$

$$\#A_4 \rightarrow A_4 a, \quad \#A_4 \rightarrow A_6 a, \quad \begin{array}{c} A_5 \\ \# \end{array} \rightarrow \begin{array}{c} a \\ A_5 \end{array}, \quad \begin{array}{c} A_5 \\ A_6 \end{array} \rightarrow \begin{array}{c} a \\ A_6 \end{array}, \quad \begin{array}{c} A_6 \\ \# \end{array} \rightarrow \begin{array}{c} a \\ A_7 \end{array},$$

$$\left. \begin{array}{c} A_7 \\ \# \end{array} \rightarrow \begin{array}{c} a \\ A_7 \end{array}, \quad A_7 \rightarrow a \right\}.$$

```
                aaa
[1,1] →    aaa     aa → [1,8]
           a        a
           a        a
           a        a
           a        a
           a        a
[7,1] →    aa      a → [7,7]
           a  aaaa
           a
             a
             a
             a
           a
           a
```

(a) noisy array p

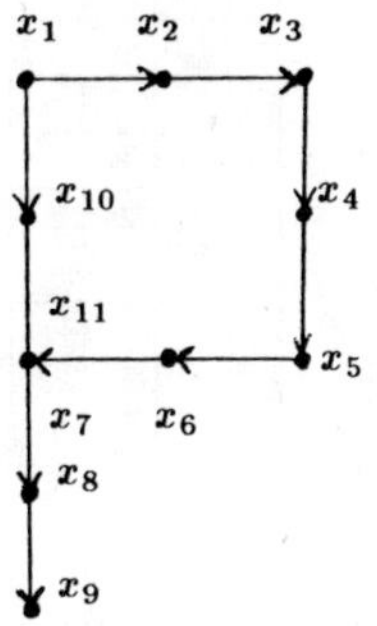

(b) smoothed parsing track of array p

Figure 5.6

```
              [1,1]
             /      \
        [1,2]        [2,1]
      [1,3]            [3,1]
    [0,4]                [4,1]
       \                 /
        [0,5]        [5,1]
      [0,6]            [6,1]
    [1,7]                [7,1]
       \
        [1,8]
      [2,8]
    [3,8]
       \
        [4,8]
      [5,7]
    [6,7]
       \
        [7,7]
      [8,6]
    [8,5]
       \
        [8,4]
      [8,3]
    [7,2]
    [7,1]
       \
        [8,1]
      [9,1]
    [10,2]
       \
        [11,2]
      [12,2]
    [13,1]
    [14,1]
```

Figure 5.7. Parsing tree for array p shown in Figure 5.6

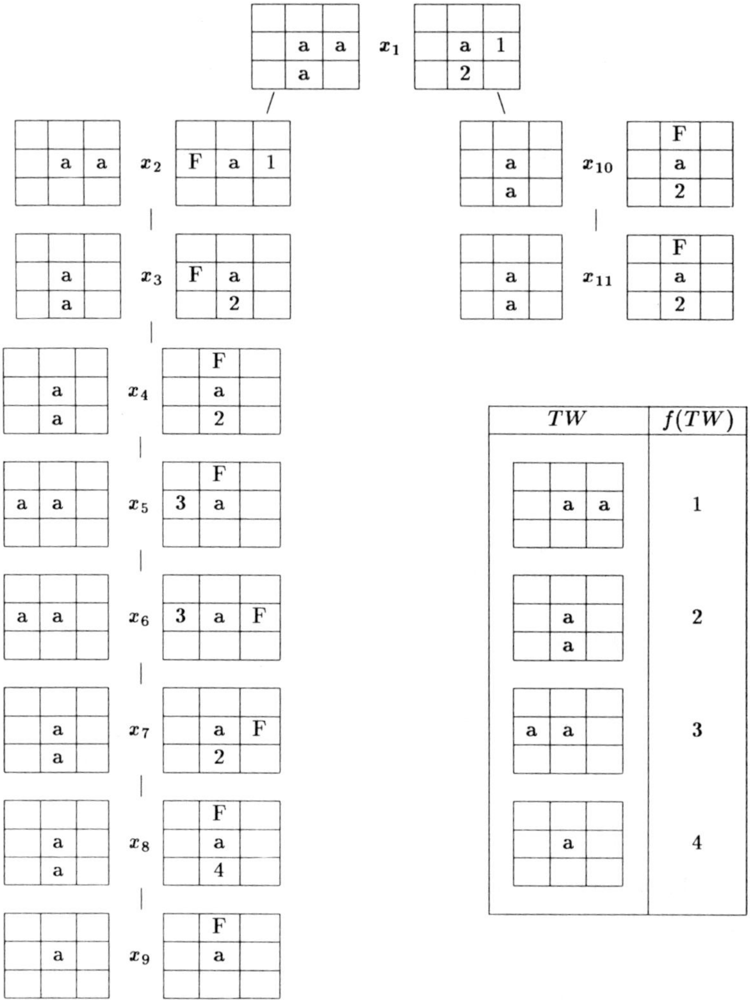

Figure 5.8. The parsing tree with true windows and parsing windows for the smoothed array p shown in Figure 5.6

<table>
<tr><th>$x'_r s$</th><th>true window</th><th>parsing window</th><th>production rules</th><th>comment for variables</th><th>stack ST</th></tr>
<tr><td>initially $Y = *$
given $[i, j]$
$= [1, 1]$</td>
<td><table><tr><td></td><td></td><td></td></tr><tr><td></td><td>a</td><td>a</td></tr><tr><td></td><td>a</td><td></td></tr></table></td>
<td><table><tr><td></td><td></td><td></td></tr><tr><td></td><td>a</td><td>1</td></tr><tr><td></td><td>2</td><td></td></tr></table></td>
<td>$S\# \rightarrow aR_3$
$\# \rightarrow R_5$</td>
<td>$R_3 := \beta([1,2])$
$R_5 := \beta([2,1])$</td>
<td>|______|</td></tr>
<tr><td>$Y = S, sr = 3$
$x_1 = [1, 2]$ x'_1
$x_2 = [1, 3]$
$x_3 = [0, 4]$</td>
<td><table><tr><td></td><td></td><td></td></tr><tr><td></td><td>a</td><td>a</td></tr><tr><td></td><td></td><td></td></tr></table></td>
<td><table><tr><td></td><td></td><td></td></tr><tr><td>F</td><td>a</td><td>1</td></tr><tr><td></td><td></td><td></td></tr></table></td>
<td>$(g = 7)$
$q = 1$
$q' = 3$
$Y' = S$</td>
<td>$R_8 := \beta([1,8])$</td>
<td></td></tr>
<tr><td>$x_4 = [0, 5]$ x'_2
$x_5 = [0, 6]$
$x_6 = [1, 7]$</td>
<td><table><tr><td></td><td></td><td></td></tr><tr><td></td><td>a</td><td>a</td></tr><tr><td></td><td></td><td></td></tr></table></td>
<td><table><tr><td></td><td></td><td></td></tr><tr><td>F</td><td>a</td><td>1</td></tr><tr><td></td><td></td><td></td></tr></table></td>
<td>$A_2\# \rightarrow aA_2$
$A_2 \rightarrow a$
$\# \rightarrow R_5$</td>
<td>substitute
$\beta([1,2]) := A_2$
in
S-productions</td>
<td></td></tr>
<tr><td>$x_7 = [1, 8]$ x'_3
$x_8 = [2, 8]$
$x_9 = [3, 8]$</td>
<td><table><tr><td></td><td></td><td></td></tr><tr><td></td><td>a</td><td></td></tr><tr><td></td><td>a</td><td></td></tr></table></td>
<td><table><tr><td></td><td></td><td></td></tr><tr><td>F</td><td>a</td><td></td></tr><tr><td></td><td>2</td><td></td></tr></table></td>
<td>$q = 3$
$q' = 5$
$Y' = A_2$</td>
<td>$R_7 := \beta([7,8])$</td>
<td>⇓</td></tr>
<tr><td>$x_{10} = [4, 8]$ x'_4
$x_{11} = [5, 7]$
$x_{12} = [6, 7]$</td>
<td><table><tr><td></td><td></td><td></td></tr><tr><td></td><td>a</td><td></td></tr><tr><td></td><td>a</td><td></td></tr></table></td>
<td><table><tr><td></td><td>F</td><td></td></tr><tr><td></td><td>a</td><td></td></tr><tr><td></td><td>2</td><td></td></tr></table></td>
<td>$A_3 \rightarrow a$
$\# \rightarrow A_3$
$\#A_3 \rightarrow R_7a$</td>
<td>substitute
$\beta([1,8]) := A_3$
in
A_2-productions</td>
<td></td></tr>
<tr><td>$x_{13} = [7, 7]$ x'_5
$x_{14} = [8, 6]$
$x_{15} = [8, 5]$</td>
<td><table><tr><td></td><td></td><td></td></tr><tr><td>a</td><td>a</td><td></td></tr><tr><td></td><td></td><td></td></tr></table></td>
<td><table><tr><td></td><td>F</td><td></td></tr><tr><td>3</td><td>a</td><td></td></tr><tr><td></td><td></td><td></td></tr></table></td>
<td>$q = 5$
$q' = 7$
$Y' = A_3$</td>
<td></td>
<td></td></tr>
<tr><td>$x_{16} = [8, 4]$ x'_6
$x_{17} = [8, 3]$
$x_{18} = [7, 2]$</td>
<td><table><tr><td></td><td></td><td></td></tr><tr><td>a</td><td>a</td><td></td></tr><tr><td></td><td></td><td></td></tr></table></td>
<td><table><tr><td></td><td></td><td></td></tr><tr><td>2</td><td>a</td><td>F</td></tr><tr><td></td><td></td><td></td></tr></table></td>
<td>$\#A_4 \rightarrow A_4a$</td>
<td>$R_7 := \beta([7,1])$</td>
<td></td></tr>
<tr><td>$x_{19} = [7, 1]$ x'_7
(entering point)</td>
<td><table><tr><td></td><td></td><td></td></tr><tr><td></td><td>a</td><td></td></tr><tr><td></td><td>a</td><td></td></tr></table></td>
<td><table><tr><td></td><td></td><td></td></tr><tr><td></td><td>a</td><td>F</td></tr><tr><td></td><td>2</td><td></td></tr></table></td>
<td>$\#a_4 \rightarrow R_7a$</td>
<td>substitute
$\beta([7,8]) := A_4$
in
A_3-productions</td>
<td>$|7, 1, A_4|$</td></tr>
</table>

<table>
<tr><td>(continued)</td><td></td><td></td><td></td><td></td></tr>
<tr>
<td>$Y = S, sr = 5$
$x_1 = [2,1]\ x_1'$
$x_2 = [3,1]$
$x_3 = [4,1]$

$x_4 = [5,1]\ x_2'$
$x_5 = [6,1]$

$x_6 = [7,1]\ x_3'$</td>
<td>
<table><tr><td></td><td></td><td></td></tr><tr><td></td><td>a</td><td></td></tr><tr><td></td><td>a</td><td></td></tr></table>
<table><tr><td></td><td>F</td><td></td></tr><tr><td></td><td>a</td><td></td></tr><tr><td></td><td>2</td><td></td></tr></table>

<table><tr><td></td><td></td><td></td></tr><tr><td></td><td>a</td><td></td></tr><tr><td></td><td>a</td><td></td></tr></table>
<table><tr><td></td><td>F</td><td></td></tr><tr><td></td><td>a</td><td></td></tr><tr><td></td><td>2</td><td></td></tr></table>

<table><tr><td></td><td></td><td></td></tr><tr><td></td><td>a</td><td></td></tr><tr><td></td><td>a</td><td></td></tr></table>
<table><tr><td></td><td>F</td><td></td></tr><tr><td></td><td>a</td><td></td></tr><tr><td></td><td>2</td><td></td></tr></table>
</td>
<td>$(g = 3)$
$q = 1$
$q' = 3$
$Y' = S$

$A_5 \quad \to \quad a$
$\# \qquad\quad A_5$

$A_5 \quad \to \quad a$
$\# \qquad\quad R_5$</td>
<td>$R_5 := \beta([7,1])$

substitute
$\beta([2,1]) := A_5$
in
S-productions</td>
<td>⇓

$|7,1,A_5|$
<u>$|7,1,A_4|$</u></td>
</tr>
<tr>
<td>pop $[7,1,A_4]$
$Y = A_4$
$[i,j] = [7,1]$
(entering
point)</td>
<td>
<table><tr><td></td><td></td><td></td></tr><tr><td></td><td>a</td><td></td></tr><tr><td></td><td>a</td><td></td></tr></table>
<table><tr><td></td><td></td><td></td></tr><tr><td></td><td>a</td><td>F</td></tr><tr><td></td><td>2</td><td></td></tr></table>
</td>
<td>$A_6 \quad \to \quad a$
$\# \qquad\quad R_5$</td>
<td>$R_5 := \beta([8,1])$
$ntsymbol([7,1])$
$:= A_6$
substitute
$\beta([7,1]) := A_6$ in
A_4-productions</td>
<td>⇓
<u>$|7,1,A_5|$</u></td>
</tr>
<tr>
<td>$Y = A_6, sr = 5$
$x_1 = [8,1]\ x_1'$
$x_2 = [9,1]$
$x_3 = [10,2]$

$x_4 = [11,2]\ x_2'$
$x_5 = [12,2]$
$x_6 = [13,1]$

$x_7 = [14,1]\ x_3'$</td>
<td>
<table><tr><td></td><td></td><td></td></tr><tr><td></td><td>a</td><td></td></tr><tr><td></td><td>a</td><td></td></tr></table>
<table><tr><td></td><td>F</td><td></td></tr><tr><td></td><td>a</td><td></td></tr><tr><td></td><td>2</td><td></td></tr></table>

<table><tr><td></td><td></td><td></td></tr><tr><td></td><td>a</td><td></td></tr><tr><td></td><td>a</td><td></td></tr></table>
<table><tr><td></td><td>F</td><td></td></tr><tr><td></td><td>a</td><td></td></tr><tr><td></td><td>4</td><td></td></tr></table>

<table><tr><td></td><td></td><td></td></tr><tr><td></td><td>a</td><td></td></tr><tr><td></td><td></td><td></td></tr></table>
<table><tr><td></td><td>F</td><td></td></tr><tr><td></td><td>a</td><td></td></tr><tr><td></td><td></td><td></td></tr></table>
</td>
<td>$(g = 3)$
$q = 1$
$q' = 3$
$Y' = A_6$

$A_7 \quad \to \quad a$
$\# \qquad\quad A_7$

$A_7 \quad \to \quad a$</td>
<td>substitute
$\beta([8,1]) := A_7$
in
A_6-productions</td>
<td>⇓

<u>$|7,1,A_5|$</u></td>
</tr>
<tr>
<td>pop $[7,1,A_5]$
$Y = A_5$
$[i,j] = [4,1]$
(entering point)
$ntsymbol[4,1]$
$= A_6$</td>
<td>
<table><tr><td></td><td></td><td></td></tr><tr><td></td><td>a</td><td></td></tr><tr><td></td><td>a</td><td></td></tr></table>
<table><tr><td></td><td>F</td><td></td></tr><tr><td></td><td>a</td><td></td></tr><tr><td></td><td>2</td><td></td></tr></table>
</td>
<td>$(mx = 1)$
$Y' = A_5$</td>
<td>In
A_5-productions
modify

$\begin{matrix} A_5 & \to & a \\ \# & & R_5 \end{matrix}$ to $\begin{matrix} A_5 & \to & a \\ A_6 & & A_6 \end{matrix}$</td>
<td>$|\_\_\_\_|$
⇓
$|\_\_\_\_|$</td>
</tr>
</table>

Table 5.1

6. CONCLUSIONS AND DISCUSSIONS

Algorithm 5.1 is tested on VAX8650/VMS using PASCAL in Appendix 1. We have described the basic concepts and techniques for the two-dimensional grammatical inference. An approach for the two-dimensional grammatical inference, especially for the digitized line-drawing patterns has been explored. This approach tends to infer a grammar which generates a language much closer to the canonical language than the language of the grammar inferred by the successor method [11]. It involves much fewer nonterminal symbols than the canonical grammar. The inference algorithm involving multiple input array patterns has been presented. Several examples of the two-dimensional grammatical inference have been illustrated. In the future, we would like to develop techniques of the two-dimensional grammatical inference for the input involving noisy patterns and compare the top-down approach with other approaches[21].

BIBLIOGRAPHY

[1] Aizawa, K. and Nakamura, A., "Direction-Independent Applications of Productions on Two-Dimensional Arrays", Information Processing Letters, **22**, 295-301 (1986).

[2] Brayer, J.M. and Fu, K.S., "Some Multidimensional Grammar Inference Method", Pattern Recognition, and Artificial Intelligence, C.H. Chen (Ed), Academic Press, 29-60 (1976).

[3] Cook, C.R. and Wang, P.S.P., "A Chomsky Hierarchy of Isotonic Array Grammars and Languages", Computer Graphics and Image Processing **8**, 144-152 (1978).

[4] Evans, T.G., "Grammatical Inference Techniques in Pattern Analysis", Software Engineering, J.T.Tou (Ed), Vol. 2, Academic Press, 183-202 (1971).

[5] Fu, K.S., Syntactic Pattern Recognition and Applications, Prentice-Hall, Chapter 10, 349-410 (1982).

[6] Fu, K.S. and Booth, T.L., "Grammatical Inference: Introduction and Survey-Part I", IEEE Trans. on Systems, Man, and Cybernetics, Vol. SMC-5, No. 1, 95-111 (1975).

[7] Fu, K.S. and Booth, T.L., "Grammatical Inference: Introduction and Survey-Part II", IEEE Trans. on Systems, Man, and Cybernetics, Vol. SMC-5, No. 4, 409-423 (1975).

[8] Fu, K.S. and Lu, S.Y., "A Clustering Procedure for Syntactic Patterns", IEEE Trans. on Systems, Man, and Cybernetics, Vol. SMC-7, 734-742 (1977).

[9] Mercer, A. and Rosenfeld, A., "An Array Grammar Programming System", CACM, **16**, 299-305 (1973).

[10] Pavlidis, T., Structural Pattern Recognition, Springer Verlag (1980).

[11] Richetin, M. and Vernadat, F., "Efficient Regular Grammatical Inference for Pattern Recognition", Pattern Recognition, Vol. 17, No. 2, 245-250 (1984).

[12] Rosenfeld, A., Picture Languages: Formal Models for Picture Recognition, Academic Press, New York (1979).

[13] Siromoney, R., "Array Languages and Lindenmayer Systems - A Survey", The Book of L, Rozenberg, G. and Salomaa, A. (Ed), Springer Verlag, 413-426 (1985).

[14] Smith III, A.R., "Two-Dimensional Formal Languages and Pattern Recognition by Cellular Automata", 12th IEEE Symp. on Switching and Automata Theory, 216-224 (1970).

[15] Smith III, A.R., "Cellular Automata and Formal Languages", 11th IEEE Symp. on Switching and Automata Theory, 144-152 (1971).

[16] Wang, P.S.P., "Hierarchical Structures and Complexities of Parallel Isometric Languages", IEEE Trans. on Pattern Analysis and Machine Intelligence, Vol. PAMI-5, No. 1, 92-99 (1983).

[17] Wang, P.S.P., "An Application of Array Grammars to Clustering Analysis for Syntactic Patterns", Pattern Recognition, Vol. 17, No. 4, 441-451 (1984).

[18] Wang, P.S.P., "Parallel Context-Free Array Grammar Normal Forms", Computer Graphics and Image Processing, **15**, 296-300 (1980).

[19] Wang, P.S.P., "Some New Results on Isotonic Array Grammars", Information Processing Letters, Vol. 10, No. 3, 129-131 (1980).

[20] Wang, P.S.P. (Ed), Intelligent Systems, Imaging Technology, and Software Engineering, Sung Kang Computer Book Co., 37-71 (1984).

[21] Wang, P.S.P. and Dai, X.W., "A Grammatical Inference Algorithm for Digitized Array Patterns", Proc. ICPR'86, Paris, 129-131 (1986).

[22] Wang, P.S.P., and Lin, H.J., "A Pumping Lemma for Two-Dimensional Array Languages", Proc. ICPR'86, Paris, 126-128 (1986).

[23] Wang., P.S.P. and Lin., H.J., "A Top-Down Approach for Two-Dimensional Grammatical Inference", Proc. of the Workshop on Syntactical and Structural Pattern Recognition, Pont-a-Mousson, France, 200-212 (1988).

[24] Yodogawa, E., "A Note on Array Grammars", Information Processing Letters, **18**, 51-54 (1984).

Appendix 1. Programming Testing for Array Grammatical Inference

INPUT 1

```
20 20
1 1
1
.....................
.yyyyyyyy......yyyyy.
.y.......yyyyyy......
.y...................
.y...................
.y...................
.y...................
..y..................
..y..................
..yyyyyy.............
..y.....yyyyy........
..y..................
..y..................
.y...................
.y...................
.y...................
.y...................
.y...................
.y...................
.y...................
.....................
S
A
B
C
D
E
F
```

OUTPUT 1

```
S#  ->  yA
#       B

A#  ->  yA

A   ->  y

B   ->  y
#       B

B   ->  y
#       C

C#  ->  yA
#       D

D   ->  y
#       D

D   ->  y
```

INPUT 2

```
20 20
1 1
1
.....................
.yyyyyxx.............
.y......xxxxyyyyyyy..
.y................x..
.y................x..
..y...............x..
..y...............x..
..y...............x..
..xyyyyyy.........x..
..x......yyyyyyyyyy..
..x..................
..x..................
.x...................
.x...................
..x..................
..x..................
..x..................
.....................
.....................
.....................
.....................
S
A
B
C
D
E
F
G
H
I
J
K
L
```

OUTPUT 2

```
S#  ->  yA
#       F

A#  ->  yA

A#  ->  yB

B#  ->  xB

B#  ->  xC

C#  ->  yC

C   ->  y
#       D

D   ->  x
#       D

D   ->  x
#       E

#E  ->  Ey

#E  ->  Gy

F   ->  y
#       F

F   ->  y
G       G

G   ->  x
#       H

H   ->  x
#       H

H   ->  x
```